DSM-IV-TR™
in Action

DSM-IV-TR™
in Action

SOPHIA F. DZIEGIELEWSKI

John Wiley & Sons, Inc.

For Mary Dziegielewski

This book is dedicated to the memory of my mother, Mary Dziegielewski, who passed away during the writing of this manuscript. My mother, a Polish immigrant, taught me how to survive in the face of adversity, but most of all she taught me to take chances through unconditional love. In watching her personal sacrifices I have become convinced that all things remain possible . . . when you never give up.

Contents

SECTION II

Applications: Selected *DSM-IV-TR* Disorders

Chapter 6   Conduct Disorder 169

Shirleyann Amos and Sophia F. Dziegielewski

Chapter 7   Substance Disorders: Alcoholism 192

Julie Wenglinsky and Sophia F. Dziegielewski

Chapter 8   Eating Disorders: Anorexia Nervosa   221

Sophia F. Dziegielewski and Janet D. Murray

Chapter 11   Mood Disorders: Bipolar Disorders   297

*Shirleyann Amos, Jennifer Loflin, Karen Simons, and
   Sophia F. Dziegielewski*

Preface

In the pages that follow, you will be introduced to the diagnostic assessment, with its obvious strengths as well as its limitations. This book is designed to support the practitioner with the current application principles relating psychopathology to clinical mental health practice. In addition, the application chapters of the book extend beyond the traditional diagnostic assessment supporting efforts to enhance behaviorally based biopsychosocial practice strategy. Although the concept of the diagnosis and assessment is rich in tradition, the connection between diagnostic procedures and behaviorally based outcomes is embedded in linking the mind with body or person in environment. This makes it paramount to continually assess and reassess how to best address context changes reflecting emotional, physical, and situational factors related to client well-being.

Mental health practitioners believe strongly in allowing ethical principles and a respect for cultural diversity to guide all practice decisions. In the diagnostic assessment, individuals are acknowledged while individual dignity, worth, respect, and nonjudgmental attitudes provide the cornerstones from which all intervention stems. Many times these concepts remain subjective and require professional acknowledgment, interpretation, and application extending beyond the diagnostic assessment to efficient and effective practice strategy. To accomplish this, the practitioner needs to understand this information and how to incorporate it into the use of diagnostic tools such as the *DSM-IV-TR*. Furthermore, this handbook encourages an environment for health and mental health practitioners that extends beyond the diagnostic assessment and allowing the best service possible acknowledging the needs of the client and his or her system.

The first section of the book is dedicated to the concept and application of the diagnostic assessment found in today's behaviorally based biopsychosocial field of practice. The first four chapters introduce the reader to the major diagnostic assessment schemes utilized in the profession, along with support and resistance issues. In Chapter 1, diagnosis and assessment are exemplified in relation to how these terms are applied in current health and mental health practice. A historical perspective is explored and the type of diagnostic assessment most utilized today is outlined. In Chapter 2, as exemplified in the multidisciplinary or interdisciplinary teams, client information is examined and applied to completion of a comprehensive diagnostic assessment to ensure quality care. In Chapter 3, the multiaxial diagnostic assessment is defined along with current practice concerns such as accurate record keeping, time-limited services, managed care requirements, and quality assurance and improvement procedures. Information in regard to the *DSM-IV-TR* is provided and each axis is described allowing practitioners to clearly identify and apply each step of the diagnostic system. In Chapter 4, the linkage is made between the diagnostic assessment and how it provides the foundation for the treatment planning and practice strategy that will follow.

The second section of the book follows with an overview of practice strategy and direct application to several common mental health conditions designed to apply and refine practitioner skills. Practice strategy is highlighted and considerations for future exploration and refinement are noted.

This section of the book takes the information provided in the first four chapters and applies diagnostic and psychotherapeutic considerations directly to practice. Selected mental health conditions include reactive attachment disorder, conduct disorder, substance disorders, eating disorders such as anorexia nervosa, schizophrenia and the psychotic disorders, obsessive compulsive disorder, mood disorders such as the bipolar disorders, and borderline personality disorder.

Two appendixes feature a glossary of general medical terms and sample treatment plans.

This book challenges the practitioner to synthesize information into a complete diagnostic assessment that includes practice strategy. Each chapter, along with the Quick Reference Boxes, are designed to give the health and mental health practitioner a sense of "hands-on" learning and participation. This book is not all-inclusive of the many aspects of a mental disorder. This book provides a quick reference for application of the mental health diagnostic assessment along with chapters on specific applications designed to show how to best apply the diagnostic framework toward current practice strategy.

Creating a practice handbook of this nature is never easy—nor should it be. Practice wisdom must be grounded in evidenced-based practice. The actual drafting of chapters from the first proposal to the end product covered a span of well over two years with numerous rewrites and edits. This book represents over 20 years of professional practice and teaching experience. In addition, the contributing authors of the application chapters—all fellow practitioners—spent countless hours working on how best to transcribe practice experience into the written word.

All the contributors of this text feel strongly about their passion for the health and mental health professions and that much needs to be learned from the clients served. Case examples are used throughout this book to help define the interface between what is written in the text and how it applies to practice. Many of the struggles that other professionals have noted are highlighted and the case examples present information in a practical and informative way that is sensitive to the client's best interests, while taking into account the reality of the practice environment.

There is a subjective nature to diagnosis and assessment, just as there is a subjective nature to individuals and the best intervention strategy to be employed. This handbook is intended to take the practitioner beyond the diagnostic assessment and ignite a creative fire for practice strategy and implementation, similar to what it has done for the authors of this manuscript.

SOPHIA F. DZIEGIELEWSKI

Acknowledgments

I am very grateful for all the help I have received from the coauthors on the applications chapters included in this text. For each of them this is their first publication and, as practitioners sharing their firsthand experiences in these areas, their contributions have been invaluable. As mental health practitioners, regardless of discipline, we have a clear path set before us to deal not only with the challenges of this changing environment, but we bear the burden of exploring and subsequently influencing how these changes will affect our professional practice.

I would like to thank my clients for teaching me the importance of going beyond what is expected and recognizing the uniqueness of each individual we have the privilege of serving.

Furthermore, I would like to express my sincere thanks to all the individuals who helped in the production of this book. First, I would like to thank Tracey Belmont, Acquisitions Editor at John Wiley & Sons. Her high energy level, drive, ambition, and perseverance have made her a wise teacher, mentor, colleague, and now my friend. I would also like to thank my husband, Linden Siri, who assisted me with so many of the technical aspects of getting this book ready. I would especially like to thank my niece Barbara Vunk and my dear friend Jan Ricks who as fellow practitioners provided me with unconditional support and encouragement.

I want to thank my family members, colleagues, and friends who understood and supported me when I said I couldn't because I had to work on this book. I have been blessed with knowing and working with so many caring and supportive family members, colleagues, and friends. With that encouragement and support, all things really are possible.

UTILIZING THE *DSM-IV-TR*

Assessment, Planning, and Practice Strategy

CHAPTER

1

Getting Started

This chapter introduces the concepts and current application principles relating psychopathology to clinical mental health practice. This application is supported through the use and explication of diagnosis–assessment skills found in today's behaviorally based biopsychosocial field of practice. To start this endeavor, we introduce the major diagnostic-assessment schemes utilized in the profession, along with support and resistance issues. Diagnosis and assessment are applied to current mental health practice. A historical perspective is explored and the type of diagnostic assessment most utilized today is outlined. Practice strategy is highlighted and considerations for future exploration and refinement are noted.

BEGINNING THE PROCESS

The concept of formulating and completing a diagnostic assessment is embedded in the history and practice of the clinical mental health counseling strategy. In practice, this rich tradition has been emphasized clearly by compelling demands to address practice reimbursement (S. R. Davis & Meier, 2001). To facilitate this process, numerous types of diagnosis and assessment measurements are currently available—many of which are structured into unique categories and classification schemes. All mental health professionals need to be familiar with the texts often referred to by those in the field as the "bibles" of mental health treatment. These resources, representing the most prominent methods of diagnosis and assessment, are the ones that are most commonly used and accepted in the area of health service delivery. Although it is beyond our scope to describe the details and applications of all of these different tools, being familiar with the ones most commonly utilized is essential. Furthermore, this book takes the practicing professional beyond assessment by presenting the most current and up-to-date methods used to support the diagnostic assessment, introducing interventions based on current practice wisdom, while focusing on the latest and most up-to-date evidence-based interventions being utilized in the field.

3

MENTAL HEALTH ASSESSMENT TOOLS

In practice today, few professionals would debate that the most commonly used and accepted sources of diagnostic criteria are the *Diagnostic and Statistical Manual of Mental Disorders-Fourth Edition Text Revision (DSM-IV-TR)* and the *International Classification of Diseases-Tenth Edition (ICD-10)*. These books are generally considered reflective of the official nomenclature in all mental health and other health-related facilities in the United States. The *DSM-IV-TR* (2000) is the most current version of the APA's *Diagnostic and Statistical Manual,* the revision to this edition *(DSM-V)* is expected to be completed in 2005.

Today, the *DSM* is similar to the *ICD* in terms of diagnostic codes and the billing categories that result; however, this wasn't always the case. As late as the 1980s, clinical practices often used the *ICD* for billing but referred to the *DSM* to clarify diagnostic criteria. It was not uncommon to hear psychiatrists, psychologists, social workers, and mental health technicians complain about the lack of clarity and uniformity in both of these texts. Later versions of these texts responded to the professional outcry of dissatisfaction over the disparity between the two texts by using similar criteria when outlining descriptive classification systems that cross all theoretical orientations. Historically, while most clinicians are knowledgeable about both books, the *DSM* appears to have gained the greatest popularity in the United States and is the resource most often used by psychiatrists, psychologists, psychiatric nurses, social workers, and other mental health professionals. For example, a past survey reported that for clinical social workers working in the area of mental health the *DSM* is the publication used most often (Kutchins & Kirk, 1988). Furthermore, in terms of licensing and certification of most mental health professionals, a thorough knowledge of the *DSM* is considered essential for competent clinical practice.

Since all professionals working in the area of mental health need to be capable of service reimbursement and to be proficient in diagnostic assessment and treatment planning, it is not surprising that the majority of mental health professionals support the use of this manual (Corey, 2001a). Nevertheless, some professionals such as Carlton (1989), a social worker, questioned this choice. Carlton believed that all health and mental health intervention needed to go beyond the traditional bounds of simply diagnosing a client's mental health condition. From this perspective, social, situational, and environmental factors are considered key ingredients for addressing client problems. To remain consistent with the "person-in-situation" stance, utilizing the *DSM* as the path of least resistance might lead to a largely successful fight—yet would it win the war? Carlton, along with other professionals of his time, feared the battle was being fought on the wrong battlefield and advocated for a more comprehensive system of reimbursement that took into account environmental aspects. Furthermore, research findings have suggested that when engaging in clinical practice many professionals did not use *DSM* to direct their interventions at all. Rather, the focus and use of the manual was primarily limited to ensuring third-party reimbursement, qualifying for agency service, or to avoid placing a diagnostic label. For these reasons, clients were being given diagnoses not based solely on diagnostic criteria, and the diagnostic labels assigned were being connected to unrelated factors such as reimbursement. Therefore, some mental health professionals were more likely to pick the most severe diagnosis so that their clients could qualify for agency services or insurance reimbursement. However, other mental health professionals engaged in the opposite behavior by assigning clients the least severe diagnosis to avoid stigmatizing and labeling them (Kutchins & Kirk, 1986). Although use of the *DSM* is clearly evident in mental health practice, there are those professionals who question whether it is being utilized properly.

Regardless of the controversy in mental health practice, the continued and increased popularity of the *Diagnostic and Statistical Manual of Mental Disorders (DSM)* makes it the most frequently used publication in the field of mental health.

The publisher of the *DSM* is the American Psychiatric Press, a professional organization in the field of psychiatry. Nevertheless, the majority of copies are bought and used by individuals who are not psychiatrists. Furthermore, early in the introductory pages of the book, the authors remind the reader that the book is designed to be utilized by professionals in all areas of mental health, including psychiatrists, physicians, psychiatric nurses, psychologists, social workers, and other mental health professionals (American Psychiatric Association [APA], 2000). Since most mental health professionals believe there is a need for a system that accurately identifies and classifies biopsychosocial symptoms as a basis for assessing mental health problems, it is no surprise that this book continues to gain popularity.

For some professionals such as social workers, however, the controversy over using this system for diagnostic assessments remains. Regardless of the school of thought or specific field of training a mental health practitioner ascribes to, most professionals would agree that there is no single diagnostic system that is completely acceptable by all. Furthermore, some degree of relative skepticism and questioning of the appropriateness of the use of this manual is useful. Placing a diagnostic label needs to reach beyond ensuring service reimbursement and can have serious consequences for the individual client. Knowledge of how to properly use the manual is needed. In addition, there must also be knowledge, concern, and continued professional debate about the appropriateness and the utility of certain diagnostic categories to discourage abuse.

HISTORY AND RESERVATIONS ABOUT THE *DSM*

The APA published the first edition of the *DSM* in 1952. This edition was an attempt to blend the psychological with the biological and to provide for the practitioner a unified approach known as the psychobiological point of view. With the popularity of this first edition, the second edition of the book was published in 1968. Unlike its predecessor, the *DSM-II* did not reflect a particular point of view. Rather, it attempted to frame the diagnostic categories in a more scientific way. Both *DSM-I* and *DSM-II,* however, were criticized by many for being unscientific and for increasing the potential for negative labeling in the clients who were served (Eysenck, Wakefield, & Friedman, 1983). There was so much diagnostic play within the categories that the diverse professionals and differing backgrounds of those who utilized the manual could result in destructive negative labels being placed on the clients served.

This fear of potentially harming clients by attaching diagnostic labels to them made many professionals cautious. They warned of the dangers of using guides such as the *DSM* by arguing that the differences inherent in the basic philosophy of mental health practitioners could lead to interpretation problems. For example, Carlton (1984) and Dziegielewski (1998) felt that social workers, one of the major providers of mental health services, differed in purpose and philosophical orientation from psychiatrists. Since psychiatry is a medical specialty, the focus of its work would be based on pathology and linked to the traditional medical model, a

---

QUICK REFERENCE

BRIEF HISTORY OF THE *DSM*

- *DSM-I* was first published by the American Psychiatric Association (APA) in 1952 and reflected a psychobiological point of view.
- *DSM-II* (1968) did not reflect a particular point of view. Many professionals criticized both *DSM-I* and *DSM-II* for being unscientific and for encouraging negative labeling.
- *DSM-III* (1980) tried to calm the controversy by claiming to be unbiased and more scientific. Even though many of the earlier problems still persisted, these problems were overshadowed by an increasing demand for *DSM-III* diagnoses being required for clients to qualify for reimbursement from private insurance companies or from governmental programs.
- *DSM-III-R* (1987) utilized data from field trials that the developers claimed validated the system on scientific grounds. Nevertheless, serious questions were raised about its diagnostic reliability, possible misuse, potential for misdiagnosis, and ethics of its use.
- *DSM-IV* (1994) sought to dispel earlier criticisms of the *DSM*. The book included additional cultural information, diagnostic tests, and lab findings and was based on 500 clinical field trials.
- *DSM-IV-TR* (2000) does not change the diagnostic codes or criteria from the *DSM-IV;* however, it supplements the current categories with additional information based on the research studies and field trials completed in each area.

perspective very different from the focus of social work. In social work, a strengths-based perspective (i.e., clients are helped to manage their lives effectively under conditions of physical or mental illness and disability) is stressed.

According to Carlton (1984), "Any diagnostic scheme must be relevant to the practice of the professionals who develop and use it. That is, the diagnosis must direct practitioners' interventions. If it does not do so, the diagnosis is irrelevant. *DSM-III,* despite the contributions of one of its editors, who is a social worker, remains essentially a psychiatric manual. How then can it direct social work interventions?" (p. 85).

Furthermore, other professionals in the 1980s argued over the alleged masculine bias of the system and the lack of supportive research (M. Kaplan, 1983a, 1983b; Kass, Spitzer, & Williams, 1983; Williams & Spitzer, 1983). The biggest argument in this area came from the contention that research conducted on the *DSM-III* (1980) was less biased and more scientific. Many professionals believed that the earlier problems still persisted; however, these problems were overshadowed by an increasing demand for use of the *DSM-III* for clients to qualify for reimbursement from private insurance companies or from governmental programs. The major complaint against this edition of the *DSM* was that the information was not well grounded in evidence-based practice.

The APA was challenged to address this issue by an immediate call for independent researchers to be allowed to critically evaluate the diagnostic categories and test its reliability. Soon after this call for increased evaluation, the developers initiated a call of their own seeking research that would support a new and improved revision of this edition of the manual to be called the *DSM-III-R* (APA, 1987). Some professionals who had originally challenged the foundations of this edition felt that this immediate designation for a revised manual circumvented these attempts for independent research by aborting the process, making these attempts obsolete because of the proposed revision. Therefore, all the complaints about the lack of reliability in regard to the *DSM-III* now became moot because all attention now focused on the revision.

The resulting revision, the *DSM-III-R* (1987) did not end the controversy. Despite data from field trials that the developers claimed validated the system on scientific grounds, serious questions were raised about its diagnostic reliability, possible misuse, potential for misdiagnosis, and ethics of its use (M. P. Dumont, 1987; Kutchins & Kirk, 1986). Researchers such as Kutchins and Kirk (1993) noted that although the new edition preserved the same structure and all of the innovations of the *DSM-III,* there were many changes in specific diagnoses. These changes resulted in over 100 categories being altered, dropped, or added. The complaint was that no one would ever know whether the changes improved or detracted from diagnostic reliability when comparing the new manual with the old. Furthermore, attempts to follow-up on the original complaints about the actual overall reliability of the *DSM-III* were not addressed, nor were any attempts made to test the overall reliability of the *DSM-III-R,* even after it was published.

Once again, the APA heard these comments and less than one year after the publication of the *DSM-III-R* the APA initiated the next revision. *DSM-IV* was originally scheduled for publication in 1990 and was grounded in research. A four-volume *DSM-IV Sourcebook* provided a comprehensive reference work that supported the research and clinical decisions made by the work groups and the task force responsible for updating the *DSM.* This publication included the results of over 150 literature reviews as well as reports outlining the data analysis and re-analysis and reports from the field trials. In addition, the four volumes of the sourcebook culminated the final decisions made by the task and work groups, presenting the rationale in an executive summary (APA, 1995). However, because of this emphasis on evidence-based diagnostic categories and the resulting criteria, publication was delayed until May 1994. Questions continued to be raised about the new edition after it was published. Some professionals questioned whether the *DSM-IV* would detract attention and efforts toward substantiating earlier versions of the manual. It was felt that simply adopting this newer version of the *DSM* without clearly addressing problems of the earlier version (*DSM-III-R*) could have the same disruptive impact on research in regard to the overall reliability (Zimmerman, 1988).

DSM-IV-TR: THE LATEST REVISION

The latest revision of the *DSM,* the *Diagnostic and Statistical Manual of Mental Disorders (Fourth Edition) Text Revision (DSM-IV-TR),* upon which this text is based, was published in 2000. Although Chapter 2 will discuss this version of the text in detail, a brief summary of the *DSM-IV-TR* is provided here. In 1997, the work and assignments for the new task groups for the text revision were assigned. Since the *DSM* has historically been used as an education tool, it was felt that recent research might be overlooked if a revision wasn't published prior to *DSM-V,* which is anticipated to publish in 2005. Surprisingly, however, even with the addition of much new research and information the *DSM-IV* continued to be relatively up to date.

Basically, in formulating the text revisions none of the categories, diagnostic codes, or criteria from the *DSM-IV* was changed. However, more supplemental information is now provided for many of the current categories. In addition, more information is provided on many of the field trials that were introduced in the *DSM-IV* but were not yet completed or required updated research findings to be applied. Furthermore, special attention was paid to updating the sections in terms

QUICK REFERENCE

INTENT OF THE *DSM-IV-TR* REVISIONS

According to the American Psychiatric Association, the intent of the latest revision is:

- To correct any factual errors that were identified in the printing of the *DSM-IV.*
- To review information to ensure that information is up to date, including the latest research and supporting information available.
- To make educational improvements to enhance the value of the *DSM* as a teaching tool.
- To be sure the new *ICD-9-CM* codes were included in the text, as many of these codes did not become available until 1996—the year after publication of the *DSM-IV.*

of diagnostic findings, cultural information, and other information to clarify the diagnostic categories (APA, 2000).

DIAGNOSTIC LABELS

Regardless of the controversy surrounding the use of the current and earlier versions of the *DSM* as a diagnostic assessment tool, the use of this and other similar measures continues. One of the biggest concerns remains: that categorizing an individual with a mental health diagnosis can result in a psychiatric label that is difficult to remove. In fact, some mental health professionals feel so strongly against the idea of labeling clients that some continue to resist the use of this assessment scheme in their practice. For example (as will be discussed later in this text), if a child is given the diagnosis of *Conduct Disorder* in youth, many professionals believe that this condition will continue into adulthood resulting in the life-long mental health condition known as *Antisocial Personality Disorder.* Such a label, whether accurately or inaccurately placed, can be very damaging to the client because of the negative connotations that characterize it. Furthermore, the negative connotations that sometimes accompany the diagnostic label of *Conduct Disorder* (i.e., generally nonresponsive to intervention, lack of moral standards, and lack of guilt) may result in the conduct-disordered behaviors (i.e., severe aggression toward people or animals). These types of behaviors are unacceptable by all societal standards yet if part of a diagnosis and the client has no control, the behaviors may be viewed as acceptable or unchangeable in the individual. Therefore, these behaviors are accepted or tolerated because they are related to a mental disorder.

> ## QUICK REFERENCE
>
> ### *DSM-IV-TR:* POSITIVE ASPECTS (PRO) AND NEGATIVE ASPECTS (CON)
>
> **PRO:** Leads to uniform and improved diagnosis.
> **CON:** Can lead to diagnostic labels.
>
> **PRO:** Improves *informed* professional communication through uniformity.
> **CON:** Provides limited information on the relationship between environmental considerations and aspects of the mental health condition.
>
> **PRO:** Provides the basis for a comprehensive educational tool.
> **CON:** Does not describe intervention strategy.

In utilizing mental health assessment schemes, the placement of a label remains. This is an issue that all clinical practitioners struggle with as they try to balance the needs of the most appropriate assessment criteria with what is most reimbursable for service. In the ideal situation labels would not exist, nor would the treatment for certain mental health conditions be more likely than others to be reimbursed. Often in health and mental health practice much of the assessment and diagnosis process is completed based on service reimbursement needs. All health care professionals feel pressure to focus on diagnostic categories that are most likely to be reimbursed. For mental health practitioners, this requires careful evaluation of what is actually happening with the client and, regardless of reimbursement, what will cause the least difficulty for the client in terms of overcoming a diagnostic label with negative connotations or a label for which treatment is typically not reimbursed.

ANOTHER MENTAL HEALTH ASSESSMENT MEASURE

So great was the discontent with the possibility of placing an unfair label that some professionals decided to create their own diagnostic approach. One such group was social workers who believed strongly in and base all practice strategy on the recognition of the person in environment or person in situation (Colby & Dziegielewski, 2001). The individual is believed to be part of the social environment and his or her actions cannot be separated from this system. The individual is influenced by environmental factors and in turn the individual can influence environmental factors.

Impetus toward the development of such a perspective was based on criticisms such as Carlton's (1984), which pointed out that since mental health practitioners had not developed their own classification and diagnostic system they were forced to use psychiatric-based typologies. This reliance was problematic because psychiatric typologies developed for classification of mental illness were not adequate for taking into account the environmental influences. Since these existing categories did not involve psychosocial situations or units larger than the individual, problems were not viewed from an environmental context thereby reducing the problems to being classified as a mental illness (Carlton, 1984). This absence of an accepted system of classification and diagnosis for social work created a burden for practitioners. Since insurance companies required a medical diagnosis before service reimbursement, social workers, as well as psychologists and other mental health professionals, waged a long and difficult fight to use *DSM* independently for third-party payment purposes.

Support for a new diagnostic classification scheme emerged (Karls & Wandrei, 1996a). This new system was designed to focus on these aspects (psychosocial situations, units larger than the individual) and was called the Person-in-Environment Classification System or PIE (Karls & Wandrei, 1996a, 1996b). The PIE was developed through an award given to the California Chapter of the National Association of Social Workers (NASW) from the NASW Program Advancement Fund (Whiting, 1996). Basically, the PIE is built around two major premises: recognition of social considerations and the person-in-environment stance—the cornerstones on which all social work practice rests.

When the PIE was created, it was originally designed to support the use of the *DSM-IV,* not substitute for it. Its purpose was to evaluate the social environment and to impact the revisions of the *DSM.* Therefore, the PIE adopted features of the *DSM* multiaxis system in its assessment typology and had a notable influence on the revisions of the *DSM,* particularly in the area of recognizing environmental problems. One concrete example of the PIE's influence on the *DSM-IV* is when Axis IV of the diagnostic system was changed to reflect "psychosocial and environmental problems," from the previous focus of the *DSM-III-R* Axis IV, which listed the "severity of psychosocial stressors."

> The PIE system calls first for a social work assessment that is translated into a description of coding of the client's problems in social functioning. Social functioning is the client's ability to accomplish the activities necessary for daily living (for example, obtaining food, shelter, and transportation) and to fulfill major social roles as required by the client's subculture or community. (Karls & Wandrei, 1996a, p. vii)

Therefore, the PIE was formulated in response to the need to identify the problems of clients in a way that health professionals can easily understand (Karls & Wandrei, 1996a, 1996b). As a form of classification system for adults, the PIE provides:

1. Common language for social workers in all settings to describe their clients' problems in social functioning.

2. A common capsulated description of social phenomena that could facilitate intervention or ameliorate problems presented by clients.
3. A basis for gathering data needed to measure the need for services and to design human service programs to evaluate effectiveness.
4. A mechanism for clearer communication among social work practitioners, administrators, and researchers.
5. A basis for clarifying the domain of social work in human service fields.

In professional practice, tools such as the PIE can facilitate the identification and assessment of clients in a way that health professionals can easily understand (Karls & Wandrei, 1996a, 1996b).

These practitioners believe that usage of the PIE, when compared to the *DSM-IV* and the *DSM-IV-TR,* allows mental health professionals a way to further codify the numerous environmental factors that must be considered when looking at an individual's situation. Classification systems such as the PIE offer mental health professionals a way to systematically address social factors in the context of the client's environment. Systems such as this can assist professionals in obtaining a clear sense of the relationship the problem has to the environment in a friendly and adaptable way.

DSM-IV IN ACTION: UTILIZATION OF MENTAL HEALTH ASSESSMENT

Mental health professionals have a unique role in assessment and diagnosis that cannot be underestimated.

As part of either an interdisciplinary or multidisciplinary team, the mental health professional brings a wealth of information in regard to the environment and family considerations essential to practice strategy. If the mental health professional takes the perspective that emphasizes client skill building and strength enhancement, he or she will be well equipped to play a key role in the psychosocial assessment of the client as well as to establish the treatment plan that will guide and determine future service delivery (Slomski, 2000).

For practitioners, the hesitancy and reluctance to differentiate between what constitutes a diagnosis or diagnostic impression and what constitutes a thorough assessment can create obvious difficulties in practice focus and strategy. Therefore, one major purpose of this chapter is to explore the relationship between diagnosis and assessment and determine exactly what the differences are, and when it is best to use one term or the other. To facilitate practice strategy, a combination approach utilizing the meaning inherent in each term is suggested.

DIAGNOSIS AND ASSESSMENT: IS THERE A DIFFERENCE?

The formulation of an assessment that leads to the diagnosis of a client's mental health problems has been a serious source of debate within the profession. According to Carlton (1984), the debate stems from the fact that there are no clear differences when defining what is meant by the terms *diagnosis* and *assessment*.

When looking specifically at the features inherent in the diagnosis, the same features remain and actually overlap in the definition of the assessment. In today's practice environment, it is not uncommon to use these words interchangeably (Dziegielewski, 1996, 1998; Dziegielewski & Holliman, 2001). When documenting treatment for reimbursement, however, it is probably better to use *assessment* or *diagnostic assessment* in place of *diagnosis* (Dziegielewski & Leon, 2001a). The primary reason for this is that assessment is often not directly related to the medical model, whereas historically the term diagnosis often is (Barker, 1995).

In the application of mental health practice, when two elements within the same process are not considered distinct, confusion can result. This allows the concepts inherent in each to blur and overlap in terms of application. This is further complicated by the multiplicity of meanings that can be applied to the terms used to describe each aspect. When applied directly to behaviorally based practice, the major difficulty occurs in differentiating clearly within the professional intervention "what constitutes an assessment" and "what constitutes the diagnosis." Furthermore, this lack of clarity of definition can result in health and mental health professionals applying social, personal, and professional interpretations that are varied and nonuniform.

Diagnosis

It is easy to see how the actual definition, criteria, and subsequent tasks of assessment and diagnosis can be viewed as very similar. This overlap of definition and criteria, however, is not always shared among the other professions. For example, in nursing assessment often has been viewed as precluding the diagnosis. In this interpretation, the assessment is the building block on which the diagnosis is established (Rankin, 1996). Since many health and mental health practitioners subscribe to the medical model, this idea of separate and unique functions between assessment and diagnosis requires further exploration. No matter what it is called, or regardless of whether a health or mental health practitioner truly subscribes to or supports this distinction between assessment and diagnosis, awareness of the blurring that exists in defining the two terms is critical.

The most widely accepted definition of diagnosis is based on the medical model. Based on this model, diagnosis is guided by

> **diagnosis:** [t]he process of identifying a problem (social and mental, as well as medical) and its underlying causes and formulating a solution. In early social work delineation, it is one of the three processes, along with social study and treatment. Currently, many social workers prefer to call this process assessment because of the medical connotations that often accompany the term "diagnosis." Other social workers think of diagnosis as the process of seeking underlying causes and assessment as having more to do with the analysis of relevant information. (Barker, 1995, p. 100)

three related activities: (1) the determination of the identity of a disease or illness supported by concrete somatic, behavioral, or concrete features; (2) ascertaining the cause or etiology of the illness or disease based on these features; and (3) making any diagnostic impression based on a systematic scientific examination (Carlton, 1984).

In fields such as social work and counseling, however, diagnosis is perceived and generally interpreted in a broader sense. Corey (2001b) states that the purpose of diagnosis in counseling and psychotherapy is to "identify the disruptions in a client's presenting behavior and lifestyle" (p. 52). Furthermore, Corey believes that diagnosis and assessment cannot be separated and must be conceived as a continual process that focuses broadly on understanding the client. To further bridge the gap between viewing diagnosis in isolation, Perlman (1957) warned social workers not to perceive that determining and formulating a diagnosis ". . . would magically yield a cure to a reluctance to come to any conclusion beyond an impression . . . grasping at ready made labels" (p. 165). Perlman defined diagnosis as the identification of both *process* and *product*. According to Perlman, the diagnostic process was defined as ". . . examining the parts of a problem for the import of their particular nature and organization, for the interrelationship among them, for the relationships between them and the means to their solution" (p. 164).

Carlton (1984) further exemplified the issue of process in the diagnostic procedure:

> To be effective and responsive, any clinical social work diagnosis must be a diagnosis "for now" a tentative diagnosis. It is the basis of joint problem solving work for the clinician and client. To serve this purpose, the diagnosis must be shared with the client(s) and, as their work gets underway and proceeds through the various time phases of clinical social work process, the diagnosis must change as the configuration of the elements of the problem change. Thus clinical social work diagnosis is evolutionary in character and responsive to the changing nature of the condition or problem in which it relates. (p. 77)

In addressing the diagnostic process, the *diagnostic product* must be obtained. The diagnostic product is generally identified as what is obtained after the counseling professional utilizes the information gained through the diagnostic assessment. This includes drawing inferences and reaching conclusions based on scientific principles that are logically derived from the information obtained. Corey (2001b) suggested that certain questions be asked:

- What is happening in the client's life now?
- What does the client want from therapy?

- What is the client learning from therapy?
- To what degree is the client applying what is learned?

Corey believed that questions such as these allow for assessment and diagnosis to be joined in a tentative hypothesis, and that these educated hunches can be formed and shared with the client throughout the treatment process. Therefore, to establish a firm foundation for the diagnostic process, the professional therapist must be skilled in obtaining and interpreting the information acquired. In identifying the diagnostic process, Carlton (1984) stressed the importance of recognizing three factors: the biomedical, psychological, and social. He felt that it was essential for professionals to understand the biopsychosocial approach to health care practice and that balance must be obtained between these factors. The balance between these factors, however, does not have to be equal and the area of emphasis can change. It is always the situation experienced by the client that places the most importance on what area must be addressed first.

For example, a client diagnosed with HIV has many issues that must be addressed. First, the emphasis for diagnosis may be placed in the biomedical area. The client may need immediate information to determine whether the medical test used is positive. Medical tests can determine whether the t-cell count (a type of body protection factor) has been obtained. Information yielded by this test can help to establish a baseline for current and future levels of self-protection from illness and opportunistic infectious diseases. Once these tests have been run, the client will need educational services to provide information on the effects of the disease, what infection means, and what to expect as the illness continues.

Once this is addressed, emphasis on the diagnostic focus may shift to the social aspects related to the client's condition. Since this disease is often sexually transmitted, the partners who are or have been sexually active with the client need to be considered. The focus is how to best tell loved ones what has happened and address issues related to what this illness will mean for future social relationships. Later, the emphasis for treatment may shift to the individual client and dealing with many other personal issues that need be resolved. In diagnosis, regardless of what area is emphasized and with what intensity, understanding and integration of the biopsychosocial approach is considered essential.

Once the process has been established, attention has traditionally been focused on the diagnostic product. In measuring the diagnostic product, Falk (1981, as cited in Carlton, 1984), suggested fourteen areas that need to be addressed in providing diagnostic impressions—life stage, health condition, family and other memberships, racial and ethnic memberships, social class, occupation, financial situation, entitlements, transportation, housing, mental functioning, cognition (personal), cognition (capability), and psychosocial elements. Utilizing a biopsychosocial perspective, the areas are further broken down into three primary categories: biomedical, psychological, and social factors. Since all mental professionals are responsible for assisting with the provision of concrete services, recognition of these factors is often considered part of the practitioner's role in assessment with the addition of a fourth area that addresses the functional/situational factors that affect the diagnostic process.

In summary, historically it has always been essential that the activity of diagnosis be related to the client's needs. A diagnosis is established to help better understand and prepare to address the probable symptoms relative to the mental disorder. Factors that result from the diagnostic procedure are shared with the client when needed and assist in self-help or continued skill building. From a medical perspective, the diagnostic process has been used to examine the situation and provide the basis to initiate the helping process. Later in the treatment regime, the formal diagnostic process will yield and contribute to formal assessment that is based on the information learned. The diagnostic information gathered is used to facilitate the establishment of the intervention plan.

Overall, the mental health professions have embraced the necessity for diagnosis in practice—although this need is often recognized with caution. Furthermore, while accepting the requirement for completion of a diagnosis, much discontent and dissatisfaction among professionals continue to exist. For some mental health professionals, when the diagnosis is referred to in the most traditional sense, reflective of the medical or "illness" perspective, some fear that it will be inconsistent with professional values and ethics. For these professionals, an illness-focused perspective detracts from an individual's capacity for initiative based on self-will or rational choice. Today, however, this view is changing. Many mental health professionals, struggling for practice survival in a competitive, cost-driven health care system, disagree. They feel that practice reality requires that a traditional method of diagnosis be completed in order to receive reimbursement. It is this capacity for reimbursement that influences and determines who will be offered the opportunity to provide service (Steps Taken to Watchdogs for Managed Care, 1997).

Assessment

Currently, most mental health practitioners are active in obtaining and completing assessment within the general context of gathering diagnostic considerations (Corey, 2001a, 2001b). According to Barker (1995), assessment involves "determining the nature, cause, progression, and prognosis of a problem and the personalities and situations involved" as well as understanding and making changes to minimize or resolve it (p. 27). Assessment requires thinking and formulating from the facts within a client's situation to reach tentative conclusions regarding their meaning (Sheafor, Horejsi, & Horejsi, 1997). Therefore, assessment is viewed as an essential ingredient to start the therapeutic process and is the hallmark of all professional (as opposed to lay) activity. Furthermore, Corey (2001a, 2001b) reminds us that, ideally, assessment is a collaborative process as it becomes part of the interaction between client and therapist. From this perspective, assessment controls and directs all aspects of practice, including the nature, direction, and scope. Corey (2001b) warns, however, that assessment and diagnosis cannot be separated and must be continually updated as part of the intervention process.

For professional practitioners who often fill many different roles as part of the interdisciplinary team, it remains expected that the process of assessment must reflect diversity and flexibility. For the completion of an accurate assessment, environmental pressures and changes in client problem situations make the need to examine and reexamine the client's situation critical. If, in the mental health setting, the process of assessment is rushed, superficial factors may be highlighted and significant ones deemphasized or overlooked. Professionals bear administrative and economic pressures to make recommendations for consumer protection while preserving health care quality.

In general, the problem of differentiating between diagnosis and assessment is not unique to any one of the counseling disciplines. Since none of the helping professions developed in isolation, the assessment process has been influenced by all, including medicine, psychiatry, nursing, psychology and social work, marriage and family therapy as well as other counseling professionals. Historically, assessment has been referred to as *diagnosis* or the *psychosocial diagnosis* (Rauch, 1993). Although Rauch admits there are similarities in the two terms and warns professional helpers not to accept them as interchangeable. In this perspective, diagnosis focuses on symptoms and assigns categories that best fit the symptoms the client is experiencing. Assessment on the other hand is broader and focuses on the person-in-situation or person-in-environment stance.

In practice today, regardless of the exact meaning of the term *diagnosis,* it is often used interchangeably with the term *assessment* (Corey, 2001a, 2001b; Dziegielewski, 1998). This blurring of terminology is becoming so accustomed that even the *DSM-IV* (1994) and *DSM-IV-TR* (2000) use both words, and at times it appears that these words are interchangeable throughout the book when used to describe the diagnostic impression. Therefore, this terminology as well as the helping activities and the practice strategy that result appear to be forced to adapt to the dominant culture (Dziegielewski, 1998). Since these expectations generally deal with reimbursement for service, whether conscious or not, they influence and guide practice intervention and strategy. Unfortunately, pressure within the environment supports the expectation to reduce services to clients, treat only those who are covered by insurance or can pay privately, or terminate clients because the services are too costly (Ethics Meet Managed Care, 1997). Therefore, the role of assessment and diagnosis, regardless of what we call it, is a critical one because it can determine what, when, and how services will be provided.

A COMBINATION APPROACH: REALIZATION OF THE NEW ASSESSMENT

Dziegielewski (1998) outlined five factors that guide the initiation of accurate assessment that will ultimately relate to the implementation of practice strategy. When working with individuals and preparing to complete an assessment, the following should always be considered:

1. *Examine carefully how much information the client is willing to share and the accuracy of that information.* The information the client is willing to share and the accuracy of what is shared is essential to ensure the depth and application of what is presented as well as the subsequent motivation and behavioral changes that will be needed in the intervention process. Gathering information from the *DSM* and matching it to what the client is reporting requires an awareness of this phenomena and how it can relate to the symptoms that are being reported. Special attention needs to be given not only to what the client is saying but also the context in which this information is revealed. What is going on in the client's life at this time? What are the systemic factors that could be influencing certain behaviors? What will revealing the information mean to family and friends, or how will it affect the client's support system? Gathering this information is important especially since a client may fear that stating accurate information could have negative consequences. For example, clients may withhold information if they feel revealing the information may have legal ramifications (they will be sent to jail), social consequences (rejection of family or friends), or medical implications (re-hospitalization).

2. *As accurate a definition of the problem as possible needs to be gathered as it will not only guide the diagnostic impression, it will also guide the approach or method of intervention that will be used.* Furthermore, the temptation should always be resisted to let the diagnostic impression or intervention approach guide the problem, rather than allowing the problem to guide the approach (Sheafor et al., 1997). This is critical since so much of the problem identification process in assessment is an intellectual activity. Therefore, the professional practitioner should never lose sight of the ultimate purpose of the assessment process, which is to complete an assessment that will help to establish a concrete service plan that can best address a client's needs.

3. *All professional practitioners need to be aware of how their beliefs can influence or affect the interpretation of the problem or both.* An individual's worldview or paradigm helps to shape the way the world is viewed. Most professionals agree that it is what an individual believes that creates the foundation for which he or she is and how he or she learns. In ethical and moral professional practice, it is essential that these individual influences do not directly affect the assessment process. Therefore, the practitioner's values, beliefs, and practices that can influence treatment outcomes must be clearly identified from the onset of treatment. It is important for the professional practitioner to ask, "What is my immediate reaction to the client and the problem expressed?" Clients have a right to make their own decisions, and the helping professional must do everything possible to ensure this right and not allow personal opinion to impair the completion of a proper assessment. In addition, since counseling professionals often serve as part of an interdisciplinary team, the beliefs and values of the members of the team must also be considered. This makes the awareness of value conflicts that might arise among the other team members essential. Awareness is critical in order to prepare for how personal feelings and resultant opinions might inhibit practitioners from accurately assessing what a client is doing and how the client perceives issues. As part of a team, each member holds the additional responsibility of helping others on the team be as objective as possible in the assessment process. Helping practitioners should always be available to assist these other professionals, and always advocate for how best to serve the client's needs. Values and beliefs can be influential in identifying factors within individual decision-making strategies, and remain an important factor to consider and identify in the assessment process.

4. *Issues surrounding culture and race should be addressed openly in the assessment phase to ensure that the most open and receptive environment is created.* Simply stated, the professional practitioner needs to be aware of his or her own cultural limitations, open to cultural differences, and recognize the integrity and the uniqueness of the client, while utilizing the client's own learning style, including his or her own resources and supports (Dziegielewski, 1996, 1997a).

For example, when utilizing the *DSM-IV,* cultural factors are stressed prior to establishing a diagnosis. The *DSM-IV-TR* (2000) emphasizes that delusions and hallucinations may be difficult to separate from the general beliefs or practices that may be related to a client's specific cultural custom or lifestyle. For this reason, an entire appendix is included in the *DSM-IV-TR* that describes and defines culturally bound syndromes that might affect the diagnosis and assessment process (APA, 1995, 2000).

5. *The assessment process must focus on client strengths and highlight the client's own resources for addressing problems that affect his or her activities of daily living and for providing continued support.* Identifying strengths and resources and linking them to problem behaviors with individual, family, and social functioning, however, may not be as easy as it sounds. Many people have a tendency to focus on the negatives and rarely praise themselves for the good they do.

This is further complicated by time-limited intervention settings where mental health professionals must quickly identify individual and collectively based strengths. The importance of accurately identifying clients' strengths and support networks is critical as later they will also be implemented into the intervention plan that is suggested as a means of continued growth and maintenance of wellness after the formal treatment period has ended.

COMPLETING THE DIAGNOSTIC-ASSESSMENT PROCESS

To initiate the process, it is assumed that the new type of assessment referred to here as the diagnostic assessment begins with the first client-professional practitioner interaction. The information gathered provides the database that will assist in determining the requirements and direction of the helping process. In assessment, it is expected that the professional will gather information about the present situation, a history of past issues, and anticipate service expectations for the future. This assessment should be multidimensional and always include creative interpretation of perspectives and alternatives for service delivery. Information gathered needs to follow a behavioral biopsychosocial approach to practice.

In this type of assessment, the biomedical factors are highlighted including information about the general physical health or medical condition of the client. Information should be considered from the practitioner's perspective as well as the client's perception. In addition, all information gathered needs to show the relationship between the biological or medical factors as well as the functioning level attained by these factors expressed in the ability to complete certain behaviors that maximize independence. In addition, concrete tasks are identified for the focus of increased future change efforts.

The second area to be considered is psychological factors. In this area, psychological functioning as noted through mental, cognitive health functioning is recorded along with how it affects occupational and social functioning. Another

---

QUICK REFERENCE

BIOMEDICAL FACTORS IN ASSESSMENT

General medical	The physical disability or illness the client reports and what specific ways it effects the client's social and occupational functioning and activities of daily living.
Perceived overall health status	Be sure to encourage the client to assess his or her own health status and assess what he or she is able to do to facilitate the change effort.

QUICK REFERENCE
PSYCHOLOGICAL FACTORS IN ASSESSMENT

Mental functioning	Describe the client's mental functioning. Complete a mental status measurement. Learn and utilize the multiaxis assessment system.
Cognitive functioning	Does the client have the ability to think and reason what is happening to him or her? Are they able to participate and make decisions in regard to their own best interest?
Assessment of lethality	Would the client hurt him- or herself or anyone else because of the perception of the problem he or she is experiencing?

important area that must also be addressed is lethality. For example, specific questions about whether the client is at risk for suicide or harming others must be asked and processed. If needed, immediate action may be warranted. It is in this portion of the assessment process that information as outlined in the *DSM-IV-TR* multiaxis system is clearly outlined. Chapters 2 and 3 will describe in depth how this is completed.

Last, when incorporating the behaviorally based biopsychosocial approach to assessment emphasis needs to be placed on identifying social and environmental factors. Most professionals would agree that environmental considerations are very important in measuring and assessing all other aspects of a client's needs. Identifying family, social supports, and cultural expectations are all important in helping the client ascertain what is the best course of action.

Generally, the client is seen as the primary source of data. As stated earlier, be sure to take the time to assess the accuracy of the information and determine whether the client may be either willingly or inadvertently withholding or exaggerating the information presented. Assessment is usually gathered through verbal and written reports. Verbal reports may be gathered from the client, significant others, family, friends, or other helping professionals. Critical information can also be derived from written reports such as medical documents, history and physical, previous clinical assessments, lab tests, and other clinical and diagnostic methods. Furthermore, information about the client can be derived through direct observation of verbal or physical behaviors or interaction patterns between other interdisciplinary team members, family, significant others, or friends. When seeking evidence-based practice, recognizing directly what a client is doing can be a critical factor in the diagnostic assessment process. Viewing and recording these patterns of communication can be extremely helpful in later establishing and developing strengths and resources as well as being utilized in the linking of problem behaviors

---

QUICK REFERENCE

SOCIAL AND ENVIRONMENTAL FACTORS IN ASSESSMENT

Social/societal help-seeking	Is the client open to outside help? What support system or helping networks are available to the client from those outside the immediate family or the community?
Occupational participation	How does a client's illness or disability impair or prohibit functioning in the work environment? Is the client in a supportive work environment?
Social support	Does the client have support from neighbors, friends, or community organizations (i.e., System church membership, membership in professional clubs)?
Family support	What support or help can be expected from relatives of the client?
Ethnic or religious affiliation	If the client is a member of a certain cultural or religious group, will this affiliation affect medical intervention and compliance issues?

---

to concrete indicators that reflect a client's performance. Remember that in addition to verbal reports, written reports that are reflective of practice effectiveness will almost always be expected. Often background sheets, psychological tests, or tests to measure health status or level of daily function may be utilized to establish more concrete measurement of client problem behaviors.

Although the client is perceived as the first and primary source of data, the current emphasis on evidence-based practice strategy, which necessitates gathering information from other sources, cannot be overstated. This means talking with the family and significant others to estimate planning support and assistance. It might also be important to gather information from other secondary sources such as the client's medical record and other health care providers. To facilitate assessment, the practitioner must be able to understand the client's medical situation. Knowledge of what certain medical conditions are and when to refer to other health professionals for continued care is an essential part of the assessment process.

In completing a multidimensional diagnostic assessment there are four primary steps for consideration:

1. *The problem must be recognized as interfering with daily functioning.* Here the practitioner must be active in uncovering problems that affect daily living

QUICK REFERENCE

**IMPORTANT CONSIDERATIONS FOR COMPLETING THE
NEW DIAGNOSTIC ASSESSMENT**

1. The problem must be recognized and linked to interference of daily functioning.
2. Special consideration must be given to the environmental context in which the behaviors are occurring.
3. Cultural considerations for both the client and the practitioner should be addressed and when possible discussed openly. Once problem behaviors are noted, criterion for the diagnostic impression is important only as it leads to assisting with identifying the needs of the client for a problem-solving strategy.
4. A complete diagnostic assessment involves more than the diagnostic impression, it involves utilizing the information gathered to best help the client and thereby, guide, enhance, and, in many cases, determine the course of treatment.

and engaging the client in self-help or skill building, changing behaviors, or both. It is important for the client to acknowledge that the problem exists, because once this is done ". . . the boundaries of the problem become clear, and exploration then proceeds in a normal fashion" (Hepworth, Rooney, & Larsen, 1997, p. 205).

2. *The problem must be clearly identified.* The problem of concern is what the client sees as important; after all, the client is the one who is expected to create the behavior change. In practice, it is common to receive referrals from other health care professionals. Special attention should always be given to referrals that clearly recommend a course of treatment or intervention. This type of focused referral may limit both the scope and intervention possibilities available to the client and when accepting these types of referrals the best interest of the client should always be paramount. Often focused referrals that limit the scope of the intervention can also provide the basis for reimbursement as well. Although referral information and suggestion should always be considered in your discussion with the client in identifying the problem, in terms of assessment and the resulting plan, the best interests of the client should always be paramount and the client should participate and help to identify the end result.

3. *Problem strategy must be developed.* Here the professional practitioner must help to clearly focus on the goals and objectives that will be followed in the intervention process. In the initial planning stage, identification of mutually agreed on and measurable goals and objective and concrete indicators that the goals and objectives have been reached will assist both the client and the practitioner to ensure practical, useful, and productive changes have been made.

4. *Once the problem strategy and plan are clearly identified, a diagnostic assessment plan must be implemented.* According to Sheafor, Horejsi, and Horejsi (1997) the plan of action is the ". . . bridge between the assessment and the intervention" (p. 135). Therefore, the outcome of the diagnostic assessment process is the completion of a plan that will guide, enhance, and in many cases determine the course of treatment to be implemented (Dziegielewski, 1998). With the complexity of human beings and the problems that they encounter, a properly prepared multidimensional diagnostic assessment is the essential first step for ensuring quality service delivery.

In summary, regardless of what type of tool is used to assist in the diagnostic assessment process, none of these classification systems suggest treatment approaches; they only provide diagnostic and assessment classifications. The intervention plan is derived after the assessment and depends on the practitioner's interpretation. Furthermore, regardless of what type of diagnostic assessment tool is utilized, all practitioners need to be able to: (1) choose, gather, and report this information systematically; (2) be aware and assist other multidisciplinary or interdisciplinary team members in the diagnostic process; (3) interpret and assist the client to understand what the results of the diagnostic assessment mean; and (4) assist the client to choose evidence-based and ethically wise modes of practice intervention.

PROFESSIONAL TRAINING IN THE PROFESSIONAL COUNSELING FIELDS

This book is written as a guide for several different disciplines of health and mental health professionals. Similar to the *DSM,* this book is designed to highlight use in medicine and psychiatry, psychology, social work, nursing, and counseling. This type of integration with so many diverse yet similar fields is no easy task since different professions follow different practice models and methods. Yet, regardless of which discipline a professional was trained in, he or she often has great overlap of therapeutic knowledge and skill. In the next chapter special attention will be given to how to apply the multiaxial diagnostic framework.

In the future, if professional practitioners are going to continue to utilize diagnostic assessment systems there are major implications for professional training and education. MacCluskie and Ingersoll (2001) are quick to remind us that if professionals of different disciplines are going to use the *DSM* each one must be trained and adequately prepared in its use in both classroom instruction and as part of a practicum or internship. This requires a more homogeneous approach to education and application be adopted among all the helping disciplines.

To provide this homogeneity from a practice perspective the answer is clearer since there is one goal that almost all professional helpers share: to "help clients manage their problems in living more effectively and develop unused or underused opportunities more fully" (Egan, 1998, p. 7). In today's practice environment, few would argue that the interdisciplinary approach of professionals working together to help the client is here to stay. Now, to extend unification and also ensure competent, ethical practitioners, these helping disciplines will also need to unite in terms of professional education. The first principle for the unification of professional education across disciplines is that (regardless of whether it is for social work, psychology, or other fields of professional counseling) training programs need to be more uniform and specific about what professional training entails; and, what effect the training has on those who participate? When training can be defined in a reasonably specific manner and measured empirically, these professions will be better able to assess its effects on client behavior. With the contemporary emphasis of professional accountability, the effort to predict and document specific outcomes of professional training is timely as well as warranted. The data also suggest that one way in which professional training can be further enhanced is through differential selection of specified treatment methods. Training in these different treatment methods will allow for different causative variables (i.e., feelings and actions) to be identified in the course of assessing the client's behavior. Some researchers believe that sticking primarily to traditional methods, which still comprise a great part of professional training that emphasizes dispositional (i.e., the direct relationship of the diagnosis and how it will relate to discharge) diagnoses, may result in diminishing accuracy of behavior assessment (Case & Lingerfelt, 1974; Dziegielewski, 1998).

Educators can improve the accuracy of client behavioral evaluations through the introduction of specific training in behavioral assessment. This may be the primary reason that in health care the behaviorally based biopsychosocial approach has gained in popularity. Clinical assessment, particularly when it emphasizes client behaviors, is a skill that can easily be taught, transmitted, and measured. Therefore, it is recommended that professional training include behavioral observation training on how to construct observable and reliable categories of behavior, and training in various systems of observation. This highlights the need for professional education to question training future practitioners in traditional methods when the likely consequence is that accuracy in behavioral assessment will decrease.

SUMMARY

The concept of formulating and completing a diagnosis, assessment, or the diagnostic assessment is richly embedded in the history and practice of many of the professional fields of helping. The exact definition of what constitutes diagnosis and what constitutes assessment remains blurred and overlapping. In professional practice the words continue to be used interchangeably, which can be confusing as the functions were originally intended to be separate (Dziegielewski, 1996, 1997a, 2001). For all professional practitioners, compelling demands to address practice reimbursement has clearly emphasized this rich tradition. Furthermore, despite the differences that currently exist between the disciplines, the degree to which a professional has power in the therapeutic marketplace rests on the degree to which a profession is licensed to use the *DSM* for diagnosis (MacCluskie & Ingersoll, 2001).

One of the most valid criticisms about the provision of counseling services is the lack of information about quality outcomes (K. Davis, 1998). To address this concern, numerous types of diagnosis and assessment measurements are currently available. Many of these are structured into unique categories and classification schemes. This makes it essential for the practitioner to be familiar with some of the major formal methods of diagnosis and assessment, especially the ones that are most commonly used and accepted in the area of mental health service delivery (S. R. Davis & Meier, 2001). All mental health practitioners, regardless of discipline, need to utilize this information for systematic ways to interpret and assist the client to understand what the results of the diagnostic assessment mean and how best to select empirically sound and ethically wise modes of practice intervention.

No matter whether we call what professional practitioners do assessment, diagnosis, or a combination of these resulting in the diagnostic assessment, the function remains a critical part of the helping process. As Dziegielewski (1998) stated, based on the general context of reimbursement or fee-for-service, is it wise for all professionals to continue to struggle for differentiation between the diagnosis and assessment? Once this issue and the differences between the two terms have been brought successfully to the forefront, the question arises about who is eligible to make a diagnosis or an assessment. If this happens in the current turbulent service environment, all professionals may be forced to lobby for providing and justifying something that they have been doing since the early development of the field. Do the various helping professions really want to embark on this quest?

Diagnosis and assessment constitute the critical first step that is essential to formulating the plan for intervention (Dziegielewski & Leon, 2001b; Dziegielewski, Johnson, & Webb, in press). Thus, it is the plan for intervention that sets the entire tone and circumstance to be included in the professional helping process.

To compete in today's current practice environment, the role of the professional practitioner is twofold: (1) to ensure that quality service is provided to the client and (2) that the client has access and is given an opportunity to see that his or her health and mental health needs are addressed. Neither of these tasks is easy or popular. The push is for behaviorally based practice to be conducted with limited resources and services. The resultant competition to be the one designated as the provider has changed the role of the practitioner as a service provider. Amid this turbulence, the role and necessity of the services the professional practitioner provides in the area of assessment and intervention remain clear. All helping professionals must know and utilize the tools relative to the diagnostic assessment. Proper completion of the diagnostic assessment is the first step in the treatment hierarchy, and it is crucial that health and mental health professionals have comprehensive training in this area.

—————— QUESTIONS FOR FURTHER THOUGHT ——————

1. Is there a difference between the terms *diagnosis* and *assessment?*
2. Are these terms treated differently and assumed to have different meanings if the practitioner is in a particular health or mental health setting?
3. What do you believe is the most helpful aspect of using manuals such as the *DSM-IV-TR* in the diagnostic process?
4. What do you feel are the least helpful aspects of using manuals such as the *DSM-IV-TR* in professional practice?
5. As a diagnostic/assessment tool, do you believe that use of the *DSM* will facilitate your practice experience? Why or why not?

2

Basics and Application

The concept of formulating and completing a diagnostic assessment is richly embedded in the history of mental health practice. Furthermore, for many practitioners, the desire to master this process has been emphasized by compelling demands to address practice reimbursement. Therefore, all mental health practitioners need to become familiar with the major formal methods of diagnostic assessment, especially the ones used and accepted in the area of health and mental health service delivery. The information gathered during the diagnostic assessment is important for identifying and classifying mental health disorders and reporting this information systematically to insurance companies for reimbursement. The practitioner, as well as other multidisciplinary or interdisciplinary team members, can also utilize the information gathered from a comprehensive diagnostic assessment to ensure quality care. Furthermore, the information can be utilized to better understand the client and in turn better help the client understand him- or herself. Once completed, the diagnostic assessment becomes the foundation for identifying the problem and can be utilized in establishing treatment plan considerations and the best course of intervention for a particular client.

As emphasized in Chapter 1, the *International Classification of Diseases-Tenth Edition (ICD-10)* and the *International Classification of Diseases-Ninth Edition-Clinical Modification (ICD-9-CM)* along with the *Diagnostic and Statistical Manual of Mental Disorders-Fourth Edition-Text Revision (DSM-IV-TR;* American Psychiatric Association [APA], 2000), reflect the official nomenclature used in mental health and other health-related facilities in the United States.

Diagnostic assessment systems such as the *DSM,* the *ICD,* and the *PIE* are examples of three descriptive (categorical) classification schemes that cross all theoretical orientations. This text demonstrates the application of these classification

---

QUICK REFERENCE

CONVERSION TABLES FOR *ICD 8, 9,* AND *10*

To review the conversion tables that list the various changes between the different versions of the *International Classification of Diseases* (ICD), go to the Web site:

http://www.who.int/msa/mnh/ems/icd10/convtab/intro.htm

schemes and describes how assessment, treatment planning, and intervention become intertwined. Since assessment and treatment are primarily based on the practitioner's clinical judgment and interpretation, a thorough grounding in these classification systems will help the practitioner to make relevant, useful, and ethically sound evaluations of clients.

Since most fields of practice utilize the *DSM* as the basis of the formal diagnostic assessment system, this text focuses on this classification scheme. This chapter introduces the *DSM-IV-TR* and its use in mental health practice. The multiaxis diagnostic system is described from both a technical and clinical viewpoint. In Chapter 3, the basics presented here will be applied to establishing a multiaxis diagnosis that leads to good, accurate documentation and treatment planning.

DEVELOPMENT OF THE *DSM* CLASSIFICATION SYSTEM

The *DSM* was originally published in 1952, with the most recent version the *DSM-IV-TR* being published in 2000. The publications of the *DSM* correspond to the publications of the *ICD* with the next version of the *DSM* scheduled for 2005, anticipated to follow the publication of the *ICD-10-CM* by the World Health Organization in 2004.

Originally, the American Psychiatric Association developed the *DSM* for statistical, epidemiological, and reporting purposes. Today, with the revisions to the *DSM* that have been made over the years, the *DSM-IV-TR* is designed to be compatible with (but not identical to) the issues presented in the *International Classification of Diseases (ICD)*. The *ICD* is credited as the first official international classification system for mental disorders. The first edition was published in 1948.

In the United States, most health-related and mental health practitioners use the *DSM* to classify mental health problems. However, the *DSM* has been designed for assessment purposes only and does not suggest treatment approaches. This makes the *DSM* essential as a starting point for determining the nature of a client's problem but also requires that mental health practitioners become familiar with the latest and most effective forms of intervention available once the diagnostic criteria have been met.

Although the *ICD-10* and the *ICD-9-CM* are often used interchangeably, the *ICD-9-CM* is most commonly referenced in the United States because of its direct relevance to clinical management. The *DSM-IV-TR*'s specific diagnostic coding system is most similar to the categories utilized in the *ICD-9-CM*. In fact, the *ICD* clinical modification was developed to facilitate its use in practice and made it more relevant for practice in the United States. Many other countries, however, now use the *ICD-10*. Thus, it is a good idea for mental health practitioners to be familiar with both editions of the *ICD,* in addition to the *DSM*.

DSM-IV-TR: WHY ANOTHER TEXT REVISION?

There were multiple reasons for this latest version of the text revision. First, the authors corrected factual errors that cropped up in the *DSM-IV*. For example, under Pervasive Developmental Disorder Not Otherwise Specified an error was corrected that allowed the diagnosis to be given in cases in which there was a pervasive impairment in only one developmental area rather than multiple related areas (APA, 2000). Other areas in which factual inconsistencies were corrected included Personality Change Due to a General Medical Condition and Bipolar Disorders with Melancholic Features.

Second, the authors also updated the information in the *DSM-IV* with the latest supporting documentation. For example, better examples of the different types of behavior were added under Autistic Disorder. Similar data were added to many of the diagnostic categories to assist practitioners in forming a more accurate diagnostic impression.

Third, at the time the *DSM-IV* was published in 1994, some of the field trials and literature reviews were still underway. The *DSM-IV-TR* includes the latest research results and integrates how this information relates to the clinical diagnostic category. The majority of the categories and information from the *DSM-IV* remained up to date without modification.

Fourth, since the *DSM* is often used in educational settings to teach professionals about diagnostic categories, more information was added to support this use.

Finally, not all the *ICD-9-CM* codes were available until 1996, thus those who bought early copies of the *DSM-IV* did not receive the complete *ICD* coding. Later printings included the *ICD* update. It is easy to check whether the *ICD* codes are included in the *DSM-IV,* simply look at the front cover. If the coding update is included, the cover should have a round orange stamp stating "Updated with *ICD-9-CM* Codes." The *DSM-IV-TR* incorporates the *ICD-9-CM* codes into the text.

QUICK REFERENCE

REASONS FOR CHANGE IN *DSM-IV-TR*

1. Corrected factual errors.
2. Allowed the work study groups to review each of the diagnostic categories to ensure that information was timely and updated.
3. Incorporated new information from literature reviews and research studies.
4. Enhanced the educational value of the book.
5. Incorporated the updated coding changes from *ICD-9-CM.*

Making the Mind-Body Connection

In using the *DSM-IV-TR*, there are several issues that need to be explored. First, and perhaps most important, is to remember the importance of *linking the mind and the body*. Individuals are complex beings and when a categorical approach to identifying and classifying disorders is utilized, such as that presented in the *DSM*, the temptation is great to apply concrete and discrete criteria that do not include the full range of an individual's existence or situation. In professional practice, it is easy to see how the line between what constitutes good *physical health* and what constitutes good *mental health* might be blurred (Dziegielewski, 1998). Just as it is impossible to separate the mind from the body, the concept of wholeness must also be considered. This means that a diagnosis alone is never enough to assess a situation completely. System and environmental variables must always be considered as well.

In the *DSM-IV-TR*, a classification system is used to assist health and mental health professionals to complete a comprehensive diagnostic assessment. To start this process, the practitioner must be clear on what exactly constitutes a mental disorder. This definition can help to guide decisions that determine the boundary between normality and pathology (APA, 2000). However, this definition is only provided to facilitate the diagnostic process and practitioners must be careful not to be too quick in categorizing an individual's problems because this may result in an inaccurate diagnostic label. The symptoms with which an individual may present for treatment may vary based on numerous variables, including psychological, social, cultural, and environmental circumstances.

One common misconception about the *DSM* diagnostic scheme is that "the classification of mental disorders classifies people, when actually what are being classified are the disorders that people have" (APA, 2000, p. xxxi). Professionals must be sensitive to the labels they use when referring to people who suffer from a mental health disorder. For example, never refer to an individual as "a schizophrenic" but rather as "an individual with Schizophrenia." Consideration should always be used to ensure that terms are not used incorrectly and that individuals who suffer from a mental disorder are not referred to or treated in a careless or derogatory manner. It is important to guard against this type of labeling and to remind others of this as well.

Who Can Use the DSM-IV-TR?

The *DSM-IV-TR*, states clearly that it was designed to be used in a wide variety of settings, including inpatient and outpatient settings as well as consultation and liaison work. Use of the diagnostic system is also encouraged for practitioners or clinicians with very different training and expertise. Furthermore, the book

---

QUICK REFERENCE

mental disorder: A mental disorder is conceptualized as a clinically significant behavior or psychological syndrome or pattern that occurs in an individual and is associated with present distress (e.g., a painful symptom) or disability (i.e., impairment in one or more areas of functioning) or with a significantly increased risk of suffering death, pain, disability, or an important loss of freedom. In addition, this symptom or pattern must not be merely an expectable and culturally sanctioned response to a particular event ... whatever its source it must currently be considered a manifestation of a behavioral, psychological, or biological dysfunction in the individual (APA, 2000, p. xxxi).

---

endorses the importance of the application of clinical skill and judgment and stresses that many different orientations can be highlighted in the intervention strategy once the diagnostic assessment has been completed. The practitioner may reference intervention approaches such as biological, psychodynamic, cognitive, behavioral, interpersonal, family systems, or a combination of these. Chapter 3 highlights the completion of the diagnostic assessment whereas Chapter 4 assists the practitioner to move beyond the diagnostic assessment phase and consider appropriate practice strategy based on a variety of practice frameworks.

The *DSM-IV-TR* was not designed for use by the lay public. A practitioner should never suggest that a client use the *DSM* to read more about a disorder. The *DSM* is very complex and could overwhelm a patient unfamiliar with the technical jargon. The role of the professional is to interpret the diagnostic criteria and work with the client on what the best course of action would be.

The professional practitioners who use the *DSM-IV-TR* include psychiatrists and other physicians, psychologists, social workers, occupational and rehabilitation therapists, and other health and mental health professionals. These professionals need to be trained in how to use this categorical approach as well as being aware of the potential for misuse that exists before putting it into practice. Special care and consideration should always be given to protect the rights of clients while helping to identify issues that need to be addressed to ensure that client benefit and progress are obtained.

DSM-IV-TR *Alone Is Not Enough*

For a diagnostic assessment to be completed, the actual information presented in each one of the criteria sets must be utilized. When the work groups of the *DSM-IV* and *DSM-IV-TR* were created, specific emphasis was given to ensure that the professionals engaging in this process had the latest in terms of information based in research and evidence–based practice. This allowed for work teams to complete:

(1) comprehensive and systemic reviews of the published literature; (2) reanalysis of the already collected data sets; and (3) extensive issue-focused field trials (APA, 2000, p. xxvi). Projective testing alone was insufficient as supporting evidence for placement in a diagnostic category. Furthermore, in forensic settings the use of a diagnostic label, regardless of the supporting criteria, cannot be utilized as a legal definition of a mental disorder or mental disability. Nor can a diagnosis of a mental disorder alone be used to determine competence, criminal responsibility, or disability. Information needs to clearly describe a person's behavioral problems and other functional impairments.

DSM-IV-TR *Is Based in Research and Evidence-Based Practice*

One of the major weaknesses in earlier editions of the *DSM* is that they generally focused on descriptive (i.e., a cookbook) rather than etiological (i.e., underlying cause related) factors. It is important to note, however, that in the *DSM-IV* this shortfall was addressed and it was further modified in the *DSM-IV-TR*. As indicated earlier, the latest version of the *DSM* is now based on (1) literature reviews, (2) data analysis and reanalysis, and, (3) field trials.

Literature reviews were conducted to elicit clinical utility, reliability (i.e., did the same criteria continue to present from case to case), descriptive validity (did it actually describe what it was meant to describe), and psychometric performance criteria (were common characteristics of performance on psychometric tests listed in the criterion). Furthermore, a number of validating variables were identified and studied. This research, including systematic and computerized reviews, ensured that evidence–based information was utilized to support the suggestions made by the individual work groups.

A second area of research support included data analysis and reanalysis. Information from this source was particularly important when there was a lack of evidence available to support work group recommendations. In addition to the original field trials in the *DSM-IV,* over 40 data sets were reexamined. The data reanalysis compared the impact of the probable changes suggested.

QUICK REFERENCE

THE BASIS FOR CHANGES IN THE *DSM-IV-TR*

The *DSM-IV-TR* changes are based on:

1. Literature reviews,
2. Data analysis and reanalysis, and
3. Field trials.

Finally, twelve field trials were also completed, each with 5 to 10 different sites and over 1000 participants (APA, 2000). The purpose of the field trials was to combine the knowledge gained from clinical practice with evidence-based procedures and research. Thus, the two most recent editions of the *DSM,* unlike their predecessors, have made efforts to incorporate the best mix of practice wisdom and research for determining the criteria and characteristics of categories presented.

Meaning of Clinically Significant

In completing the diagnostic assessment, practitioner interpretation is critical. The practitioner needs to be well versed in the use of the *DSM* and other situational factors that need to be part of the diagnostic assessment process. Once identified, the practitioner needs to know how to address these factors in clinical practice. Furthermore, the practitioner must have knowledge of the potential damage that can occur from placing a diagnostic label inappropriately. The term *clinically significant* indicates that a practitioner has clearly linked the symptoms present in the mental disorder with how the symptoms either stop or impair a client's current level of functioning. For example, an individual may at times exhibit the symptoms that match the criterion of a mental disorder yet individual, social, or occupational functioning is not impaired. When this occurs, a diagnosis should not be given. A diagnosis should only be given when the client's symptoms are severe enough to either interfere with or disturb functioning. This makes the incorporation of environmental circumstances essential to either support or negate the use of a diagnostic category. In this chapter, important sections and diagnostic features associated with the *DSM-IV-TR* are introduced. Remember, however, that regardless of the diagnostic symptoms a client is experiencing and whether these symptoms are related to factors such as culture, age, and gender, if the behavior is not considered clinically significant, no diagnosis should be given.

IMPORTANT SECTIONS IN THE *DSM-IV-TR*

For each disorder in the *DSM-IV-TR,* the authors describe the primary characteristics of the disorder and, when available, provide additional diagnostic information. When additional information is available, the diagnostic criteria are divided under separate headings, such as *Diagnostic Features* and *Associated Features and Disorders. Diagnostic Features* consists of examples of the disorder and the tests available to determine etiology (APA, 2000). When separate from the Diagnostic Features, the *Associated Features and Disorders* is generally subdivided into three sections including descriptive features, laboratory findings, and information associated with features related to the physical examination or general medical conditions. For example, under the disorder Vascular Dementia (a type of dementia generally related to stroke) the diagnostic criteria are outlined. Under the associated features the text further highlights tests (e.g., CT-computerized tomography of the head) that will help to demonstrate or confirm the existence of the disorder. Based on the information available, the Diagnostic Features section may be either combined or separate from the section on Associated Features and Disorders.

When associated features and lab findings are presented in the text, the following types of information are included: (1) The descriptive features of the mental disorder are presented as well as predisposing factors and complications. (2) Associated laboratory findings (this section is divided into three types of laboratory findings: diagnostic, abnormal to this group, and associated) are listed. (3) The physical exam and general medical conditions that generally accompany this condition are noted. The section on associated lab findings is further broken down into three areas: diagnostic (tests available to determine etiology); confirmatory of the diagnosis (tests that support or are associated with the diagnosis but do not necessarily reveal the cause or etiology); and complication(s) of the disorder (not directly related to the diagnosis per se but often found in conjunction to it or as a result of it (e.g., electrolyte imbalance with the eating disorder anorexia). In the diagnostic assessment, the practitioner should be alert to these factors and how they can affect the diagnostic criteria that the client exhibits.

QUICK REFERENCE

Diagnostic and Associated Features

Diagnostic features provide illustrative examples of the disorder being reviewed.

Associated Features and Disorders:

- **Associated Descriptive Features and Mental Disorders** includes features associated with the disorder but not critical to making the diagnosis.
- **Associated Features and Lab Findings** are not clearly categorized in the text but generally consist of the following types of information. These tests may be helpful but are not required for diagnosis.

  Diagnostic: These tests explain or confirm the cause or etiology of the disorder.

  Confirmatory of the Diagnosis: Most tests are in this category and are associated with the diagnosis but do not necessarily reveal the cause or etiology (e.g., computerized tomography (CT) scans to assist in classification of type of dementia).

  Findings Associated as Complication(s) of the Condition: Factors not directly related to the diagnosis per se but often found in conjunction with it or as a result of it (e.g., electrolyte imbalance with the eating disorder anorexia).

- **Associated Physical Exam Findings and General Medical Conditions** are findings related to the disorder that have significance in treatment.

CULTURE, AGE, AND GENDER-RELATED INFORMATION

Each diagnostic category seeks to be sensitive to issues related to culture, age, and gender and the effects these variables can have on the symptoms with which a client presents. This is particularly important in terms of cultural diversity. Possessing knowledge of and being sensitive to cultural aspects that can contribute to a client's overall diagnostic picture is critical in completing an accurate diagnostic assessment. To facilitate this, each category briefly addresses cultural variables. For additional information, clinicians are referred to an outline for cultural formulation and culturally bound syndromes found in Appendix I of the *DSM-IV-TR*.

Every culture has processes, healers, medications, and prescribed medical practices that enter into the shared view of what constitutes daily living. These shared lifestyle patterns are reflected in daily behaviors. Patterns of response can easily be misinterpreted for something they are not (i.e., reflective of pathology).

Being culturally sensitive in completing the diagnostic assessment is twofold: First, the assessment must clearly outline the client's culturally based behaviors that correspond to diagnostic criteria for mental disorders, thereby helping to rule out disorders for which the client might otherwise qualify. This becomes more and more difficult as cultural practices and mores of different races and ethnic groups overlap. Although researchers have gathered information on race and ethnicity concurrently, the difference between the two is pronounced. In race the attributes of the individual are partially based on physical characteristics of genetic origin (Helms, 1990); ethnicity, on the other hand, encompasses a much broader range of commonalties such as religion, customs, geography, and historical events. Ethnic identity is generally defined as a common thread of heritage, customs, and values unique to a group of people (Casas, 1984; Queralt, 1996; Worden, 1999). The commonalties between individuals define and bond members thereby producing an ethnic backdrop to everyday life. Ethnicity can influence thinking and feeling and pattern behaviors in both obvious and subtle ways. Generally, however, most individuals remain unaware of the influence of ethnicity as it remains natural and consistent with their daily behaviors (e.g., what they eat, how they react).

The development of *ethnic identity,* or how an individual identifies and reacts relative to his or her ethnic group, is not automatic. Rather, it stems from the continuum of acceptance of a person's ethnicity. Many individuals either embrace or reject their ethnicity, relating it to personal and ascribed identity or a particular reference group, which dictates the primary support group to which one turns for clarity of decisions (Helms, 1990). Furthermore, no two people seem to experience their culture in the same way. This means that counselors must be careful not to approach the client with any preconceived bias, or textbook definitions of exactly what to expect (Swartz-Kulstad & Martin, 1999).

The practitioner needs to work with the client to help him or her examine issues related to *personal identity,* where the individual sees himself in a certain way(s); and, *ascribed identity,* where the individual indicates how the society values or perceives behaviors and actions. Although it constitutes a potent factor in intervention counseling, ethnic identity is not easily identified and the degree to which it can influence life factors and behavior changes assessed in the diagnostic interview can remain elusive. Further, disparities related to poverty and the lack of health care insurance as well as the lack of cultural training available to professionals can leave individuals without competent health care (Sutton, 2000).

When assessing cultural aspects of the client, remember that both the client and the practitioner are products of the society in which they live. Societal influences therefore can directly affect individual cultural mores and beliefs predominant in the environmental system. Culture can influence not only the client's behaviors but also the practitioner's behaviors. In general, most of the beliefs and values that helping professionals hold reflect those of the greater society. Based on this assumption, practitioners from other ethnic groups, as well as those with heritage in a similar cultural group, may look at the client's behaviors through his or her own cultural lens. This "culturally limited lens" may prevent the professional from gaining a clear picture of the importance of helping the client to identify behaviors that are based in maintaining his or her cultural and ethnic heritage rather than being based on a particular disorder. Professional helpers must be aware of a tendency to assess the client based on the professional's own values, beliefs, societal biases, and stereotypes (Boyd–Franklin, 1989; Dupper, 1992). If practitioners do not take care to avoid this bias, the lack of awareness of client ethnicity and culture may lead to distorted perceptions of these clients and their family dynamics.

QUICK REFERENCE

IDENTIFYING CULTURAL ASPECTS

Practitioners need to help the client:

- Identify and discuss the impact of present life circumstances that can affect daily functioning.
- Identify and acknowledge any psychological problems stemming from adaptation to a new environment.
- Identify and explore the degree to which the client has positive and supportive peer relationships that can contribute or reduce feelings of isolation and facilitate transition.
- Identify willingness to explore new coping skills that will help negotiate his or her environment.

The key to completing the best diagnostic assessment rests with addressing how to work best with the client in his or her cultural context (Marin, 1993). Some considerations for completing the diagnostic assessment and integrating helping activities with clients from different cultural backgrounds include: (1) becoming familiar with the client's cultural values and points of reference; (2) being aware of and sensitive to the traditional role of the client when in the client's environment; (3) identifying areas of conflict that can result from changes in environmental considerations; and (4) gaining familiarity with how the client is encouraged to express feelings of grief, stress, or unhappiness. To accomplish this, the mental health practitioner must first recognize aspects of the client's culture and incorporate this meaning into the diagnostic assessment and any change efforts to follow.

Countertransference problems may present challenges for both the client and the practitioner, especially when the practitioner is not familiar with the norms and mores of the client's culture. If unfamiliar with the culture, the best-meaning practitioner may assess and treat the client using his or her own cultural lens. It is also important to avoid countertransference related to overidentification with the client's culture and values, which may cause the practitioner to lose objectivity and not encourage the client to examine and make changes that improve psychological well-being. It is important not to accept a dysfunctional pattern as a cultural one because with this acceptance the practitioner may not help to identify alternative coping strategies. This concept will be discussed further in the next section; however, the danger rests in the potential violation of the client's right to self-determination (Hepworth & Larsen, 1993). Completing an ethnic-sensitive diagnostic assessment requires that the practitioner very clearly assess the client and his or her family and the role that culture, environment, and family play on the client's behaviors and responses.

In terms of training professionals, in a recent study of 500 professional counselors the majority perceived themselves to be culturally competent yet they also reported that they found their multicultural training to be less than adequate (Holcomb-McCoy & Myers, 1999). In a similar study with social workers, A. Kaplan and Dziegielewski (1999) examined attitudes of MSW students that directly addressed issues of spirituality and religion and the degree to which these attitudes were incorporated into social work practice. In this survey, most graduate students stated that they valued the role of spirituality and religion in their personal and professional lives. These social workers, however, similar to the professional counselors, reported the lack of adequate training and preparation during graduate education to deal with issues such as culture supported by identification with spiritual or religious ties.

Therefore, if mental health practitioners are truly committed to enhancing the lives of people—as individuals, groups, families, and communities—they must also

---

QUICK REFERENCE

CREATING CULTURAL COMPETENCE IN PRACTITIONERS

- Learn to value diversity in all individuals and the strengths that can be found in differences.
- Seek out experiences and training that will facilitate the understanding of the needs of diverse populations.
- Conduct a cultural self-assessment, where the values, beliefs, and views of the practitioner are identified.
- Be sure to include aspects of cultural identity and the influences it can have on each phase of the diagnostic assessment.
- Become aware of the limits of what he or she has competence and expertise in. If the problem behavior(s) the client is experiencing is beyond the understanding of the practitioner, it is up to the practitioner to seek ethnic group consultation or to make referrals to the more appropriate services or helping professionals.

---

be committed to enabling clients to maximize their capabilities as full and effective participants in society. Therefore, if there is a spiritual aspect of human life, and if this aspect is interrelated with other aspects of life, then practitioners need to be trained in how to best understand this in order to help clients reach their goals and potential. Furthermore, although many practitioners may accurately assess relevant cultural, religious, or spiritual issues, he or she may not understand the relevance of a client's spiritual beliefs, values, perceptions. What a client believes can influence the way he or she responds and these behaviors may be inseparable from the environmental system. Without specific education and preparation in this area, mental health practitioners are ill equipped to practice just as they would be if professional training did not include aspects on how to deal with policy issues or other types of psychological problems. Mental health practitioners need to be aware of their own strengths and limitations while remaining active in seeking education to prepare themselves to deal effectively with cultural and spiritual or religious issues (or both) in the lives of the clients they serve.

CULTURAL-BOUND SYNDROMES

As stated earlier, it is important for clinicians to be aware that viewing a client through a narrow "cultural lens" can lead to misinterpreting a client's cultural traditions and problem–solving processes as abnormal or dysfunctional. When examining the revisions and changes in the *DSM-III-R* (1987), *DSM-IV* (1994), and *DSM-IV-TR* (2000), experts clearly acknowledged that powerful cultural influences can and often do negate a mental health diagnosis. Taking a client's overall cultural influences into account, however, does not equate directly to a culture-bound syndrome.

The term *culture-bound syndrome* denotes recurrent, locality-specific patterns of behavior that can result in troubling experience(s) that may or may not be linked to a particular *DSM-IV* diagnostic category (APA, 2000). Culture-bound syndromes are examples of extreme forms of cultural expression that may be seen as dysfunctional in mainstream society. Furthermore, unless clinicians are sensitive to these culture-bound syndromes, they may inaccurately assess such symptoms as being related to one of the *DSM-IV-TR* diagnostic categories.

In the culture-bound syndrome, cultural beliefs and mores influence the symptoms, course, and social response to the behaviors. Practitioners must understand that each family system seeks to maintain a homeostatic balance that is functional and adaptive for that system. The practitioner therefore must guard against impulses to reorganize a client's family system based on his or her expectations or based on the standards set by the larger society.

Being aware of cultural differences and acceptance of diversity are essential in establishing a culturally sensitive practice. This awareness can prevent an inappropriate diagnostic label being given to a client. Appendix I of the *DSM-IV-TR* lists some of the best-studied culture-bound syndromes and idioms of distress that may be encountered in clinical practice in North America and includes relevant *DSM-IV-TR* categories when data suggest that they should be considered in a diagnostic formulation. The quick references provided here give only some of the possible types of culture-bound syndromes that have been identified.

In summary, a comprehensive diagnostic assessment needs to take into account the cultural identity of the client being served. This is particularly important for immigrants and ethnic minorities who may have communication problems in terms of language understanding and content (Leon & Dziegielewski, 1999). The practitioner must also be sensitive to the predominant idioms of distress through which problematic behaviors are identified or communicated, especially when clients report problems with nerves, being possessed by spirits, multiple somatic complaints, and a sense of inexplicable misfortune. The meaning that these symptoms have to the client in relation to norms of his or her cultural reference group, which could be related to a culture-bound syndrome, need to be explored. When examining these factors, it is also important to directly make the connection of how these factors can be related to psychosocial environment and the client's level of individual, social, or occupational functioning. Be sure to note differences in culture and social status between the client and the practitioner and the problems that these differences may cause in the diagnostic assessment. The

QUICK REFERENCE

SELECTED CULTURE-BOUND SYNDROMES

Generally Related to American Indians

ghost sickness: A preoccupation with death and the deceased (sometimes associated with witchcraft) frequently observed among members of many American Indian tribes. Various symptoms can be attributed to ghost sickness, including bad dreams, weakness, feelings of danger, loss of appetite, fainting, dizziness, fear, anxiety, hallucinations, loss of consciousness, confusion, feelings of futility, and a sense of suffocation.

Generally Related to Regions of West Africa and Haiti

boufée delirant: This French term (West Africa and Haiti) refers to a sudden outburst of agitated and aggressive behavior, marked confusion, and psychomotor excitement. Visual and auditory hallucinations or paranoid ideation may sometimes accompany it. These episodes may resemble an episode of brief psychotic disorder.

brain fag: A term initially used in West Africa to refer to a condition experienced by high school and university students in response to the challenges of schooling. Symptoms include difficulties in concentrating, remembering, and thinking. Students often state that their brains are "fatigued." Additional somatic symptoms are usually centered on the head and neck and include pain, pressure or tightness, blurring of vision, heat, or burning. "Brain tiredness" or fatigue from "too much thinking" is an idiom of distress in many cultures, and resulting syndromes can resemble certain anxiety, depressive, and somatoform disorders.

Generally Related to Hispanic Individuals

ataque de nervios: An idiom of distress principally reported among Latinos from the Caribbean but recognized among many Latin American and Latin Mediterranean groups. Commonly reported symptoms include *uncontrollable shouting, attacks of crying, trembling, heat in the chest rising into the head, and verbal or physical aggression.* Dissociative experiences, seizure like or fainting episodes, and suicidal gestures are prominent in some attacks but absent in others. A general feature of an ataque de nervios is a sense of being out of control. Ataques de nervios frequently occur as a direct result of a stressful event relating to the family (e.g., news of the death of a close relative, a separation or divorce from a spouse, conflicts with a spouse or children, or witnessing an accident involving a family member). People may experience amnesia for what occurred during the ataque de nervios, but they otherwise return rapidly to their usual level of functioning. Although descriptions of some ataques de nervios most closely fit with the *DSM-IV* description of Panic Attacks, the association of most ataques with a precipitating event and the frequent absence of the hallmark symptoms of acute fear or apprehension distinguish them from Panic Disorder. Ataques span the range from normal expressions of distress not associated with having a mental disorder to symptom presentations associated with the diagnoses of anxiety, mood, dissociative, or somatoform disorders.

QUICK REFERENCE *(Continued)*

locura: A term used by Latinos in the United States and Latin America to refer to a severe form of chronic psychosis. The condition is attributed to an inherited vulnerability, to the effect of multiple life difficulties, or to a combination of both factors. Symptoms exhibited by persons with locura include incoherence, agitation, auditory and visual hallucinations, and inability to follow rules of social interaction, unpredictability, and possible violence.

nervios: A common idiom of distress among Latinos in the United States and Latin America. A number of other ethnic groups have related, though often somewhat distinctive, ideas of "nerves" (such as *nevra* among Greeks in North America). Nervios refers both to a general state of vulnerability to stressful life experiences and to a syndrome brought on by difficult life circumstances. The term *nervios* includes a wide range of symptoms of emotional distress, somatic disturbance, and inability to function. Common symptoms include headaches and "brain aches," irritability, stomach disturbances, sleep difficulties, nervousness, easy tearfulness, inability to concentrate, trembling, tingling sensations, and *mareos* (dizziness with occasional vertigo like exacerbations). Nervios tends to be an ongoing problem, although variable in the degree of disability manifested. Nervios is a broad syndrome that spans the range from cases free of a mental disorder to presentations resembling adjustment, anxiety, depressive, dissociative, somatoform, or psychotic disorders. Differential diagnosis will depend on the constellation of symptoms experienced, the kind of social events that are associated with the onset and progress of nervios, and the level of disability experienced.

Source: Selected definitions reprinted with permission from the *Diagnostic and Statistical Manual of Mental Disorders, Fourth Edition, Text Revision.* Copyright 2000. American Psychiatric Association.

diagnostic assessment should always conclude with an overall cultural assessment acknowledging how these factors can either directly or indirectly influence behavior and further comprehensive diagnosis and care.

DIAGNOSTIC ASSESSMENT FACTORS RELATED TO AGE

Regardless of their cultural or racial background, individuals both young and old use their cultural experiences to interpret their immediate surroundings, the interaction of others, and the interpersonal patterns of society (Bruner, 1991; Salesby, 1994). Similarly, culture and family are the first two powerful influences that determine how all individuals understand, internalize, and act on what is expected of them by their family, community, and the larger society. In the case of minority individuals, discriminatory experiences may provide additional information and feelings to decipher and understand. During times of emotional or psychological turmoil, human nature is such that all individuals, regardless of age, will strive for meaning in their lives using their "cultural lens," values, beliefs, and experiences. In the case of both the elderly and children in therapeutic situations, the practitioner must first accept that these individuals present a rich and complex picture that requires them to examine biological, psychological, and social factors within a historical and cultural framework. During the diagnostic assessment, it is important to ensure that a lack of historical and cultural sensitivity by helping professionals does not hinder the good intentions of the intervention or the research process.

Recognizing age and culture in the diagnostic assessment are similar: Both areas need to be assessed and treated effectively and rapidly. To carry out this task efficiently, practitioners must be aware of their own stereotypes in regard to age and aging and how not recognizing these discriminatory practices can affect the welfare and progress of the individual for whom assessment or treatment is provided (Dupper, 1992; Gaw, 1993; Willie, Kramer, & Brown, 1973).

DIAGNOSTIC ASSESSMENT WITH CHILDREN

To develop age-sensitive practice and provide effective services, practitioners need to recognize, understand, and appreciate the effects that geographic and regional differences can have on children. When assessing children, the family's place of origin should not be minimized. Family values may reflect differences in urban versus rural expectations and traditions. Congress (1997) recommends that practitioners identify appropriate tools to conduct culturally sensitive assessments. Children's actions are guided by the values and norms established within the family system. For example, if a child's family of origin is not supportive of mental health treatment and holds negative beliefs surrounding professional assistance, a child may not independently ask for help. The practitioner needs to know that if a parent does not support assessment or treatment for the child, it may be more complicated than simply having an uninvolved parent (Boyd-Franklin, 1989). Although

---

QUICK REFERENCE

DIAGNOSTIC ASSESSMENT WITH CHILDREN

- Carefully assess changes in self-esteem or confidence levels.
- Assess dysfunctional behavioral patterns being sure to take into account family system and other support system influences (including peer pressure).
- Always be aware that the child may not have directly caused many of the difficulties encountered, understanding the role that cultural differences and expectations can play.

atypical, it may be possible to obtain a more accurate assessment in the parent's own home, or by collaboratively engaging other significant people in the community (e.g., clergy) in the diagnostic assessment process who are part of the family's extended helping network and trusted by the family (Congress, 1997; Harrison, Thyer, & Wodarski, 1996).

DIAGNOSTIC ASSESSMENT WITH OLDER ADULTS

Growing old often is viewed negatively in our society by those who are not yet old, as well as by many health and mental health care professionals. Older adults themselves are also victimized by societal attitudes that devalue old age. Many individuals (young and old) will do almost anything to avoid or deny old age. Such prejudices are the result of both rational and irrational fears. Rational fears about declining health, income, loss of loved ones, and social status can be exaggerated by negative stereotypes of older adults, and irrational fears such as changes in physical appearance, loss of masculinity or femininity, and perceived mental incompetence also can be exaggerated. Older adults continue to be oppressed by myths and misinformation and by real obstacles imposed by various biological, psychological, social, and economic factors.

When working with older adults, practitioners need to examine their own attitudes toward aging. Practitioners should not contribute, directly or indirectly, to discrimination based on age, which results in ineffective and unethical practice. Practitioners need to recognize older adults as valuable resources in our society and to provide services and advocacy that will assist them in maximizing their degree of life satisfaction and well-being. Many older adults fear activity loss and may deny the actual occurrence of such loss. Older adults may suffer from chronic conditions where probability of the condition getting better is unlikely. They may also suffer from many life stresses including widowhood, social and occupational losses, and progressive physical health problems. Older adults with psychiatric problems generally go to community mental health centers for checkups and medication. However, many of these individuals may not have access to these services if it requires leaving their home.

It is critical for practitioners to be knowledgeable of the problems that elderly individuals face. For example, in our society many men and women fear that aging will eventually prevent them from having sexual intercourse (Kelly & Rice, 1986). Such attitudes often cause the sexual needs of the elderly individual to be ignored by family, friends, peers, caregivers, and society in general (Hodson & Skeen, 1994). Furthermore, there is a tendency to deny that problems may be terminal. Family members, and some professionals, may tell aged individuals that a condition will get better, rather than helping them develop ways to cope with a problem. A diagnostic assessment should take into account the individual's health conditions and environmental factors among other aspects of their lives.

Last, the role of the practitioner in assessing lethality when dealing with a potentially suicidal older client is essential. Older adults may not openly discuss feelings of hopelessness and helplessness and the practitioner must carefully screen for this. If an older client expresses suicidal ideation or thoughts of suicide and mentions a concrete plan (the way to carry out the suicidal act), steps to ensure hospitalization must be conducted immediately, similar to measures necessary for any client at serious risk for suicide. Unfortunately, many older adults may not be forthcoming with situational criteria and the practitioner may remain uncertain of the seriousness of the client's thoughts with regard to his or her actions. Regardless of whether the client's behavior is action focused or not, some type of immediate protective measures need to be employed. This topic will be discussed in detail in the chapters on intervention strategy.

QUICK REFERENCE

DIAGNOSTIC ASSESSMENT WITH THE ELDERLY

Identify life circumstances that can complicate the diagnostic assessment process:

- **Retirement issues:** Identify problems with work role transition and retirement status.
- **Chronic conditions:** Identify chronic medical conditions that an individual may suffer from and how these conditions can affect an individual's level of daily functioning.
- **Physical health conditions:** Identify physical health conditions, especially vision and hearing problems, that can complicate or magnify current problems.
- **Mental health complaints:** Identify mental health problems and look for signs such as feelings of sadness, loneliness, guilt, boredom, marked decrease or increase in appetite, change in sleep behavior, and a sense of worthlessness. Be aware that many times signs of depression in the elderly can be situational (e.g., the etiology of the depression is related to life circumstances) and screen for problems related to tragic life experiences including the loss of loved ones, job, status, independence, and other personal disappointments. Also, screen for confusion that may be a sign of dementia.
- **Medication use and misuse:** Identify the use and misuse of prescription medication because commonly prescribed medications can present side effects such as irritability, sexual dysfunction, memory lapses, a general feeling of tiredness, or a combination of these.
- **Sexual problems:** Be open to the identification of sexual problems.
- **Suicide:** Identify the probability of accumulated life losses and be cognizant of a client's abilities and/or problems in coping with grief.

DIAGNOSTIC ASSESSMENT FACTORS RELATED TO GENDER

Most professionals would agree that girls and boys are often subjected to early differential treatment and identification. Both parents and the larger societal network deal differently with girls and boys, and children often are expected to model themselves according to accepted gender lines. To date, most of the inquiry made into gender has focused on the importance of outlining the "actual" differences between male and female characteristics and whether there are true physical, cognitive, and personality differences among the sexes. From a medical-biological perspective, most professionals would say such differences do exist. Although the physical differences (e.g., physical structure and anatomy) between males and females are obvious, other differences are not. For example, in medication use, when controlling for most factors (e.g., size, dose), therapeutic response to certain drugs can differ between males and females (PDR, 2001). Furthermore, when viewing gender divergence from a social-psychological perspective, "broader social issues relating to sex and gender stereotyping can lead to unfair practices of sexism" (Dziegielewski, Resnick, & Krause, 1995, p. 169).

Because gender as evidenced through sex roles remains part of an individual's beliefs, during the completion of the diagnostic assessment it is difficult to avoid gender bias. Even though "gender neutral" influences may be considered, as products of the society at large, individuals continue to have definite ideas about sex role deviance. Therefore, it is critical to acknowledge the influences that gender may have on the diagnostic assessment process. Practitioners must be careful to rule out bias such as viewing the male as the "doer" who is always rational, logical, and in control and the female as the "nurturer" who is often emotional, illogical, and needy.

To accomplish a gender-sensitive diagnostic assessment, behaviors must be reinterpreted to include gender as a naturally occurring phenomena. From a feminist perspective, gender and power relations are paramount to effective assessment and intervention. To summarize the methodology of feminism in our society, five elements are generally considered: (1) gender inequality is highlighted and many times women are oppressed by this patriarchal society; (2) the individual experiences of men and women are considered the cornerstone of all social science understanding; (3) this method has a social action component where the primary emphasis is to improve the conditions that women experience; and (4) feminism acknowledges that gender bias exists and, as products of the society, practitioners cannot be objective observers (Concian, 1991). Whether one agrees with the feminist perspective or not, it is clear that feminist contributions have been a major force in stimulating and rethinking the traditional methods of assessment and intervention, and for developing new areas of inquiry and practice (Burck & Speed, 1995; Gilbert, 1991; E. Jones, 1995; Lott, 1991).

To be gender sensitive in the diagnostic assessment process, the practitioner must first identify what behaviors are adaptive or maladaptive (Liberman, 1973). The primary focus is placed on the actual behavior exhibited and the influences that affect it. When dysfunctional behaviors occur in the family system, they are generally viewed as learned responses. Therefore, if a difficulty arises in the family unit, it is generally explored in relation to how it has been reinforced.

Second, environmental or interpersonal circumstances that currently support the problematic behavior must be identified, which is often referred to as a *functional analysis* (Liberman, 1973). Gender issues can contribute to the social reinforcement of behavior patterns. All behaviors are learned and reinforced within the social, societal, and cultural climate in which individuals live (Smyrnios & Kirkby, 1992).

When completing the diagnostic assessment, gender needs to be considered as a basic building block, along with such concepts as generation (age) and ethnic and cultural implications. Operating with this foundation or mind-set, practitioners can assess the behavior patterns that are reinforced in this contingency pattern.

In the diagnostic assessment process, the practitioner is responsible for interpreting and finding meaning in what the client says, and this interpretation is not based solely on what the client has stated. The practitioner must listen and respond by helping the client to problem solve what is determined to be the "real" situation. Developing rapport during the diagnostic assessment is critical because it makes clients feel more comfortable and gives them permission to state how they feel and how those feelings are affecting behavior (Friedman, 1997).

QUICK REFERENCE

GENDER AND THE DIAGNOSTIC ASSESSMENT

The practitioner needs to:

- Identify the individual's perception of gender and how this belief can affect perceptions, values, beliefs, and behaviors.
- Identify an individual's traditional roots and acknowledge how that can influence perceptions and the way issues are addressed and discussed.
- Identify the behaviors that are adaptive and maladaptive.
- Identify the environmental or interpersonal circumstances that support the behavior.
- Help the individual to acknowledge what he or she perceives to be the family or societal perception of his or her behavior and how that influence may detract or contribute to problem behaviors.

> ## QUICK REFERENCE
>
> ### GENDER AND THE DIAGNOSTIC ASSESSMENT II
>
> Practitioners:
>
> - Must realize that individuals are products of their family and societal context and the practitioner must make a conscious attempt to recognize his or her own "behavior paradigms" and the sexual stereotypes that may either consciously or unconsciously exist.
> - Must strive to be as objective and tolerant as possible of the uniqueness of clients and their right, acknowledging that the behavioral paradigm of the practitioner is not necessarily the correct or ideal one.
> - Need to be aware of how gender (the practitioner's or the client's) can affect the diagnostic assessment process and the information shared.
> - Must be aware that the personalities of those in the family can have a significant effect on how things are viewed and how the client acts and performs his or her activities of daily living.

In summary, the practitioner must realize that there are many different interpretations of gender. Practitioners need to explore the full range of possible gender interpretations possible as interpreted by the family system (Terry, 1992) and to use this systemic information to achieve the most accurate diagnostic assessment possible.

Although differences between men and women do exist, many of these perceived differences can be traced to the situations in which men and women find themselves; and when in these situations even if they behave identically they may be judged by different standards (Aronson, 1988). The practitioner must remember that he or she is also a product of the social environment and is influenced by the culture that is natural to him or her. It is important not to impose double standards of interpretation, or worse yet, interpretation without realizing the influence of gender at all. The inclusion of gender is imperative within the foundation or mind-set incorporated in diagnostic assessment.

SUBTYPES AND COURSE SPECIFIERS

In using the *DSM-IV-TR,* the use of *subtypes* and *course specifiers* is encouraged. A subtype helps clarify a diagnosis where the criteria are mutually exclusive and jointly exhaustive (APA, 2000). For example, in schizophrenia, the *DSM-IV* (1994) clearly establishes that there are five subtypes identified (e.g., paranoid type, disorganized type, catatonic type, undifferentiated type, and residual type). The subtypes are defined by the prominent symptomolgy at the time of evaluation (see Chapter 9 for further analysis and application).

This example represents one of the major changes between the *DSM-IV* and the *DSM-IV-TR*. Based on the latest research, it appears that the subtypes of schizophrenia appear to be limited in terms of stability and prognostic value. Therefore, these subtypes are being evaluated and in the *DSM-V* may be condensed to more accurately reflect the research field trial results.

The second grouping in this area in the *DSM-IV-TR* for diagnostic categories is the *course specifier*. Contrary to the diagnostic subtype, the course specifier is not considered mutually exclusive and exhaustive. It is provided to show how criteria are similar and can be grouped. These homogenous (or similar) subgroupings can highlight certain shared features. For example in the condition of *major depressive disorder* the specifier *with melancholic features* can be added. Additional specifiers that may be listed after the diagnosis include mild, moderate, and severe, in partial remission, in full remission, and prior history. Since these specifiers help to clarify, specify, and note recurrence of a diagnostic mental disorder, the qualifiers of mild, moderate, and severe should only be used when the full criteria for the diagnosis is met.

When it is considered important to the diagnostic assessment, the practitioner can note the recurrence of a mental disorder. For example, if an individual has suffered from major depressive disorder in the past yet currently does not satisfy the time criteria for the disorder, it is considered appropriate to use the qualifier *recurrent,* in this case, noted as *major depressive disorder, recurrent.* The use of the term recurrent is particularly useful in assisting the practitioner when the criteria for a past disorder are not currently met, yet it appears supported by the clinical judgment of the practitioner that the criteria will be met.

When applying any of the additional qualifiers, or specifiers, the practitioner needs to make sure the application is related to the current level of problem behavior and clearly document the frequency, intensity, and duration of why the specifier

---

QUICK REFERENCE

SEVERITY AND COURSE SPECIFIERS

Practitioners use these qualifiers to clarify or specify a diagnosis, noting the recurrence and prior history of diagnoses:

- Is the condition mild, moderate, or severe?
- Is the condition in remission (i.e., partial or full remission)?
- Is there a prior history of the condition and can this prior history have an effect on current level of functioning?

was noted. As will be discussed in more detail in the next chapter, diagnostic codes, usually 3 to 5 digits, are often utilized to report statistical information and to facilitate retrieval of information. The fourth and fifth digits of the code can be assigned to the subtype.

To code to facilitate reimbursement, many of the subtypes and specifiers listed in the *DSM* are not listed in the *ICD-9-CM* system, thus, there are no corresponding codes for these subtypes and specifiers. In such cases, when the practitioner wants to further specify a client problem by utilizing the subtype or specifier, simply write it out (e.g., in the condition of obsessive compulsive disorder include three–digit code, the subtype is referred to as *With poor insight*).

USE OF THE PRINCIPLE AND PROVISIONAL DIAGNOSIS

The reason an individual is being seen by a mental health professional or admitted to an inpatient facility is often referred to as the *principle diagnosis*. Many times, however, when a client is interviewed and the initial diagnostic assessment is completed, a principle diagnosis cannot be determined. In these cases a *provisional diagnosis* can be assigned. A provisional diagnosis (often referred to in the field as the best educated clinical guess) is based on clinical judgment and reflects a strong suspicion that an individual suffers from a type of disorder yet for some reason or another the actual criteria are either not met or not available. In practice, a provisional diagnosis can be particularly helpful when information from family or the support system is not available to confirm the diagnosis. Furthermore, there are some disorders for which specific time frames must be met to assign a diagnosis. For example, in schizophrenia, regardless of the subtype, the criteria state that the duration of the illness must be approximately six months or more. With the first episode or the onset of the disorder, all criteria may be met except this one. Therefore, the provisional diagnosis allows the practitioner to use the term schizophreniform disorder which also meets the same criteria as schizophrenia but has a lesser time frame (e.g., less than six months and remission does not occur). The most important thing for the practitioner to remember, however, is that a provisional diagnosis is *temporary.* This means that once a provisional diagnosis is given, every attempt must be made to monitor its course. When the needed information is gathered or the suggested time frame has been met, the provisional diagnosis should be changed to the primary diagnosis most relevant to current problem behaviors and future treatment.

Several other diagnostic categories can also be used when diagnostic uncertainty as to an exact condition is noted. When completing a diagnostic assessment, there are times when there may not be a specific diagnosis relevant to a client's behaviors or actions, or the information gathered is so inadequate that the diagnostic criteria cannot be applied. At these times, simply coding *no diagnosis* or *diagnosis deferred* would be sufficient.

USE OF NOT OTHERWISE SPECIFIED

Since it is sometimes impossible for the practitioner completing the diagnostic assessment to categorize all the symptoms that a client is experiencing into one diagnostic category, the term *Not Otherwise Specified* (NOS) was introduced. There are at least four situations in which a client with a disorder may be given this diagnosis. This option is provided at least once for every diagnostic category listed in the *DSM-IV-TR*. Also, even though the criteria for when to use it is outlined, the criteria remain so subjective that clinical judgment is often the key factor to consider when making the determination for use.

The four situations that qualify for use of the NOS category include:

1. The client appears to meet the general guidelines for a disorder yet all of the criteria have not been met or some of the ones that are present are not considered clinically significant.

2. Significant behaviors are noted that affect social and occupational functioning but are not considered part of the usual presentation for a disorder.

3. Uncertainty about etiology or the cause of the disorder exists. This is especially important when it is suspected that the disorder may be related to a general medical condition.

4. Insufficient information exists to fully support assigning behaviors to a particular mental disorder in the category, but the general criteria for the category of disorders are evident. For example, it is clear that an individual suffers from a type of bipolar disorder but the specific criteria for a particular type cannot be clearly identified.

There are many reasons why the practitioner may have inaccurate information, beginning with having insufficient time to gather assessment information, to the individual client being unable to report symptoms accurately, and no family or support system individuals are available to help complete the accurate and comprehensive information needed for the assessment.

Although using the NOS category is encouraged in the *DSM-IV-TR* when these considerations are met, a caution from an experienced practice reality must be noted. In billing and within reimbursement practices, the NOS category is often very carefully scrutinized. Managed care companies and service providers are well aware of the criteria that *do not have to be present* for a diagnosis to be utilized for

---

QUICK REFERENCE

USE OF THE NOT OTHERWISE SPECIFIED CATEGORY

Practitioners need to be sure when this category is utilized that the problem behaviors can clearly be linked to one of these reasons for its use:

1. The client appears to meet the general guidelines for a disorder yet all of the criteria have not been met or some of the behavioral symptoms present are not considered clinically significant.

2. The symptoms noted affect social and occupational functioning, but these symptoms are not considered part of the usual presentation for a particular disorder in that category.

3. There is uncertainty about etiology or the cause of the disorder, especially when it might be related to a medical condition.

4. There is not sufficient information to fully support assigning behaviors to a particular mental disorder in the category, but the general criteria for the category of disorders is evident.

QUICK REFERENCE

DSM-IV-TR APPENDICES

A—Decision Trees for Differential Diagnosis: Utilizes decision trees to help the practitioner facilitate differential diagnosis.

B—Criteria Sets and Axes Provided for Further Study: Discusses several disorders that are being considered for possible inclusion as well as alternative dimensional criteria that can be used to support the diagnostic assessment process.

C—Glossary of Technical Terms: Particularly helpful in defining certain terms that are listed under the various disorders.

D—Annotated Listing of Changes in the *DSM-IV* Text Revision: Highlights the additions, modifications, and changes that were made within the latest revision of the *DSM*.

E—Alphabetical Listing of *DSM-IV-TR* Diagnoses and Codes: Lists both the *DSM-IV-TR* codes and the matching codes in the *ICD-9-CM*.

F—Numerical Listing of *DSM-IV* Diagnoses and Codes: The same as Appendix E, except that the codes are listed numerically rather than alphabetically. In billing, this Appendix can be very helpful especially when all a provider may be given is the diagnostic numerical code. Most practitioners do not memorize all the code numbers, although they may be very familiar with the diagnostic category once they see the name. Therefore, this appendix allows the practitioner to look up the code directly and see what diagnostic category is associated with it.

G—*ICD-9-CM* Codes for Selected General Medical Conditions and Medication Induced Disorders: Lists the general medical conditions and matches these conditions with the *ICD-9-CM* codes. This section also allows for coding in regard to certain medications (prescribed at therapeutic doses) that can cause substance-induced disorders. The effects of these medications are coded (E-codes) as optional and when used would be listed on Axis I.

H—*DSM-IV* Classification with *ICD-10* Codes: Since much of the world is still using the *ICD-9-CM* clinical codes, it is expected that soon they will be replaced with the *ICD-10-CM* that is due in 2004. Until that time, the *ICD-10* codes are listed in this appendix for clinical convenience.

I—Outline for Cultural Formulation and Glossary of Culture-Bound Syndromes: Divided into two parts, this outline facilitates cultural assessment and an actual glossary of culture-bound syndromes. The culture-bound syndromes often present similar to a mental disorder but, as discussed earlier in this chapter, are related directly to an individual's cultural beliefs.

J—*DSM-IV* Contributors: Lists the names of those who contributed to the formulation and development of the *DSM-IV* published in 1994.

K—*DSM-IV-TR* Advisers: Lists the names of those who contributed to the formulation and development of the *DSM-IV-TR* published in 2000.

Source: Reprinted with permission from the *Diagnostic and Statistical Manual of Mental Disorders, Fourth Edition, Text Revision.* Copyright 2000. American Psychiatric Association.

reimbursement. This means that medical reviewers will be looking closely to see that the client who is given an NOS category clearly needs to be given that diagnosis. They will want to determine what circumstances make this diagnostic category more appropriate than the others in the same classification. Practice reality dictates the use of this diagnostic category cautiously. Practitioners must clearly link the choice of the NOS category to one of the four accepted reasons.

SUMMARY

This chapter gives the mental health practitioner the background information needed to complete the most accurate diagnostic assessment possible using the *DSM-IV-TR*. An accurate diagnostic assessment is the critical first step to identifying behaviors that disturb individual, occupational, and social functioning and formulating the plan for intervention. Thus, it is the diagnostic assessment that sets the tone for therapy. To compete in today's current mental health care service environment, the role of the practitioner is twofold: (1) to ensure that quality service is provided to the client, and (2) to ensure that the client has access and is given an opportunity to see that his or her health needs are addressed. Neither of these tasks is easy or popular in today's environment. The push for mental health practice to be conducted with limited resources and services and the resultant competition to be the provider have changed and stressed the role of the mental health service practitioner. Amid this turbulence, however, the role and necessity of the diagnostic assessment remains clear. Chapter 3 discusses in detail the application of the multiaxis diagnostic system in terms of documentation and the development of treatment plans that can assist and guide with the intervention process.

QUESTIONS FOR FURTHER THOUGHT

1. Is it really important for mental health practitioners to be aware of the *DSM* and the *ICD,* and if so, why?
2. Why was the *DSM-IV-TR* published? What are the substantial changes between the *DSM-IV* and the *DSM-IV-TR?*
3. Why is it critical to realize and incorporate the mind–body connection when completing the diagnostic assessment?
4. What is a culture-bound syndrome? Can you give an example how this concept could be applied to the diagnostic assessment?
5. When is best to use a principle diagnosis?
6. When is best to use a Not Otherwise Specified diagnostic category?

3 Documentation and the Multiaxial Diagnostic Assessment

The purpose of this chapter is to use the multiaxial diagnostic assessment within the parameters of current mental health practice. Professional record keeping by all mental health practitioners in the twenty-first century is characterized by time-limited services, managed care requirements, and quality assurance and improvement procedures (Browning & Browning, 1996; Dziegielewski & Leon, 2001, Dziegielewski & Powers, 2000; Frager, 2000; Rudolph, 2000; Wambach, Haynes, & White, 1999). Therefore, when diagnostic systems such as the multiaxial approach presented in the *DSM-IV-TR* are used, practitioner training in how to best utilize this system is mandatory. Furthermore, skill in professional documentation in this area becomes essential for social workers, psychologists, mental health therapists, professional counselors, and other helping professionals. Training in this area constitutes a functional building block for effective, efficient, and cost-controlled service provision as well as representing the legal, ethical, and fiscal concerns inherent in all service provision (Mitchell, 1991; Sheafor et al., 1997).

In addition to presenting information on how to best utilize the multiaxial system, this chapter will outline the changes between *DSM-III-R* (1987), *DSM-IV* (1994), and *DSM-IV-TR* (2000). Each axis is described and changes between the earlier and later versions of the *DSM* are described. The application of this information is highlighted allowing practitioners to clearly identify and apply each step of the diagnostic system.

INTRODUCTION TO THE MULTIAXIAL ASSESSMENT SYSTEM

The information presented in this chapter is not meant to be inclusive of all the possibilities available for use of the *DSM-IV-TR* assessment system. It is, however, designed to give professional practitioners a practical introduction to facilitate and identify this multiaxial diagnostic system in the practice setting. Proper use of the

---

QUICK REFERENCE

DSM-IV-TR: MULTIAXIAL ASSESSMENT

Axis I: Clinical disorders.
             Other conditions that may be the focus of clinical attention.

Axis II: Personality disorders.
             Mental retardation.

Axis III: General medical conditions.

Axis IV: Psychosocial and environmental problems.

Axis V: Global assessment of functioning.

DSM-IV-TR requires diagnostic classification on a multiaxial system that involves five separate axes. This chapter described each axis, and compares and contrasts what is required today within the assessment process to what was required in the past.

When and How to Use the Multiaxial System

The *DSM-IV-TR* is a multiaxial assessment system that identifies five separate axes. In many practice settings in the 1980s and 1990s, the first three axes were considered sufficient to constitute the formal diagnostic process. The practitioner would complete a diagnostic impression of the client that involved Axis I, II, and III, leaving the use of Axis IV and V as optional. With the later additions of the *DSM (DSM-III* and *DSM-III-R),* however, it was recommended that all five axes be addressed as part of the diagnostic assessment. In current practice, when utilizing the multiaxial system, the first three axes alone are no longer considered acceptable as a practice standard. Therefore, with the advent of the *DSM-IV* in 1994, and in the *DSM-IV-TR* in 2000, working with the multiaxial framework requires addressing all five axes. Today, in most professional practice settings, a comprehensive diagnostic assessment should include all five areas, especially Axis IV and V because it relates directly to the practice plans that are derived.

Nevertheless, there are times when use of the multiaxial diagnostic assessment does not seem appropriate. For some practitioners, especially those who work with specialized groups such as troubled youth or in specialized settings such as assisted residential care with the elderly, the formal diagnostic assessment with diagnostic related treatment plans may not be required. Thus, use of the multiaxis diagnostic system may seem unnecessary. For example, practitioners in some counseling agencies may focus their efforts directly on problem solving that entails helping individuals to gain the resources needed to improve their functioning.

Nonformal Multiaxial Assessment System

In situations where groups, settings, or agency function does not require it, the formal use of the multiaxial assessment system may not be needed. Nonetheless, there may be interest in documenting some of the conditions or issues relative to the diagnostic assessment that may prohibit improved problem-solving strategy. For example, if a client suffers from depression and this mental health condition is severe enough to impair occupational or social functioning, he or she may not be able to actively engage in problem-solving strategy. Therefore, in such cases, a modified form of the multiaxial assessment system can be helpful. In these types of situations the practitioner is urged to consider the use of the *nonformal multiaxial assessment system*. This nonformal system can be beneficial when the multiaxial format is not outlined but the specific categories are used to identify or classify the problems that a client may experience. To illustrate, the *Other conditions that may be the focus of clinical attention* generally coded on Axis I, may be of assistance. This category of mental health conditions is not considered representative of a major clinical syndrome, although the symptoms that the client is experiencing may be severe enough to initially make the professional consider assigning a diagnosis. For example, an elderly client's reaction to the death of a loved one may be significant enough to meet the criteria for *bereavement* (coded as V62.82), which is appropriate when the focus of clinical attention is related directly to the loss of a loved one (American Psychiatric Association [APA], 2000). As people age they are more likely to experience repeated losses of partners, family, and friends. Repeated losses and the constant adjustment process can easily lead to feelings of sadness, disturbed sleep, and loss of appetite that resemble depression and, although the individual will eventually learn to cope with these changes and losses, the responses that occur in the adjustment process vary considerably. The nonformal multiaxial system can help the client and significant others (i.e., family and friends within his or her support system), as well as other professional and nonprofessional helpers, understand why a client is acting in a certain way.

It may also be helpful when working in settings where the full multiaxial diagnosis is not needed to use a categorical approach to describe other mental disorders such as alcohol abuse or major depressive disorder or to list a general medical condition that might be troubling the individual. In these cases, the practitioner is urged to simply list the conditions that apply. The two guidelines to follow when using a nonformal assessment system are: (1) when there is more than one mental health condition, list the principle diagnosis or reason for visit first; and (2) list the mental disorders that interfere with functioning first and afterward list the general medical condition(s) that in the formal multiaxial system would be placed on Axis III.

Coding within the Multiaxis Assessment System

All mental health practitioners must be familiar with the numeric coding that is utilized in the *DSM-IV-TR*. This coding provides quick and consistent recording that leads to service recognition and reimbursement. Furthermore, coding can assist with describing the injury or illness a client suffers from; it can be helpful in gathering prevalence and research information; and it can assist other health care professionals in providing continuity of care (Rudman, 2000). When a mental health practitioner completes or assists in completing a claim form, the proper diagnostic and procedural claim codes must be utilized. To facilitate this process, the creators of the *DSM-IV-TR* (APA, 2000) and the *ICD-9-CM* (World Health Organization with updates in coding provided by the American Medical Association) have collaborated to establish similar codes for each diagnostic system. When a mental health practitioner uses the *DSM-IV-TR* codes for reimbursement, he or she is in effect also using the *ICD-9-CM* codes.

There are two primary types of coding: *diagnostic* (what a client suffers from) and *procedural* (what will be done to treat it). The *DSM-IV-TR* and the *ICD-9-CM* are most concerned with the diagnostic codes. *Current procedural terminology* (CPT) are the services that mental health practitioners often use. Although closely linked to the *ICD-9-CM* codes, these codes correspond to procedures rather than diagnostic categories.

CPT codes are divided into four procedural categories: (1) evaluation and management services, (2) surgical care, (3) diagnostic services, and (4) therapeutic services (Rudman, 2000). For example, when billing for Medicare reimbursement, the CPT codes are primarily responsible for documenting practice strategy.

GUICK REFERENCE

HELPFUL HINTS: DIAGNOSTIC CODING

To purchase an updated CPT or *ICD-9-CM* manual, call the American Medical Association at (800) 621-8335.

E-mail Address for APA, which may be helpful in obtaining coding changes:
   http://www.apa.org/practice/cpt.html and
   http://www.apa.org/practice/pointer1295.html

Copies can also be obtained through the government relations office at:
(202) 336-5889.

CPT codes and the *ICD-9-CM* codes are updated regularly, therefore, keeping abreast of the latest procedural codes is a good idea. The CPT coding manual dated 1998 or later has the most comprehensive codes on the psychiatric disorders (APA Online, 2001a). The *DSM-IV-TR* also has been updated with the latest diagnostic codes. Updated CPT codes assist with procedural recording in the inpatient and outpatient setting, denoting the setting where the service is provided (APA Online, 2001b). One myth in the practice setting is that since the CPT codes represent procedure, the use of certain CPT codes can restrict reimbursement. Although there is some truth to this statement, it is not the code itself that restricts reimbursement—it is the reimbursement provider. Therefore, each insurance company or service reimbursement system will determine what service is covered and what is not. This makes it critical for the mental health practitioner who practices or facilitates billing to be aware of not only what the major service reimbursement systems utilized will cover but also which providers are authorized to dispense these services.

AXIS I AND AXIS II: MULTIAXIAL ASSESSMENT SYSTEM

In the *DSM-IV-TR,* all *clinical disorders* are coded on Axis I (e.g., mood disorders, schizophrenia, dementia, anxiety disorders, substance disorders, disruptive behavior disorders). In addition, all other codes that are not attributed to a mental disorder but are the focus of intervention known as *Other conditions that may be focus of clinical attention* are also coded on Axis I. Axis II is used to code *personality disorders* in adults, (this can also include those of children and adolescents) and *mental retardation.*

For practitioners who are just learning to use the *DSM-IV-TR,* it may seem daunting to try to establish where to place a diagnostic condition. One simple way to do this is to first remember that all diagnostic mental health conditions and disorders, regardless of type, will be categorized on either Axis I or Axis II. Second, if the professional cannot remember all of the Axis I disorders, simply remember what is to be placed on Axis II (personality disorders and mental retardation). All other mental health conditions should be placed on Axis I.

Remembering where to place the diagnostic category of *mental retardation* (with the subtypes mild, moderate, severe, or profound) is easy to remember. Many professionals, however, get confused when is comes to what constitutes a personality disorder.

This may seem simple, yet some practitioners may remember when this axiom was not followed. For example, the disorder currently known as *dissociative identity disorder* (where an individual has more than one distinct personality) was called *multiple personality disorder* in *DSM-III-R*. Even though it ended in the words personality disorder, it was not classified as a personality disorder. It always has been and remains a clinical disorder to be coded on Axis I. To avoid confusion, the name of the disorder was changed in the *DSM-IV*. Now all mental disorders listed in the *DSM-IV-TR* that end in the words **personality disorder** represent personality disorders and need to be coded on Axis II. For example, if an individual suffers from obsessive compulsive disorder, what Axis would it be coded on? If an individual suffers from obsessive compulsive personality disorder, what Axis would it be coded on? The answer to the first question is Axis I, and the answer to the second is Axis II.

There is a myth that Axis I diagnoses are the most serious. *This is not true.* The multiaxial system is not based on severity of the illness; it is merely a classification system. Therefore, an Axis I diagnosis is not necessarily more serious than an Axis II diagnosis. This point is well supported when the two categories of mental health conditions listed on Axis I are examined. For example, Axis I lists the *clinical disorders* and the *other conditions that may be the focus of clinical attention.* Both categories have many similar presenting symptoms and these conditions can

---

QUICK REFERENCE

HELPFUL HINTS: CODING ON AXIS I AND AXIS II

When a professional is learning to use the *DSM-IV-TR* and is not sure where a diagnosis is to be placed and whether it should be placed on Axis I or Axis II, remember these simple rules.

- All diagnostic mental health disorders must be placed on either Axis I or Axis II.
- If the practitioner can remember that goes on Axis II (mental retardation and the personality disorders), everything else will go on Axis I.
- All disorders listed in *DSM-IV-TR* that end in **personality disorder** should be coded on Axis II.

QUICK REFERENCE

AXIS I: COMPARISON OF *DSM-III-R* AND *DSM-IV-TR*

DSM-III-R Clinical Syndromes and V Codes.

Changed to:

DSM-IV Clinical disorders.
    Other disorders that may be focus of clinical treatment.

AXIS II: COMPARISON OF *DSM-III-R* AND *DSM-IV-TR*

DSM-III-R Developmental disorders and personality disorders.

Changed to:

DSM-IV Personality disorders and mental retardation.
    Borderline intellectual functioning.*

---

* It remains unclear whether this category should be included on Axis II, in the *DSM-IV-TR* (p. 29), it is not listed but in the descriptive text (p. 25 and p. 740), it states it is to be listed on Axis II. Until this is clarified by the American Psychiatric Association, place this diagnosis based on practitioner judgment on either Axis I or Axis II.

QUICK REFERENCE

AXIS I: CLINICAL DISORDERS WITH MAJOR SUBSECTION HEADINGS

Disorders Usually First Diagnosed in Infancy, Childhood, and Adolescence

Learning disorders.

Communication disorders.

Motor skills disorders.

Pervasive developmental disorders.

Attention-deficit and disruptive behavior disorders.

Feeding and eating disorders of infancy or early childhood.

Tic disorders.

Elimination disorders.

Other disorders of infancy, childhood, and adolescence.

Delirium, Dementia, and Amnestic and Other Cognitive Disorders

Delirium.
Dementia.
Amnestic disorders.
Other cognitive disorders (NOS coded 294.9).

QUICK REFERENCE *(Continued)*

Mental Disorders Due to a General Medical Condition Not Elsewhere Classified

Substance Related Disorders

Alcohol-related disorders.

Caffeine-related disorders.

Cocaine-related disorders.

Inhalant-related disorders.

Opioid-related disorders.

Sedative-, hypnotic-, or anxiolytic-related disorders.

Polysubstance-related disorders.

Amphetamine- (or Amphetamine-like) related disorders.

Cannabis-related disorders.

Hallucinogen-related disorders.

Nicotine-related disorders.

Phencyclidine- (or phencyclidine-like) related disorders.

Other (or unknown) substance-related disorders.

Schizophrenia and the Other Psychotic Disorders

Mood Disorders

Depressive disorders.
Bipolar disorders.

Anxiety Disorders

Somatoform Disorders

Factitious Disorders

Dissociative Disorders

Sexual and Gender Identity Disorders

Sexual dysfunctions.
Paraphilias.
Gender identity disorders.

Eating Disorders

Sleep Disorders

Primary sleep disorders.
Sleep disorders related to another mental disorder.
Other sleep disorders.

Impulse Control Disorders Not Otherwise Classified

Adjustment Disorders

Source: Information modified from the *Diagnostic and Statistical Manual of Mental Disorders, Fourth Edition, Text Revision.* Copyright 2000. American Psychiatric Association.

cause problems that are significant enough to affect individual, occupational, and social functioning. *Other conditions that may be the focus of clinical attention,* however, are not considered mental disorders at all. Furthermore, although a mental disorder (e.g., major depressive disorder) may coexist with one of these conditions that may be the focus of clinical attention (e.g., bereavement), the focus of clinical attention (i.e., the reason for the visit) should not be the mental disorder. As explained earlier in this chapter, if we look at individuals who suffer from *bereavement* (formerly known as *uncomplicated bereavement*), although initially the symptoms may mimic depression, if the symptoms are related to the death of a loved one, they will diminish as adjustment progresses. Another example, of this category and how it can be utilized is in the category *malingering* (coded as V65.2). Although a client may present with multiple severe individual, occupational, and social problems, if the client meets the criteria for the condition of *malingering,* careful evaluation and documentation are required. Since malingering is not a mental disorder and it involves ". . . the intentional production of false or grossly exaggerated symptoms physical or psychological symptoms, motivated by external incentives such as avoiding . . ." (APA, 2000, p. 739), the practitioner must be sure to document clearly the external incentives.

To apply this further, imagine that a client wants to qualify for disability so he or she can receive a disability check. Therefore, the client feigns or grossly exaggerates what he or she is feeling. In actuality, this client would not qualify as having a mental disorder related to the reason for visit and his or her behaviors would be viewed as primarily manipulative in nature. In all fairness, and in support of the need for a thorough and comprehensive diagnostic assessment, this category should not be used haphazardly. The practitioner needs to be sure that the criteria to justify the diagnostic category are met. Often to support this effort, as will be discussed later in this chapter, supporting information gained through psychometric testing such as rapid and self-administered assessment instruments needs to be considered.

All practitioners need to be careful not to assume that an Axis I diagnosis is more severe than an Axis II diagnosis. All diagnostic listings on the multiaxial system are merely for categorical purposes.

The coding of several disorders has changed significantly with the new editions to the *DSM-IV* and *DSM-IV-TR.* (See box on page 62.) For example, the classification of *developmental disorders* in the *DSM-III-R* included mental retardation, pervasive developmental disorders (e.g., autistic disorder), and the specific developmental disorders (a.k.a. academic skill disorders), which were all listed on Axis II (APA, 1987). This coding changed when the *pervasive developmental disorders, learning disorders, motor skills disorders* and *communication disorders,* were moved from Axis II to Axis I in *DSM-IV.* Although, there are no diagnostic or multiaxial changes between the *DSM-IV* and *DSM-IV-TR,* it is a good

QUICK REFERENCE

AXIS I: OTHER CONDITIONS THAT MAY BE A FOCUS OF CLINICAL ATTENTION

Psychological Factors Affecting Medical Condition
Medication-Induced Movement Disorders

Neuroleptic-induced parkinsonism.	Coded 332.1
Neuroleptic malignant syndrome.	Coded 333.92
Neuroleptic-induced acute dystonia.	Coded 333.7
Neuroleptic-induced acute akathisia.	Coded 333.99
Neuroleptic-induced tardive dyskinesia.	Coded 333.82
Medication-induced postural tremor.	Coded 333.1
Medication-induced movement disorder NOS.	Coded 333.90

Other Medication Induced Disorder
Relational Problems

Relational problems associated with a general medical condition.	Coded V61.9
Parent-child relational problem.	Coded V61.20
Partner relational problem.	Coded V61.10
Sibling relational problem.	Coded V61.8
Relational problem NOS.	Coded V62.81

Problems Related to Abuse or Neglect

Physical abuse of a child.	Coded V61.21
Sexual abuse of a child.	Coded V61.21
Neglect of a child.	Coded V61.21
Physical abuse of an adult.	——
Sexual abuse of an adult.	——

Additional Conditions That May Be a Focus
of Clinical Attention

Noncompliance with treatment.	Coded V15.81
Malingering.	Coded V65.2
Adult antisocial behavior.	Coded V71.01
Child or adolescent antisocial behavior.	Coded V71.02
Borderline intellectual functioning.*	Coded V62.89
Age-related cognitive decline.	Coded 780.0
Bereavement.	Coded V62.82
Academic problem.	Coded V62.3
Occupational problem.	Coded V62.2
Identity problem.	Coded 313.82
Religious and spiritual problem.	Coded V62.89
Acculturation problem.	Coded V62.4
Phase of life problem.	Coded V62.89

————

* Can also be listed on Axis II.

Source: Listing of topics reprinted with permission from the *Diagnostic and Statistical Manual of Mental Disorders, Fourth Edition, Text Revision.* Copyright 2000. American Psychiatric Association.

idea to be sure to update professional knowledge and expertise in this area regularly as these coding systems can and do change.

Documentation of Information on Axis I

When documenting conditions on Axis I, the reason for the visit, generally referred to as the principle diagnosis, is listed first. When this is not the case and the principle diagnosis needs to be coded on Axis II, it would simply be listed there. One of the questions that professionals ask is: Why do most of the principle diagnoses almost always occur on Axis I rather than Axis II? The answer to this is not difficult but it requires knowledge of both practice application (what diagnoses are placed on a particular axis) and some of the circumstances that surround why diagnoses are coded there.

In practice, most clients usually present with a principle diagnosis relative to Axis I. In adults, one of the major reasons for this prevalence is that many of the diagnoses coded on Axis II (i.e., the personality disorders) generally start in childhood or adolescence and persist in a stable form into adulthood with nonexistence or limited periods of remission. This would make it more unlikely, although not impossible, for an adult to come in for intervention with a presenting condition needing to be coded on Axis II. Furthermore, if an adult suffers from mental retardation (coded on Axis II), this is considered a lifelong condition that, although possible, usually would not in itself constitute the presenting problem. In addition, if the individual develops a condition that resembles mental retardation in adulthood, it would not be diagnosed as mental retardation but rather as a specific type of dementia (both of these conditions will be discussed in further detail in subsequent chapters). In this case, once again an Axis I diagnosis would most likely result.

One example of an exception to this assumption is when an adult is given a principle diagnosis on Axis II such as *borderline personality disorder*. Individuals diagnosed with this condition often have a pattern of "instability of interpersonal relationships, self-image, and affects and marked instability" that might result in ". . . frantic efforts to avoid abandonment [that] may include impulsive actions such as self-mutilating or suicidal behaviors . . ." (APA, 2000, p. 706). Therefore, in this case, although the presenting diagnosis would be placed on Axis II because of self-harming behaviors such as self-mutilating or suicidal threats or actions, the client likely would warrant admission for inpatient observation. This would make the Axis II diagnosis of a personality disorder the actual reason for admission. When the principle diagnosis is listed on Axis II, it is always good practice to place the words (principle diagnosis) in parentheses after it (see Example 1 for further clarification).

In children, the same prevalence holds and the presenting diagnosis is also more likely to be placed on Axis I. The reasons for this remain very similar to those of adults as previously stated. There is one additional reason, however, that is particularly important to remember when working with children. Since the personality disorders are generally considered to be representative of lifelong patterns of behavior, children often are too young to meet the foundational criteria for assignment of the personality disorders.

Regardless of whether the practitioner is working with adults or children, acceptable proficient documentation of the provisional diagnosis requires that if more than one diagnosis is noted (on either Axis) the principle diagnosis should always be listed *first*.

As demonstrated in Example 1, whether a diagnosis is noted on Axis I or not, some type of coding will *always* need to be placed there. Therefore, the Axis I diagnosis should never be left blank. If there is no Axis I diagnosis, the practitioner should code *No diagnosis on Axis I* (V71.09). If the practitioner is uncertain of what diagnosis to place because of insufficient information (as explained in Chapter 2) he or she should code *Diagnosis or condition deferred on Axis I* (coded 799.9).

In completing the diagnostic assessment when working with Axis I conditions, the following situations need to be examined. First, the practitioner should note the major psychiatric symptoms a client is displaying. In the *DSM-IV-TR* each diagnostic category has specific criteria that are associated with it. Second, these presenting symptoms should be clearly noted and documented especially in regard to *frequency, intensity,* and *duration.* When looking at issues of frequency, it is critical to document how often the problem behaviors are happening (i.e., the rate of occurrence) during a specific time period. Are the behaviors happening, for example,

---

QUICK REFERENCE

EXAMPLE 1: DOCUMENTATION OF PRINCIPLE DIAGNOSIS

When major depressive disorder is the principle diagnosis and there are two Axis I diagnoses, the reason for visit or principle diagnosis is listed first.

Axis I: Major depressive disorder 296.xx.
            Alcohol dependence 303.90.

When the reason for visit or principle diagnosis is an Axis II diagnosis, be sure to identify it as the reason for the initial visit.

Axis I: V71.09 No diagnosis.

Axis II: Borderline personality disorder 301.83 (Principle Diagnosis).

QUICK REFERENCE

Coding on Axis I

Practitioners need to be aware that:

- Some type of coding is always expected on Axis I.
- No diagnosis on Axis I is coded: V71.09.
- Lack of, or inaccurate information for, an Axis I diagnosis is to be coded: 799.9 (Diagnosis or condition deferred on Axis I).

---

once a week, or once a day; and how does the frequency of occurrence of these problem behaviors directly affect individual, occupational, or social functioning? Many of the diagnostic categories say that the behaviors must occur once or more and others say it must be a frequent occurrence. Therefore, to be safe, always document the frequency of the behavior and relate it directly to level of functioning.

Intensity is another critical aspect that needs to be clearly identified when assessing diagnostic criteria. To address intensity, the practitioner must gather information in regard to the magnitude of the strength, power, or force with which a problem behavior is occurring and relate this directly to the way it affects daily functioning. For duration, the practitioner should document the time between the onset and the offset of the behavior (Ciminero, Calhoun, & Adams, 1986). Specifically, addressing duration requires that the period of time that something lasts or exists be measured. This time frame is very important in terms of identifying the criteria for a disorder because often specific time frames must be met (e.g., for schizophrenia the symptoms must last approximately six months; if less than six months the diagnosis of schizophreniform is utilized). Suggested measures, and standardized tools that can assist the mental health practitioner to measure incidents and problem behaviors in terms of frequency, intensity, and duration are presented later in this chapter along with the other rapid assessment instruments.

Last, when substantiating the categorization of diagnostic criteria supportive of the Axis I diagnosis, environmental, cultural, and social factors must always be assessed. As discussed in Chapter 2, it can be difficult to separate out behaviors that are culturally based from those that are not. It is critical to *not* diagnose Axis I disorder(s) when an individual's behaviors are related a culture-bound syndrome. In the diagnostic assessment process, if the practitioner believes the behavior is "culture" related, no clinical syndrome or formal diagnosis constituting a mental disorder based on those symptoms alone is given. Practitioners should code an individual's behaviors that they consider to be culturally related under the category of other conditions that may be a focus of clinical attention as an acculturation problem (coded V62.4). They *should not* be diagnosed with a mental disorder.

QUICK REFERENCE

AXIS I: QUESTIONS TO GUIDE THE PROCESS

- What are the major psychiatric symptoms a client is displaying?
- What are the frequency, intensity, and duration of the symptoms or problem behavior?
- Have environmental factors such as cultural and social factors been considered as a possible explanation?

Even though this condition is not considered a mental disorder, it would still be coded on Axis I.

Documentation of Information on Axis II

Axis II is used for reporting mental retardation and the personality disorders. Mental retardation is listed in terms of four degrees of severity (e.g., mild, moderate, severe, and profound with an additional classification when it is believed that mental retardation is present but the degree of severity cannot be assessed). Previously in the *DSM-III-R,* it was clearly documented that an additional condition called *borderline intellectual functioning* (coded V62.89) could also be coded on Axis II. Borderline intellectual functioning is one of the additional conditions that may be a focus of clinical attention. The main criterion for this category is the results of a standardized intelligence test. In borderline intellectual functioning, the Intelligence Quotient (IQ) range is between 71 and 84. This is the category of IQ scores directly above Mild Retardation and directly below what would be considered to fall within the normal intelligence range (85–115). Originally, this diagnosis was placed on Axis II because it was similar to the other disorders in that the personality traits present are believed to be enduring and pervasive. In *DSM-IV* and *DSM-IV-TR* (pp. 26, 27, and 29), it is no longer listed as a condition to be listed on Axis II. However, in the descriptive text within the *DSM-IV-TR* (APA, 2000) in the classification system (p. 25), and in the description of the disorder (p. 740), it states that it is to be coded on Axis II. Therefore, most practitioners choose to put it on Axis II, but until the text is clarified clearly, from a practice standpoint coding it on either Axis I or Axis II would suffice.

The second group of disorders that are listed on Axis II, are the *personality disorders.* As mentioned earlier in this chapter, if a disorder is designated as a personality disorder in the *DSM-IV* and the *DSM-IV-TR,* the diagnosis will end in the two words "personality disorder." In the *DSM-IV-TR,* although personality disorders continue to be grouped in clusters, the manual urges practitioners to be cautious using the cluster system. Although, the cluster system may be helpful in terms of general categorizing of symptoms, in research and in educational settings these

---

QUICK REFERENCE

AXIS II: TYPES OF MENTAL RETARDATION

Mild mental retardation	(IQ level 50–55 to approximately 70)	Coded 317
Moderate retardation	(IQ 35–40 to 50–55)	Coded 318.0
Severe retardation	(IQ level 20–25 to 35–40)	Coded 318.1
Profound mental retardation	(IQ level below 20 or 25)	Coded 318.2
Mental retardation, severity unspecified		Coded 319
Borderline intellectual functioning	(IQ level 71–84)	Coded 62.89

---

groupings have not been proven to accurately measure what is expected (APA, 2000). Furthermore, in the *DSM-IV* and the *DSM-IV-TR* there are now 11 different conditions related to personality. This is one less than was reported in the *DSM-III-R* (APA, 1987). The personality disorder known as *passive aggressive personality disorder* was removed from the *DSM-IV* and *DSM-IV-TR* diagnostic categories and placed in the section with the *criteria sets* and *axes provided for further study.*

In completing the diagnostic assessment when working with the conditions to be listed on Axis II, the following factors need to be examined. First, the practitioner should note the major psychiatric symptoms a client is displaying. Just as the conditions on Axis I, the conditions on Axis II also have similar criteria. The greatest predictor related to conditions on Axis II is whether there is a lifelong pattern of behavior or whether the onset of the condition occurred before the age of 18. This lifelong pattern is true for most individuals who suffer from mental retardation and those who suffer from the personality disorders. In mental retardation the practitioner should immediately look for significantly subaverage intelligence (IQ of 70 or below) with an age of onset younger than age 18. Also, it is critical to link the subaverage intelligence to concurrent problems in adaptive individual and social functioning.

With personality disorders individuals will often present with long-standing or enduring patterns of behavior and inner experiences that deviate markedly from expectations within the individual's cultural context. These behaviors remain pervasive and inflexible and cause the individual distress or impairment (APA, 2000, p. 685) Again, as with all diagnoses, the symptoms presented must be related directly to either adaptive or functional impairment.

QUICK REFERENCE

AXIS II: TYPES OF PERSONALITY DISORDERS

Cluster A: Characteristic of Odd and
Eccentric Behaviors

Paranoid personality disorder	Coded 301.0
Schizoid personality disorder	Coded 301.20
Schizotypal personality	Coded 301.22

Cluster B: Characteristic of Dramatic,
Emotional, and Erratic Behaviors

Antisocial personality disorder	Coded 301.7
Borderline personality disorder	Coded 301.83
Histrionic personality disorder	Coded 301.50
Narcissistic personality disorder	Coded 301.81

Cluster C: Characteristic of Anxious and
Fearful Behaviors

Avoidant personality disorder	Coded 301.82
Dependent personality disorder	Coded 301.6
Obsessive-compulsive personality disorder	Coded 301.4
Personality disorder NOS	Coded 301.9

Source: Listing of topics reprinted with permission from the *Diagnostic and Statistical Manual of Mental Disorders, Fourth Edition, Text Revision.* Copyright 2000. American Psychiatric Association.

Similar to Axis I, all presenting symptoms for Axis II conditions should be clearly noted and documented especially in regard to frequency, intensity, and duration of the problem behavior. That is, be sure to note the rate of occurrence of the problem behavior (frequency); the magnitude of the strength, power, or force (intensity) with which a problem behavior is occurring; and the period of time the

QUICK REFERENCE

AXIS II: QUESTIONS ABOUT MENTAL RETARDATION

In completing the diagnostic assessment for mental retardation, the following considerations should be taken into account:

- Is there a lifelong pattern of behavior with an onset of the condition prior to age 18?
- Is there significantly subaverage intelligence (IQ of 70 or below)?
- Is the subaverage intelligence concurrent with problems in adaptive functioning?
- What are the frequency, intensity, and duration of the presenting behaviors?

behavior exists (duration). When the symptoms exist but neither create marked distresses nor disturb or impair functioning, application of any diagnostic category is inappropriate. Similar to Axis I, Axis II needs to have a plan for addressing the disorders coded.

AXIS II: APPLICATION OF DEFENSE MECHANISMS

Defense mechanisms are a type of mental process or coping style that results in automatic psychological responses exhibited as a means of protecting the individual against anxiety. These coping styles and patterns of behavior help to safeguard the individual by keeping perceived internal and/or external stresses away from the individual's awareness (APA, 2000; Barker, 1999). Since it is believed that many individuals either consciously or unconsciously develop defense mechanisms that can influence the diagnostic condition and impede progress, these psychological occurrences, when noted in the client, should be listed on Axis II. When present, it is very important for the practitioner to be aware and recognize how these defense mechanisms may influence treatment because often the individual who is experiencing them is unaware of how these processes can affect his or her behavior. Defense mechanisms can influence an individual's reaction to emotional conflicts as well as responses displayed toward internal and external stressors found in daily living. Therefore, identification and subsequent documentation of the defense mechanism(s) can facilitate the most accurate diagnostic assessment. When present, these mechanisms should be documented regardless of the fact that this type of coding holds no value in the billing process and is not considered a mandatory part of the multiaxial system.

QUICK REFERENCE
CODING ON AXIS II

Practitioners need to be aware that:

- Similar to Axis I, some type of coding is always expected on Axis II.
- No diagnosis is to be coded: V71.09   Diagnosis on Axis II.
- Lack of, or inaccurate, information is to be coded: 799.9   Diagnosis or condition deferred on Axis II.
- Defense mechanisms can be coded on Axis II.

In the *DSM-IV-TR,* the Defensive Functioning Scale, located in the appendix section of the *DSM-IV-TR,* can prove to be very helpful as a reference for practitioners. The Defensive Functioning Scale identifies the defense mechanisms that an individual might develop as well as establishing the degree to which the defense mechanism or coping style may protect against anxiety or stress. Interpretation of defense mechanisms tends to be very subjective and the definitions and subsequent application of these concepts can differ based on the source of the professional reference. Therefore, it is important when using the defense mechanisms to identify coping styles and behaviors that can affect mental health related behaviors utilizing similar definitions. Since most professionals in mental health use the *DSM* in practice, it makes sense to use the definitions of the terms described in the *DSM-IV-TR* to represent the coding that is placed within the multiaxis system. When noted, documentation of the occurrence of defense mechanisms in clients is usually listed in order of prevalence and severity and placed on Axis II. Generally, the defense

---

QUICK REFERENCE		
EXAMPLE: RECORDING OF DEFENSE MECHANISMS		
Axis I:	V71.09	No diagnosis.
Axis II:	301.83	Borderline personality disorder. Splitting (current defense mechanism).
Axis III:	881.02	Lacerations of wrist.
Axis IV:		Loss of employment.
Axis V:		GAF = 45 (current).

mechanisms are listed beginning with those defenses or coping styles that are pre-dominant and most representative of the client's current level of functioning.

To use the defense mechanisms, the Defensive Functioning Scale divides these coping styles into related groups referred to as *defense levels*. At the first defense level, the defensive mechanisms are related to *high adaptive functioning*. In this level of functioning, an individual is aware of what he or she is experiencing and uses it to promote a healthier sense of well-being. (See the Quick Reference for samples and definitions of the defense mechanisms that might occur at this level.) For example, a common situation encountered is when a client uses the defense mechanism known as *suppression*. According to the *DSM-IV-TR* suppression is defined as an ". . . individual who deals with emotional conflict or internal or external stressors by intentionally avoiding thinking about disturbing problems, wishes, feelings, or experiences (APA, 2000, p. 813). In this case, an individual may refuse to think about something that is painful and thereby refuse to discuss it. This can complicate the history taking of the diagnostic assessment directly impacting the accuracy and relevance of what the client states as the presenting problem. This type of defense mechanism is considered higher level in terms of adaptive functioning since the client is cognizant of the suppression. It can also be helpful for professionals working to help the client to address this coping style in subsequent treatment planning and intervention strategy. Other defense mechanisms that are considered to be of the highest adaptive level are affiliation, altruism, anticipation, humor, self-assertion, self-observation, and sublimation.

The second level of defense is referred to as *mental inhibitions (compromise formation)*. When a client utilizes coping behaviors at this level, he or she is attempting to keep potentially threatening ideas, feelings, memories, wishes, or fears out of awareness (APA, 2001). For example, *repression* is a defense mechanism where "the individual deals with emotional conflict or internal or external stressors by expelling disturbing wishes, thoughts, or experiences from conscious awareness . . . [and] the feeling content may remain detached from its associated ideas" (APA, 2000, p. 813). Therefore, when an individual practices these coping styles at this level, he or she may not be aware of what is happening (unconscious) although the feelings may come out in other ways. For example, in repression a client may report that he loves and wants to protect his parents but is actually very angry and wants to punish his parents. He may report that he is very close and wants to protect his family, yet the client continually practices behaviors that put his parents at risk. Other examples of defense mechanisms in this area include *displacement, dissociation, intellectualization, isolation of affect, reaction formation,* and *undoing* (see quick reference for this level of functioning and definitions).

The third level of defense mechanisms identified in the *DSM-IV-TR* is *minor-image distorting*. Clients who utilize coping styles and behaviors representative of this level of functioning exhibit behaviors that are characterized by distortions

---

QUICK REFERENCE

DEFENSE LEVELS AND INDIVIDUAL DEFENSE MECHANISMS

high adaptive level: Coping styles and behaviors are in the conscious awareness of the client being served and result in optimal adaptation in the handling of stressors.

Selected definitions and examples of common defense mechanisms at this level include:

affiliation: The individual deals with emotional conflict or internal or external stressors by turning to others for help or support. This involves sharing problems with others but does not imply trying to make someone else responsible for them.

altruism: The individual deals with emotional conflict or internal or external stressors by dedication to meeting the needs of others. Unlike the self-sacrifice sometimes characteristic of reaction formation, the individual receives gratification either vicariously or from the response of others.

anticipation: The individual deals with emotional conflict or internal or external stressors by experiencing emotional reactions in advance of, or anticipating consequences of, possible future events and considering realistic, alternative responses or solutions.

humor: The individual deals with emotional conflict or external stressors by emphasizing the amusing or ironic aspects of the conflict or stressor.

self-assertion: The individual deals with emotional conflict or stressors by reflecting on his or her own thoughts, feelings, motivation, and behavior, and responding appropriately.

self-observation: The individual deals with emotional conflict or stressors by reflecting on his or her own thoughts, feelings, motivation, behavior and responding appropriately.

sublimation: The individual deals with emotional conflict or internal or external stressors by channeling potentially maladaptive feelings or impulses into socially acceptable behavior (e.g., contact sports to channel angry impulses).

suppression: The individual deals with emotional conflict or internal or external stressors by intentionally avoiding thinking about disturbing problems, wishes, feelings, or experiences.

Source: Reprinted with permission from the *Diagnostic and Statistical Manual of Mental Disorders, Fourth Edition, Text Revision.* Copyright 2000. American Psychiatric Association.

---

in self-image or self-esteem as well as distortions related to the way he or she perceives his or her body. For example, the defense mechanism *idealization* is defined as when an ". . . individual deals with emotional conflict or internal or external stressors by attributing exaggerated positive qualities to others. In this case, when completing the diagnostic assessment it may be difficult to assess the family and social influences that might affect a client's behavior because he or she cannot avoid or simply cannot accept the general perceptions of reality as shared by others.

QUICK REFERENCE

DEFENSE LEVELS AND INDIVIDUAL DEFENSE MECHANISMS

mental inhibitions (compromise formation) level: Coping styles and behaviors utilized at this level require that the client try to keeps potentially threatening ideas, feelings, memories, wishes, or fears out of awareness.

Selected definitions and examples of common defense mechanisms at this level include:

displacement: The individual deals with emotional conflict or internal or external stressors by transferring a feeling about, or a response to, one object onto another (usually less threatening) substitute object.

dissociation: The individual deals with emotional conflict or internal or external stressors with a breakdown in the usually integrated functions of consciousness, memory, perception of self or the environment, or sensory/motor behavior.

intellectualization: The individual deals with emotional conflict or internal or external stressors by the excessive use of abstract thinking or the making of generalizations to control or minimize disturbing feelings.

isolation of affect: The individual deals with emotional conflict or internal or external stressors by the separation of ideas from the feelings originally associated with them. The individual loses touch with the feelings associated with a given idea (e.g., a traumatic event) while remaining aware of the cognitive elements of it (e.g., descriptive details).

reaction formation: The individual deals with emotional conflict or internal or external stressors by substituting behavior, thoughts, or feelings that are diametrically opposed to his or her own unacceptable thoughts or feelings (this usually occurs in conjunction with their repression).

repression: The individual deals with emotions, conflict, or internal or external stressors by expelling disturbing wishes, thoughts, or experiences from conscious awareness. The feeling content may remain detached from its associated ideas.

undoing: The individual deals with emotional conflict or internal or external stressors by words or behavior designed to negate or to make amends symbolically for unacceptable thoughts, feelings, or actions.

Source: Reprinted with permission from the *Diagnostic and Statistical Manual of Mental Disorders, Fourth Edition, Text Revision.* Copyright 2000. American Psychiatric Association.

When working with children, for example, idealization may be related to seeing a parent as a role model. The parent may be abusive but because the child idealizes or sees the abusive actions as part of the expression of love and concern by the parent, the abuse is considered acceptable and tolerable. As a role model, the behaviors exhibited by the abusive parent become viewed as acceptable expressions of love. The child may begin to see herself or himself as bad or undeserving of other types of love (e.g., the child may say to himself, my father beats me, I respect him, so it must be done through love). Another example that takes into account the distortions in body image that may occur when idealization is used is the condition of *anorexia*. Anorexia is an eating disorder of a client who idealizes the body image of being extremely thin and is willing to starve to achieve this perceived ideal body frame. Other examples of coping styles reflective of these types of behaviors are *devaluation, idealization,* and *omnipotence.*

At the fourth level, the individual develops defense mechanisms referred to as experiencing *disavowal,* characterized by "keeping unpleasant or unacceptable stressors, impulses, ideas, affects, or responsibility out of awareness with or without a misattribution of these to external causes" (APA, 2000, p. 809). For example, in denial, the individual cannot or will not face emotional conflict or turmoil related to internal or external stressors and based on this inability refuses to acknowledge aspects or the entire situation or event because it is too painful. Generally, this lack of acknowledgment of the problem or situation is obvious and disconcerting to others in the client's environment. At times, when the defense mechanisms in this area are very extreme, psychotic denial may result. When this happens, there is clearly gross impairment when discussing the problem or situation with the client in terms of reality testing. Noting psychotic denial is very important when completing the diagnostic assessment because the information received may be inaccurate where the client cannot or will not acknowledge it.

QUICK REFERENCE

DEFENSE LEVELS AND INDIVIDUAL DEFENSE MECHANISMS

minor-image distorting level: Coping styles and behaviors at this level are characterized by distortions in the image of the self, in terms of self-worth and self-esteem as well as body image and the coping patterns are employed to regulate self-esteem.

Selected definitions and examples of common defense mechanisms at this level include:

devaluation: The individual deals with emotional conflict or internal or external stressors by attributing exaggerated negative qualities to self or others.

idealization: The individual deals with emotional conflict or internal or external stressors by attributing exaggerated positive qualities to others.

omnipotence: The individual deals with emotional conflict or internal or external stressors by feeling or acting as if he or she possesses special powers or abilities and is superior to others.

Source: Reprinted with permission from the *Diagnostic and Statistical Manual of Mental Disorders, Fourth Edition, Text Revision.* Copyright 2000. American Psychiatric Association.

Also, recognition of these types of defense mechanisms clearly highlights the need for including environmental information from other sources such as family and other individuals in the support system to assess the reliability and validity of the information the client is sharing. Identifying these factors could also be especially helpful to other professionals who will be working with the client in terms of treatment planning and strategy. For example, if a client is in denial and the practitioner does not gather additional information to supplement what is said, important factors that could guide the treatment process could be overlooked. Other examples of coping styles and strategies at this level include *projection* and *rationalization*.

The fifth defense level is referred to as *major image distorting*. When experiencing defense mechanisms at this level, the client grossly distorts and misattributes actions or behaviors of the self or others. Examples are autistic fantasy, projective identification, and splitting. For example, when working with certain personality disorders (e.g., borderline personality disorder, which will be defined later in this text), the defense mechanism known as splitting may occur. When utilizing this coping style, the individual deals with emotional conflict or internal or external stressors by compartmentalizing opposite affect states and failing to integrate the positive and negative qualities of the self or others into cohesive images (APA,

---

QUICK REFERENCE

DEFENSE LEVELS AND INDIVIDUAL DEFENSE MECHANISMS

disavowal level: Coping styles and behaviors at this level are characterized by keeping unpleasant or unacceptable stressors, impulses, ideas, affects, or responsibility out of awareness with or without a misattribution of these to external causes.

Selected definitions and examples of common defense mechanisms at this level include:

denial: The individual deals with emotional conflict or internal or external stressors by refusing to acknowledge some painful aspect of external reality or subjective experience that would be apparent to others. The term *psychotic denial* is used when there is gross impairment in reality testing.

projection: The individual deals with emotional conflict or internal or external stressors by falsely attributing to another his or her own unacceptable feelings, impulses, or thoughts.

rationalization: The individual deals with emotional conflict or internal or external stressors by concealing the true motivations for his or her own thoughts, actions, or feelings through the elaboration of reassuring or self-serving but incorrect explanations.

Source: Reprinted with permission from the *Diagnostic and Statistical Manual of Mental Disorders, Fourth Edition, Text Revision.* Copyright 2000. American Psychiatric Association.

2000). In this practice, ambivalent feelings result and the client may focus on the extremes avoiding more balanced views and expectations from self and others. This may lead the client to act in extremes such as being overly loving at times and extremely hateful and rejecting of others. Other defense mechanisms at the major-image distorting level include *autistic fantasy* and *projective identification* (see Quick Reference for definitions).

The sixth level is referred to as the *action level*. At this level, the client learns to deal with anxiety and internal and external stressors by withdrawing and running away or leaving the situation. Acting out is a defense mechanism that can occur in clients who cannot accept or deal with certain emotions. For example, an adolescent may have extremely contradictory feelings about his or her parents and, related to this internal or external struggle, the adolescent continually runs away from home.

QUICK REFERENCE

DEFENSE LEVELS AND INDIVIDUAL DEFENSE MECHANISMS

major-image distorting level: Gross distortion or misattribution of the image of self or others characterizes coping styles and behaviors at this level.

Selected definitions and examples of common defense mechanisms at this level include:

autistic fantasy: The individual deals with emotional conflict or internal or external stressors by excessive daydreaming as a substitute for human relationships, more effective action, or problem solving.

projective identification: As in projection, the individual deals with emotional conflict or internal or external stressors by falsely attributing to another his or her own unacceptable feelings, impulses, or thoughts. Unlike simple projection, the individual does not fully disavow what is projected. Instead, the individual remains aware of his or her own affects or impulses but misattributes them as justifiable reactions to the other person. Not infrequently, the individual induces the very feelings in others that were first mistakenly believed to be there, making it difficult to clarify who did what to whom first.

splitting: The individual deals with emotional conflict or internal or external stressors by compartmentalizing opposite affect states and failing to integrate the positive and negative qualities of the self or others into cohesive images. Because ambivalent affects cannot be experienced simultaneously, more balanced views and expectations of self or others are excluded from emotional awareness. Self and object images tend to alternate between polar opposites: exclusively loving, powerful, worthy, nurturant, and kind—or exclusively bad, hateful, angry, destructive, rejecting, or worthless.

Source: Reprinted with permission from the *Diagnostic and Statistical Manual of Mental Disorders, Fourth Edition, Text Revision.* Copyright 2000. American Psychiatric Association.

It is important to note, however, that acting out is not simply defining bad behaviors, the behaviors must be related directly to conflicting emotions and conflicts. Other defense mechanisms that fall at the action level are *apathetic withdrawal, help-rejecting complaining,* and *passive aggression.*

The last level of defensive functioning identified is referred to as *defensive dysregulation.* At this level, coping styles break down in terms of the client's reaction to stressors. This breakdown is severe enough to distort perceptions of reality and cause the individual to lose objective reality. The individual denies what is happening around him or her and refuses to acknowledge the existence of certain factors related to emotional stressors or events in his or her internal or external reality. Examples of this level of defense mechanisms include *delusional projection,* where the individual holds on to beliefs even when evidence to the contrary is

---

QUICK REFERENCE

DEFENSE LEVELS AND INDIVIDUAL DEFENSE MECHANISMS

action level: Coping styles and behaviors at this level are characterized by defensive functioning that deals with internal or external stressors by action or withdrawal.

Selected definitions and examples of common defense mechanisms at this level include:

help-rejecting complaining: The individual deals with emotional conflict or internal or external stressors by complaining or making repetitious requests for help that disguise covert feelings of hostility or reproach toward others, which are then expressed by rejecting the suggestions, advice, or help that others offer. The complaints or requests may involve physical or psychological symptoms or life problems.

acting out: The individual deals with emotional conflict or internal or external stressors by actions rather than reflections or feelings. This definition is broader than the original concept of the acting out of transference feelings or wishes during psychotherapy and is intended to include behavior arising both within and outside the transference relationship. Defensive acting out is not synonymous with "bad behavior" because it requires evidence that the behavior is related to emotional conflicts.

passive aggression: The individual deals with emotional conflict or internal or external stressors by indirectly and unassertively expressing aggression toward others. There is a facade of overt compliance masking covert resistance, resentment, or hostility. Passive aggression often occurs in response to demands for independent action or performance or the lack of gratification of dependent wishes but may be adaptive for individuals in subordinate positions who have no other way to express assertiveness more overtly.

Source: Reprinted with permission from the *Diagnostic and Statistical Manual of Mental Disorders, Fourth Edition, Text Revision.* Copyright 2000. American Psychiatric Association.

strong; *psychotic denial,* where there is a complete split from reality based inter-pretation of activities and events; and *psychotic distortion* where the individual cannot see things as others see them and misinterprets much of what is happening to them. When a client is experiencing defense mechanisms at this level, informa-tion from outside sources (family, friends, social supports) is essential as the his-tory and interpretation are very likely to be confused.

AXIS III: THE MULTIAXIAL ASSESSMENT SYSTEM

Axis III lists the physical (medical) conditions that may be relevant to the condi-tion being addressed. These medical or physical conditions are referred to as *gen-eral medical conditions* in the *DSM-IV* and the *DSM-IV-TR*. Previously, Axis III referred to these conditions as physical disorders and related conditions.

Since the term *mental disorder* means a condition that is not due to a medical condition, it is important for all practitioners to have some knowledge of the medical conditions that may be listed in Axis III. Furthermore, the practitioner needs to be acquainted with the relationship that these conditions can have to a mental disorder. Pollak, Levy, and Breitholz (1999) were quick to warn that in the diagnostic assessment alterations in behavior and mood that mimic a mental disorder may be directly related to a medical illness. Since most mental health practitioners do not have extensive training in medical disorders and what to ex-pect when one occurs, the misdiagnosis of a medical disorder as a mental health disorder can be a fairly common occurrence. Clients at the greatest risk for mis-diagnosis in this area include women who are pregnant or after pregnancy (e.g., prenatal, perinatal, or neonatal); indigent individuals because of limited resources and access to continued health care; individuals who engage in high-risk behav-iors; individuals with a medical illness who exhibit symptoms that might be con-fused for mental illness; and individuals with chronic conditions such as those who suffer from major mental disorders and the elderly (Hartmann, 1995; Pol-lak, Levy, & Breitholtz, 1999). For example, clients who have been diagnosed

---

QUICK REFERENCE

AXIS III: COMPARISON OF *DSM-III-R* AND *DSM-IV/DSM-IV-TR*

DSM-III-R	Physical Disorders and Related Conditions.
Changed to:	
DSM-IV/DSM-IV-TR	General Medical Conditions.

with mental disorders such as schizophrenia or the bipolar disorders may be unable to perceive, misperceive, or simply ignore warning signs of a medical problem. Among older adults, many of the chronic conditions that these individuals exhibit may be deemphasized or ignored as a normal course of aging or chronic disease progression.

For all clients, misdiagnosis or absence of the proper diagnosis can have devastating effects. When a client is acting extremely agitated and uncooperative, the practitioner should assess to see if this type of behavior is characteristic of any other time in the client's life. If it is not, it is possible the behaviors could be related to an unknown trauma such as a closed head injury. Furthermore, nonrecognition of the medical aspects of a mental disorder could also result in severe legal, ethical, and malpractice considerations. This makes it essential for nonmedically trained mental health practitioners to have some background in the medical conditions and the particular influence these conditions can have on mental health symptoms.

To guide the diagnostic assessment and screening inquiries that help to identify the relationship that medical factors can have on mental health-related behaviors. Pollack et al. (1999) suggest following several guidelines. First, the practitioner should look for risk factors and whether the client falls into a high-risk group as identified earlier. Second, the practitioner should consider whether the presentation is suspicious or inconsistent and therefore suggestive of a neurodevelopmental or medical condition.

Last, after gathering initial screening information, the practitioner should decide whether further testing is warranted to address the physical or medical basis of the symptoms a client is experiencing. In this case, a physical exam should always be considered. Also, once the practitioner makes a referral, a signed release from the client will be needed for the physician to share this information with the mental health practitioner. It is also recommended that the practitioner use client information from previous history and physical exams, medical history summaries, radiological reports, and lab findings. The most valuable advice for the practitioner is to first establish when the client last had a physical exam. When this information cannot be verified and the practitioner is not sure whether the condition is medically based, referral for a physical exam should be made. Remember that although the mental health practitioner can assist in helping to identify and document medical conditions, the original diagnosis of any such medical condition always rests with the physician.

Pollak et al. (1999) suggest several factors that can help a practitioner to separate mental health clinical presentations that may have a medical contribution. The following should always be considered in completing the diagnostic assessment: First, give special attention to clients who present with the first episode of a major disorder. In these clients, particularly when symptoms are severe (e.g., psychotic,

---

QUICK REFERENCE

HELPFUL HINTS: CLINICAL PRESENTATIONS
SUGGESTIVE OF A MENTAL DISORDER

- Previous psychosocial difficulties not related to a medical or neurodevelopmental disorder.
- Chronic unrelated complaints that cannot be linked to a satisfactory medical explanation.
- A history of object relations problems such as help-rejecting behavior, codependency, and other interrelationship problems.
- A puzzling lack of concern on the part of the client as to the behaviors he or she is engaging in and a lack of concern with a tendency to minimize or deny the circumstances.
- Evidence of secondary gain where the client is reinforced by such behaviors by significant others, family, or members of the support system.
- A history of substance abuse problems (alcohol or medication abuse).
- A family history of similar symptoms and/or mental disorders.
- Cognitive or physical complaints that are more severe than what would be expected for someone in a similar situation.

---

catatonic, and nonresponsive), close monitoring of the original presentation, when compared with previous behavior, is essential.

Second, note if the client's symptoms are acute (just started or relative to a certain situation) or abrupt with rapid changes in mood or behavior. Examples of symptoms that would fall in this area include both cognitive and behavioral symptoms such as marked apathy, decreased drive and initiative, paranoia, lability or mood swings, and poorly controlled impulses.

Third, the practitioner should pay particular attention when the initial onset of a problem or serious symptoms occur after the age of 40. Although this is not an iron clad rule, most mental disorders become evident before the age of 40, thus onset of symptoms after 40 should be carefully examined to rule out social, situational stressors, cultural implications, and medical causes.

Fourth, note symptoms of a mental disorder that occur immediately preceding, during, or after the onset of a major medical illness. It is very possible the symptoms may be related to the progression of the medical condition. There is also the possibility that symptoms could be medication or substance related (Dziegielewski & Leon, 2001). Polypharmacy can be a real problem for many individuals who are unaware of the dangers of mixing certain medications and substances that are not considered medications by the individual (i.e. herbal preparations) (Dziegielewski, 2001).

Fifth, when gathering information for the diagnostic assessment, note whether there is an immediate psychosocial stressor or life circumstance that may contribute to the symptoms the client is experiencing. This is especially relevant when the stressors present are so minimal that a clear connection between the stressor and the reaction cannot be made. One very good general rule is to remember that anytime a client presents with extreme symptomolgy of any kind with no previous history of such behaviors, attention and monitoring for medical causes is essential.

Sixth, pay particular attention in the screening process when a client suffers from a variety of different types of *hallucinations*. Basically, a hallucination is the misperception of a stimulus. In psychotic conditions, *auditory hallucinations* are most common. When a client presents with multiple types of hallucinations such as visual (seeing things that are not there); tactile, which pertain to the sense of touch (e.g., bugs crawling on them); gustatory, pertaining to the sense of taste; or olfactory relative to the sense of smell, this is generally too extreme to be purely a mental health condition.

Seventh, note any simple repetitive and purposeless movements of speech (e.g., stuttering or indistinct or unintelligible speech), the face (e.g., motor tightness or tremors), and hands and extremities (e.g., tremor, shaking, and unsteady gait). Also note any experiential phenomena such as derealization, depersonalization, and unexplained gastric or medical complaints and symptoms such as new onset of headache accompanied by physical signs such as nausea and vomiting.

Eighth, note signs of cortical brain dysfunction such as aphasia (language disturbance), apraxia (movement disturbance), agnosia (failure to recognize familiar objects despite intact sensory functioning), and visuo-constructional deficits (problems drawing or reproducing objects and patterns).

Last, note any signs that may be associated with organ failure such as jaundice related to hepatic disease, or dyspnea (difficulty breathing) associated with cardiac or pulmonary disease. For example, if a client is not getting proper oxygen, he or she may present as very confused and disoriented and when oxygen is regulated, the signs and symptoms would begin to decrease and quickly subside. Although mental health practitioners are not expected to be experts in diagnosing medical disorders, being aware of the medical complications that can influence mental health presentations are necessary to facilitate the most accurate and complete diagnostic assessment possible.

Coding Medical Conditions on Axis III

All relevant medical conditions should be listed on Axis III. These general medical conditions should be listed when (1) the mental disorder appears to have a physiological relationship or bearing on the mental health condition coded on Axis I and/or Axis II and (2) when the medical condition actually causes or facilitates and is part of the reason for the development and continuation of the mental health condition. One sure way to establish this relationship is that when the general medical condition is resolved, the mental health condition is resolved as well. Although conclusive, it doesn't always happen so easily, or the damage from the general medical condition may not be curable. Regardless, it is important to document all related medical conditions when forming a diagnosis. For example, if an individual suffers from dementia of the Alzheimer's type, which is coded on Axis I, then it is expected that one cause of the dementia (i.e., Alzheimer's disease) would be coded on Axis III. Similarly, when a mental disorder due to a general medical condition is coded on Axis I, the medical diagnosis that caused it should

---

QUICK REFERENCE

AXIS III: GENERAL MEDICAL CONDITIONS

Diagnostic categories include:

Diseases of the nervous system.

Diseases of the circulatory system.

Diseases of the respiratory system.

Neoplasms.

Endocrine diseases.

Nutritional diseases.

Metabolic diseases.

Diseases of the digestive system.

Genitourinary system diseases.

Hematological diseases.

Diseases of the eye.

Diseases of the ear, nose, and throat.

Musculoskeletal system and connective tissue diseases.

Diseases of the skin.

Congenital malformations, deformations, and chromosomal abnormalities.

Diseases of pregnancy, childbirth, and the puerperium.

Infectious diseases.

Overdose.

Additional codes for the medication-induced disorders.

Source: Listing of topics reprinted with permission from the *Diagnostic and Statistical Manual of Mental Disorders, Fourth Edition, Text Revision.* Copyright 2000. American Psychiatric Association.

be reported on both Axis I and Axis III. (See Axis III, General Medical Conditions Quick Reference for the categories of general medical conditions listed on Axis III.) Appendix B includes the complete list of general medical conditions that use the *ICD-9-CM* codes and are featured in the *DSM-IV-TR*. Some of the conditions listed in Appendix B are further defined in the Glossary and brief descriptions are given of the medical conditions.

When making an Axis III diagnosis, mental health practitioners may find it helpful to receive support from an interdisciplinary or multidisciplinary team that includes a medical professional. Individuals who have training in the medical aspects of disease and illness can be valuable resources in understanding this mind-body connection.

Before an Axis III diagnosis is recorded, there should always be some hard evidence to support its inclusion. The practitioner should query whether a recent history and physical has been conducted and when one is available review the written summary, which can be helpful in identifying medical conditions that may be related to the symptoms and behaviors a client is exhibiting. Also, as stated earlier, if a physical exam has not been conducted prior to the assessment, it is always a good idea to either refer the client for a physical or suggest that the client see a physician for a routine examination. Furthermore, a review of the medical information available, such as lab reports and other findings, as well as consulting with a medical professional may also be helpful in identifying disorders that could complicate or prevent the client from achieving improved mental health. When utilizing this axis, mental health practitioners should be prepared to inquire into the signs and symptoms of these conditions and to assist in understanding the relationship of this medical condition to the diagnostic assessment and planning process that will evolve.

Special Considerations for Axis III

When completing the diagnostic assessment, there are two areas that are coded on Axis III that are often overlooked and neglected, yet their importance is critical to

---

QUICK REFERENCE

AXIS III: ASSESSMENT QUESTIONS

- Has the client had a recent physical exam? If not, suggest that one be ordered.
- Does the client have a summary of a recent history and physical exam that could be reviewed?
- Are there any laboratory findings or tests or any diagnostic reports that can assist in establishing a relationship between the mental and physiological consequences that result?

a well-rounded comprehensive diagnostic assessment. The first falls under diseases of the eye and has to do with *visual loss* (coded 369.9) or *cataracts* (coded 366.9). Visual loss is related to a decrease in vision (sight) yet the apparent loss or visual acuity or visual field is not related directly to substantiating physical signs. This problem may be best addressed with client reassurance (PDR Medical Dictionary, 1995). Cataracts relate to the loss of transparency in the lens of the eye. Both of these conditions result in vision impairment. Keep in mind that decreased or impaired vision may lead individuals to interpret daily events incorrectly. For example, have you ever sat near a window only to look up and be startled by your reflection? For a moment, you are shocked and frightened that someone is watching you. As you look closer, however, you realize that it is only your reflection. Now imagine that you are vision impaired and cannot see well. Or imagine that you are not wearing your glasses because you cannot remember where you put them. Or that you have developed a cataract that has grown so large your vision is obstructed, and what you can see is clouded or shadowed in appearance. Is it possible that no matter how hard you try you are still unable to tell that reflection in the window is really you? Since you are unable to distinguish the shape in the window as your own, imagine how frightened you might become as you now convince yourself that a stranger is watching your every move? Would you not be suspicious of why you were being watched, and what this person or people might be after? Now imagine how someone who is vision impaired might feel if he or she is troubled by symptoms that cannot be easily explained. The frustration with the present situation can lead to symptoms being misperceived or misinterpreted. For mental health practitioners, the most salient issue to identify once the vision difficulty is recognized or corrected is whether the problem resolves itself. As part of the diagnostic assessment, special attention should always be given to screening for vision problems that may cause distress to the client in terms of individual and social functioning.

The second medical area that is often overlooked in the diagnostic assessment is related to hearing loss (Coded 389.9). A client with hearing impairment or hearing loss will experience a reduction in the ability to perceive sound that can range from slight impairment to complete deafness (PDR Medical Dictionary, 1995). Many times a client who is having hearing difficulty may not want to admit it. Many individuals may rely on hearing enhancement devices such as hearing aids, which amplify sound more effectively into the ear. Such hearing aids may not be able to differentiate among selected pieces of information as well as the human ear. Furthermore, as a normal part of aging, high-frequency hearing loss can occur. Most noises in a person's environment, such as background noise, are low frequency. Therefore, an individual with high-frequency loss may not be able to tune out background noise such as television sets or side conversations. He or she may get very angry over distractions that other people who do not have a similar hearing loss do not perceive.

QUICK REFERENCE

AXIS III: ASSESSING HEARING AND VISION PROBLEMS

In the diagnostic assessment process for hearing and vision practitioners need to ask the client:

- Do you have any problems with your hearing or vision?
- How would you rate your current hearing and your vision?
- Can you give examples of specific problems you are having?
- When did you have your last vision or hearing checkup?

Special attention should always be given during the diagnostic assessment process to ask very specific questions in regard to hearing and vision problems as these medical problems can be misinterpreted as signs of a mental health problem.

CASE APPLICATION

The Importance of Medical Factors

In the multiaxial assessment, the importance of examining complicating or interacting medical conditions cannot be underestimated. Consider the following example. Late one night a client was brought to the Emergency Room who was extremely unkempt, delusional, and paranoid. He reported bizarre delusions stating that demons had invaded his teeth and were trying to capture his mind. The client had a past history of schizophrenia paranoid type. This time, however, the delusions he was reporting were very extreme, when compared with previous presentations. He was so convinced that demons were inside his teeth that he had started to tear at his gums with his fingers in an attempt to get at the demons inside. In his state of poor hygiene and malnourishment, it is not hard to see how he had managed to remove most of his teeth from his mouth, ripping them out with his fingers. Immediately on admission a physical exam was ordered along with an X-ray of his teeth to see the extent of the damage he had created by ripping the teeth from his mouth. The X-ray revealed that the client had an extensive sinus infection. The X-ray report made it obvious how much pain was being caused by the untreated infection. The pressure the sinus discharge was placing on the roots of his teeth were causing him extensive pain and heightening the paranoid delusion of demons occupying his teeth. The client had managed to rip most of the teeth from his mouth before the professionals were able to intervene and determine the cause of the problem. Once the sinus infection was treated, the severity of the paranoid delusions subsided. As can be seen in this example, it is critical that medical issues, especially when clients present with signs and symptoms that are extreme, be clearly assessed and documented as part of the comprehensive diagnostic assessment process.

AXIS IV: THE MULTIAXIAL ASSESSMENT SYSTEM

Axis IV is designed to address the severities of the psychosocial stressor(s) clients have experienced over the past year. Axis IV is particularly relevant when one considers the relationship between stresses in the environment and how these stresses can directly or indirectly influence mental health problems and symptoms. The use of this Axis was strongly encouraged in *DSM-III* and later in *DSM-III-R.* In the *DSM-III,* the rating system was categorical (i.e., stressors were either listed as mild, moderate, severe, or catastrophic). This later changed to a numerical scale in *DSM-III-R,* in which the rating scale asked the practitioner to rate client problems on a scale from 1 (low) to 6 (high). In addition, a list of examples to help determine the proper number was given. A "0" was given if the information was unknown or repetitive. Generally, both the stressor and the severity were listed on this axis. In the formulation of *DSM-IV,* however, it was decided that a numeric scale allowed for too much ambiguousness in terms of coding and the rating scale was discontinued. In both the *DSM-IV* and the *DSM-IV-TR,* a list of stressors as factors contributing to life stress is included, and Axis IV was renamed *Psychosocial and Environmental Problems.* In addition, the stressors can be further clarified by listing the specific problem that results. It is important to discern how long the

---

QUICK REFERENCE

AXIS IV: CHANGES BETWEEN *DSM-III-R* AND *DSM-IV* AND *DSM-IV-TR*

DSM-III-R   Severity of psychosocial stressors.
(Scale rating 1 = low to 6 = high)

Changed to:

DSM-IV-TR   Psychosocial and environmental problems.

Problems with primary support.

Problems related to social environment.

Educational problems.

Occupational problems.

Using problems.

Economic problems.

Problems with access to health care services.

Problems related to interaction with the legal system.

Other psychosocial problems.

stressor(s) has been prevalent. An acute stressor has a better prognosis for recovery. For further clarification of the differences in Axis IV between *DSM-III-R* and *DSM-IV/DSM-IV-TR* refer to the previous quick reference box.

AXIS V: THE MULTIAXIAL ASSESSMENT SYSTEM

Axis V is used to rate the client's psychosocial and occupational functioning for the past year. To complete this task a scale known as the *Generalized Assessment of Functioning* (GAF) is used. Over the years, this measurement scale has gained in importance because the scale can be used to support measurement. Therefore, an increasing number of professionals are turning to the *DSM-IV-TR* and the GAF rating scores independent of the multiaxial diagnostic system as an aid for measuring and documenting client behaviors. Use of the GAF supports the current movement to enhance the diagnostic assessment by responding to the pressure to incorporate additional forms of measurement as part of the treatment plan (Dziegielewski, 1997). The pressure to achieve evidence-based practice has led to the incorporation of factors related to the individual, family, and social rankings to be included. These factors are now included in a reporting scale that provides a practitioner–driven measure that is capable of monitoring a client's functioning that can clearly be supported through direct client observation and recording.

Although the GAF was first described in the *DSM-III-R,* the range and the scaling descriptions were different. In the *DSM-III-R* the scale ranged from 1 to 90 with the lowest scores representing poor functioning. The descriptions for each scale range were very limited. In *DSM-IV* and *DSM-IV-TR,* the scale of the GAF has been extended to 100 points; lower numbers continue to indicate lower functioning (e.g., 1 = minimal functioning, 100 = highest level of functioning). In addition, several other major changes have been made between the *DSM-IV* and the *DSM-IV-TR.* The modifications include: (1) changes related to the instructions for completing the scale; (2) minor changes and clarification in how to record the scores on the scale (i.e., past, current, at discharge); and, (3) a function component reflective of the score range was added to the description section of the text.

When utilizing the GAF, the scale allows for assigning a number that represents a client's behaviors. The scale is designed to enable the practitioner to differentially rank identified behaviors from 1 to 100, with higher ratings indicating higher overall functioning and coping levels. By rating the highest level of functioning, a client has attained over the past year and then comparing it to his or her current level of functioning, helpful comparisons can be made. For example, although the current level of functioning at time of assessment is expected, the practitioner can also gather information from the past year, upon admission or start of treatment (current level of functioning), and at discharge or termination. In this method, ratings of a client's functioning are assigned at the outset of therapy, and again upon termination. It is particularly important to note, however, that in the *DSM-IV* all assessments of functioning, current, and past, were generally made recording the client's highest level of functioning observed. This differs from what is stated in the *DSM-IV-TR*, which encourages practitioners to note not only current level of functioning, but also the lowest level of functioning assessed during the weekly period prior to hospitalization or initiation of service. When other functioning times are assessed (over the past year, or on termination) the highest level of functioning is assessed.

The *DSM-IV-TR* also gives more detailed instructions on how to apply the GAF. According to the APA (2000) there are three steps to applying the GAF. First, always start at the top of the scale, and look at the numbers that denote the highest level of functioning possible. Now compare the behaviors that the client is exhibiting to the sample behaviors that appear in that category. (See Quick Reference box on p. 92 to become familiar with the categories.)

Second, measure the individual's current level of functioning or severity of the behaviors (when looking specifically at the behaviors, if it appears more severe then outlined in that category, select a number from the next lower category). The practitioner continues down the scale's score groupings until reaching the range that is most reflective of the client's behavior. If the severity of the symptoms and the level of functioning differ, the more dysfunctional aspect should be utilized to represent the number assigned.

Last, to determine the appropriate number from the range, consider whether the individual's symptoms and level of functioning are at the higher or lower level of the range and use that information in the selection of the number. For example, many professionals feel a GAF score within the range of 41 to 50 is often considered indicative of inpatient admission. According to the given criteria for this range, individuals with this score are experiencing serious symptoms that disturb functioning. When a client has behaviors that fall into this range the behaviors need to be clearly identified. Once this is accomplished, the exact number [e.g., GAF = 45 (current)] is identified by the practitioner after assessing the symptoms and level of functioning. Next the practitioner uses this information to determine whether the client falls at the top, middle, or bottom of the range and assigns the number. Utilization of the GAF can help practitioners both to quantify client problems and to document observable changes that may be attributable to the intervention efforts. Scales such as this allow the practitioner to track performance variations across behaviors relative to client functioning.

Professionals are not expected to memorize the GAF. The scale is clearly listed in the *DSM-IV-TR* and in this text as well. Practitioners may want to keep a copy the GAF available so that it can be referred to as needed. Also, it is suggested

QUICK REFERENCE

GLOBAL ASSESSMENT OF FUNCTIONING (GAF) SCALE

Consider psychological, social, and occupational functioning on a hypothetical continuum of mental health illness. Do not include impairment in functioning due to physical (or environmental) limitations.

Code	(Note: Use intermediate codes when appropriate, e.g., 45, 68, 72)
100–91	Superior functioning in a wide range of activities, life's problems never seem to get out of hand, is sought out by others because of his or her many positive qualities. No symptoms.
90–81	Absent or minimal symptoms (e.g., mild anxiety before an exam).
80–71	If symptoms are present, they are transient and expectable reactions to psychosocial stressors (e.g., difficulty concentrating after family argument); no more than slight impairment in social, occupational, or school functioning (e.g., temporarily falling behind in schoolwork).
70–61	Some mild symptoms (e.g., depressed mood and mild insomnia) or some difficulty in social, occupational, or school functioning.
60–51	Moderate symptoms (e.g., flat affect and circumstantial speech, occasional panic attacks) or moderate difficulty in social, occupational, or school functioning (e.g., few friends, conflicts with peers or coworkers).
50–41	Serious symptoms (e.g., suicidal ideation, severe obsessional rituals, frequent shoplifting) or any serious impairment in social, occupational, or school functioning (e.g., no friends, unable to keep a job).
40–31	Some impairment in reality testing or communication (e.g., speech is at times illogical, obscure, or irrelevant) or major impairment in several areas, such as work or school, family relations, judgment, thinking, or mood (e.g., depressed man avoids friends, neglects family, and is unable to work; child frequently beats up younger children, is defiant at home, and is failing at school).
30–21	Behavior is considerably influenced by delusions or hallucinations or serious impairment in communication or judgment (e.g., stays in bed all day; no job, home, or friends).
20–11	Some danger of hurting self or others (e.g., suicide attempts without clear expectation of death, frequently violent, manic excitement) or occasionally fails to maintain minimal personal hygiene (e.g., smears feces) or gross impairment in communication (e.g., largely incoherent or mute).
10–1	Persistent danger of severely hurting self or others (e.g., recurrent violence) or persistent inability to maintain minimal personal hygiene or serious suicidal act with clear expectation of death.
0	Inadequate information.

Source: Reprinted with permission from the *Diagnostic and Statistical Manual of Mental Disorders, Fourth Edition, Text Revision.* Copyright 2000. American Psychiatric Association.

strongly that when working as part of an interdisciplinary or a multidisciplinary team, all members sit down with a copy of the GAF and outline what behaviors, based on the specific population being served, would fall in the score range. (See p. 92 in this chapter.) All professionals would be looking at the same types of behaviors and could be aware of the relationship between the behavior and level of functioning specified for the particular population group being served. Since the GAF score may be used to justify the need for additional testing or assessment, careful documentation on this axis is critical to quality client care (Pollak et al., 1999).

SUPPLEMENTS TO AXIS V

In the *DSM-IV* "Criteria Sets and Axes Provided for Further Study" there are two scales that are not required for diagnosis yet can provide a format for ranking function that might be helpful to mental health professionals. The first of these optional scales is the relational functioning scale: Global Assessment of Relational Functioning (GARF). This index is used to address the status of family or other ongoing relationships on a hypothetical continuum from *competent* to *dysfunctional* (APA, 1994). The second index is the Social and Occupational Functioning Assessment Scale (SOFAS). With this scale an ". . . individual's level of social and occupational functioning that is not directly influenced by overall severity of the individual's psychological symptoms . . ." can be addressed (APA, 1994, p. 760). The complimentary nature of these scales in identifying and assessing client problems is evident in the fact that all three scales, the GARF, GAF, and SOFAS, use the same rating system. The rankings for each scale range from 0 to 100, with lower numbers representing more severe problems. Collectively, these tools provide a viable framework within which mental health practitioners can apply concrete measures to a wide variety of practice situations. They also provide a multidimensional perspective that permits workers to document variations in levels of functioning across system sizes, including the individual (GAF), family (GARF), and social (SOFAS) perspectives. The same method of scoring as described for the GAF should also be applied for use with the GARF and SOFAS.

STANDARDIZED MEASUREMENTS

Since the GAF, GARF, and SOFAS are considered to be *therapist driven,* meaning that the practitioner uses clinical judgment to set the number and interpret all clinical information in regard to symptom severity and level of functioning, it makes good practice sense to also consider the utilization of other standardized assessments to supplement the diagnostic assessment. Furthermore, standardized

QUICK REFERENCE

GLOBAL ASSESSMENT OF RELATIONAL FUNCTIONING (GARF) SCALE

Instructions: The GARF Scale can be used to indicate an overall judgment of the functioning of a family or other ongoing relationship on a hypothetical continuum ranging from competent, optimal relational functioning to a disrupted, dysfunctional relationship. It is analogous to Axis V (Global Assessment of Functioning Scale) provided for individuals in *DSM-IV.* The GARF Scale permits the clinician to rate the degree to which a family or other ongoing relational unit meets the affective or instrumental needs of its members in the following areas:

A. *Problem solving*—skills in negotiating goals, rules, and routines; adaptability to stress; communication skills; ability to resolve conflict.

B. *Organization*—maintenance of interpersonal roles and subsystem boundaries; hierarchical functioning; coalitions and distribution of power, control, and responsibility.

C. *Emotional climate*—tone and range of feelings; quality of caring, empathy, involvement, and attachment/commitment; sharing of values; mutual affective responsiveness, respect, and regard; quality of sexual functioning.

In most instances, the GARF Scale should be used to rate functioning during the current period (i.e., the level of relational functioning at the time of the evaluation). In some settings, the GARF's Scale may also be used to rate functioning for other time periods (i.e., the highest level of relational functioning for at least a few months during the past year).

Note: Use specific, intermediate codes when possible, for example, 45, 68, and 72. If detailed information is not adequate to make specific ratings, use midpoints of the five ranges, that is, 90, 70, 50, 30, or 10.

81–100 Overall: *Relational unit is functioning satisfactorily from self-report of participants and from perspectives of observers.*

Agreed on patterns or routines exist that help meet the usual needs of each family/couple member; there is flexibility for change in response to unusual demands or events; and occasional conflicts and stressful transitions are resolved through problem-solving communication and negotiation.

There is a shared understanding and agreement about roles and appropriate tasks, decision making is established for each functional area, and there is recognition of the unique characteristics and merit of each subsystem (e.g., parents/spouses, siblings, and individuals).

There is a situationally appropriate, optimistic atmosphere in the family; a wide range of feelings is freely expressed and managed within the family; and there is a general atmosphere of warmth, caring, and sharing of values among all family members. Sexual relations of adult members are satisfactory.

61–80 Overall: *Functioning of relational unit is somewhat unsatisfactory. Over a period of time, many but not all difficulties are resolved without complaints.*

Daily routines are present but there is some pain and difficulty in responding to the unusual. Some conflicts remain unresolved, but do not disrupt family functioning.

QUICK REFERENCE *(Continued)*

Decision making is unusually competent, but efforts at control of one another quite often are greater than necessary or are ineffective. Individuals and relationships are clearly demarcated but sometimes a specific subsystem is depreciated or scapegoated.

A range of feeling is expressed, but instances of emotional blocking or tension are evident. Warmth and caring are present but are marred by a family member's irritability and frustrations. Sexual activity of adult members may be reduced or problematic.

41–60 Overall: *Relational unit has occasional times of satisfying and competent functioning together, but clearly dysfunctional, unsatisfying relationships tend to predominate.*

Communication is frequently inhibited by unresolved conflicts that often interfere with daily routines; there is significant difficulty in adapting to family stress and transitional change.

Decision making is only intermittently competent and effective; either excessive rigidity or significant lack of structure is evident at these times. A partner or coalition quite often submerges individual needs.

Pain or ineffective anger or emotional deadness interferes with family enjoyment. Although there is some warmth and support for members, it is usually unequally distributed. Troublesome sexual difficulties between adults are often present.

21–40 Overall: *Relational unit is obviously and seriously dysfunctional; forms and time periods of satisfactory relating are rare.*

Family/couple routines do not meet the needs of members; they are grimly adhered to or blithely ignored. Life cycle changes, such as departures or entries into the relational unit, generate painful conflict and obviously frustrating failures of problem solving.

Decision making is tyrannical or quite ineffective. The unique characteristics of individuals are unappreciated or ignored by either rigid or confusingly fluid coalitions.

There are infrequent periods of enjoyment of life together; frequent distancing or open hostility reflects significant conflicts that remain unresolved and quite painful. Sexual dysfunction among adult members is commonplace.

1–20 Overall: *Relational unit has become too dysfunctional to retain continuity of contact and attachment.*

Family/couple routines are negligible (e.g., no mealtime, sleeping, or waking schedule); family members often do not know where others are or when they will be in or out; there is little effective communication among family members.

Family/couple members are not organized in such a way that personal or generational responsibilities are recognized. Boundaries of relational unit as a whole and subsystems cannot be identified or agreed on. Family members are physically endangered or injured or sexually attacked.

Despair and cynicism are pervasive; there is little attention to the emotional needs of others; there is almost no sense of attachment, commitment, or concern about one another's welfare.

0: *Inadequate information.*

Source: Reprinted with permission from the *Diagnostic and Statistical Manual of Mental Disorders, Fourth Edition, Text Revision.* Copyright 2000. American Psychiatric Association.

SOCIAL AND OCCUPATIONAL FUNCTIONING ASSESSMENT SCALE (SOFAS)

Consider social and occupational functioning on a continuum from excellent functioning to grossly impaired functioning. Include impairments in functioning due to physical limitations, as well as those due to mental impairments. To be counted, impairment must be a direct consequence of mental and physical health problems; the effects of lack of opportunity and other environmental limitations are not to be considered.

Code   (Note: Use intermediate codes when appropriate, e.g., 45, 68, 72.)

Code	
100–91	Superior functioning in a wide range of activities.
90–81	Good functioning in all areas, occupationally and socially effective.
80–71	No more than a slight impairment in social, occupational, or school functioning (e.g., infrequent interpersonal conflict, temporarily falling behind in schoolwork).
70–61	Some difficulty in social, occupational, or school functioning, but generally functioning well, has some meaningful interpersonal relationships.
60–51	Moderate difficulty in social, occupational, or school functioning (e.g., few friends, conflicts with peers or coworkers).
50–41	Serious impairment in social, occupational, or school functioning (e.g., no friends, unable to keep a job).
40–31	Major impairment in several areas, such as work or school, family relations (e.g., depressed man avoids friends, neglects family, and is unable to work; child frequently beats up younger children, is defiant at home, and is failing at school).
30–21	Inability to function in almost all areas (e.g., stays in bed all day; no job, home, or friends).
20–11	Occasionally fails to maintain minimal personal hygiene; unable to function independently.
10–1	Persistent inability to maintain minimal personal hygiene. Unable to function without harming self or others or without considerable external supports (e.g., nursing care and supervision).
0	Inadequate information.

Source: Reprinted with permission from the *Diagnostic and Statistical Manual of Mental Disorders, Fourth Edition, Text Revision.* Copyright 2000. American Psychiatric Association.

measures can help to provide evidence for the development of operationally based terms. During the diagnostic assessment, symptom behaviors based on nebulous constructs such as stress, anxiety, and depression can be identified with subjective connotations. This semantic elusiveness when defining the symptom makes it very difficult to establish when change for the better has occurred. Success of the

---

PRACTICE EXERCISE

UTILIZING GAF, GARF, AND SOFAS

One of the hardest problems practitioners confront when utilizing therapist-driven scales such as the GAF, GARF, and SOFAS is ensuring that the documented behaviors are relevant to the clients who are being served. To facilitate documentation of client behaviors, try the following exercise.

1. Ask to host an in-service training or to provide a segment of continuing education for your agency, inviting members of the interdisciplinary team, or if you do not use a team approach, other colleagues and practitioners who work with the same population group as you. If you are working alone, try the same exercise by yourself.

2. Make a copy of the GAF, GARF and SOFAS for each of the individuals who will be attending.

3. Lead the discussion and start with the GAF. For your population group, what behaviors do the majority of the clients served exhibit that represent the category discussed. What are the problem-solving skills an individual would have, what type of organizational skills would the individual have, and what type of emotional climate would be expected at that level.

   For example take the GAF:

   100–91: Superior functioning in a wide range of activities, life's problems never seem to get out of hand, is sought out by others because of his or her many positive qualities. No symptoms.

   Review the criteria for this ranging and write down the behaviors and indicators that would be typical of the client group being served that the individual might engage in. Starting at the top of the scale provides the perfect opportunity for participants to focus on strength's of the client and what that means in terms of future progress and success.

4. Once done, write down the behaviors and skills that are agreed on for the group, and go to the next area. Once the GAF is done, do the same for the GARF and the SOFAS. Since coding on the GAF is considered mandatory, however, it is best to complete the GAF before trying the same activity for the other measures.

---

diagnostic assessment guiding intervention strategy relative to client progress can only be determined when problem behaviors are clearly and operationally defined. Standardized instruments can assist in this process when utilized as repeated measures to gather consistent data from baseline through termination and follow-up. Therefore, it is the responsibility of the practitioner to select, implement, and evaluate the appropriateness of the measurement instruments. Most professionals agree that standardized scales (i.e., those that have been assessed for reliability and validity) are generally preferred.

In recent years, mental health practitioners have begun to rely more heavily on standardized instruments in an effort to achieve greater accuracy and objectivity in their attempts to measure some of the more commonly encountered clinical problems. The most notable development in this regard has been the emergence of numerous brief pencil-and-paper assessment devices known as *rapid assessment instruments* (RAI). As standardized measures, RAIs share a number of characteristics in common. They are brief; relatively easy to administer, score, and interpret; and they require very little knowledge of testing procedures on the part of the clinician. For the most part, they are self-report measures that can be completed by the client, usually within 15 minutes. They are independent of any particular theoretical orientation, and as such can be used with a variety of intervention methods. Since they provide a systematic overview of the client's problem, they often tend to stimulate discussion related to the information elicited by the instrument itself. The score that is generated provides an operational index of the frequency, duration, and intensity of the problem. Most RAIs can be used as repeated measures, and thus are adaptable to the methodological requirements of both research design and goal assessment purposes. In addition to providing a standardized means by which change can be monitored over time with a single client, RAIs can also be used to make equivalent comparisons across clients experiencing a common problem (e.g., depression and marital conflict).

One of the major advantages of standardized RAIs is the availability of information concerning reliability and validity. Reliability refers to the stability of a measure. In other words, do the questions that comprise the instrument mean the same thing to the individual answering them at different times, and would different individuals interpret those same questions in a similar manner? Unless an instrument yields consistent data, it is impossible for it to be valid. But even highly reliable instruments are of little value unless their validity can also be demonstrated. Validity speaks to the general question of whether an instrument measures what it purports to measure.

There are several different approaches to establishing validity (Chen, 1997; Cone, 1998; Powers, Munaghan, & Toomey, 1985; Schutte & Malouff, 1995) each of which is designed to provide information regarding how much confidence we can have in the instrument as an accurate indicator of the problem under consideration. While levels of reliability and validity vary greatly among available instruments, it is very helpful to know in advance the extent to which these issues have been addressed. Information concerning reliability and validity, as well as other factors related to the standardization process (e.g., the procedures for administering, scoring, and interpreting the instrument), can help professionals make informed judgments concerning the appropriateness of any given instrument.

The key to selecting the best instrument to facilitate the diagnostic assessment is knowing where and how to access the relevant information concerning potentially useful measures. Fortunately, there are a number of excellent sources available to the clinician to help facilitate this process. One such compilation of standardized measures is *Measures for Clinical Practice* by Corcoran and Fischer (1999a, 1999b) and another is *Sourcebook of Adult Assessment Strategies* by Schutte and Malouff (1995). These reference texts can serve as valuable resources for identifying useful rapid assessment instruments suited for the kinds of problems most commonly encountered in mental health practice.

Corcoran and Fischer have done an excellent job, not only in identifying and evaluating a viable cross section of useful clinically grounded instruments, but also in discussing a number of issues critical to their use. In addition, Schutte and Malouff (1995) provide a list of mental health related measures for adults and guidelines for their use with different types of practice-related problems. In addition to an introduction to the basic principles of measurement, these books discuss various types of measurement tools, including the advantages and disadvantages of RAIs. Corcoran and Fischer (1999a, 1999b) also provide some useful guidelines for locating, selecting, evaluating, and administering prospective measures. Furthermore, Corcoran and Fischer divide the instruments into two volumes in relation to their appropriateness for use with one of three target populations: adults, children, or couples and families. They are also cross-indexed by problem area, which makes the selection process very easy.

To assist with identification of Axis III (general medical conditions) and Axis IV (psychosocial stressors) diagnoses, completing a neuropsychiatric history by utilizing screening instruments can be useful. These types of instruments can assist with family and health history as well as act as a checklist of neuropsychiatric complaints and symptoms. For example, health status instruments such as the SF-36 (Ware & Sherbourne, 1992) can be utilized to identify physical functioning and difficulties as well as psychiatric problems and social adaptation difficulties. The availability of these, as well as numerous other references related to special interest areas, greatly enhances the mental health professional's options with respect to monitoring and evaluation practice. Overall, the RAIs can serve as valuable adjuncts for the mental health practitioner's evaluation efforts.

The helping relationship is a complex one that cannot be measured completely through the information gathered in the diagnostic assessment. This information is meant to serve as the basis for the development of intervention strategy. Gathering information through a diagnostic assessment needs to be intervention friendly, thereby outlining and providing the ingredients for the treatment planning and strategy to follow. The practitioner should always consider incorporating a number of evidence-based tools such as direct behavioral observation techniques, self-anchored rating scales, client logs, projective tests, Q-sort techniques, unobtrusive measures, and personality tests as well as a variety of information that can be derived from mechanical devices for monitoring physiological functioning. Together these methods can provide a range of qualitative and quantitative measures for improving the overall diagnostic assessment process. Several of them are especially well suited for the assessment of practice based on the more phenomenological and existentially grounded theories. Space limitations do not permit a discussion of all of these methods in this chapter; however, there are a number of excellent sources available that discuss in detail the kinds of information you would need in order to make informed decisions regarding selection and application (Bloom, Fischer, & Orme, 1999).

ETHICAL AND LEGAL CONSIDERATIONS

Professional efforts require that all activities performed and the judgments that are made be done within an ethical and legal framework. Practitioners must avoid any hint of malpractice. Malpractice is negligence in the exercise of one's profession. It is beyond the scope of this book to outline all the legal requirements and the problems that can occur, however, professionals should: (1) be aware of the rules and requirements that govern professional practice activity in their state; and (2) be well versed with the profession's code of ethics that represents the moral consensus of the profession. It is not enough for helping professionals to assume that their ethical practice will be apparent on the basis of their adherence to their professional Code of Ethics.

> **Always Remember:** The client information you gather and document lives on and on and on.

Client information that is accurate and carefully documented and reflects the nature of the ethical client services provided can be the best way for mental health practitioners to protect against malpractice. Practitioner documents must ensure that client confidentiality and privacy are protected. One helpful rule is to remember that at any time all records may be subpoenaed in a court of law where private client information may be divulged. Regardless of the employment setting, all helping professionals should consider maintaining personal malpractice insurance in addition to what may be provided through agency auspices. Even with the best of intentions, mental health practitioners may find themselves in legal proceedings defending the content of notes, subjective assessments, or terminology used in the diagnostic assessment. It is always best to record objective data and refrain from using terminology that may be subjective in nature (i.e., what you think is happening). When documenting, always use direct client statements; do not document hearsay or make interpretations based on subjective data. The practitioner needs to be familiar with specific state statues that do not allow professionals to elicit or document specific client information. For example, AIDS patients are protected by prohibiting mental health professionals from documenting their medical condition without client consent. In record keeping, the ultimate legal and ethical responsibility of all written diagnostic and assessment based notes will always start and stop with the mental health practitioner.

PULLING IT ALL TOGETHER: USE OF THE MULTIAXIAL SYSTEM

To initiate the utilization of the multiaxial system, it is assumed that the screening begins with the first client-mental health practitioner interaction. The information gathered by the mental health practitioner is assembled into a database that facilitates the diagnostic assessment as well as determining the requirements and direction of future treatment planning and intervention efforts. The diagnostic assessment assists in ordering information on the client's present situation and history in regard to how past behaviors can relate to present concerns. This assessment is multidimensional and includes creative clinically based judgments and interpretation of perspectives and alternatives for service delivery.

Generally, the client is the primary source of data, using either a verbal or written report. This information can be supplemented through direct observation of verbal or physical behaviors; and interaction patterns between other interdisciplinary team members, family, significant others, or friends. Viewing and recording these patterns of communication can be extremely helpful in later establishing and developing strength and resource considerations. In addition to verbal reports, written reports can also be utilized such as background sheets, psychological tests, and tests to measure health status or level of daily functioning. Although the client is perceived as the first and primary source of data, the need to include information from other areas cannot be underestimated. This means talking with the family and significant others to estimate planning support and assistance. It is also important to gather information from other secondary sources such as the client's medical record and other health care providers. Furthermore, to facilitate the diagnostic assessment, the practitioner must be able to understand the client's medical situation and the relationship that the medical symptoms can have with mental health symptoms. Knowledge of what certain medical conditions are and when to refer to other health professionals for continued care is an essential part of the diagnostic assessment process.

In completing a multidimensional assessment, there are four primary steps that can be adapted in the mental health setting:

1. *Problem or behavior recognition.* Here the practitioner must explore and be active in uncovering problems that affect daily living and will later be beneficial in engaging the client in self-help or skill changing behaviors. It is important for the client to acknowledge that the problem exists, because once this is done ". . . the boundaries of the problem become clear, and exploration then proceeds in a normal fashion" (Hepworth, Rooney, & Larsen, 1997, p. 205).

2. *Problem or behavior identification.* In the diagnostic assessment, problems that affect daily functioning need to be identified. In addition, it is important to note what the client sees as the problem of concern, since this will assist later in helping the client to develop change behavior. In the mental health field, it is common to receive referrals that often provide the basis for reimbursement. Many times the referral source establishes how the problem is viewed, and what should constitute the basis of intervention. Sound, efficient, cost-effective clinical practice needs to take referral information into account and can lead to better problem identification.

3. *Treatment plan.* Once the diagnostic assessment is complete, how will the information be related to the intervention plan and strategy to follow? According to Sheafor and coworkers (1997), the plan of action is the ". . . bridge between the assessment and the intervention" (p. 135). Here the practitioner can help to clearly focus on the goals and objectives that will be followed in the intervention process. In the initial planning stage, emphasis on the outcome that is to be accomplished is essential.

The outcome of the diagnostic assessment process is the completion of a plan that will guide, enhance, and in many cases determine the course of intervention to be implemented. With the complexity of human beings and the problems that they encounter, a properly prepared multidimensional assessment is the essential first step for ensuring quality service delivery. Also, the diagnostic assessment should never be considered a static entity or it may become too narrow in focus thereby decreasing its utility, relevance, and salience. Therefore, the process of diagnostic assessment must continually be examined and reexamined to ensure the quality of the practice provided. This process should not be rushed because when it is superficial factors may be highlighted and significant ones deemphasized or overlooked. Mental health practitioners owe it to their clients to ensure that diagnostic efforts and the helping strategy that develops is quality driven, no matter what the administrative and economic pressures may be. To further support this, many mental health practitioners were active in supporting the creation of a commission to review changes in health care and make recommendations for consumer protection and health care quality (Steps to Watchdog Managed Care, 1997). This support is just one of the ways practitioners are working to not only assist in developing a comprehensive strategy to help clients, but to also ensure that quality service is made available and obtained.

SUMMARY

Mental health practitioners must be aware of how to best proceed with the diagnostic assessment that rests within the multiaxial assessment system. In mental health, all practitioners are expected to help their clients and other professionals in the area of diagnostic assessment and evaluation. For many professionals, the role of assessment leading to diagnosis in mental health counseling can be a complicated one; this can be particularly problematic for practitioners in solo practice who do not have either multidisciplinary or interdisciplinary team support to perform triage services or act as service brokers (Libassi & Parish, 1990). Regardless of the practice setting, all mental health practitioners are being called on to be more knowledgeable and interactive and to utilize evidence-based diagnostic tests to support practice strategy (Frances, Pincus, Davis, et al., 1991; Frances, Pincus, Widiger, et al., 1990; Siegelman, 1990). The role of the practitioner in regard to linking the client to environmental considerations is an essential one. As well, all mental health practitioners need to be keenly aware and alert to updates in diagnostic criteria and act as advocates for the client throughout the diagnostic assessment and intervention process.

Equipped with a basic knowledge of the use and misuse of the *DSM-IV* as a tool in the creation of a diagnostic impression, the mental health practitioner can more constructively participate in the consultation process. Knowledge of diagnostic impressions and criteria can assist the practitioner in impacting and enhancing the client's overall functioning level. Since mental health practitioners often have regular and subsequent contacts with their clients, they can be essential in helping the interdisciplinary team to reexamine or reformulate previous diagnostic impressions and the relationship these original impressions can have on the client's future treatment potential. As a team member, the mental health practitioner is keenly aware of the environment and the importance of building and maintaining therapeutic rapport with the client. This makes the practitioner's input in understanding the mental disorder an essential contribution to intervention effectiveness. The mental health practitioner remains in a key position to allay the client's and his or her family's fears as well as elicit their help and support (Bernheim, 1992).

Moreover, with the increased emphasis on managed care and limiting time frames for treatment (Anderson, Berlant, Mauch, & Maloney, 1997; Dziegielewski, 1998), it is further postulated that increased emphasis on the conditions not attributable to a mental disorder, coded on Axis I, will also gain increased acceptance.

These are mental health conditions that are not attributable to a mental disorder, yet they remain the focus of clinical treatment. These mental health conditions are often referred to by clinicians in the field as the "V" codes and are coded on Axis I. Since these conditions have historically not been considered reimbursable, some practitioners have avoided their use. Nevertheless, the current practice emphasis based on brief time-limited treatment (Dziegielewski, 1996, 1997) makes awareness of these conditions essential.

Information gathered must always extend beyond the client and, in doing so, special consideration should be given to the needs of family, significant others, and the client's identified support system. It is not uncommon for family members to have limited information in the area of mental health diagnosis and treatment. Family members may feel uncomfortable admitting to health care professionals that they believe another mode of treatment might be better (Wynne, 1987). The well-informed practitioner can correct distortions and foster cooperation in the treatment plan and among treatment team professionals (May, 1976). When practitioners are knowledgeable about the different mental health conditions, they can better serve their clients and make the most appropriate treatment decisions and system linkages. With an updated knowledge of mental health diagnosis and subsequent intervention, mental health practitioners can help prepare, as well as educate, clients and family members about the responsible use and expectations for psychiatric care. Professional schools that train mental health practitioners need to strongly encourage course work on use of the multiaxial assessment system. Since practitioners are held accountable for their own practice actions, they must strive to achieve the highest standards of their profession (Reamer, 1994, 1998).

—————   QUESTIONS FOR FURTHER THOUGHT   —————

1. Use of the nonformal multiaxial format can be helpful when identifying and addressing the mental health needs of a client. Give several examples of when, why, and where this nonformal system should be considered.

2. On Axis II, the defense mechanisms can be listed. When and why would it be advantageous to list these factors as part of the diagnostic assessment?

3. As a practitioner, what direct relationship exists between the diagnostic codes and the procedural codes? Apply a case example that highlights this relationship.

4. When utilizing the multiaxial system in the diagnostic assessment, all five axes are utilized. Why is it important to note Axis III, which involves the general medical conditions? Why are Axis IV and V important? What client information could be added to the documentation that supports the information provided on these axes?

4 Applications: Beyond the Diagnostic Assessment

When utilizing the *DSM-IV-TR* in the diagnostic assessment process, emphasis is placed on completing the initial assessment. Therefore, the diagnostic assessment providing the foundation for treatment planning and practice strategy that will follow. Accurate and successful documentation is critical to showing what progress is being made in therapy and also providing the groundwork for establishing efficiency and effectiveness of treatment. The *DSM-IV-TR* does not suggest treatment strategy or courses of action that can further highlight the intervention or treatment phases of the helping process. Since the mental health practitioner will be expected not only to assist in treatment planning but also in the selection of the intervention and practice strategy, some background knowledge in this area is essential. This chapter provides an overview of the importance of efficient and effective documentation in terms of treatment planning and practice strategy. In Section II, direct application will be made to many of the specific diagnostic conditions that will integrate many of the principles and practice techniques described in this chapter. Once the mental health practitioner has completed the diagnostic assessment, this information must be recorded and applied accordingly.

DOCUMENTATION, TREATMENT PLANNING, AND PRACTICE STRATEGY

Throughout the history of mental health practice, practitioners have relied on some form of record keeping to clearly document information on client situations and problems. Although the formats used by professionals have changed, the value of documentation in maintaining case continuity has remained a professional priority (Dziegielewski, 1998). In its most basic form, case recording provides the helping professional with a map that indicates where the client and practitioner have traveled in their treatment journey (Dziegielewski & Leon, 2001b). Because experience is dynamic and words are static, the intervention process goes beyond what written words can describe (Lauver & Harvey, 1997). Therefore, the exact words used must be chosen carefully, which makes the primary goal of case documentation an evolving process. Case documentation must also be geared toward maintaining high quality service as well as preserving continuity of service when different mental health professionals are involved (Welfel, 1998). In addition, well-documented diagnostic assessments and interventions can also protect the mental health practitioner in high-risk cases making him or her less likely to be judged negligent in the legal setting (Bernstein & Hartsell, 1998; Welfel, 1998).

Understanding and recording the client's problems, interventions used, and client progress enables the practitioner to assess the interventions provided and make necessary changes in the course of treatment. Sheafor, Horejsi, and Horejsi (1997) stated that the purpose of documentation and accurate record keeping in helping professions is multifaceted. Therefore, in the diagnostic assessment, good record keeping must: (1) provide an accurate and standardized account of the information gathered; (2) support this information with introspective and retrospective data collection; (3) provide the information needed for good practice standards that include relevant ethical, legal, billing, and agency requirements; and (4) provide clearly stated information that will withstand scrutiny by external reviewers such as accreditation bodies, ombudsmen, lawyers, insurance companies, and quality assurance/improvement and control personnel.

In the diagnostic assessment as well as throughout the intervention, practitioners must be aware that without accurate case documentation most third-party payers will not reimburse for the start or continuation of services. Therefore, it is critical that all documentation within the diagnostic assessment and subsequent practice strategy clearly identify specific information related to problem severity that will lead and guide continued intervention efforts. This emphasis on accountability and reimbursement is mandated by managed care organizations and other external reviewing bodies that monitor client services (Dziegielewski & Holliman, 2001). All mental health practitioners are expected to justify and document client eligibility for service, appropriateness for continuation of services, length of treatment, level of care, interventions provided, and the use of outcome criteria (Lowery, 1996).

Utilizing a holistic framework that stresses the client's behavioral and biopsychosocial factors allows mental health practitioners to play an important role in the efficient delivery of interdisciplinary psychological and social services. Mental health practitioners can also assist other team members to document effectively while collaborating with other interdisciplinary team members on client progress and problems. The importance of providing accurate, up-to-date, and informative records is vital to the coordinated planning efforts of the entire team.

With the advent of behaviorally based managed care, however, high caseloads and shorter lengths of stay have caused mental health practitioners to adopt a style of documentation that is brief yet informative (Dziegielewski, 1997, 1998;

Dziegielewski & Holliman, 2001). The challenge is to summarize important client information in meaningful yet concise notes and treatment plans. Given the litigious nature of our society, informative records that demonstrate treatment interventions and reflect legal and ethical values and concerns become important documents in legal proceedings that can be recalled long after the therapeutic intervention has ended (Bernstein & Hartsell, 1998). The pressure for accurate documentation rests in the growing emphasis and pressure to utilize evidence-based professional practice and justification for the course of intervention that will follow.

When utilizing evidence-based practice, clear documentation as reflected in the case record can be used for numerous purposes. Regardless of the helping discipline or practice setting, generic rules for efficient and effective documentation must always be employed.

First, clear and concise record keeping is essential to clearly document problem behaviors and coping styles. Second, the behavioral symptoms identified within the diagnostic assessment will set the tone and provide concrete justification for the goals and objectives that will be highlighted within the treatment plan. Recording supporting information in the case file is essential for supplementation of the treatment plan. The relationship between case notes and the treatment plan is critical to the justification for service delivery. Third, the treatment plan will clearly reflect progress indicators and time frames, which once again must be supported in the written case record. In this section, the review of current goals and objectives as well as whether the therapeutic tasks assigned can be completed is discussed. Fourth, the case notes and the treatment plan must clearly document and show response to

---

QUICK REFERENCE

GUIDING PRINCIPLES FOR EFFICIENT DOCUMENTATION

- Use the information gathered in the diagnostic assessment as the foundation for treatment planning and practice strategy.
- Use concrete behaviors as indicators of client progress when designing treatment or intervention plans.
- Complete periodic updates and report and change those interventions and treatment strategies that do not appear to be working for the client.
- Be sure that the goals the client is to accomplish are stated in concrete, measurable terms and that the client can complete the therapeutic tasks assigned.
- Monitor problem behaviors and behavior changes to continually review and update the intervention process.
- Be sure to always assess goal accomplishment and evaluate the efficiency, treatment, and cost effectiveness of the service delivered.

interventions and whether changes are needed to continue to help the client to progress. Last, case notes are used to assess goal accomplishment and to evaluate the efficiency, treatment, and cost effectiveness of the service delivered (Chamblis, 2000; Fischer, 1978).

Problem-Oriented Recording

Among the various types of record keeping formats, many mental health facilities commonly use problem-oriented recording (POR; Dziegielewski, 1998; Rankin, 1996). Developed first in health care or medical settings, this type of recording was used to encourage multidisciplinary and interdisciplinary collaboration and to train medical professionals. As members of either multidisciplinary or interdisciplinary teams, helping professionals find that problem-oriented case documentation enables them to maintain documentation uniformity while remaining active within a team approach to care.

POR emphasizes practitioner accountability through brief and concise documentation of client problems, services, or interventions as well as client responses. Although there are numerous formats for problem-oriented case recording, always keep comments brief, concrete, measurable, and concise. Many professionals feel strongly that problem-oriented recording is compatible with the increase in client caseloads, rapid assessments, and time-limited treatment. By maintaining brief but informative notes, practitioners are able to provide significant summaries of intervention progress. The mental health practitioner does not select the type of problem-oriented recording that will be utilized. The choice of a specific problem-oriented format for case recording is based on agency, clinic, or practice's function, need, and accountability. In today's practice environment, clear and concise documentation reflects the pressure indicative of evidence-based practice. This makes it critical that mental health practitioners be familiar with the basic types of problem-oriented recording and how to utilize this format within the case record.

One thing that all problem-oriented recording formats share in common is that they all start with a problem list that is clearly linked to the behaviorally based biopsychosocial intervention (Chamblis, 2000; Frager, 2000). This problem-oriented documentation helps the practitioner to focus directly on the presenting problems and coping styles that the client is exhibiting thereby helping to limit abstractions and vague clinical judgments. This type of documentation should include an inventory reflective of current active problems that are periodically updated. When a problem is resolved, it is crossed off the list with the date of resolution clearly designated. Noting that the active problems a client is experiencing and maintaining self-contained files are considered the basic building blocks for case recording within the problem-oriented record.

QUICK REFERENCE

INFORMATION TO BE INCLUDED IN THE POR

In a complete problem-oriented medical record, regardless of the recording format used, the following should always be included:

- Client identifying information.
- A complete behaviorally based biopsychosocial diagnostic assessment.
- A psychosocial history recording important past and present information.
- Progress notes that encapsulate intervention strategy and progress.
- A termination summary.
- Copies of supporting data and information (e.g., consent forms, releases, summaries of recent medical or physical exams, and laboratory results).

Although numerous formats for the actual progress note documentation can be selected, the subjective, objective assessment plan (SOAP) is considered the most commonly used. See the following Quick Reference box for a sample listing of the most common problem-oriented format used today.

The SOAP first became popular in the 1970s. In this format, the practitioner utilizes the S (subjective) to record the data relevant to the client's request for service and the things the client says and feels about the problem. The mental health

---

QUICK REFERENCE

SOAP, SOAPIE, AND SOAPIER RECORDING FORMATS

Subjective, Objective, Assessment, Plan (SOAP) or Subjective, Objective, Assessment, Plan, Implementation, Evaluation (SOAPIE)

S = Subjective data relevant to the client's request for service; client and practitioner impressions of the problem.

O = Objective data such as observable and measurable criteria related to the problem. If client statements are used, put the statement in quotes.

A = Assessment information of the underlying problems; diagnostic impression.

P = Plan outlines current intervention strategy and specific referrals for other needed services.

I = Implementation considerations of the service to be provided.

E = Evaluation of service provision.

R = Client's response to the diagnostic process, treatment planning, and intervention efforts.

professional can use his or her clinical judgment in terms of what appears to be happening with the client. Some professionals prefer to document this information in terms of major themes or general topics addressed rather than making specific statements about what the practitioner thinks is happening. Generally, intimate personal content or details of fantasies and process interactions should not be included here. When charting in this section of the SOAP, the mental health practitioner should always ask herself "Could this statement that I record be open to misinterpretation?" If it is vulnerable to misinterpretation or it resembles a personal rather than professional reaction to what is said, it should not be included.

The O (objective) includes observable and measurable criteria related to the problem. These are symptoms, behaviors, and client-focused problems observed directly by the practitioner during the assessment and intervention process. In addition, some agencies, clinics, and practices have started to include client statements in this section as well. If a client statement is to be utilized as objective data, however, exact quotes must be used. For example, if in the session the client states that he will not harm himself, the practitioner must document exactly what the client has said. What is said must be placed within quotation marks. Under the objective section of the summary note, it is also possible to include the results from standardized assessment instruments designed to measure psychological or social functioning. Several of these measures are described in Chapter 3 and can be helpful in supporting the objective data gathering process.

The A (assessment) includes the therapist's assessment of the underlying problems, which often involves the development of a *DSM-IV-TR* diagnostic impression. As described in Chapter 3, when utilizing the multiaxial system all five axes are utilized. In P (plan), the practitioner records how treatment objectives will be carried out, areas for future interventions, and specific referrals to other services needed by the client.

With today's increased emphasis on time-limited intervention efforts and accountability, two new areas have been added to the original SOAP format (Dziegielewski & Leon, 2001b). This extension, referred to as SOAPIE, identifies the first additional term as I (implementation considerations of the service to be provided). Here the mental health practitioner explains exactly how, when, and who will implement the service. In the last section, an E is designated to represent service provision evaluation (Dziegielewski, 1998). It is here that all health care professionals are expected to identify specific actions related to direct evaluation of progress achieved after any interventions are provided. When treatment is considered successful, specific outcomes-based objectives established early in the treatment process are documented as progressing or checked off as attained. In some agencies, a modified version of the SOAPIE has been introduced and referred to as SOAPIER. In this version, the R outlines the client's response to the intervention provided.

A second popular problem–oriented recording format used in many health care facilities today is the data, assessment, and plan (DAP) format. The DAP encourages the mental health practitioner to identify only the most salient elements of a practitioner's client contact. Using the D (data), the practitioner is expected to record objective client data and statements related to the presenting problem and the focus of the therapeutic contact. The A is used to record the diagnostic assessment intervention from the multiaxial format, the client's reactions to the service and intervention, and the practitioner's assessment of the client's overall progress toward the treatment goals and objectives. Specific information on all tasks, actions, or plans related to the presenting problem and to be carried out by either the client or the helping professional is recorded under P (plan). Also recorded under P is information on future issues related to the presenting problem to be explored at the next session and the specific date and time of the next appointment (Dziegielewski, 1998). Similar to the SOAP, the DAP format has also undergone some changes. For example, some counseling professionals who generally apply the DAP are now being asked to add an additional section. This changes the DAP into the DAPE where E reflects what type of educational and evaluative services have been conducted.

Two other forms of problem-based case recording formats are the problem, intervention, response, and plan (PIRP) and the assessed information, problems addressed, interventions provided, and evaluation (APIE). Both of these formats as described in quick reference boxes can also be utilized for standardizing case notes. Similar to the SOAP and the DAP, a similar structure is employed. All four of these popular formats of problem-oriented case recording support increased problem identification, standardizing what and how client behaviors and coping styles are reported, thus providing a greater understanding of mental health problems and the various methods of managing them. This type of problem-oriented record

---

QUICK REFERENCE

DAPE RECORDING FORMAT

Data, Assessment, and Plan (DAP) or Data, Assessment, Plan, and Education (DAPE)

D = Data that is gathered to provide information about the identified problem.

A = Assessment of the client in regard to his or her current problem or situation.

P = Plan for intervention and what will be completed to assist the client to achieve increased health status or functioning.

E = Professional education that is provided by the mental health practitioner to ensure that problem mediation has taken place or evaluation information to ensure practice accountability.

QUICK REFERENCE

PIRP AND APIE

Problem, Intervention, Response, and Plan (PIRP)

P = Presenting problem(s) or the problem(s) to be addressed.

I = Intervention to be conducted by the mental health practitioner.

R = Response to the intervention by the client.

P = Plan to address the problems experienced by the client.

Assessed Information, Problems Addressed, Interventions Provided, and Evaluation (APIE)

A = Documentation of assessed information in regard to the client problem.

P = Explanation of the problem that is being addressed.

I = Intervention description and plan.

E = Evaluation of the problem once the intervention is completed.

---

brings the focus of clinical attention to an often traditionally neglected aspect of recording that involves the recognition of a client's problems by all helping professionals to quickly familiarize themselves with a client's situation (Starfield, 1992). For mental health practitioners, utilizing a problem-focused perspective must go beyond merely recording information that is limited to the client's problems. When the focus is limited to gathering only this information, important strengths and resources that clients bring to the therapeutic interview may not be validated (Dziegielewski, 1998). Furthermore, partialization of client problems presents the potential risk that other significant aspects of a client's functioning will be overlooked in treatment planning and subsequent practice strategy. Therefore, problem-oriented forms of case recording need to extend beyond the immediate problem regardless of whether managed care companies require it (Dziegielewski, 1998; Rudolph, 2000).

Maintaining Clinical Records

Since records can be maintained in more than one medium, such as written case files, audio- or videotaped material, and computer-generated notes, special attention needs to be given to ensuring confidentiality and the maintaining of ethical release of client information. Probably the greatest protection a mental health practitioner has in terms of risk management for all types of records is maintaining accurate, clear, and concise clinical records. This means that an unbroken chain of custody between the practitioner and the file must always be maintained. Since the mental health practitioner will ultimately be held responsible for producing a clinical record in case of litigation, this policy cannot be overemphasized. Furthermore, documentation in the record should always be clearly sequenced and easy to follow. If a mistake occurs, never change a case note or treatment plan without acknowledging it. When changes need to be made to the diagnostic assessment, the treatment plan, or any other types of case recording, clearly indicate that a change is being made by drawing a thin line through the mistake and dating and initialing it. Records that are legible and cogent limit open interpretation of the services provided. In addition, the mental health practitioner will always be required to keep clinical case records (including written records and computerized backup files) safeguarded in locked and fireproof cabinets. It can also benefit the mental health practitioner to consider using archiving types of storage systems such as microfiche or microfilm to preserve records and maximize space.

As the use of computer-generated notes continues to become more common, different forms of problem-oriented case recording will be linked directly into computerized databases (Starfield, 1992). In terms of convenience, this can mean immediate access to fiscal and billing information as well as client intervention strategy, documentation, and treatment planning. When working with computerized records, Bernstein and Hartsell (1999) suggest the following: (1) when recording client information on a hard drive or disk, be sure storage is in a safe and secure place; (2) be sure to secure any passwords from detection; (3) if you are treating a

---

QUICK REFERENCE

HELPFUL HINTS: DOCUMENTATION

Since accurate and ethical documentation ensures continuity of care, ethical, and legal aspects of practice, and provides direction for the focus of intervention, every record must have the following essential information:

- Date and time of entry.
- Interview notes that clearly describe the client's problems.
- A complete diagnostic assessment that is evidence-based.
- A treatment plan with clearly established overall goals, objectives, and intervention tasks.
- Always use ink that does not run (ball point pens are best).
- Never using pencil or white-out to erase mistakes.
- Draw a line through an error, marking it "error" and initialing the error.
- Print and sign the practitioner's name, title, and credentials with each entry that is made.
- Document all information in the case record as if you might some day have to defend it in a court of law.

celebrity or a famous individual, use a fictitious name and be sure to keep the "key" to the actual name in a protected place; (4) always maintain a backup system and keep it secure; (5) be sure that everyone who will have access to the client's case file reads and signs an established protocol concerning sanctity, privacy, and confidentiality of the records; and (6) take the potential of computer theft or crash seriously and establish a policy that will safeguard what will need to happen if this should occur. The convenience of records and information now being easily transmitted electronically produces major concern. Since clinical case records are so easy to access and are portable, there is a genuine problem represented by the vulnerability of unauthorized access of the recorded information. This means that mental health practitioners who often deal with very personal and confidential information about the clients who are served take every precaution to safe guard the information that is shared. In addition, since medical records are kept for the benefit of the client, access to the record by the client is generally allowed. When engaging in any type of disclosure or transfer issues to either the client or third parties, however, a written consent from the client is expected (Lauver & Harvey, 1997).

Documentation and Treatment Planning Considerations

Once the diagnostic assessment information has been gathered, this information will be utilized to start a treatment or intervention plan. When working with the client, it is important that each treatment plan be individualized. The plan also must reflect the general as well as the unique symptoms and needs the client is experiencing. The importance of a formal treatment plan cannot be overestimated as it will help to determine the structure and provide focus for any type of mental health intervention. Furthermore, a clearly established treatment plan can deter any litigation by either the client or a concerned family member (Bernstein & Hartsell, 1998). When the treatment plan clearly delineates the intervention plan, family and friends of the client may feel more at ease and may actually agree to participate and assist in any behavioral interventions that will be applied.

In developing the treatment plan for the client who suffers from mental health problems, there are several critical steps that need to be identified (Jongsma & Peterson, 1995). First, problem behaviors, which are interfering with functioning, must be identified. In practice, it is considered essential that the client and his or her family participate and assist in this process as much as possible in terms of identifying the issues, problem behaviors, and coping styles that are either causing or contributing to the client's discomfort. Of all of the problem behaviors a client may be experiencing, the ones that should receive the most attention are those behaviors that impair independent living skills or cause difficulties in completing tasks of daily living. Once identified, these behaviors need to be linked to the intervention process. The identification of specific problem behaviors or coping styles can provide an opportunity to facilitate educational and communicative interventions that can further enhance communication between the client and family members. Involving the family and support system in treatment plan formulation and application can be especially helpful and productive since at times individuals experiencing mental confusion and distortions of reality may exhibit bizarre and unpredictable symptoms. If support systems are not included in the intervention planning process, and the client's symptoms worsen, the client-family system environment may be characterized by increased tension, frustration, fear, blame, and helplessness. To avoid withdrawing from support systems, the client, family members, and key support system members need either to be involved or at a minimum made aware of the treatment plan goals and objectives that will be utilized if the client consents to their involvement.

Second, not only do family and friends need to be aware of the treatment plan initiatives, they also need to be encouraged to share valuable input and support to ensure intervention progress and success. Family education and supportive interventions for family and significant others can be listed as part of the treatment plan for an individual client. It is beyond the scope of this chapter to discuss the multiple interventions available to the family members of the mentally ill individual; however, interested readers are encouraged to refer to J. Walsh (2000), which provides an excellent strategy for working with families with a relative who suffers from mental illness.

Next, to assist in treatment plan development, it is critical to state the identified problem behaviors in terms of behaviorally based outcomes (Dziegielewski, 1998). In completing this process, the assessment data that led to the diagnostic impression as well as the specific problems often experienced by the client need to be outlined. Once identified, the client's problems are then prioritized so that goals, objectives, and action tasks may be developed. Third, the goals of intervention, which constitute the basis for the plan of intervention, must be clearly outlined and applied. These goals must be broken down into specific objective statements that reflect target behaviors to be changed and ways to measure the client's progress on each objective. As subcomponents to the objectives, action tasks that clearly delineate the steps to be taken by the client and the helping professional to ensure successful completion of each objective must be included.

Once the problem behaviors have been identified, the mental health practitioner must identify the goals and the behaviorally based objectives that can be used to measure whether the identified problems have been addressed and resolved. If the problem behavior is ambivalent feelings that impair general task completion, the main goal may be to help the client decrease feelings of ambivalence. It is therefore important to document a behavioral objective that clearly articulates a behavioral definition of ambivalence, ways that the ambivalence will be decreased, and the mechanisms used to determine if the behavior has been

---

QUICK REFERENCE

SAMPLE OF IDENTIFIED PROBLEM BEHAVIORS

Examples of identified problem behaviors often include:

- Ambivalent feelings that impair general task completion related to independent living skills.
- Affect disturbances such as feelings of depression or a difficulty in controlling anger.
- Problem behaviors of coping styles such as poor concentration and recording of limitations for goal-directed behavior and completion of the activities of daily living.
- Associative disturbances, particularly in terms of being touched or approached by others.

---

changed. The therapeutic intervention involves assisting the client to develop specific and concrete tasks that are geared toward decreasing this behavior and consequently meeting the objective. The outcome measure simply becomes establishing whether the task was completed. Each of the chapters in the applications section of this text and Appendix C include hints on creating sample intervention plans for dealing with clients who suffer from different types of mental disorders. The treatment plan is not designed to be all inclusive, rather it is designed to provide the guidelines for effective documentation of the assessment and intervention process. Furthermore, the treatment plan must be individualized for the client outlining the specific problem behaviors and how each of these behaviors can be addressed.

In summary, the key to documenting the diagnostic assessment, treatment plan, and practice strategy is to maintain brevity while providing informative data. Documentation should record only the most salient issues relevant to client care and progress. Information should focus directly on content covered in the therapeutic sessions as well as the interplay of the client's progress with the counseling interventions. It is equally important for the practitioner to include the intervention strategies in the primary treatment plan. Always link the therapeutic interventions to the original problems, goals, and objectives identified.

Brief, accurate, and informative documentation that includes both the diagnostic assessment and the treatment plan and practice strategy requires skill and training. Mental health practitioners must learn to document important information that will assist other professionals and oversight processes in providing the most effective interventions for clients. This requires that vital client information gathered during the diagnostic assessment and intervention recommendations be combined in documentation that clearly identifies the client's problems, signs and symptoms, and past and current mental health history. While the specific type of documentation format used by mental health practitioners will often be determined by the practice setting, practitioners should closely examine the format of choice and learn to integrate biopsychosocial and spiritual information that will be helpful in understanding the client and assist in formulating an effective intervention strategy.

Outcome Measures

With the emphasis on treatment efficacy and accountability in today's practice environment, it is essential that mental health practitioners learn to include objective measures that help to evaluate the effects of medication and counseling therapies on the client's functioning. Included in these measures are standardized scales, surveys, and rapid assessment instruments (RAIs), several of which were described in Chapter 3 and are utilized in the application chapters that follow. These tools provide evidence-based data that identify the changes occurring over the course of the intervention. It is extremely important that mental health practitioners become familiar with and integrate measurement instruments in their practice and in their documentation to determine if treatment interventions have impacted baseline behaviors and problems (Dziegielewski, 1997). Gathering pre- and postdata on a client's course of treatment enables both the practitioner and the client to examine whether progress has occurred and provide regulatory agencies with tangible objective evidence of client progress or client decompensation. By using a holistic framework that stresses the client's biopsychosocial factors, mental health practitioners play an important role in the efficient delivery of interdisciplinary health and mental health services. As part of the health care team, practitioners utilize record keeping, effectively communicating and collaborating with other interdisciplinary team members on client progress and problems. The importance of providing accurate, up-to-date, informative records is vital to the coordinated health care planning efforts of the entire team and most importantly to the client's health. See the example treatment plan for bereavement on page 118 that highlights how to define the condition and breakdown problem behaviors into goals, objectives, and interventions for the client.

SELECTING AN INTERVENTION FRAMEWORK

Most counseling professionals, regardless of discipline, agree that all practitioners should be familiar with multiple practice modalities and frameworks for utilization in therapy. The mission of all helping professionals is to engage in activity that enhances opportunities for all people in an increasingly complex environment. Since mental health practitioners can work with a variety of human systems, including individuals, families, groups, organizations, and communities,

SAMPLE TREATMENT PLAN

BEREAVEMENT

Definition: Clinical attention focusing on an individual's reaction, emotionally, behaviorally, and cognitively, to the death of a loved one.

Signs and Symptoms to Note in the Record:

- Characteristics of a major depressive episode including problems sleeping and eating, weight gain or loss.
- Guilt surrounding the death of the loved one.
- Conversational superficiality with respect to the loved one's death.
- Excessive emoting when the loved one's death is discussed.
- Feelings of worthlessness.
- Difficulty concentrating due to domination of thoughts surrounding loved one's death.
- Possible psychomotor retardation.
- Functional impairment(s).

Goals:

1. Client will acknowledge and accept the death of loved one.
2. Client will begin the grieving process.
3. Client will resolve feelings over the death of loved one.
4. Client will reconnect with old relationships and activities.

Objectives:

1. Client will identify and state steps in the grieving process.
2. Client will explore and express emotions and feelings associated with this loss.
3. Client will resolve feelings of anger and guilt associated with loss of loved one.
4. Client will interact with and discuss the death of loved one with others.

Interventions:

- Therapist will educate the client on the grieving process, specifically, the stages of grief.
- Client will seek out others who have experienced the loss of a loved one to evaluate coping mechanisms used in dealing with this loss, and evaluate the use of these in individual therapy.
- Client will create a journal of emotions related to this loss to be discussed in individual therapy.
- Client will participate in "empty chair" exercise where the client will verbally express feelings not verbalized to the deceased loved one in life.
- Client will write a letter to the lost loved one expressing feelings and emotions, memories and regrets associated with loss to be discussed in individual therapy.
- Client will attend a bereavement support group.
- Client will interact with one mutual friend of the client and the deceased and share feelings about this loss, discussing the impact it has had on the living.

some type of orientation that guides practice structure is needed. This overarching framework needs to be consistent with the professional values and ethics of the practitioner's discipline as well as respect the cultural differences of all involved. Defined simply, a theoretical practice framework is the structured ideas or beliefs that provide the foundation for the helping activity that is to be preformed. Utilization and knowledge of theory that is consistent with professional values and ethics are what make the helping activities of the mental health practitioner unique.

In mental health practice, many people use the words theory and practice methods or strategy interchangeably. Since they coexist (and in practice one without the other cannot exist for long), this linking is understandable. It is important to note, however, that theory and methods of practice strategy are not the same thing. A theoretical foundation provides the practitioner with the basics or the concepts of what can be done and why it is essential. The method or practice strategy on the other hand is the "doing" part of the helping relationship. This involves the outline or the plan for the helping activity that is generally guided by theoretical principles and concepts.

In mental health practice, selecting the theoretical or methodological basis for practice remains varied (Schram & Mandell, 1997). The diversity and uniqueness of each helping relationship requires that the practitioner be well versed in theory and practice and resilient in his or her ability to adapt this foundation to the needs of the client and the situation. For mental health practitioners, a delicate balancing act exists between blending theoretical concepts and frameworks that direct practice strategy. This requires practitioners to be flexible in their approach as they deal with a multitude of different clients and different problems. To design and initiate professional practice strategy, practitioners must often go beyond the traditional bounds of their practice wisdom.

Utilizing the **DSM-IV-TR** and Selecting a Practice Framework

Although *DSM-IV-TR* is only a diagnostic tool, it can help practitioners develop an appropriate intervention plan for individual clients. Developing an intervention plan and selecting appropriate practice strategies is beyond the scope of this book; however, helping professionals can use the information gathered from the diagnostic assessment to decide how to formulate the intervention plan and identify the best ways to engage the client. To begin this process, helping professionals must first be aware of the theoretical principles that underlie certain types of helping activity. Practitioners need to be prepared to pick and choose which theoretical concepts and practice strategies will offer the greatest assistance in formulating the helping process. Thus, practitioners should review the theoretical principles in terms of their application to the problem behaviors noted.

First and foremost, any helping strategy employed must be firmly based within the reality of the client's environment. At times, however, making this link may seem difficult or time consuming. Regardless, considering the impact of the client's environment on the practice method selected remains essential. For example, if a client is diagnosed with substance abuse and after receiving treatment is discharged back into an environment that is conducive for him to once again begin abusing a substance, much of the influence of the intervention would be negated. In one case, a client diagnosed with substance dependence was admitted repeatedly to alcohol rehabilitation and treatment centers. The client always responded well to treatment while in the program but upon discharge quickly relapsed. After numerous intervention failures with this client, the mental health practitioner thoroughly assessed his situation and home environment. The practitioner quickly learned that the client was unable to maintain a bank account as a result of his instability and troubles with alcohol. So when it came time for him to cash his social security check, he used the local bar as his home address. When his check arrived each month, there was only one place to cash it—the local bar. To complicate matters even further, the bar had a policy that they would cash checks only if a purchase was made, which led to the client's relapse. Being aware of the client's environment was a critical component in applying an appropriate helping strategy. Thus, anticipating the relationship that a client's environment can have on intervention outcome is essential (Colby & Dziegielewski, 2001).

In selecting a framework for the practice strategy, a second ingredient that is essential for formulating constructive helping activity is that all efforts be guided by theoretical concepts that are consistent with the needs and desires of the individual, group, family, or community being served. Furthermore, the theoretical framework must be consistent and reflective of the values and ethics of the practitioner's profession. It is important to recognize that selection of a theoretical framework to guide the interaction may not be as simple as knowing what models and methods are available and selecting one. When choosing a method of practice, it is not uncommon to feel influenced and subsequently trapped within a system that is driven by social, political, cultural, and economic factors. With the numerous demands that are encountered in today's practice environment, it is difficult not to be influenced by these factors, and often they can dictate the practice basis that is employed. Mental health providers are often presented with problems as diverse as the individuals being treated. Once identified, these problems must be addressed within the framework of a client's unique circumstances (e.g., indigent or disadvantaged clients or clients who are culturally different form the majority culture in terms of ethnicity, race, or sexual orientation). How might all or any of these factors affect the helping relationship and practice strategy? How do mental health practitioners maintain the dignity and worth of each client served and balance their own feelings and possible prejudices so that those feelings and prejudices do not compromise the helping relationship? To address each of these questions thoroughly would fill several books. In short, each situation must be dealt with individually and mental health practitioners should take care to identify potential problems and seek supervisory help when needed.

PRACTICE STRATEGY AND APPLICATION

Selecting the most appropriate practice method requires helping professionals to consider a multitude of factors relative to the individual, his or her family, and their support system. In addition to recognition of the support system, the general provision and recognition of the importance of counseling and the services that practitioners provide in regard to enhancing overall client well-being needs to be addressed. Clients or their families may be resistant to counseling and remain unconvinced that this type of intervention is necessary. In addition, other helping professionals may also not recognize the importance of mental health professionals in improving clients' functioning (Cowles & Lefcowitz, 1992). Although, as mental health services are demystified and affirmed by the media, public policy makers, and the general public, access to these types of services will continue to improve. Most clients and their families as well as other helping professionals now recognize the importance of counseling (Dziegielewski, 1997a; Gross, Rabinowitz, Feldman, & Boerma, 1996).

A basic assessment, intervention plan, and referral process initiated by the mental health professional can help clients promote and protect their physical, as well as mental, health. How to best handle a client's situation in the helping relationship, no matter how seasoned a practitioner may become, will never be an easy task. It requires a constant process of assessing, reassessing, and collaborating with other professionals. Furthermore, when working as part of a professional team, professional opinions on how to interpret, best select, and apply these strategies for helping will vary.

Although, it is beyond the scope of this chapter to explain how to select from among the many theoretical and practice frameworks available to mental health practitioners, a brief presentation of several of the most common methods of practice, and how they can be related to client intervention, follows. Practice principles are presented to stress the importance of inclusion prior to embarking on the direct application of process to outcome when selecting a practice method.

Mixing Art and Science: Utilizing an Empowering Approach

In most schools that train mental health practitioners, students have traditionally been taught that the practice application can be defined in phases (even when not clearly established) with each application having a beginning, middle, and end. This is the format that is often presented in many time-limited practice models. One of the greatest lessons that professionals learn is that many times when applying the *science* of practice (i.e., identifying clear goals, objectives, and indicators for practice strategy), the intervention process will have a predictable beginning, middle, and end. At the same time, however, the *art* of practice acknowledges that at times nothing is predictable and even the best-made intervention plans will need constant modification and renegotiating. Balancing these two factors requires understanding that addressing and subsequently assisting to solve the problems of clients served will never be as easy as it might seem to the untrained observer.

In mental health practice today, *client empowerment* is very important. It is the uniqueness of the individual that must always be accentuated and highlighted in each step of the helping process, regardless of the method of practice that is selected. Almost all clients respond favorably when they are acknowledged for their strengths and challenged to maximize their own potential.

Utilizing Time-Limited Practice and Managed Care

Mental health practitioners must recognize that current practice will be brief. There are many reasons for this trend. For example, to receive reimbursement, practitioners must follow the expectations and subsequent limitations to service imposed by insurance reimbursement patterns. Insurance companies usually will not pay for long-term treatment. To ensure that practitioners will be reimbursed for their services, very specific time-limited approaches are essential. In defense of this trend, many clients (especially the poor) simply do not have the time, desire, or money for long-term treatment. Many times individuals are not willing to commit the extra time or energy needed to go beyond addressing what is causing the problem. For many mental health practitioners who believe in long-term and comprehensive types of clinical helping relationships, this trend is very frustrating. Today, little emphasis exists in terms of amorphous clinical judgments and vague attempts at making clients "feel better," as these efforts will no longer be supported. In most areas of mental health practice, the days of insurance covered long-term therapy encounters have ended.

For all professionals, starting the helping activity can be complicated by the fact that in today's turbulent and changing practice environment selecting a practice framework remains dependent on more than just what is best for the client. With the advent of health care from a "managed care" perspective, this practice strategy must always be guided by balancing quality and effectiveness of the care provided with the cost effectiveness of the service being delivered. Since it is hard at times to quantify the helping benefits that clients receive, many professionals believe that when there is a battle between them it is generally cost effectiveness that wins. Therefore, even the most seasoned practitioners are now being forced to battle the expectation of providing what they believe is the most beneficial and ethical practice possible, while being pressured to have completed it as quickly and efficiently as reasonable.

A further complication when selecting a method of practice in mental health is that defending a type of treatment that is viewed as being in the best interest of the client may not truly reflect the client's wishes. The promise of lower premiums and less health care expenditures (Burner, Waldo, & McKusick, 1992) has changed clients' perspectives and expectations for treatment. Clients now may request a specific type of intervention or that therapy address only certain problems because they are concerned about whether or not the service they need will be covered. For many clients, it is not uncommon to be more interested in receiving a service that is time limited or reimbursable, regardless of the expected benefit that may be gained from an alternate, possibly longer term, intervention strategy.

Regardless of what practice framework is employed, practice reality dictates that the duration of most practice sessions, regardless of the methodology used or the orientation of the mental health practitioner, remain relatively brief. In general clinical practice, most of these therapeutic encounters generally range from six to eight sessions (Wells & Phelps, 1990); however, as many as 20 have been noted (Fanger, 1994). For many practitioners, only seeing a client once is becoming commonplace. Furthermore, in health and mental health settings, so much of what practitioners do can no longer fall under the heading of brief therapy because much of intervention no longer has clear beginnings and endings. This has led the formal types of brief therapy to be replaced by intermittent types of therapy where intervention is provided when a client comes in and each session is considered to stand alone. Regardless of exactly what type of theoretical framework is to be utilized, a realization that most practice encounters are going to be brief and self-contained is essential. Planning for this short time or the single-session duration in implementing the helping strategy is critical. Without it a lack of planning can result in numerous unexpected and unplanned endings for the client (Wells, 1994). It can also contribute to feelings of failure and decreased job satisfaction for the mental heath and health care professionals (C. Resnick & Dziegielewski, 1996).

Time-Limited Brief Therapies

Many mental practitioners who practice traditional forms of psychotherapy, particularly those who support psychoanalytic therapy, believe that managed care policies and subsequent counseling practice remain biased against them. For many practitioners trained in the more traditional forms of therapy and counseling, it is a common belief that making changes in a person takes time and that rushing into changes could lead to complications in a client's future health and wellness. Advocates for long-term approaches urge practitioners to realize this danger and advocate strongly for its continuance before it becomes an extinct mode of practice delivery in today's "big business" practice environment (Alperin, 1994).

For many practitioners, conducting traditional forms of psychotherapy remains problematic. Long-term therapy presents a particular problem for the poor and the disadvantaged. These individuals generally do not have the time or finances to afford long-term therapy, which has been referred to in some circles as a long-term luxury. Today, the majority of those in practice have for years shunned the more traditional approaches for a preferred emphasis on the applicability and effectiveness of time-limited methods of practice (B. L. Bloom, 1992; Dziegielewski, 1997, 1998; Epstein, 1994; Mancoske, Standifer, & Cauley, 1994; Wells, 1994).

Based on the turbulence in our current practice environment, it is easy to see how time-limited therapies have gained in popularity, based on the overall objective of bringing about positive changes in a client's current lifestyle with as little face-to-face contact as possible (Fanger, 1994). It is this emphasis on effectiveness and applicability leading to increased positive change that has helped to make time-limited brief interventions popular. In general, time-limited approaches are the most often requested forms of practice in use today.

The major difference between traditional psychotherapy and time-limited or intermittent approaches is that the foundation for both is quite different. This difference requires practitioners to reexamine some basic premises that have been taught in regard to long-term therapeutic models utilized in a more traditional format. According to Dziegielewski (1997b), there are seven factors that can be identified that highlight the difference between these two methods.

First, there is the primary difference in the way the client is viewed. Traditional psychotherapeutic approaches often linked individual problems to personal pathology. This is not the case from a time-limited perspective where the client is seen as a basically healthy individual with an interest in increasing personal or social changes or both (Budman & Gurman, 1988; Roberts & Dziegielewski, 1995). In current mental health practice, the focus on empowerment extends the belief that clients are not only capable of change, but they can be aware and active participants in this process. Traditional psychoanalytic approaches emphasize that the client is often unaware and unable to access this information because it lies beneath the surface of the client's awareness and is defined as a preconscious or unconscious level of awareness. These approaches make empowerment difficult to engage and do not highlight the strengths of the client in becoming an active participant in the practice strategy employed.

Second, time-limited approaches are most helpful when administered during critical periods in a person's life (Roberts & Dziegielewski, 1995). This provides a basic difference from the use of traditional psychotherapies that are seen as necessary and ongoing over a much longer period of time. Third, in time-limited brief treatment, the goals and objectives of therapy are always mutually defined by both the client and the therapist (Wells, 1994). In traditional psychotherapeutic approaches, goals are often first recognized and defined by the therapist and later shared with the client (Budman & Gurman, 1988).

Fourth, in time-limited therapy goals are concretely defined and are often addressed outside the actual therapy session in the form of homework or other activities (Epstein, 1994). One example of this is *bibliotherapy*, the use of outside reading materials as an adjunct to office sessions. In traditional psychotherapeutic approaches, issues are generally addressed during the sessions only—not generally outside of them (Budman & Gurman, 1988). This is because the presence of the therapist is seen as the catalyst for change.

The fifth difference between brief approaches and traditional psychotherapy is one of the hardest to accept for mental health practitioners who were educated with a traditional psychotherapeutic methodology. Simply stated, in time-limited intervention, regardless of the model, little emphasis is placed on insight. This is very different from traditional psychotherapy where development of problem-oriented insight is considered necessary before any type of meaningful change can take place.

Sixth, time-limited approaches to practice are seen as active and directive. Here the mental health practitioner often goes beyond just active listening and assumes a consultative role with the client (Wells, 1994). This results in the development of concrete goals and problem-solving techniques and is very different from traditional psychotherapeutic approaches that emphasize a more nebulous inner representation of satisfaction.

QUICK REFERENCE

DEFINITIONS OF THEORETICAL CONCEPTS

psychotherapy: A form of therapy that involves understanding the individual in regard to his or her personal situation.

cognitive-behavioral therapy: This method of practice uses the combination of selected techniques incorporating the theories of behaviorism, social learning theory, and cognition theories to understand and address a client's behavior.

crisis intervention: A practice strategy used to help clients in crisis regain a sense of healthy equilibrium.

educative counseling: A loosely defined approach to practice that focuses on helping the client to become an "educated consumer" and through this information is better able to address his or her own needs.

interpersonal therapy: A form of time-limited treatment often used in the medical setting. Generally, an assessment that includes a diagnostic evaluation and psychiatric history. The focus of treatment is directed toward interpersonal problem areas such as grief, role disputes, role transitions, or deficits.

The last difference is the process of termination. In brief time–limited settings, termination is discussed early in the therapeutic process (Wells, 1994). Often the practitioner begins to plan for termination in the first session and termination issues are discussed continually throughout the intervention process. By contrast, traditional psychotherapy may never address termination issues in advance. Preparation for termination is not typically considered an essential part of the therapy process.

TYPES OF TIME-LIMITED THERAPY IN MENTAL HEALTH PRACTICE

This section reviews several models usually linked to the provision of time–limited counseling services; however, these models do not represent all the major models of practice for mental health counseling. This review describes the types of models and methods available as well as the tradition from which they were developed. In the applications section of this text, each of the mental health disorders and conditions presented describes a currently accepted treatment or intervention strategy for the problem. To assist and provide an overview of several current therapeutic approaches, the following models for practice will be briefly summarized: *interpersonal psychotherapeutic or psychodynamic approaches, strategic or solution-oriented therapies, cognitive-behavioral approaches, crisis intervention,* and *health, education, and wellness counseling.* Cases are used to highlight each of these approaches. In the psychodynamic aspects of therapeutic practice, emphasis is placed on understanding the internal workings of the individual. In the solution-focused therapies, the solution (or course of action) is identified and specific attempts are made to attain it. In the cognitive-behavioral approaches, the focus is on understanding the complex relationship between socialization and reinforcement as it affects thoughts and behaviors in the current environment. The final application is a form of time-limited therapy in which practitioners focus on providing health counseling and education based on the principle of creating and maintaining wellness.

Before discussing these methods, it is important to note that there is no method of practice that can alone call itself a "clean" mental health practice theory. In mental health practice, there has been a blending of ideas and theoretical concepts that are mixed and altered to best serve the client. Thus, there is substantial overlap in the information that is presented for each approach and although the practitioner may first start using one mode of practice, pieces of the other methods of intervention may also be incorporated to assist the client in the most efficient and effective way possible. Very often the mental health practitioner will be expected to mix and match practice strategies thereby using what works to help the client. Pieces or techniques alone, however, are not considered enough. There also needs to be some theoretical understanding of why certain techniques are being used, and how selecting these methods must be consistent with the practitioner's professional ethics and standards.

Psychodynamic Approaches

Psychodynamic approaches allow for past experiences to be blended with present ones. This approach is often credited with being the foundation of mental health casework and its premise is that focusing on history and past issues can lend credence to current problem-solving efforts. Furthermore, when utilizing a "biopsychosocial" perspective, this form of intervention has gained credibility and recognition among many health care professionals as an interdisciplinary approach. For example, historically this type of approach to practice was used in medical settings where interdisciplinary teams assisted clients in addressing their needs. In this practice framework, helping professionals are seen as active, supportive, and a contributing factor in therapeutic gain (Fimerson, 1996; Rounsaville, O'Malley, Foley, & Weissman, 1988). In general, these models are often used to directly address symptom removal and prevention of relapse and help clients having difficulty relating to significant others, careers, social roles, and/or life transitions (Karasu et al., 1993).

Psychodynamic approaches focus clinical attention on the conscious (individual awareness) and the unconscious (beyond individual awareness). Next, these factors are identified, outlined, reviewed, and addressed as part of the practice strategy. For the most part, as evidenced by the following case (pp. 128–129), most of the psychodynamic approaches used in practice today portray the unconscious as immediately accessible and changeable (Ecker & Hulley, 1996).

As in the case of John, the intervention addressed the client's present situation and focused on the "here and now" (Klerman et al., 1994). Similar to what was done in this case, the focus of the intervention is on recent interpersonal events (the death of John's mother) with a clear effort to link the stressful event to John's current mood and actions (crying out for attention by making obscene phone calls).

Information is gathered in the diagnostic assessment along with a psychiatric history. When completing the diagnostic assessment, the mental health practitioner is expected to pay particular attention to the family and support system interactions by the client, including changes in relationships proximal to the onset of symptoms. In general, the focus of treatment is directed toward interpersonal problem areas such as grief, role disputes, role transitions, or deficits (Fanger, 1994). Focusing on one of these interpersonal areas will allow the practitioner to identify problems in the interpersonal and social context that need to be addressed (Klerman et al., 1994).

———————   **THE CASE OF JOHN**   ———————

Mr. Jones brought his 12-year-old son John in for assessment after he discovered that his son had been making obscene phone calls. John had never been in trouble before and after being charged legally and sent to court a judge decided that John could benefit from a mental health assessment rather than proceeding with further legal action. It was obvious during the interview that the father was extremely frustrated with the situation and could not understand why John had been engaging in this type of behavior. During his interview, John became very nervous. He seemed embarrassed to talk about what he had done and kept his head down looking directly at the floor as he spoke.

The mental health practitioner asked John what had happened. John described exactly what he had done, the phone calls he had made, and the obscene comments he had made to the women who answered the phone. John seemed embarrassed by his behavior but appeared honest in telling what he had done. When asked how he had gotten caught making the calls, John calmly stated that when asked he gave his name. The practitioner was surprised by this and tried to clarify what he said and again John stated that when the recipient of the obscene phone call asked who was calling, John told her his name. After hearing John tell of what he had done and how he had gotten caught, John's father voiced his frustration, anger, and shock with his son's behavior. He openly stated that he was alarmed by his son's behavior and could not understand it. The fact that John was leaving his name when asked caused the practitioner to feel that there was more here than simply "acting out" as the father had stated.

In gathering information for the diagnostic assessment, the practitioner asked if John had ever been in trouble before. John and his father agreed that he had not. Since this appeared inconsistent with his behavior, the practitioner asked if anything out of the ordinary had happened to upset John or disturb him. John stated he was not aware of anything. When asked specifically if there had been any changes in the past few months, John's father responded. According to the father, John's mother had died approximately six weeks before. Once the practitioner began to explore the death of the mother and the feelings of the child, it became clear that John was indeed having difficulty adjusting to the death of his mother. It appeared as though John was making the phone calls and leaving his name as an attempt at crying out for attention or help. After beginning to discuss the death of his mother with the practitioner, John was also able to voice his fear that his father might die as well and leave him alone. The practitioner concluded that John did not suffer from a mental disorder at all but rather was suffering from bereavement (related to the death of his mother) and his reaction was an adolescent antisocial act (making the obscene phone calls).

The role of the mental health practitioner is to gather a comprehensive assessment exploring why things are happening as they are. In this case, many issues surrounding the death of the mother remained unresolved. Furthermore, it also appeared as though the child might in his own way be crying out for help and attention from the father. The approach the practitioner took in this case was to explore the relationship between John and his father as well as to look at how their past relationship could balance and strengthen the present one. This approach utilized the concepts relevant in ego-psychology, a form of psychodynamic therapy. In this approach, the practitioner helped to address the situation, plant a seed as to what was

——————— **THE CASE OF JOHN** *(Continued)* ———————

happening, create a release of tension and energy for John and his father, and later help them to reintegrate, address, and discontinue the problematic behaviors that had resulted. It is important to note: Although trained professionals do engage in these types of psychodynamic approaches, graduate level training and expertise is usually required. Helping professionals without graduate training should refer clients to a qualified practitioner if they believe this type of approach would best serve the client. Overall, however, as can be seen in this case, the more a mental health practitioner knows in terms of practice strategy and frameworks, the more she or he can pick and choose the best helping approach.

For John, exploring the reasons for his making the phone calls and the relationship between the problem behavior and the death of his mother was a crucial link. In making this connection, John was helped to address his feelings and he was able to stop making the phone calls as a means of getting attention.

The mental health practitioner and the client work together to identify issues for the treatment plan and establish the goals and objectives that will later be addressed in the practice strategy. Practice strategy must be directly related to the identified interpersonal problem. For example, if a role conflict exists between a client and his or her family member in regard to substance use and abuse, practice strategy would begin by clarifying the nature of the dispute. Discussion of the problem would result in an explanation of usual limitations that often are beyond the client's control. Limitations that are causing the greatest disagreements are identified and options to resolve the disputes are considered. If resolution does not appear possible, strategies or alternatives to replace the problematic behaviors are contemplated. In some cases, application manuals can be acquired and followed that give specific practice steps for approaching certain interpersonal problem areas (Klerman et al., 1994).

When applying the psychodynamic method of practice, mental health practitioners are expected to help clients identify issues of concern and provide the groundwork for how they can be addressed. Many times this includes helping the client to learn how to recognize the need for continued help and assistance through counseling, especially when problems seem greater than what the client is capable of handling at the time (Dziegielewski & Leon, 2001a). Regardless of who is actually assisting the client, the role of the practitioner in this form of practice is an important one. Most importantly, the practitioner must always remain influential in helping the client feel comfortable about seeking additional help when needed. This help-seeking behavior is an important step in establishing and maintaining a basis for continued health and wellness.

Solution-Focused Approaches

Solution-focused models are different in focus from the more traditional problem-solving methods in practice because they do not spend much time on problem identification as the key ingredient to the practice encounter. Solution-focused models assume that clients are basically healthy individuals who possess the skills they need to address their problems and remain capable of change (deShazer, 1985). Thus, this method focuses on identifying solutions to resolving the client's stated concern. This popular treatment strategy does not require there to be a causal link between the antecedent (what comes before the problem behavior) and the actual problem. Since this causal connection is not made, a direct link need not be established between the problem and the solution (O'Hanlon & Weiner-Davis, 1989).

THE CASE OF JIM

Jim was referred for a mental health assessment requesting help because he was having difficulty interacting with his child. His wife constantly complained that he did not show enough attention and concern for their handicapped child. Jim stated he loved his son very much but was not particularly comfortable showing it. He did not like the way his son who was moderately mentally retarded always demanded to be hugged after completing tasks. When asked whether he believed that it was important to show affection he agreed but stated that he just was not sure how to go about it. Furthermore, he felt that his son was expecting too much love and attention and should be able to function without always requiring that it be given.

When Jim sought intervention assistance, he made it very clear that his insurance company would only allow three sessions and that was what he was going to stick with. After completing a diagnostic assessment, the mental health practitioner felt that a solution-focused approach to intervention would be best for Jim. Although his symptoms were problematic, they did not seem severe enough to affect Jim's overall functioning. In helping Jim to develop a change strategy, the practitioner (1) focused on what Jim saw as the problem, (2) let Jim establish what he perceived as the desired outcome, (3) helped Jim to begin to analyze and develop solutions focusing on his own individual strengths, (4) helped Jim to develop and implement a plan of action, and (5) assisted with termination and follow-up issues if needed (Dziegielewski, 1997b).

In summary, in this case, the mental health practitioner was active in helping the client to find and identify strengths in his current functional patterns of behavior. A dialogue of "change talk" was created rather than "problem talk" (Walter & Peller, 1992). In change talk, the problem was viewed positively with patterns of change highlighted that appear successful for the client. Positive aspects and exceptions to the problem are explored allowing for alternate views of the problem to develop. Once the small changes have been highlighted, the client becomes empowered to elicit larger ones (O'Hanlon & Weiner-Davis, 1989; Walter & Peller, 1992). Jim looked at what he was doing and the practitioner helped him to establish alternative ways of acting and behaving when his son approached him. They also developed ways for him to discuss his feelings and his strategy for building independence in his son with his wife.

Cognitive-Behavioral Approaches to Mental Health Practice

Cognitive-behavioral therapy often involves concrete and focused strategies to help clients change irrational thoughts or behaviors that can complicate the helping process. This type of practice approach gained popularity in the early 1970s when the focus was originally on the applied behavior and the power of reinforcement on the influence of human behavior (Skinner, 1953). However, many theorists believed that behavior alone was not enough and that human beings acted or reacted based on an analysis of the situation and the thought patterns that motivated them. Here the thought process, and how cognitive processes and structures influence individual emotions, was highlighted (Roberts & Dziegielewski, 1995). This process results in the development of a schema, referred to as the cognitive structure that organizes experience and behavior (Beck, Freeman, and Associates, 1990).

Overall, cognitive-behavioral approaches to practice focus on the present and seek to replace distorted thoughts and/or unwanted behaviors with clearly established goals (Fanger, 1994). In the cognitive-behavioral approach, the setting of goals and objectives are crucial for measuring the effectiveness of treatment provided (Brower & Nurius, 1993). In cognitive-behavioral therapy, these goals should always be stated positively and realistically so that motivation for completion will be increased. Also to facilitate the measurement of effectiveness of what is being done, objectives must be stated in concrete and functional terms. In setting appropriate objectives, the focus is not necessarily on process but rather on the outcome that is desired (Roberts & Dziegielewski, 1995). Adapting cognitive and behavioral principles in the time-limited framework creates a viable climate for change.

—————————— THE CASE OF JILL ——————————

Jill sought the assistance of a mental health professional after becoming extremely frustrated with her ability to take tests in college. She often became so anxious that she could not focus or concentrate thereby rendering her unable to put on paper what she really did know in her head. After interviewing Jill, the practitioner decided it would probably be best to use a type of cognitive-behavioral therapy to address Jill's test anxiety.

As the first step in this helping process, the practitioner asked the client to keep a diary. In the diary she was asked to record the specific thoughts, feelings, and emotions that she experienced when she was put in stressful situations—particularly testing situations. Jill kept the diary for seven days and brought it to her next session. At that session, the practitioner reviewed the comments Jill had written and realized much of what was noted was self-defeating phrases and thoughts. For example, Jill often reported feeling stupid and useless. She also stated that she could remember her older brothers telling her how stupid she was.

(continued)

THE CASE OF JILL *(Continued)*

Jill's schema revolved around her feelings of inadequacy and that she believed she was not smart enough to succeed in college. Once this was triggered by the stress of a test, she could no longer function. It was her interpretation of these events that influenced her reaction resulting in cognitive distortion when interpreting a current situation or event (Beck, 1967; Burns, 1983). Therefore, the role of the mental health practitioner in this type of framework is to help Jill identify her negative and self-defeating thoughts and to replace them with more productive and fruitful ones.

The mental health practitioner helped Jill to look at each of the statements in her diary and analyze them. Many times they practiced rewriting the statements or inserting more positive self-statements in the process. Basically, the practitioner helped Jill to rethink the comments she was saying to herself and replace them with more positive and productive statements.

In working with client problems such as those experienced by Jill, a cognitive-behavioral approach can be very helpful. This is especially true for professionals who must deal with clients who are suffering from a variety of personal and situational problems. Thoughts can be difficult to control and often clients may become extremely frustrated with their inability to control their own actions and behaviors and perform in areas in which they previously were proficient. When faced with a medical situation, they may develop negative schemas or ways of dealing with the situation that can clearly cause conflicts in their physical, interpersonal, and social relationships. Specific techniques such as identifying irrational beliefs, utilizing cognitive restructuring, behavioral role rehearsal, and systematic desensitization can assist the client to adjust and accommodate to the new life status that will result. Cognitive and behavioral techniques can help the client to recognize these needs for change as well as assist with a plan to provide the behavior change needed for continued health and functioning.

Crisis Intervention Approaches to Mental Health Practice

Crisis intervention addresses acute problem situations and can help clients discover an adaptive means of coping with a particular life stage, tragic occurrence, or problem that generates a crisis situation. Crisis intervention techniques are employed in many settings: social and relief agencies, the military, private practice, shelters, hospitals (especially hospital emergency rooms), public health agencies, hospice services, home health care agencies, and almost all other agencies and services that utilize mental health professionals. Professionals have used crisis intervention techniques with migrant workers, rape survivors, domestic violence victims, death and dying, mental illness, event trauma such as plane crashes, floods, tornado, and in numerous other ways when immediate help and assistance is needed.

For professionals, the first criterion in this method of service delivery is that all practice approaches are of short or limited duration. Brief time-limited intervention is important because crisis is by its nature self-limiting (Roberts & Dziegielewski, 1995). Time-limited practice is intended to accomplish a set of therapeutic objectives within a sharply limited time frame and its effectiveness in crisis management appears to be indistinguishable from that of long-term treatment (B. L. Bloom, 1992). According to Parad and coworkers (1990) utilizing minimum therapeutic practice strategy during the brief crisis period can often produce the maximum therapeutic effect. For those suffering from a crisis, an emphasis on utilizing supportive social resources and focused intervention techniques to facilitate practice effectiveness is highlighted (Parad & Parad, 1990).

THE CASE OF JUAN

Juan was referred for a mental health assessment after a devastating tornado. After the tornado, Juan was found wandering the neighborhood in a state of shock. For weeks he would return and wander through the rubble of what was once his home looking for belongings (now treasures) of a previous time. Although it had been a month since the event, Juan reported that he could not put it behind him and move forward. Juan sought intervention because his wife was very concerned about his behavior. He often woke up in the middle of the night in a cold sweat and could not go back to sleep. Juan reported that since his home was destroyed by the tornado he often felt like he was in a daze. He reported having recurrent flashback episodes during the day and the night where he would relive the night the tornado destroyed his home. He reported that he now avoided driving to the construction site where his home was now being rebuilt. Whenever he tried to go there, he would feel overwhelmed with anxious feelings and have to stop his car.

After completing a diagnostic assessment, the mental health practitioner felt that Juan was experiencing a stress reaction such as acute stress disorder (308.3). Although Juan was able to go to work, it was apparent that his reaction was severe enough to impair his overall functioning.

As part of the helping strategy, crisis intervention requires a dynamic form of practice that focuses on a wide range of phenomenon affecting individual, group, or family equilibrium. For Juan, the crisis was defined as a temporary state of upset and disequilibrium characterized chiefly by his inability to cope with a particular situation. During this crisis period, Juan's usual methods of coping and problem solving simply did not work. Juan's perception was that the tornado was so devastating and intolerable that he could not cope with it. Juan viewed the tornado as a hazardous threatening event that left him vulnerable. He stated that no matter how hard he tried he could not seem to control his fears.

To help Juan, crisis intervention techniques were applied to help him reformulate the crisis situation within the context of growth. Ultimately, the mental health practitioner needed to help Juan reach a healthy resolution where he could emerge with greater strength, self-trust, and a greater sense of freedom than before the crisis event (Gilliland & James, 1993). When applied with clients such as Juan, crisis intervention techniques are centered on the assumption

(continued)

THE CASE OF JUAN *(Continued)*
---

that acute crisis events can be concretely identified, controlled, and lessened. Successful resolution is therefore achieved when the practitioner helps Juan to successfully reach a more healthy resolution of the problem.

For Juan, learning to deal with the physical devastation that resulted from the recent tornado was an area that needed to be addressed. A crisis such as this one was so unexpected that many families, similar to Juan's, lost their homes, their personal possessions, and in some cases the lives of their loved ones, neighbors, and friends. Juan worried repeatedly what he could have done differently and why this had to happen to him. With such an unanticipated catastrophe, Juan was concerned with understanding why this happened or how he could prevent it in the future. In situations such as these, the role of the helping professional is clear: To help Juan once again return to that previous level of coping and adjustment.

For many clients the psychological suffering that they experience following a traumatic event can be understood as an "affliction of the powerless" (Herman, 1992, p. 33). These are basically healthy people who are so disturbed by the event that functioning is impaired. If they are afraid of something, the threat to life and bodily integrity overwhelms normal adaptive capabilities, producing extensive symptomatology. For the mental health practitioner, an active problem-addressing and supportive role is essential. The practitioner helps the client to become empowered, recognizing that the symptoms that are being experienced can be viewed as signs of strength. The symptoms a client is experiencing are better related to understanding coping techniques developed by the survivor to adapt to a toxic environment (Roberts & Dziegielewski, 1995).

Educative Counseling

Through the document *Healthy People 2000* (N. L. Thomas, 2000), health promotion has been incorporated into the nation's health delivery agenda. However, despite the growth and emphasis placed in this area, health promotion remains fragmented. Often its implementation is characterized by "poor communication between the many disciplines contributing to this area and little interaction between the research and the practitioner communities" (O'Donnell, 1994, p. ix).

Many times mental health professionals are called upon to participate in a type of counseling that is not considered traditional. This type of counseling can include many different techniques, however at a minimum, it must be time-limited, goal-directed, and objective-focused and assist clients to address present and future health and wellness issues. More and more mental health practitioners are being called upon to provide "educative counseling," yet rarely is it openly discussed and accepted as a method of providing practice. Nor is its importance generally stressed or addressed in formal education through the curriculum in most schools.

THE CASE OF BILL

Mental health practitioners can assist in providing education to clients in many different areas. Consider the case of Bill, who would not follow his diabetic diet. The medical condition resulting from his noncompliance was so severe that he was hospitalized repeatedly. During each hospitalization, he met with a dietitian and was given a copy of his diet before discharge, but was later readmitted for noncompliance. Upon referral to the mental health practitioner, a family assessment was completed. The practitioner discovered that the client's wife was responsible for preparing the family's meals. His wife had been handed the diet but was not really sure of the relevance of strict adherence to his continued health. After meeting with the family and helping to educate his wife about the need for assisting, Bill's diet compliance increased dramatically.

This is just one example of how practitioners can assist clients by educating not only them and their families but also other members of a delivery team. It is also important for practitioners to be willing to educate clients in areas such as child abuse, domestic violence, and incest dynamics. Practitioners need to go beyond the traditional bounds of counseling and assist in educating clients to be better prepared for maintaining safety, security, and preparing for health and wellness for not only themselves but their entire family system.

Openly acknowledging the importance of client education can assist practitioners in identifying the need for this commonly provided service. Mental health practitioners are in a unique position to participate in education, particularly in the areas of prevention and continued health and wellness. The overall practice of education in mental health is safety- and health-oriented both conceptually and philosophically. This makes the mental health practitioner the link between the person and a system of support that maintains health (Skidmore, Thackeray, & Farley, 1997).

SUMMARY

Case documentation and using the information gathered to provide the basis for intervention planning and the practice strategy to follow is never simple. Numerous cases and individual situations arise that professionals are not sure how to handle. It is never easy to decide where to begin, what to write, and what not to write in the case record, and what goals and objectives to process and apply to practice strategy. The science of intervention is important in starting the process, but it is the art that will carry it to a successful end. This always takes a delicate balancing act between the needs of the client, the demands of the environment, and the skills and helping knowledge available to the mental health practitioner.

Furthermore, the art and science within practice strategy is more involved than being familiar with the practice frameworks and simply choosing what works. It takes knowing the client and the strategies and methods available as well as how and when to best apply the theoretical foundations that underlie the practice techniques selected. In today's environment, there are a multitude of complicated problems that need to be addressed and a real urgency to address them as quickly and effectively as possible. All mental health professionals, regardless of their discipline, need to be trained in these methods of helping. This training cannot be viewed as static. All professional helpers must continue learning and growing in order to anticipate the needs of our clients.

Dziegielewski (1998) identified the following five expectations or factors that need to guide the initiation of the diagnostic assessment, treatment planning, and the practice strategy:

1. *Clients need to be active and motivated in the diagnostic assessment, treatment plan formulation, and intervention strategy.* Support and participation by the client will increase the likelihood of participation and completion of change efforts. Generally, the issues and behavioral problems a client is exhibiting may require serious energy to be exerted in attempting to make behavioral change. This means that clients must not only agree to participate in the assessment process, but must be willing to embark on the intervention plan that will result in behavioral change.

2. *The information gathered in the diagnostic assessment will be used to guide the approach or method of intervention used.* Once symptoms are identified different methods and approaches for clinical intervention can be selected, however, the approach should never guide the intervention chosen. Sheafor et al. (1997) warn against practitioners becoming over involved and wasting valuable clinical time by trying to match a particular problem to a particular theoretical approach, especially since so much of the problem identification process in assessment is an intellectual activity. The practitioner should never lose sight of the ultimate purpose of the assessment process. Simply stated, the purpose is to complete an assessment that will help to establish a concrete service plan to address a client's needs.

3. *The influence and effects of values and beliefs should be made apparent in the process.* Each individual, professional or not, is influenced by his or her own values and beliefs (Colby & Dziegielewski, 2001). It is these beliefs that create the foundation for who we are and what we believe. In mental health practice, however, it is essential that these individual influences do not directly affect the assessment process. Therefore, the individual values, beliefs, and practices that can influence intervention outcomes must be clearly identified from the onset of treatment. For example, consider an unmarried client at a public health clinic who finds out she is pregnant. The practitioner assigned to her case personally believes that abortion is "murder" and cannot in good conscience recommend it as an option to the client. The client, however, is unsure of what to do and wants to explore every possible alternative. The plan that evolves must be based on the client's needs and desires, not the mental health practitioner's. Therefore, the practitioner ethically should advise the client of her prejudice and refer her to someone who can be more objective in exploring abortion as a possible course of action. Clients have a right to make their own decisions, and mental health professionals must do everything possible to ensure this right and not allow personal opinion to impair the completion of a proper assessment.

In addition to the beliefs held by the practitioner and the client, the beliefs and values of the members of the interdisciplinary team must also be considered. It is not uncommon for helping professionals to have value conflicts. These team members need to be aware of how their personal feelings and resultant opinions might inhibit them from addressing all of the possible options to a client. For example, in the case of the unmarried pregnant woman, a physician, nurse, or any other member of the health care delivery team who did not believe in abortion, would also be obligated to refer the client. This is not to assume that mental health practitioners are more qualified to address this issue, or that they always have an answer. The point is that mental health practitioners should always be available to assist other helping professionals and advocate for how to best serve the needs of the client. Values and beliefs can be influential in identification of factors within individual decision making strategy and remain an important factor to consider and identify in the assessment process.

4. *Issues surrounding culture and race should be addressed openly in the assessment phase.* The mental health practitioner needs to be aware of his or her own cultural heritages as well as the client's to ensure the most open and receptive environment is created. Dziegielewski (1997) suggested the following considerations be established on the part of the health and mental health professionals: (1) be aware of his or her own cultural limitations; (2) be open to cultural differences; (3) recognize the integrity and the uniqueness of the client; (4) utilize the client's learning style including his or her own resources and supports; and (5) implement the behaviorally based biopsychosocial approach to practice from an integrated and as nonjudgmental a format as possible. For example, when utilizing the *DSM-IV-TR,* cultural factors should be stressed prior to establishing a formal diagnostic condition. As stated earlier in this book, delusions and hallucinations may be difficult to separate from the general beliefs or practices that may be related to a client's specific cultural custom or lifestyle. For this reason, the mental health practitioner should not forget that an appendix is included in the *DSM-IV-TR* that describes and defines culturally bound syndromes that might affect the diagnosis and assessment process and subsequent intervention strategy (American Psychiatric Association [APA], 2000).

5. *The assessment must focus on client strengths and highlight the client's own resources for providing continued support.* One of the most difficult things for most individuals to do is to find, identify, and plan to use their own strengths. People, in general, have a tendency to focus on the negatives and rarely praise themselves for the good they do. With the advent of behavioral managed care, health and mental health care workers must quickly identify the individual and collectively based strengths of our clients. Once this has been achieved, highlight these strengths and incorporate them into the treatment plan that is suggested. The information gathered is utilized in the assessment and stressed in regard to the importance of individual support networks for the client. In this time-limited intervention environment, individual resources are essential for continued growth and maintenance of wellness after the formal intervention period has ended.

One such example in need of support and attention from practitioners is that of individuals suffering from acquired immune deficiency syndrome (AIDS). According to the Joint United Nations program on HIV/AIDS, 58 million people around the globe have been affected with HIV, the virus that causes AIDS and 22 million have already died from the virus that rendered their immune system defenseless (Bullers, 2001). Many individuals are forced to either confront this generally terminal illness in themselves or see it progress in a loved one. Misconceptions and fear based on lack of education can often stop family and friends from being supportive to individuals when they need their care and support the most. Practitioners must actively work to help these individuals and encourage support for them in their time of need. In this situation, the practitioner needs to be exposed not only to varied theoretical approaches but be able to select which one to use and when. Psychodynamic approaches can be used to help clients to feel better about themselves and to help address previous relationship experiences that are affecting the development of new or current ones. Solution-focused methods can help individuals develop new ways of changing behavior, focusing positive energy and attention on how to make things better. Cognitive-behavioral approaches can help individuals and family members to look at dysfunctional thought patterns and how they complicate current interactions. The crisis intervention approach can assist the client and his or her family to return to a previous or healthier level of coping. Education can provide client empowerment while enhancing independence and control. Being aware of the multiple frameworks and practice methods available to practitioners is essential in helping them to become better equipped in the helping activity.

———— QUESTIONS FOR FURTHER THOUGHT ————

1. In this chapter, supporting information beyond that related directly to the diagnosis is essential. List the types of supporting information that are most helpful for inclusion and explain why.

2. Apply the basics of the POR to a client you have seen or are seeing. Break down the factors in the case into either the SOAP or SOAPIE format.

3. Take a problem that a client could face and describe how you would approach it utilizing:

   Psychotherapy/psychodynamic.

   Cognitive behavioral.

   Crisis intervention.

   Educative counseling.

   Interpersonal therapy.

4. Compare and contrast the different types of therapy in handling clients.

SECTION II

APPLICATIONS

Selected *DSM-IV-TR* Disorders

5 Reactive Attachment Disorder

Heather T. Forbes and Sophia F. Dziegielewski

Since first being introduced in the *Diagnostic and Statistical Manual of Mental Disorders* 20 years ago, reactive attachment disorder of infancy or early childhood (RAD) continues to raise many questions regarding its validity, criteria, and impact on children. Today in clinical practice, most seasoned practitioners will agree that there is a "muddy" consensus as to what defines RAD among researchers and professionals who work with children and adolescents who suffer from attachment difficulties. Attachment theory, based on the early work of John Bowlby, provides a basis for treating these children, yet few longitudinal studies are available to legitimize current treatment modalities. One such treatment method, *holding therapy,* is an emotionally driven and intense therapeutic intervention that is applied to the case presentation and described in the intervention section of this chapter. With an increase in international adoptions, this therapy should be considered for treatment of the young client who is suffering from the residual effects of beginning life in an orphanage where bonding with the caretaker and physical touch have not been present. Holding therapy is also used as an intervention to resolve conflicts between the child's parents and the child's extended family members. Further discussion of RAD, from a community and societal perspective, identifies how critical it is that clinicians complete a thorough diagnostic assessment, treatment plan, and practice strategy that can efficiently embrace, identify, and effectively treat RAD to reduce the magnitude of disturbances this disorder can have on our society.

REACTIVE ATTACHMENT DISORDER (RAD)

Jeffrey Dahmer, Edgar Allen Poe, Hitler, Ted Bundy, Saddam Hussein, and Ted Kaczynski, the Unabomber—what do all of these infamous individuals have in common? All had attachment breaks in their childhood and did not receive therapeutic help (N. L. Thomas, 2000, p. 67). Basically, an *attachment break* can happen to any child or adolescent at any time during the human growth and development cycle. When bonding is generally discussed in any of the human growth and development theories, it usually involves the mother who is often noted as the primary caretaker. However, it is also possible that when the primary caretaker is someone other than the mother, attachment breaks could occur. In the literature, this break typically happens in the bonding relationship between the mother and child. When such a break occurs and is not resolved or healed, pathological disturbances are believed to occur. N. L. Thomas quotes a profound example:

> The first clue is something that happened when Kaczynski was only six months old. According to federal investigators, little "Teddy John," as his parents called him, was hospitalized for a severe allergic reaction to a medicine he was taking. He had to be isolated—his parents were unable to see him or hold him for several weeks. After this separation, family members have told the Feds, the baby's personality, once bubbly and vivacious seemed to go "flat." (1996, p. 29).

DSM-IV-TR: *Definition of RAD*

Thus RAD was added to the American Psychiatric Association 1980 edition of the *Diagnostic and Statistical Manual of Mental Disorders* (*DSM-III*) to identify children who have not been able to attach appropriately to a primary caregiver (Benedict, 1998) and to address the manifestations of a child's attachment break. The original version of RAD in *DSM-III* (1980) is markedly different from the current criteria outlined in the *DSM-IV-TR* (2000). In the *DSM-III,* early criteria identified for RAD postulated that symptom onset occurs prior to the age of 8 months (an age younger than when a child is developmentally able to form an

---

QUICK REFERENCE

TWO PRIMARY TYPES OF RAD

The essential diagnostic feature of RAD is markedly disturbed and developmentally inappropriate social relatedness in most contexts, beginning before age 5 years, associated with grossly pathological care (Criterion A).

Two Subtypes:

- **Inhibited type:** Refers to a persistent failure to initiate and to respond to most social interactions in a developmentally appropriate way.
- **Disinhibited type:** Refers to predominant disturbances in social relatedness, indiscriminate sociability, from or lack of selectivity in the choice of attachment figures.

Source: Summarized criteria from the *Diagnostic and Statistical Manual of Mental Disorders, Fourth Edition, Text Revision.* Copyright 2000. American Psychiatric Association (p. 128).

attachment) and the criteria also included infants and children who experienced a *failure to thrive.* The revised version of RAD in the *DSM-III-R* (APA, 1987) reworked the criteria to focus attention on issues commensurate to social relatedness and dysfunctional patterns (Boris & Zeanah, 1999). The criteria from *DSM-III-R* remains similar to the later versions of the *DSM,* yet there continues to be much disagreement among practitioners as to what exactly defines this disorder and what specific criteria best represent this disorder.

Currently, the *DSM-IV* and the *DSM-IV-TR* list the essential diagnostic feature of RAD to be a "markedly disturbed and developmentally inappropriate social relatedness in most contexts, beginning before age 5 years and is associated with grossly pathological care (Criterion A)" (APA, 2000, p. 127). The subtypes of RAD include the inhibited type and the disinhibited type. The inhibited type is described as "persistent failure to initiate and to respond to most social interactions in a developmentally appropriate way." The disinhibited type is used if the

---

QUICK REFERENCE

MENTAL RETARDATION

Abbreviated Guidelines

- If this condition is present, the practitioner should always diagnose it.
- Individuals must have significantly subaverage intelligence and deficits in adaptive functioning.
- Definition is compatible with AAMR definition except for subtyping.
- Onset prior to age 18, if later the proper diagnosis is dementia.
- Must have IQ of 70 or below on an individual intelligence test (IQ).
- This disorder is slightly more common in males.

Borderline Intellectual Functioning: IQ 71–84, Can code on Axis II.

Mild: IQ approximately (50–55) 55–70, considered *educable,* able to perform at sixth grade level, can use minimal assistance, may need some supervision and guidance, can live in community or in supervised settings.

Moderate: IQ approximately (35–40) 35–55 (50–55), considered trainable, able to perform at second grade level, with moderate supervision can attend to their own personal care, can perform unskilled or semiskilled work, can live in the community.

Severe: IQ approximately (20–25) 20–35, (35–40) generally institutionalized, has little or no communicative speech, possible group home.

Profound: IQ below 20, generally total care required.

Note: All IQ score categories can have a margin of error, equivalent to a five-point overlap.

Source: Summarized criteria from the *Diagnostic and Statistical Manual of Mental Disorders, Fourth Edition, Text Revision.* Copyright 2000. American Psychiatric Association.

QUICK REFERENCE

PERVASIVE MENTAL DISORDERS

Pervasive mental disorders involve multiple functions and behaviors that are not considered normal at any age. Qualitative impairment in reciprocal interaction, verbal and nonverbal skills, imaginative activity, and intellectual skills.

autistic disorder: Severe form, onset in infancy or childhood, self-stimulating, self-injuring behaviors often present (i.e., rocking, spinning, head banging), poor prognosis, age of onset requirement in *DSM-IV-TR* is age 3.

New pervasive developmental disorders listed in *DSM-IV* (1995) and *DSM-IV-TR* (2000) include:

Rett's disorder: Only in females, deceleration of head growth, start out normal, problems develop at 5 to 24 months, loss of previously acquired hand skills, loss of social engagement, appearance of stereotyped movements, impaired language functioning generally associated with severe or profound mental retardation.

childhood disintegrative disorder: Normal development for two years then a drastic decline, followed by a loss of previously acquired skills, and development of autistic-like symptoms.

asperger's disorder: Autistic-like symptoms without language impairment, severely impaired social interaction.

Source: Summarized criteria from the *Diagnostic and Statistical Manual of Mental Disorders, Fourth Edition, Text Revision.* Copyright 2000. American Psychiatric Association.

"predominant disturbance in social relatedness is indiscriminate sociability or lack of selectivity in the choice of attachment figures" (APA, 2000, p. 128).

Criterion B states that the disorder cannot be diagnosed if the condition is solely related to a developmental delay (as in mental retardation, see Quick Reference) or a pervasive developmental disorder (see Quick Reference).

In addition to deficits in sociability, the child must meet the criteria that the *DSM-IV-TR* outlines for pathogenic care. Criterion C notes pathogenic care required if "(1) persistent disregard of the child's basic emotional needs for comfort, stimulation, and affection, (2) persistent disregard of the child's basic physical needs, and (3) repeated changes of primary caregiver that prevent formation of stable attachments (e.g., frequent changes in foster care)" (APA, 2000, p. 130).

THE DEFINITION USED IN PRACTICE

Since the criteria for RAD, as outlined in the *DSM-IV-TR,* is often considered too narrow in its scope, in practice a more inclusive clinical definition is often considered. Many seasoned practitioners who work in the area of attachment suggest that the current definition is limited because it focuses primarily on the sociability of a child and in practice appears to fall short in terms of covering the reactive behaviors of many children dealing with attachment issues (Zeanah, 2000). The result is that although the diagnosis of RAD is still taken from the *DSM-IV-TR,* it is being used in a freer and less stringent manner than most would expect, deviating from time to time from the specific criteria outlined in the *DSM-IV-TR.* In practice, "children exhibiting a multitude of behavior problems, problems that extend far beyond the *DSM-IV* [and *DSM-IV-TR*] criteria, are being diagnosed with RAD" (Hanson & Spratt, 2000, p. 139). In other words, it appears as if some practitioners have silently agreed to either modify or disagree with the *DSM-IV-TR* and move beyond the published criteria in order to realistically assess and treat children suffering from this debilitating illness. For example, Boris and Zeanah (1999), at the Tulane University School of Medicine, have developed alternative criteria for RAD. They write that, "in preliminary data from cases of infants and toddlers referred to an outpatient clinic, the alternative criteria were more reliably applied by clinicians than current *DSM-IV* criteria" (p. 5).

Furthermore, published journal articles on attachment research and books authored by attachment specialists go beyond those outlined in the *DSM-IV-TR* for RAD and indicate a wider range of behavioral symptoms for a child with attachment difficulties. The boxed chart gives examples of such behavioral lists from experts such as Daniel Hughes, Gregory Keck and Regina Kupecky, and Foster Cline and C. Helding. These lists, as well as others, vary from one another, yet a thread of consensus runs through all of them. These children have difficulties with relationships based on multiple problems with attachment that are severe enough to disturb individual, family, and social functioning.

Overall, the behavior of children with severe attachment difficulties is characterized as being aggressive, controlling, and attention seeking. In their attempts to control the external environment, children with severe attachment difficulties demonstrate a blatant disregard for authority. Children who have not had their needs met, develop more aggressive strategies in satisfying their needs, such as screaming, charming, or manipulating, all in an effort to gain control over others (Hughes, 1999). Many of the behaviors of children with attachment problems also include cruelty to others and animals; persistent lying, stealing, and self-destructive behaviors; thoughts about fire, blood, or gore; and refusal to accept responsibility for consequences or actions (Cline & Helding, 1999).

Another criticism of the *DSM-IV-TR* criteria for RAD is that it focuses on social behavior and not on the child's attachment to the primary attachment figure (Boris & Zeanah, 1999). The *DSM-IV-TR* diagnosis of RAD only captures part of the disorder: disturbances in the child's social abilities and the child's ability to

QUICK REFERENCE

FACTORS BEYOND *DSM-IV-TR*: INDIVIDUALS WITH SEVERE ATTACHMENT DIFFICULTIES

Children or adolescents with severe attachment difficulties:

- Often have a compulsive need to control others in the family and support system.
- May engage in intensive lying even when caught in the act.
- Exhibit poor response to attempts at discipline.
- Address physical contact, wanting too much or too little.
- Become indiscriminately friendly, often with strangers.
- Have easily discontinued or replaced relationships.
- Have poor communication, with many nonsense questions and chatter.
- Have difficulty learning and poor problem solving.
- Have poor eye contact, unless discussing being caught in a lie.
- Lack of empathy with little evidence of guilt or remorse.
- Often have the ability to see only in extremes, all bad or all good.
- Have habitual dissociation or habitual hypervigilance.
- Experience pervasive shame and difficulty reestablishing a bond following conflict.

Source: Compiled from Federeci (1998), Hughes (1997), and Reber (1996).

relate in a social context. Although mothers of children diagnosed with RAD will agree that the child's social abilities are disturbed, most would argue that the core of the issue lies in the mother-child relationship. Children with RAD typically project their anger, resentment, and sadness onto the mother; the mother becomes the main target. Attachment theory explains this reaction in its definition of the mother's job: to keep the child safe. For children with RAD, their mothers did not keep them safe. Thus, RAD is a disorder that occurs within the construct of relationships, namely between a child and his or her mother, and many argue that the diagnosis should place more of its emphasis on the relationship between the primary attachment figure and the child.

Attachment specialist Dr. Elizabeth Randolph proposed that the criteria for RAD be reserved for children who have been maltreated but do not have true attachment problems. She is suggesting that a new disorder be added to the *DSM* to address children's attachment difficulties that are a result of severe traumatization. This new disorder, a clinical syndrome already recognized by many attachment therapists, is identified as "attachment disorder." Dr. Randolph's research suggests that RAD is a disorder that deals with a child's social relatedness, where attachment disorder goes beyond the child's rage to be more comprehensive in addressing both the child's neurological difficulties and behavioral problems. Attachment disorder focuses on the behavioral issues of the child (those symptoms meeting the criteria for oppositional defiant disorder), the neurological development of the child, the child's history of placements, and brain injuries brought about from alcohol and/or drug exposure (E. M. Randolph, personal communication, August 2001). It is important to note that much of the literature written today does not make a distinction between RAD and attachment disorder. A great deal of the literature erroneously uses the two terms interchangeably. These two disorders are distinct from one another. As more research is conducted and the *DSM* becomes revised in the future to reflect this research, the difference in the two disorders will become clearer and more distinguishable, thus allowing practitioners to be more accurate in their diagnoses.

Thus, there is an overwhelming consensus within the attachment profession that a more legitimate and comprehensive description of RAD is necessary. It may take revising the criteria for RAD, or as Dr. Randolph has suggested, defining a new and separate disorder all together. For this chapter to address these practice and research concerns, yet work within the parameters currently defined by the *DSM-IV-TR,* the term RAD used from this point includes both the criteria defined in the *DSM-IV-TR* combined with the clusters of behavioral symptoms accepted among professionals treating these children.

STANDARDIZED MEASUREMENT AND
THE DIAGNOSTIC ASSESSMENT

Research indicates "there is no standardized or even widely accepted assessment protocol used to validate this diagnosis" (Hanson & Spratt, 2000, p. 140). However, one standardized tool that can assist in the diagnostic assessment is the measure adopted by attachment specialists known as the Randolph Attachment Disorder Questionnaire (RADQ). The RADQ was developed to measure the severity of a child's attachment disorder through identifying behaviors. It is important to make the distinction that the RADQ was developed to measure attachment disorder, not RAD (E. M. Randolph, personal communication, August 2001). Yet again, because the current *DSM-IV-TR* does not make a distinction between attachment disorder and RAD, the RADQ is discussed in this chapter as a means of identifying certain behaviors and behavioral patterns. Recall that "proponents of the diagnosis have suggested that RAD is the underlying cause of behavior problems" (Hanson & Spratt, 2000, p. 140). If the behaviors can be identified and grouped together as a related set of symptoms, an understanding of what is causing these behaviors can be reached, thus allowing for a better diagnostic assessment, more accurate intervention planning, and, thus, more effective treatment.

MISDIAGNOSIS AND TREATMENT

The behavioral lists developed by attachment specialist are similar to behaviors associated with other childhood disorders. Many children with RAD are typically misdiagnosed with these disorders instead. These include conduct disorder, oppositional defiant disorder, disruptive behavior disorder, posttraumatic stress disorder, and separation anxiety disorder (Reber, 1996). What differentiates RAD from these other disorders is a single factor: a history of attachment disruptions. Critics of the *DSM-IV-TR* definition of RAD argue that it is "problematic to make an assumption that the prevalence of abuse serves as a benchmark for the prevalence of RAD. Researchers do no rely on estimates of the number of sexual assault victims, for example, to derive estimates of posttraumatic stress disorder" (Hanson & Spratt, 2000, p. 140).

To further illustrate this point, a research study was conducted involving adopted children who had experienced deprivation in infancy. It compared these children with other adopted children who had not experienced deprivation in infancy. The study challenged "the notion that 'pathogenic parental care' is necessary for the diagnosis and suggests that the field may have some way to go in defining what constitutes a clinical case" (Boris & Zeanah, 1999, p. 6). Thus, practitioners must take this into consideration when diagnosing a child with RAD. They must not diagnosis children simply because they have a history of pathogenic parental care and conversely, they must not rule out the diagnosis of RAD simply because a child does not have a history of pathogenic parental care.

The risk is high when attachment disorders are left untreated. Although more longitudinal studies are necessary, there seems to be great potential for children with serious attachment problems to be later diagnosed as an adult with avoidant personality disorder, narcissistic personality disorder, borderline personality disorder, or other psychopathologies (Benedict, 1998, p. 34; Boris & Zeanah, 1999, p. 4). Many of the criteria for these disorders are remarkably similar to the behavioral characteristics of children with RAD. For example, antisocial personality disorder is described as a "pervasive pattern of disregard for and violation of the rights of others" (APA, 2000, p. 706). Many characteristics of this disorder include societal conformity issues, impulsivity, aggressiveness, lack of remorse, and repeated lying. In comparison to the behaviors listed on the RADQ, these behaviors have a chilling similarity.

In addition to the potential for mental disorders, when RAD is left untreated, children are at risk as adults for relational problems. "It is suggested that when children do not partake in interactive emotionally charged experiences with their primary caregiver that they are at risk for chronic relationship difficulties" (Boris & Zeanah, 1999, p. 5). These children are likely to grow up and have "serious problems developing and maintaining attachments with their spouses and children" (Hughes, 1999, p. 558).

ATTACHMENT THEORY

To fully understand the attachment disordered child, or the child diagnosed with RAD, a discussion of attachment theory along with the working models a child develops is warranted. "Much of the research examining mother-child interactions in neglectful families has been conducted within the attachment theory model" (Hanson & Spratt, 2000, p. 138). Attachment theory addresses and helps to comprehensively explain RAD.

The genesis of attachment theory is from the work of John Bowlby. Bowlby's writings, including the *Attachment Trilogy,* grew out of psychoanalytic theory in order to emphasize "the role of the child-parent relationship in the development of the personality and psychopathology" (C. George, 1996, p. 412). As seen by Bowlby, the basic nature of the child's tie to his or her mother is protection. A child's attachment behavior is activated in times of "pain, fatigue, and anything frightening, and also by the mother being or appearing to be inaccessible" (Bowlby, 1988, p. 3). This idea led Bowlby to propose that in order for a child to grow in a secure manner, the child and the mother must participate in a reciprocal relationship, with the primary function being that of protection. Thus, normal development occurs in a social context (Welch, 1988), which begins for a child in the mother-child relationship at birth.

Bowlby theorized that within this mother-child relationship, control systems are in place. He explained that the "simplest form of a control system is a regulator, the purpose of which is to maintain some condition constant." A simple metaphoric example Bowlby gave is that of a thermostat. A thermostat is designed "to switch on heat when temperature falls below the set level and switch it off when temperature rises above that level" (Bowlby, 1982, p. 42).

Thus, the attachment system is maintained by a system of reciprocal feedback between the mother and child, in which the child uses the mother as a secure base, thus using her as a regulator (Benedict, 1998).

A child who is scared or has needs such as hunger, instinctively searches to satisfy that need from his mother; the mother acts as the regulator and satisfies this need. Thus the child is gratified, is receptive to his mother's gratifying efforts, and returns to a state of homeostasis (Figure 5.1). Through these interactions, the child develops trust and, most importantly, fills the mother and child with joy, merriment, and full engagement (Levy & Orans, 1998; Hughes, 1997). Thus, attachment is not something mothers *do* to their children, but rather something that is

FIGURE 5.1 Attachment Cycle

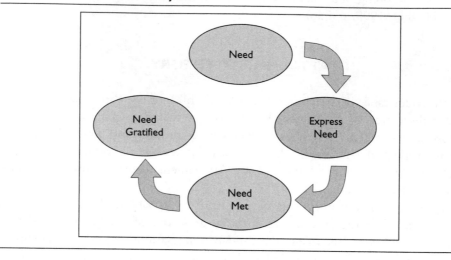

created together between the mother and the child. When this attachment cycle is not repeated, literally thousands of times (Hughes, 1997) in the mother–child relationship in the first two years, attachment problems are likely to occur.

The majority of children with RAD have experienced abusive or neglectful environments in which the attachment cycle was not completed. There is evidence that other factors can contribute to an impaired attachment as well. These include social parental risk factors such as partner violence, parental substance abuse, and adolescent parenthood (Boris & Zeanah, 1999). "Furthermore, factors such as prematurity, a difficult temperament, prolonged medical illness, physical anomalies, problematic feeding interactions, persistent colic, as well as developmental and neurological conditions (e.g., sensory loss, mental retardation, autism, and communication disorders) can contribute to impaired attachment and influence the likelihood that a child will react pathogenically to maltreatment" (Hanson & Spratt, 2000, p. 150).

Treatment Efficacy

Attachment theory can provide a foundation for the implementation of practice strategy in treating RAD and attachment disorders because it clearly explains the source of patterned behaviors exhibited by children that develop early in infancy. According to attachment theory, the foundation for a child's future experiences is laid within the first years of the child's life. This foundation is reflected in the mother–child relationship and serves as the ". . . basis for the full development of the child. All aspects of the child's development—neurological, physical, emotional, behavioral, cognitive, and social—are fundamentally effected by the quality of this unique relationship" (Hughes, 1997, pp. 11–12). Thus, attachment theory is a vital working model for clinicians to effectively understand, identify, and treat childhood attachment disorders.

Attachment theory refers to a pattern of behavior within a relationship. Attachment theory is not just a theory of outcome; it is a theory of process. Thus, attachment is not merely a developmental task to achieve; it is an experience that builds a framework in which children relate to their external environment. It is also important to recognize that the attachment system is part of the behavioral system. Too often, professionals neglect this concept and work solely with the behaviors of a child, not assessing or addressing the child's emotional state or attachment state. Within the attachment framework, it is understood that the behaviors are simply the manifestation of the feelings beneath the expression of a strained attachment. "What is not given enough attention is understanding the roots of the symptoms, which, when we are talking about traumatized children, lie among the thousands of experiences that occurred during the first two years of life" (Hughes, 1998). Attachment theory directly identifies these troubling behaviors as symptomatic of insecure attachments. These manifestations can be divided into four "internal working models" that a child uses in functioning in his or her social environment. These four internal working models defined by researchers, as a continuum to Bowlby's work, are critical components in working with attachment stressed children.

Internal Working Models

Bowlby's theoretical idea of attachment centered itself on the clinical concept of "internal working models" (Sroufe, Carlson, Levy, & Egeland, 1999). Bowlby proposed the idea that children will extract from their previous experiences in future experiences. This concept means that children's early attachment history will be reflected in how they will later react in their development; children's internal working models will define their approach to social situations and their reactions to others. It means that children will "approach new situations with certain preconceptions, behavioral biases, and interpretive tendencies" (Sroufe et al., 1999, p. 5). Thus, the internal working model serves as a blueprint for all current and future relationships (Levy & Orlans, 1998).

For clinicians, the use of attachment theory, as defined through the concept of internal working models, allows them to easily assess a child's attachment pattern and the parent-child relationship. Four attachment categories have been developed from empirical studies (Figure 5.2). These include (1) secure, (2) resistant/ambivalent, (3) disorganized/disoriented, and (4) avoidant. Children with a secure attachment are

FIGURE 5.2 Attachment Types

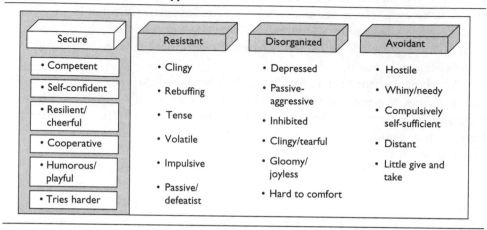

Secure	Resistant	Disorganized	Avoidant
• Competent	• Clingy	• Depressed	• Hostile
• Self-confident	• Rebuffing	• Passive-aggressive	• Whiny/needy
• Resilient/cheerful	• Tense	• Inhibited	• Compulsively self-sufficient
• Cooperative	• Volatile	• Clingy/tearful	• Distant
• Humorous/playful	• Impulsive	• Gloomy/joyless	• Little give and take
• Tries harder	• Passive/defeatist	• Hard to comfort	

Source: Adapted from M. G. Welch, videotape series: Creating and Repairing Attachment with Direct Synchronous Bonding, 1999.

organized in their behavior and thought, thus allowing them to maintain a functional relation with others. Bowlby argued that when the internal relationships are balanced, children develop a sense of security (Boris & Zeanah, 1999, p. 4). A securely attached child has developed a set of coherent and organized rules, based on experience that predicts and guides future behavior. These children have the ability to control impulses and emotions and are cooperative and compassionate. Securely attached children have a high level of self-esteem with positive core beliefs (Levy & Orlans, 1998, p. 45). They are appropriate in responsiveness and flexibility. Thus, securely attached children exhibit interest and ability in exploring their environments. They are also agreeable and competent in social interactions.

The insecure child (the child falling into the attachment categories of resistant/ambivalent, avoidant, and disorganized-disoriented), and thus, the child with attachment difficulties, has a negative self-concept and feels "I am bad, unwanted, worthless, helpless, unlovable." Since the insecure child's needs were not met in the past by the mother, the child has developed a model in which all those in authority are viewed as being unresponsive, insensitive, hurtful, and untrustworthy. In general, the insecure child perceives the world as an unsafe place and believes life is not worth living.

The resistant/ambivalent child is characterized by a child who becomes extremely distressed by the separation of the mother, yet is difficult to soothe upon the reunion of the mother and child. "Such children are inconsolable, yet obsessed with the parent, and vacillate between the need for closeness and anger at the parent" (Reber, 1996, p. 84). They are overly demanding of affection, seek closeness, and are clingy with the mother. They are also impulsive and volatile in their behaviors (Welch, 1999).

Children with avoidant attachments tend to be less affectionate, have an aversion to physical contact and touch, and tend to mask their anger with indifference. These children, when distressed, will not seek out the mother and, without fear, will be willing to be taken home by a stranger (Reber, 1996). Their behaviors against the mother tend to be more passive-aggressive. As avoidant children experienced rejection themselves, they subsequently expect rejection from others, as well as from themselves (Sroufe et al., 1999). And by avoiding others close to them, they are avoiding situations that have the potential for yet more rejection. Thus, they become compulsively self-sufficient and distant (Welch, 1999).

Children with disorganized/disoriented attachment patterns tend to exhibit the characteristics of both the resistant/ambivalent and the avoidant types. These children have no coherent coping strategies so they display diverse and sometimes contradictory behaviors. These behaviors may be incomplete and can include strong avoidance; undirected expressions of fear, distress, apprehension, or confusion; and dazed or disoriented expressions. They are typically depressed, anxious, and difficult for the parents to comfort (Welch, 1999).

Intergenerational Concerns

The clinician must also be aware of the concept that attachment is passed down from one generation to the next, primarily through the mother. The mother's inner working model of her early attachment experiences influences her responsiveness to the child's attachment signals. This, in turn, influences and sets the child's attachment pattern as shown in Figure 5.3. Thus, attachment is intergenerational and the type of maternal behavior experienced by the child directly influences the type of internal working model the child develops.

As discussed earlier, attachment theory proposes that children form internal working models of themselves based on the responsive nature of their mother. Children who are maltreated by their mother may form an internal working model of the mother as unresponsive, unavailable, and rejecting, thus feeling themselves to be unworthy and incompetent. It has also been discussed that this early relationship guides, or is the blueprint, for future relationships. Thus, it is of great concern that these children will continue this cycle when they themselves become parents. They will predictably be unable to form secure relationships with their own children.

Some researchers have pointed to the central role of fear of the mother in the attachment process. It has been noted that some mothers engage directly in frightening behaviors toward their infants. Others appear themselves to be frightened of

FIGURE 5.3   Maternal Behavior and Patterns of Attachment

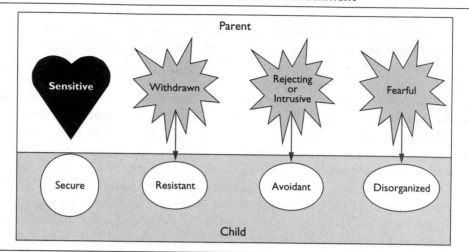

their infants. "Main and Hesse proposed that frightened parental behavior occurs spontaneously and is triggered internally, stemming from parents' thoughts or from events or objects in the environment associated with the parent's own traumatic experiences" (Broberg, 2000, p. 38). A frightening or frightened mother presents a dichotic problem for the child. The child's internal attachment behaviors are activated by the fear of the mother, yet it is the mother to whom the child is "programmed" to seek comfort. Thus, the mother is "at once the source of and the solution" (Broberg, 2000, p. 38) to the attachment response.

THE CASE OF JOSEPH

Joseph was adopted from an orphanage in Russia in 1996, at the age of 2½ years. At birth, his birth parents signed over their parental rights to the Russian Federation. Joseph was later transferred from a Russian hospital to a children's orphanage and remained in the same orphanage for his first 2½ years. Joseph's adoptive parents first met him in the Russian orphanage and brought him to his adoptive home in the United States five days after their initial contact. From the moment Joseph was adopted, he completely rejected his adoptive mother. For the first few months they were together, Joseph actively resisted physical contact with her. Joseph did, however, appear to initially bond with his new adoptive father. Joseph has been living with his adoptive parents for four years and is now 6½ years old.

Joseph's adoptive parents report that he exhibits behavior that has been very difficult to control for both parents, especially for his mother. He blatantly disregards his parents as authority

——————— THE CASE OF JOSEPH *(Continued)* ———————

figures. His parents describe their life with him as characterized by serious and intense control battles. Joseph often becomes oppositional and simply will not do what is asked of him. When Joseph is frustrated he quickly becomes very aggressive, outraged, and physically attacks or charges after either his mother or father. This happens often but is particularly likely to occur when he is forced to handle disruptions or changes in his daily schedule. Large amounts of stimulation, excitement, or emotion put Joseph into a chaotic state and he is typically hyperactive and has difficulties sitting still. Joseph's frustration tolerance is extremely low and he becomes easily agitated at the smallest difficulty. No amount of comforting from his father or mother can settle him down when he is upset, scared, or hurt. Joseph is extremely demanding of attention, especially from his mother and episodically wets his bed. Joseph has a constant need to be engaged in conversation with his mother and these communications are characterized by constant and incessant questioning. Joseph often comforts himself by sucking his two fingers and rocking himself to sleep. When apart from his mother, Joseph appears to do well in school, but upon initially returning home to his mother his behaviors markedly worsen.

The mother reports that all of these behaviors are experienced on an almost daily basis, at a high level of intensity. She also reports that many of these behaviors will last for two to three hours at a time (states of anger, aggression, and hyperactivity). Typical parenting strategies, such as time-out, depriving, rewards, and "talking it out," have proven futile. The mother has in the past implemented physical punishment such as spanking, yet reports that this resulted in the child becoming more aggressive and physically abusive back to his mother. Currently, the mother's only method of discipline that works is to contain the client physically by either wrapping her arms and legs around him, or holding him down while lying on top of him. During these times, Joseph resorts to hitting, biting, spitting, hair pulling, clawing, kicking, and head banging in his fight to be freed. Joseph has never been placed on medication and it is the desire of the mother to avoid medications.

According to his parents, past treatments have been unsuccessful and in some cases, worsened the behavior. For example, Joseph's parents sought the counsel of a behavioral analyst and used the intervention of "extinction." This technique was employed at times when Joseph would refuse a parental instruction. The extinction technique required that the instruction become the entire focus until Joseph conformed. According to the parents, Joseph became completely oppositional and outraged with this intervention. At times, it would take Joseph up to 3 hours to follow a simple instruction such as putting on his shoes. Joseph's response to this treatment became so severe that he smashed a window with his bare hands, charged at his mother with a pair of scissors, and continually threw objects at her. Joseph has also been seen by a childhood psychiatrist and a medical doctor specializing in childhood behavioral problems. According to the parents and the recorded treatment information available, these interventions proved to be unsuccessful as well for Joseph.

Gathering a Family History

Although the parent's commitment is intact, they are currently feeling overwhelmed by their child. At this point the mental health practitioner asked the mother to help complete a genogram for the child. In this way a better sense of family history could be obtained. As evidenced by the genogram, the mother stated that she especially was feeling depressed and highly stressed over her lack of control with her child. Her inability to comfort her child, to effectively discipline her child, and to satisfy her child's needs has left her depleted and frustrated. The mother has also stated that the rejection she faces daily with her own child has resurfaced many of her own unresolved childhood wounds. The mother states that the insensitivity she experienced in her family, with both her alcoholic father and alcoholic mother, are affecting her ability as a caring and sensitive mother. She states that the combination of these family of origin issues with her helplessness as a mother to her son has put her at her "screaming edge." As shown in Figure 5.4, the mother's family is rampant with divorce, abuse, and alcoholism. Joseph's father is supportive of his wife, yet has been unable to comfort her adequately. The couple has a stable and loving marital relationship but it has been overly stressed due to their child's behavior.

Application of the Multiaxial Diagnostic Assessment System

Due to a history of multiple caregivers in an environment in which his emotional, physical, and cognitive needs were not met, Joseph needs to be assessed for reactive attachment disorder, inhibited type, on Axis I (according to the attachment types listed previously from empirical studies, Joseph appears to have resistant attachment). Also on Axis I, Joseph appears to have posttraumatic stress disorder (PTSD), complex-unresolved, because the stress occurred during the

FIGURE 5.4 Client's Genogram

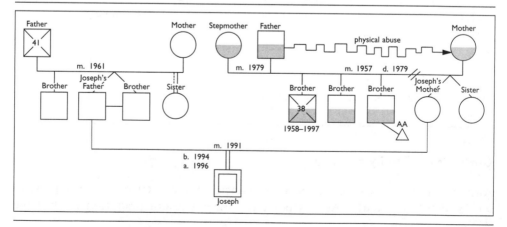

first two years of his life. Although Joseph would meet and exceed the minimum criteria for oppositional defiant disorder (ODD), it is believed that this symptomolgy is not due to this other disorder and rests with the attachment disorder only. It appears that the ODD is simply a by-product of the RAD and that these behaviors will be resolved upon treatment for RAD. In addition, Joseph could also be assessed with enuresis, nocturnal only. It is possible that it may be secondary to the diagnosis of RAD and will be included in the intervention planning because of the extensive tension it is creating in the family system. Bed-wetting often ceases after four to six weeks of attachment therapy (Welch, 1988, p. 228).

In Axis II, no diagnosis will be given. Joseph's disorder is not a personality disorder, nor is his intellectual functioning below normal. Medical records indicate that the client is in excellent physical condition, thus, Axis III will also not be given a diagnosis.

Axis IV will indicate that the client has a history of neglect and multiple caregivers with ambivalent attachment patterns. Adding this to Axis IV will help to explain why the PTSD has not been resolved. Under the framework of attachment theory, Joseph's attachment skills are still weak and he lacks the ability to utilize the stable and caring environment of his adoptive home. He also lacks the ability to trust or rely on his parents for a secure attachment base, and thus continues to use his own self-reliant ways of coping, which are ineffective, destructive, and socially unacceptable (Hughes, 2000).

The Global Assessment Functioning (GAF) Scale on Axis V will currently be scored at a 35. Client presents with major impairments in family relations. As mentioned, he frequently attacks his mother and he is deliberately defiant at home. This score is solely based on a subjective interpretation of the rating scale outlined

---

QUICK REFERENCE

JOSEPH'S MULTIAXIAL ASSESSMENT

Axis I: 313.89 Reactive Attachment Disorder, Inhibited Type (resistant attachment).
            39.81 Posttraumatic Stress Disorder (PTSD), Chronic (complex-unresolved).
            307. 6 Enuresis, Nocturnal Only (provisional).

Axis II: V71.09 No Diagnosis.

Axis III: None.

Axis IV: History of neglect and multiple caregivers with ambivalent attachment pattern.

Axis V: 35 (current).

in the *DSM-IV-TR,* as it is designed primarily for adults and does not specifically address young children. Although Joseph is frequently violent, a lower score will not be given considering his young age. If Joseph were older and more physically capable of harm, a lower GAF score would be considered.

Treatment Plan Considerations

Intervention efforts will need to focus on developing Joseph's ability to accept and enter into a relationship with his mother and father. Helping him to gain more security and comfort in his relationships will further help him resolve the trauma of his early childhood and will help to strengthen his ability to engage in a reciprocal, loving relationship. From this perspective, intervention efforts will be family centered and use attachment theory as the theoretical basis.

Goals for Joseph to accomplish include the following:

- Contain and reduce aggressive behaviors.
- Allow Joseph to express and identify his anger and other difficult emotions in a productive and less hurtful manner.
- Allow Joseph to experience a reciprocal parent-child interaction within a safe and loving environment.
- Joseph will develop a positive self-concept.
- Joseph will relinquish control to his parents, reframing his destructive equation that equates survival to control.
- Joseph will learn that the home is a safe and secure base.

Goals for Joseph's mother and father to accomplish include the following:

- Mother to address and resolve her family-of-origin issues.
- Parents to regain sense of control over their child.
- Mother and father to improve their communication, understanding, and ability to console each other in their marital relationship.
- Mother and father to learn effective parenting techniques of children with RAD, with skills to regulate and to facilitate attachment with their child.
- Information about RAD will be provided to the parents in order to educate, restore hope, and reduce anxiety.
- Referral for attendance in support groups (in person or Internet) for parents with children who have RAD.

Once the goals of the intervention process have been identified, the objectives must be identified. Proper implementation of the objectives listed below requires the full participation and commitment of the family, especially the mother. Working under the attachment model, it is the mother who needs to be the primary facilitator of the stated goals, and thus will be required to fully participate and accomplish the objectives. It is believed that with her active participation and support, she will be able to reach Joseph at an emotional level and will be able to teach him to express his emotions verbally with her in order to develop a healthier level of bonding for them both. The father's role is to be a support for the mother and as a parent assist and encourage his child.

Intervention Objectives:

- Mother will continue to physically contain the client when he becomes anxious, angry, or aggressive, yet through a safer and more effective means. To accomplish this she will watch a video tape and role-play the demonstrations of more passive restraint.
- Mother will provide a safe, honest, and loving environment for the child to resolve and understand his emotions.
- Mother is to join adoptive support group through the Internet.
- Mother is to allow the client to verbally and physically release his anxieties, frustrations, fears, and sadness with her.
- Mother will verbally and physically release her anxieties, frustrations, fears, and sadness with her husband.
- Mother is to remove her child from school and register her child for home school status with the local school system.
- Mother is to seek professional help to confront her family of origin issues with both her mother and father.
- Mother and father are to read from a recommended reading list of attachment books and articles.
- Mother and father are to watch a recommended series of videos with parenting strategies for how to best handle children with RAD.

Joseph was given a provisional diagnosis of enuresis because of his repeated incidents of bed-wetting (enuresis) at night. This diagnosis was given provisionally for two reasons. First, the enuresis may be a direct result of the RAD and may be resolved through successful treatment of RAD. The second reason relates to the "art" of clinical judgment. If the diagnosis of enuresis is related directly to the RAD, it may get better with or without intervention. Helping the family along in this process by setting up a treatment plan that is doable may help to build confidence for all involved. Joseph may start to feel better about himself if he can learn to control his urine at night. In turn, providing intervention in this area may help his parents to become less frustrated and also experience the same sense of progress and success. Regardless, since there is not enough information at this time to determine whether he clearly has the disorder or not, giving the provisional diagnosis and beginning to address the condition in practice could be beneficial to all. See sample treatment plan for ideas in formulating goals and objectives in this area.

ELIMINATION DISORDER, ENURESIS/NOCTURNAL ONLY

Definition: Enuresis is repeated voiding of urine during the day or at night into bed or clothes. Diurnal is voiding of urine only during waking hours. Involuntary urination in children aged older than 5.

Signs and Symptoms to Note in the Record:

1. Voiding of urine has been occurring at least twice a week for the past three months.
2. Significant distress or impairment in social, academic, or other important areas of functioning.
3. Voiding of urine is not directly related to a medical condition.
4. Individual will be at least 5 years old.
5. Reoccurring urinary tract infections.

Goals:

1. Eliminate incidents of urination in bed.
2. Client will learn proper toileting routine before bedtime.
3. Urinate in the toilet independently during the night, without being woken by parents.

Objectives	Interventions	Time Frame
Client will complete developmental, mental, nutritional, physical, and psychosocial examination, to rule out organic etiology.	Practitioner will make referrals and will assist parents to arrange medical appointments, and testing.	1 month for physical, 2 months for other appointments.
Parents will monitor how many times accidents occur.	Practitioner will teach parents to create diary. Parents will markdown every time child has wet the bed.	
Parents will set up a toileting schedule during the sleeping hours.	Practitioner and parents will review charted information and set up a toileting schedule during the times when the child is most likely to have an accident during the night.	
Parents will assist in taking child to the toilet during scheduled times at night.	The parent will take child to the toilet during the times charted on the schedule.	
Parents will reward child when he has successfully urinated not wet the bed.	Parents will praise as reward.	
Child will practice good personal hygiene before bedtime (i.e., toileting skills).	If child has accident, parents will guide child to clean up the mess.	Continue until no longer having accidents.
Maintain dry bed for at least 7 hours per night.	Void before going to bed. Restrict fluid intake at least 3 hours before going to bed. Log successes in journal each morning upon rising from bed. Tally number of dry nights per week in journal. Reward successes with praise.	2 months.

Practice Strategy

To meet these established goals and objectives, the application of the concepts of attachment therapy is recommended. Since so many of these children live in an inner world of anger and fear, attachment therapy is needed to release the internalized rage in order for the child to be able to accept love. Unfortunately, research and literature reviews report, "significant attachment problems tend to be quite resistant to therapeutic change" (Hughes, 1999, p. 556). "Traditional psychological treatment techniques which are supportive, reflective, and depend on insight are ineffective for children with RAD" (Reber, 1996). These types of therapy work on the premise that the individual can trust authority, has sufficient concern for others, and feels enough anxiety or guilt to want to change. These therapies are typically based on cognitive theory and will not reach and change a child at the depth of an emotional disorder such as RAD (Pickle, 2000). Behavioral modification techniques, as seen with Joseph, can be just as unsuccessful and, in fact, can amplify the child's anger-filled behaviors. Thus, attachment therapy may provide the best alternative.

It is important to note at this point that the goals, objectives, and interventions are not community-based. In fact, they are on the opposite end of the continuum. Joseph is currently having his difficulties inside of the home, not outside of the home, and in this case a community-based approach would be detrimental to Joseph's treatment. Outside interactions with Joseph would only serve to distract him from his mother and allow him to withdraw even further. Instead, the focus needs to be contained within the home itself. The goals and objectives are solely based on the relationship between Joseph and his mother (and his father). The mother is to stay with the client 24 hours a day, 7 days a week, with the child having no direct interaction with friends, teachers, or baby-sitters.

In utilizing attachment therapy, the current research on effective attachment interventions is limited (Hanson & Spratt, 2000). It is believed, however, that in order for the therapy to be effective, it has to be long term and it needs to be targeted at deep structural changes aimed at the representational level for the client. Change for Joseph has to occur in the internal working models developed from his past orphanage experiences of inconsistent and unsympathetic care giving. "It is such preverbal experiences that Bowlby (1973) emphasized in his discussion of the enduring effects of early attachment relationships" (Sroufe et al., 1999, p. 4). These missing early attachment experiences need to be re-created.

Bowlby described the emotion that accompanies attachment behavior as "intense" (Bowlby, 1988) and as stated earlier, secure attachments develop with intense emotionally charged interactions. Thus, reaching a child at this level takes intense radical relationship-focused intervention and for these reasons, the chosen treatment for Joseph is holding therapy. There are several different types of holding therapy being practiced in attachment therapy and all are limited in published and proven effectiveness. However, most practitioners in the attachment field would argue that it is the only therapy that offers hope for true change. There are several different types of holding therapy being used and it is important to recognize the differences. Some attachment therapist use holding therapy whereby the therapist does the holding with the child, not the parent. Others direct the parent to do the holdings with the child, yet use a soft approach with limited confrontation. Martha G. Welch has developed a more directive type of holding whereby only the mother holds the child, never the therapist, in order for a synchronized bonding to be created between the dyad. This type of holding is known as Welch Method Direct Synchronous Bonding (DSB).

Holding therapy, in general, is a controversial form of intervention being practiced today for children with RAD. If one were to watch a therapeutic hold for the first time, without an understanding behind the technique, he or she might perceive it to be abusive or coercive. Critics believe it is a violation of the child's rights to be held and that therapy should always follow the child's lead. Many critics further believe that strong confrontation is bad for children. However, many proponents of holding therapy believe it to be exactly the opposite. Some attachment professionals believe that children with RAD need strong confrontation in order to break through the child's overdeveloped defenses. Other attachment professionals believe that physical touch is necessary in their therapeutic experiences in order for deep interior changes to happen because children with RAD are so skillful at keeping people at a distance.

In this case presentation, Welch Method DSB is the particular type of holding therapy being advocated for Joseph. Welch Method DSB has been chosen because of its emphasis on the direct, intense interaction of the mother, where the mother becomes the catalyst for change. Welch Method DSB allows both the mother and the child to release their anger; it uses anger in a positive way in order to help reach all the other emotions buried within the pair. Welch Method DSB addresses both the needs of the child and the mother. It is "only when the needs of both mother and child are met will the child's behavior improve" (Welch, 1999). Attachment is not something that can be taught to either the mother or child. As Bowlby explained, it is a process both the mother and child must experience simultaneously. Thus, therapeutic holding interventions aimed at the child alone, without the mother, were not chosen.

Welch Method DSB is a nurturing and maternally sensitive technique. With Welch Method DSB, the mother-child hold begins with the mother taking the child into her arms and holding him closely. If the child is too large for this cradle hold, the child lies down on his or her back and the mother lies on top of him or her, with her face facing the child's. This physical contact is imperative to the success of this intervention. "Synchrony can only be achieved when mother and child interrelate with direct physical contact" (Welch, 1999). Several stages generally follow and the mother continues to hold the child until there is final resolution between the child and the mother. At the beginning, the child has a short period of feeling good in the mother's arms. Then the child begins to want out of the hold and becomes angry and attempts to get free. The child then works through this conflictual stage with the mother, usually with a full range of emotions from yelling to crying to attempts at biting or hitting. It is at this stage that the anger and conflict is used in a positive way in order to reach resolution. Once the anger is expressed by both the mother and child, the deeper emotions beneath can then be explored. Having the child then express his or her sadness verbally along with other emotions, allows the final stage to happen. The child finally becomes accepting of the mother and they end the hold with resolution. The child is then able to fully respond to the mother's love and touch, and this then allows the mother to regulate her child. This also leaves the mother feeling calmer and more loving toward her child (Reber, 1996). In correlation to Bowlby's concept that regulation between the mother and child is part of the attachment process, Welch Method DSB directly and intensely activates this behavioral system, creating an environment conducive to attachment.

In this case presentation, the therapist believes that Welch Method DSB will allow Joseph to feel his hurt and sadness within a protected atmosphere. Joseph's internal working model has been structured to communicate to him that feeling sad, angry, scared, or shameful makes him vulnerable and thus, he has learned to fear his emotions and his needs. As he continues to fear his needs and to avoid his emotions, the denial of them leads to anger, aggression, tantrums, opposition, withdrawal, and/or low self-esteem (Welch, 1999). This process is cyclical. If Joseph feels hurt, then he becomes afraid. He then does not want to feel these emotions. He then fights for his life in order to keep from being hurt and from feeling these emotions. Welch Method DSB will allow Joseph to work through his past emotions and push him to express his buried feelings while being loved during the cathartic experience of the hold. He is safe within the embrace of his mother. With his mother doing the holding, he will then be allowed to begin to understand that his mother is there to love him, not hurt him, thus redefining his negative earlier experiences, redefining his internal working models. Welch Method DSB will also teach him that when he experiences negative emotions in the future, his mother will be there to help him, and thus, he will begin to trust her as well (Reber, 1996).

Joseph's treatment is to first begin with two full-day sessions under the therapist's direction. This will ensure that the parents receive proper instructions for the therapy as well as for them to receive the needed support as they begin this emotionally draining therapy. The parents are to continue the therapy at home, daily, and are also to continue to meet with the therapist for weekly sessions. In order to assess the effectiveness of this therapy, the mother will keep a daily journal of

Joseph's behaviors. It is expected that significant and permanent changes will be apparent within six months.

The Welch Method DSB will also be used to help the mother and father improve on their marital relationship. Welch Method DSB for this adult relationship would be conducted in the same manner, with the husband physically on top of the mother and with the two embracing each other in the hold. Again, the confrontation and anger are used as a tool in order to reach deep emotions that have been buried and it will help the couple to find some of their "honeymoon" connections that have been lost. Communication between the two will improve once the anger and frustrations are released, allowing resolution to happen at a deeper level. Thus, each other's needs can be fully met.

Special Considerations: Involvement of Extended Family

As much of the success of treatment relies on the mother, it is often important to take into consideration the mother and father's history with their extended family as well. Mothers especially, often have an attachment problem which has been carried over from their earlier childhood. When the mother is trying to parent a child who refuses to be parented, these childhood issues can be triggered by the stress of being rejected by her own child. This serves to further complicate the situation and interferes with the mother's ability to attach (M. G. Welch, personal communication, June 2000). It is necessary to first break the intergenerational cycle of insecure attachments for the mother to achieve sensitive responsiveness to her child (Broberg, 2000, p. 39). In this case, it is evident that Joseph's mother is having difficulties stemming from her childhood. Direct involvement from her mother (Joseph's maternal grandmother) and her father (Joseph's maternal grandfather) is imperative. Treatment would include holding sessions with these grandparents with the mother in order to resolve the issues of the past. These intergenerational holds will allow the mother to be liberated from her past pains to be emotionally available to Joseph, even during times of his complete rejection.

Additional support is also needed for the mother as the treatment involves isolation in the home with her child. Although the isolation is imperative for the child, it will be extremely difficult for the mother. The mother will be encouraged to meet with outside support systems, such as those at her church or within her inner social circle, to explain to them the situation and treatment she and her family will be under going. The mother must use these support systems, along with her husband and extended family, to receive the emotional support she needs during this treatment period. If the mother finds that she is not receiving enough support through theses channels, individual therapy is recommended either weekly or every other week, while the father takes care of Joseph in her short absence.

SUMMARY AND FUTURE DIRECTIONS

Unlike some of the other childhood disorders listed in the *DSM-IV-TR*, RAD is an emotionally intense social disorder, occurring in the context of relationships. A child's ability to form an attachment begins within the confines of the home environment in the simplest of all community units: the family. As evident in the examples given at the beginning of this chapter, however, the repercussions of this disorder do not stay contained within the walls of the home. It is society that later suffers from these individuals' unstable home environments. In Bowlby's early work, he researched the backgrounds of 44 thieves and found a "consistent background of early parental privation in the lives of these young men. He reasoned that this was no mere coincidental association but, rather, had causal implications" (Sroufe et al., 1999, p. 1).

With the awareness of the impact of unresolved attachment patterns, it becomes evident that mental health professionals, and society as a whole, need to address these risk factors. "The costs of ignoring this problem are great, both on a financial level and in terms of human lives" (Pickle, 2000, p. 262). Preventative work needs to be community based and needs to place its focus in three areas: biological factors, familial factors, and societal factors. These costs are already evident in our criminal justice system, our mental health systems, our domestic violence systems, and in our homeless population. Children with attachment difficulties grow up taking only what they need, taking it when they want it, and taking it without considering the rights of others. They do not recognize authority and do not like to be told to do anything. These characteristics do not make for productive and happy members of society.

Currently, RAD is not fully recognized in our society as a severe and legitimate disorder. The significance of attachment has been known since the 1950s, yet it has not been incorporated in the curriculum of most schools preparing professionals who will be working with and treating these children. School systems, medical professionals, social service agencies, and other community systems need to acknowledge and embrace the seriousness of attachment-related problems. "There are a limited number of professionals who have a good understanding of attachment disorder and who have the training and expertise to effectively work with the child who has attachment disorder and his/her family" (Pickle, 2000, p. 267). More efforts need to be made in order to educate, train, and supervise therapists in the field of attachment work.

All three components regarding attachment are relatively new: attachment theory, the diagnosis of RAD, and attachment therapy. The diagnosis of RAD was developed out of the need to address children with attachment disorders and will be revised and redefined as more research is concluded. To free the sufferings of these children, more longitudinal research needs to be undertaken in order for helping professionals and their professional associations to form a consensus as to the definition and criteria of RAD or other disorders created to adequately address this illness. Continuity between the professional community, the research community, and the APA is imperative. More research and more studies are also desperately needed to substantiate treatments for RAD currently in practice or to provide other viable treatment modalities for these children and their families.

Treatment for RAD has the potential of saving these children from growing into other mental disorders and treatment is needed for these children to experience inner freedom of safety and love and the healthy development of their whole selves. The short-term implications of treatment can be seen in the single family structure, but the long-term implications of successful attachment therapy can be seen throughout society. RAD as a mental disorder clearly needs to be studied further and needs to be redefined to address the severe attachment difficulties of the children that suffer from this disorder.

6 Conduct Disorder

SHIRLEYANN AMOS AND SOPHIA F. DZIEGIELEWSKI

Conduct disorder is a diagnosis first made during childhood or adolescence and can result in barriers to individual and social functioning. Since first being introduced in the *Diagnostic and Statistical Manual of Mental Disorders (DSM-III)*, the diagnosis of conduct disorder continues to raise many questions for practitioners. Concerns center around its validity and application of criteria, as well as the negative impact that this diagnosis can have on children. Most practitioners agree that there is a "muddy" consensus as to what defines conduct disorder and how it will progress over time. Furthermore, the actual etiology (cause) of this condition continues to remain a mystery even though research studies are ongoing. Thus, it is essential for practitioners to keep updated on what is happening in controlled field trials, and how this can affect condition identification and progress.

To understand conduct disorder, we start with an overview of the disorder focusing on the risk factors and symptoms, the diagnostic criteria, the problems identifying the disorder, and the different interventions that have been used for treatment. Children or adolescents with conduct disorder demonstrate behaviors that violate societal norms or the basic rights of others. These negative behaviors can result from particular risk factors that have been noted to be precursors to conduct disorder. Some of the risk factors associated with the development of conduct disorder include cognitive deficits, academic failure, confrontational aggressive parent-child interaction, familial dysfunction, and environmental issues. Since one risk factor does not necessarily determine that a child or adolescent will have behavior problems, it is essential for the practitioner to be aware that when the risk factors are combined, they magnify the possibility for conduct disorder.

Once the risk factors are identified and understood, intervention support and efficacy in terms of parenting and developmental education classes can be utilized to improve the likelihood that a child diagnosed with attention-deficit/hyperactivity disorder (ADHD) will be less likely to develop conduct disorder. Inclusion of this type of supportive intervention may prevent the resulting behaviors from becoming severe enough to result in a dual diagnosis such as ADHD and conduct disorder.

When an individual is diagnosed with conduct disorder, intervention options can vary. This chapter is discusses conduct disorder from a community and societal perspective. In order to reduce the magnitude of disturbances this disorder can have on the individual, the family, and society it is critical that practitioners complete a thorough diagnostic assessment, treatment plan, and practice strategy that can efficiently embrace, identify, and effectively treat individuals who suffer from conduct disorder.

USE OF THE *DSM-IV-TR* MULTIAXIAL SYSTEM

According to the *DSM-IV-TR* (American Psychiatric Association [APA], 2000), conduct disorder refers to a diverse cluster of problem behaviors involving persistent violations of the rights of others and of major social rules. Children and adolescents with this disorder often behave aggressively toward people and animals. For example, they may initiate frequent fights; bully, intimidate, or threaten others; or torture animals. In some cases, acts of aggression include rape, assault with a deadly weapon, or homicide. Children and adolescents with conduct disorder tend to engage in destructive behavior that results in loss or damage to other peoples' property. These children may vandalize public buildings, set fires, or break up furniture in the family home. They may also engage in deceitfulness as evidenced by chronic lying, breaking promises, or stealing. Finally, children with conduct disorder tend to violate important rules set by parents and school officials resulting in behaviors such as staying out late, running away overnight, or repeatedly failing to attend school. Overall, most children with conduct disorder tend to lack empathy for others, show poor frustration tolerance, and high levels of irritability.

Associated Conditions and Problems

Children and adolescents who suffer from conduct disorder often experience pervasive problems in social and academic functioning. Children with conduct disorder tend to show lower intelligence, achievement, and school adjustment than their peers who do not suffer from conduct disorder (APA, 2000). In addition, reading disabilities are especially prominent. Furthermore, these symptoms of emotional and behavioral maladjustment often lead to a high degree of overlap between conduct disorder and attention–deficit/hyperactivity disorder. Children with conduct disorder suffering from a dual diagnosis, display more severe and persistent antisocial behaviors than those with a single diagnosis. Furthermore, dually diagnosed children are also more likely than others to have fathers with severe antisocial psychopathology. Finally, a significant number of children with conduct disorder qualify for a diagnosis of depressive disorder, particularly during adolescence.

Generally, these cognitive and academic behavior problems begin early in life and remain chronic throughout the individual's school career. Children with conduct disorder show equally broad-ranging problems in their social adjustment. Conduct problems tend to co-occur with a diverse range of overlapping familial and social-ecological stressors, including poor child management skills, parental psychopathology, marital distress and discord, poverty, and social isolation (First, Frances, & Pincus, 1995; Frances & Ross, 1996; Thyer & Wodarski, 1998).

Moreover, children with conduct disorder experience high levels of peer rejection with their aggressive and annoying behaviors. Over time, peers begin to counterattack and provoke these children, thereby creating a negative spiral of aggression and rejection. In addition, children with conduct disorder often tend to have poor and nonsupportive relationships with their teachers and many significant individuals in their lives including parents, significant others, family members, and school personnel. Not surprisingly, parents and school officials often clash over how to best address and deal with the child's behavior problems (First et al., 1995; Frances & Ross, 1996; Thyer & Wodarski, 1998).

Historical Aspects and Application

Conduct disorder was first included in the *DSM-III* (APA, 1980). In *DSM-IV* and *DSM-IV-TR,* the age of onset of antisocial symptoms was added and is now used to subtype conduct disorder. Early–onset conduct disorder requires that at least one criterion characteristic (1 of 15 antisocial behaviors) is present before age 10 years, whereas if the first antisocial behavior occurs at or after 10 years, the case is classified as adolescent onset (APA, 1994). The adoption of this subclassification in the *DSM-IV* was stimulated by reports of differences between early- and adolescent-onset cases suggesting different causal pathways.

Early–onset cases are more likely than adolescent-onset cases to be boys, to be aggressive, and to have attention-deficit/hyperactivity disorder. They may also be more inclined to evolve to conduct disorder from oppositional defiant disorder or from neuropsychological deficits, academic failures, poor school attendance, or family disadvantage. The *DSM-IV-TR* describes the difference between oppositional defiant disorder and subsequent development of childhood-onset type of conduct disorder by explaining that those with conduct disorder have a persistent pattern of more serious forms of behavior, such as violating basic rights of others or age–appropriate societal norms or rules.

This subtyping has been enthusiastically embraced even though it is based chiefly on early work involving delinquent adolescents and on a limited longitudinal study of children with diagnosed conduct disorder. Additional risk factors for developing conduct disorder such as genetic and environmental factors are also included.

Gender differences are also found in the varying types of conduct problems. Boys more commonly display confrontational aggression whereas girls tend to use

---

QUICK REFERENCE

CONDUCT DISORDER

- Individuals who suffer from conduct disorder often exhibit a pattern of behavior that violates rights of others.
- Symptoms are grouped in four categories:
    1. Aggression to people and animals.
    2. Destruction of property.
    3. Deceitfulness or theft.
    4. Serious violations of rules.
- Two criteria were added to increase applicability to females: staying out at night and intimidating others.
- There are new subtypes based on age of onset: childhood and adolescent (onset prior to age 10 has a poor prognosis).
- Historically, when a child turned 18 diagnosis was changed to antisocial but now can remain conduct disorder into early 20s.
- Remember, not all conduct disorders become antisocials and this diagnosis is clearly more common in males.

Source: Summarized criteria from the *Diagnostic and Statistical Manual of Mental Disorders, Fourth Edition, Text Revision.* Copyright 2000. American Psychiatric Association.

---

more nonconfrontational behaviors. For example, boys frequently exhibit fighting, stealing, vandalism, and school discipline problems, and girls are most likely to exhibit running away, substance use/abuse, truancy, lying, and prostitution (APA, 2000).

THE CASE OF CHARLIE

An 11-year-old Caucasian boy named Charlie was always in trouble and had been brought to the attention of school authorities since age 7 for truancy, fights, and petty thefts. He is currently staying in a juvenile detention facility after hitting his older brother in the head with a can of soda while he was sleeping. Charlie is the youngest of three brothers and one sister. His mother and father stated that since Charlie attended first grade, they have received numerous calls and consultations for disruptive and aggressive behavior, school problems, and difficulties with peer relationships. They state that they are unable to control him. They report Charlie is a "fibber" and when questioned about the truth of his statements he becomes defiantly irate and walks away. In defiance of his parent's attempt to control his behaviors and actions, Charlie frequently stays out with friends, without telling his parents where he is going or where he has been. His mother reported that he has run away twice from home after arguments with her and his dad. She also suspects that he often takes money from her purse or his father's wallet without permission.

THE CASE OF CHARLIE (*Continued*)

Charlie was diagnosed with attention-deficit/hyperactivity disorder in the first grade because of home, school, and social disruptions. His behavior was reported to be inattentive, hyperactive, and impulsive and involved verbal and physical fights and disruptions in classrooms such as inattention, yelling, running, and jumping. More recently, he was expelled from school when he and two friends were fighting in the school hallway and he and friends set fire to school property. He began stealing in the second grade, had been held back two years in elementary school, and now was failing in the fourth grade.

He refused to do homework when he was in school because he stated that schoolwork was boring and openly preferred to play video games that revolved around violence with "blood and guts." After school on several occasions, he chased classmates who had angered him. Charlie reports that he often thinks about killing someone, and when he does the police will finally take him out of his house.

A series of thefts from neighborhood stores and classmates, fighting in the hallways at school, and the incident in which he and a companion set a fire at school resulted in pending criminal charges. The judge placed him in a juvenile detention facility and sent him to a mental health facility for evaluation. In the juvenile detention facility, Charlie originally appeared to befriend other adolescents and several staff members; however, soon the staff reported that he was demanding, manipulative, and volatile. He frequently stormed out of supportive therapeutic groups and care plan meetings when decisions were made that did not go his way. He tried hard to ensure that all activities revolved around him and was enthusiastic about them at first. Later, however, he appeared angry and moped around when he was not permitted to monopolize the activity. Beneath his apparent bravado, however, the staff found him insecure and dependent.

Charlie slashed his wrist two months ago and ended up in the psychiatric ward of the hospital for an attempted suicide. He reported that he did not feel he could do anything right and being expelled from school put him over the edge.

Environmental stresses increased six years ago, when Charlie's parents both had to take on extra work to adequately support the family. When Charlie was five, his father had difficulty keeping employment because of his alcohol problem. It was not until Charlie was eight that his father began treatment for alcoholism. Although Charlie wants to get along with his father, his father finds it difficult to cope with Charlie's willfulness and anger. When verbal efforts at discipline fail, his father resorts to harsh corporal punishment, often with a switch. The family is plagued with financial hardships and moved six months ago for better paying jobs and employment opportunities.

Charlie was court ordered for an evaluation, assessment, and presentation of intervention options to this mental health agency. Once completed and an intervention plan established, the judge has agreed to court order Charlie to engage in and complete counseling and to remain in juvenile justice detention for the remainder of his probation period. Charlie's parents and his siblings are fearful of him and no longer trust Charlie's unpredictable behavior and want to discuss out-of-home placement options when he is ready for discharge.

QUICK REFERENCE

IDENTIFY PRIMARY AND PRESENTING PROBLEM

Primary Problem:	Conduct disorder/childhood-onset type, severe.
Presenting Problems:	Court ordered mental health evaluation due to his involvement in thefts and fire setting.

COMPLETION OF THE DIAGNOSTIC ASSESSMENT

The diagnostic assessment began with the collection of biological and psychosocial information. Charlie is an 11-year-old boy with a history of attention-deficit/hyperactivity disorder that was present at age 5, with escalating disciplinary problems since age 7. He is the youngest of three brothers and one sister. There is a family history of antisocial disorder and alcoholism suggestive of a biological basis for attention-deficit/hyperactivity disorder that may place him and his other siblings at higher risk for developing conduct disorder. Charlie denies use of any illicit drugs or substances. He is currently in a juvenile detention facility after expulsion from his home by both the judge and his parents as a result of him hitting an older brother over the head with a full can of coke while his brother was sleeping.

Once the primary and presenting problems have been identified the first task of the mental health practitioner, especially with the child's history of violence toward self and others, is to complete a risk assessment. Key questions need to identify the potential for suicide risk, violence to others risk, and child abuse risk. These questions are asked in a straightforward and direct manner. Once identified, this information needs to be clearly recorded.

The second step for the mental health practitioner is to identify client strengths and behaviors that contribute to impairment in daily functioning. In addition, the clinician should observe the client's appearance, mood, attitude, affect, speech, motor activity, and orientation. Mental functioning should be assessed in terms of the client's ability to complete simple calculations, serial sevens, immediate memory,

QUICK REFERENCE

RISK ASSESSMENT

Document and assess suicide risk:	No evidence or none.
Document and assess violence risk:	Slight.
Document and assess child abuse risk:	Slight.

remote memory, general knowledge, proverb interpretation, and recognition of similarities and differences. In addition, questions in regard to higher order abilities and thought form and content need to be processed.

Mental Status Description

Presentation	Mental Functioning	Higher Order Abilities	Thought Form/Content
Appearance: Unkempt	Simple Calculations: Mostly accurate	Judgment: Impulsive	Thought Process: Logical and organized
Mood: Anxious		Insight: Intact	
Attitude: Guarded	Serial Sevens: Accurate	Intelligence: Low	Delusions: None
Affect: Appropriate	Immediate Memory: Intact		Hallucinations: None
Speech: Normal	Remote Memory: Intact		
Motor Activity: Restless	Gen. Knowledge: Mostly accurate		
Orientation: Fully oriented	Proverb Interpretation: Mostly accurate		
	Similarities/Differences: Mostly accurate		

APPLICATION OF THE MULTIAXIAL SYSTEM

Charlie is given the Axis I diagnosis conduct disorder/childhood-onset type, severe (312.82). The placement of this diagnosis is supported by the fact that in the past 12 months Charlie has exhibited more than three criteria of the disorder. During this time period, Charlie has practiced serious violations of rules by staying out at night; being truant from school; destroying siblings' and family belongings; being physically cruel to people; bullying, threatening, deceiving, and intimidating others; stealing from friends and family; and breaking into homes. Charlie also presented with more than one criterion present in the past six months reflective of aggression toward people. He states that he often gets what he wants through threats and intimidations of others, including starting verbal and physical fights. He has been caught destroying property such as deliberately setting fire to school property. Other problematic behaviors include deceitfulness and theft by breaking into homes and the school, and stealing from parents. Charlie has a history of repetitive and persistent patterns of disturbed peer relationships, disobedience, and opposition to authority figures, lying, shoplifting, physical fighting, exhibition fighting, fire setting, stealing, vandalism, and school discipline problems since age 7. These conduct problems impair social and academic functioning as evidenced by few friends, poor grades, school suspension, and being involved in numerous fights.

A second diagnosis to be included on Axis I is adjustment disorder, with depressed mood/acute (309.0). This second diagnosis is also placed on Axis I since Charlie demonstrates a typical pattern with depressive symptoms and suicidal ideation, and his behaviors rapidly escalate when he is frustrated or confronted by authorities after being caught in wrongdoing. This is supported by a suicide attempt he made two months ago by slashing his wrist. Self-esteem is low, despite the image of toughness presented to the public. Charlie's depression frequently manifests in his concurrent conduct and impulsivity problems. The co-occurring symptoms of conduct and attention-deficit/hyperactivity disorders are indicators of his depression. Other depressive symptoms appear related to the family's move, his disturbances in the home, and his statements that he is bored with school and schoolwork. The client's parents' report that Charlie isolated himself in his room for the past five months, has stopped being around friends, and has clinically significant impairment in social and academic functioning. Currently there are no severe symptoms to meet the criteria for a depressive disorder. For this reason, an additional diagnosis of adjustment disorder with depressed mood appears the most appropriate and provisional status to be considered.

On Axis II, No diagnosis (V71.09) will be recorded since there are no apparent personality disorders, borderline intellectual functioning, or mental retardation present. Defense mechanisms that can be coded on this Axis include the following. His dealing with emotional conflict and internal and external stressors indicates omnipotence by feeling or acting as if he possesses special powers and abilities and is superior to others. His dealing with emotional conflict and internal and external stressors indicates devaluation by attributing exaggerated negative qualities to self and others. His dealing with emotional conflict and internal and external stressors indicates idealization by attributing exaggerated positive qualities to gang leaders and troublemakers. His dealing with emotional conflict and internal and external stressors indicates projection identification by falsely attributing his own unacceptable feelings, impulses, and thoughts toward someone else. Charlie remains aware of his own impulses but misattributes them as justifiable reactions to the other person. He induces the very feelings in others that were first mistakenly believed to be there, making it difficult to clarify who did what to whom first. His dealing with emotional conflict and internal and external stressors indicates acting out by actions rather than reflections or feelings. His dealing with emotional conflict and internal and external stressors indicates denial by refusing to acknowledge some painful aspects of external and subjective experiences that would be apparent to others. His dealing with emotional conflict and internal and external stressors indicates rationalization by concealing the true motivations for his own thoughts, actions, and feelings through elaboration of reassuring and self-serving but incorrect explanations. This client's defense is at the minor image-distorting level as characterized by distortions in the image of the self, body, and others that are employed to regulate self-esteem.

On Axis III (F54), lacerations of the left wrist are noted from Charlie's attempted suicide two months ago.

On Axis IV, the clinician can note the following: Charlie was recently arrested for setting a fire and fighting in school. The family moved six months ago. Charlie exhibits education deficits due to school change and nonattendance in class. His father admits using harsh discipline. Relationship conflicts are due to aggressive and annoying behaviors and peer-rejection exist along with expulsion from home by judge and parents for brutally hurting his brother. Charlie is experiencing social environmental pressures due to low income and a poor living environment. There is support group deficiency due to limited access to social welfare support and few family members or friends. Current stress severity rating is moderate.

On Axis V the *global assessment of functioning (GAF)* rating for current = 30 is noted. Family routines of mealtime and sleeping do not meet the needs of the children because rules are grimly adhered to or blithely ignored. Lifecycle changes generate painful conflict and there are obvious frustrating failures of problem solving. Parental decision making is tyrannical and ineffective. The unique characteristics of individuals are unappreciated or ignored, and there are confusing fluid coalitions among family members. Infrequent periods of enjoyment of family life together due to frequent distancing and hostility reflect significant conflicts that remain unresolved and quite painful.

DIAGNOSTIC SUMMARY

The diagnosis for Charlie is conduct disorder, childhood-onset type, severe. Charlie has a seemingly charming personality, but from an early age has been unable to follow home, school, or society's rules on a consistent basis. Incorrigibility, delinquency, and school problems such as truancy mark his childhood. Charlie's behavior problems affect every life area of functioning. There are numerous complaints from parents and school that the child fights, lies, steals, starts fires, cheats, and is abusive and destructive. Charlie glibly claims to have guilt feelings, but he does not appear to feel genuine remorse for his behavior. Charlie complains of multiple somatic problems and has made a suicide attempt, and the manipulative nature of all his interactions with others makes it difficult to decide whether his complaints are genuine. Charlie has many conduct problems in excess of those required to make the diagnosis and the conduct problems have caused serious harm to his brother.

The additional diagnosis of *adjustment disorder with depressed mood/acute* appears appropriate. A mood disorder along with conduct disorder often gets missed. There are usually so many pressing problems to sort out and so many different stressors, that it is not until suicide is tried or talked of that many families, physicians, and other health professionals consider comorbid depression. Recent studies of teenagers who have committed suicide have found that these children were about three times more likely to have conduct disorder and 15 times more likely to abuse substances. Suicide is worth worrying about in those diagnosed with conduct disorder and also must be a part of treatment planning. In Charlie's case he has attempted suicide, has low-self esteem, and is diagnosed

---

QUICK REFERENCE

MULTIAXIAL DIAGNOSTIC ASSESSMENT (*DSM-IV-TR*)

Axis I: 312.82   Conduct disorder/childhood-onset type, severe.
          309.0   Adjustment disorder, with depressed mood.

Axis II: V71.09   No diagnosis.
          A.   Current defenses or coping styles:
               1.   Omnipotence.
               2.   Devaluation.
               3.   Idealization.
               4.   Projection identification.
               5.   Acting out.
               6.   Denial.
               7.   Rationalization.
          B.   Predominant current defense level: Minor image-distorting level.

Axis III: Lacerations of left wrist.

Axis IV: Recent arrest for setting a fire and school fights.

           Family move six-months ago.

           Educational deficits due to truancy and school change.

           Harsh discipline by father.

           Relationship conflicts with peers due to aggressive and annoying behaviors.

           Expulsion from home by parents and court.

           Social environment pressures of low income and poor environment.

           Support group deficient: Few family or friends and lack of access to social services.

           Stress Severity Rating: 3 (Severe).

Axis V: GAF = 30 (current).
           GAF = 45 (past six months).
           GAF = 50 (past year).

with adjustment disorder with depressed mood. This is supported by symptoms of depressed mood, tearfulness, and current feelings of hopelessness (APA, 2000).

CONTRIBUTING FACTORS

The family history of antisocial disorder, physical abuse, and alcoholism suggests the possibility of a biological basis for attention-deficit/hyperactivity disorder and conduct disorder for the client. Also, the client has a history of attention-deficit/hyperactivity disorder that was present at age 5. Charlie's family and environmental surroundings are poor. Conflicting punitive measures and assistance from parents, teachers, and the legal system complicate the problems experienced by this client. Charlie has a poor frustration tolerance; irritability, temper outburst, and recklessness are common.

FURTHER INFORMATION NEEDED

School and juvenile records will be requested to further validate the diagnosis and assist in treatment planning. Charlie's previous mental health records will be requested to see whether symptoms he had then could be those of depression when diagnosed with attention-deficit/hyperactivity disorder. Hospitalization records of the client's admittance to a mental health facility for suicide attempt will be requested. Educational testing and Intelligence tests will be requested to rule out pervasive problems in academic function. Referral for a medical exam and blood work will be requested of the parents.

DECISION PROCESS FOR *DSM* DIAGNOSIS

In diagnostic formulation, the following target symptoms require consideration: (1) biopsychosocial stressors (especially sexual and physical abuse, separation, divorce, or death of key attachment figures); (2) educational potential, disabilities, and achievement; (3) peer, sibling, and family problems and strengths; (4) environmental factors including disorganized home, lack of supervision, presence of child abuse or neglect, psychiatric illness (especially substance abuse) in parents, and environmental neurotoxins (e.g., lead intoxication); and (5) adolescent or child ego development, especially ability to form and maintain relationships.

A decision on the subtype of the disorder (childhood onset versus adolescent onset; overt versus covert versus authority; underrestrained versus over-restrained; socialized versus undersocialized; severity specifier of mild, moderate, or severe) is needed. Also, it is important to examine if there are any other possible alternate primary diagnoses with conduct symptoms complicating their presentation, especially in adolescents. To prevent a wrong diagnosis, it is essential to look carefully at these syndromes that might be confused or concurrent with conduct disorder: (1) attention-deficit/hyperactivity disorder; (2) oppositional defiant disorder; (3) intermittent explosive disorder; (4) substance use disorders; (5) mood disorders (bipolar and depressive); (6) posttraumatic stress disorder and dissociative disorders; (7) borderline personality disorder; (8) adjustment disorder; (9) dementia or delirium and seizure disorder; (10) narcissistic personality disorder; (11) specific developmental disorders (e.g., learning disabilities); (12) mental retardation; and (13) schizophrenia (APA, 2000; First et al., 1995).

TREATMENT PLAN AND INTERVENTION COMPONENTS

In formulating the treatment plan, Charlie and his parents were interviewed together and separately to go over the history and check out all other possible contradictory information and comorbid conditions. School reports helped to verify truancy, behavior problems, and educational status. It is important for the practitioner to gather a comprehensive history that includes schoolwork, some parts of the physical exam, and both the child and parents' perspective. As noted earlier, lab tests and X-rays are needed to rule out neurological and/or biological components. In addition, the referral for a blood test will detect use or abuse of drugs or hormonal problems. Problem behaviors must be clearly identified, as these are the behaviors that will be reflected in terms of the intervention efforts.

Treatment time can vary among individuals with conduct disorder; however, it is rarely brief since establishing new attitudes and behavior patterns take time. However, early intervention offers Charlie a better chance for considerable improvement and hope for a more successful future. Charlie's treatment will combine medication, individual therapy, group therapy, behavioral therapy, social skills training, family support and family therapy, and, potentially, remedial education. While medication may be an important component of treating Charlie's behavior disorders, especially early on, it will work best as an adjunct to psychotherapy. Individual therapy can help Charlie gain greater self-control and insight into his social conduct and develop more thoughtful and efficient problem-solving strategies. Most important, it gives him the opportunity to understand and express his feelings with words instead of through behavior. Charlie's treatment will include behavior modification techniques, such as social skill training, through which he can learn to evaluate social situations and adjust his behavior accordingly. In addition, Charlie may need to have some kind of remedial education or special tutoring to compensate for any learning difficulties or to

---

QUICK REFERENCE

BEHAVIORAL DEFINITIONS

- Persistent failure to comply with rules or expectations in the home, school, and community.
- Excessive fighting, intimidation of others, cruelty and violence toward people, and deliberate fire setting with intention of causing damage and destruction of school property.
- History of breaking and entering and stealing from family, classmates, and neighbors.
- School adjustment characterized by repeated truancy, disrespectful attitude, and suspensions for misbehavior.
- Repeated conflict and confrontation with authority figures at home, school, and in the community.
- Failure to consider the consequences of actions, taking inappropriate risks, and engaging in thrill-seeking behaviors.
- Numerous attempts to deceive others through lying, conning, or manipulating.
- Consistent failure to accept responsibility for misbehavior accompanied by a pattern of blaming others.
- Little or no remorse for past misbehavior.
- Lack of sensitivity to the thoughts, feelings, and needs of other people.

---

address any reading disorders, learning disabilities, or language delays that may be indicated following testing.

Family therapy is an important component to treating conduct disorder. Family therapy and behavioral therapies, such as parent training programs, will address the family stress normally generated by living with a child with conduct disorder. These treatment modalities will provide strategies for managing Charlie's behavior, and may help the parents encourage appropriate behaviors in their children and discipline them more effectively. By involving the entire family, this treatment will foster mutual support, positive reinforcement, direct communication, and more effective problem solving within the family (Braithwaite, Duff, & Westworth, 1999; Brunk, 1999).

Many target symptoms that may not have been apparent or acknowledged during the client interview may be discovered following interviews with parents, juvenile detention staff, and teachers. It is essential for the therapist to obtain additional information on the client and evaluate the following: (1) capacity for attachment, trust, and empathy; (2) tolerance for and discharge of impulses; (3) capacity for showing restraint, accepting responsibility for actions, experiencing guilt, using anger constructively, and acknowledging negative emotions; (4) cognitive functioning; (5) mood, affect, self-esteem, and suicide potential; (6) peer relationships (loner, popular, drug-, crime-, or gang-oriented friends); (7) disturbances of ideation (inappropriate reactions to environment, paranoia, dissociate episodes, and suggestibility); (8) history of early, persistent use of tobacco, alcohol, or other substances; and (9) psychometric self-report instruments. In addition, Charlie's school records will provide a great deal of information such as his academic functioning (IQ, achievement test data, academic performance, and behavior). Additional data may be obtained in person, by phone, or through written reports from appropriate staff, such as school principal, psychologist, juvenile detention personnel, teachers, and school nurse. Any standard parent- and teacher-rating scales of the patient's behavior would be useful. The practitioner should also make any referral for IQ, speech and language, and learning disability and neuropsychiatric testing if available test data are not sufficient. It may be necessary to look at physical evaluations, particularly any physical examination within past 12 months (i.e., baseline pulse rate). A part of the treatment plan is to collaborate with the family doctor, pediatrician, or other health care providers. It is also important to conduct vision and hearing screenings. As records become available, it is necessary to evaluate medical and neurological conditions (e.g., head injury, seizure disorder, and chronic illnesses). The therapist will review any urine and blood drug screening, especially when clinical evidence suggests substance abuse that the client denies (Dziegielewski, 1998; Thyer & Wodarski, 1998).

Treatment should be provided in a continuum of care that allows flexible application of modalities by a cohesive treatment plan. Some outpatient treatment is planned for Charlie, including intervention in the family, school, and peer group. The predominance of externalizing symptoms in multiple domains of functioning call for both the interpersonal psychoeducational modalities (rather than an exclusive emphasis on intrapsychic) and psychopharmacological approaches. Because Charlie's conduct disorder is severe it may require an extensive treatment and long-term follow-up. In preparing the treatment plan, the clinician considered (a) treatment of comorbid disorders (e.g., attention-deficit/hyperactivity disorder, specific developmental disabilities, intermittent explosive disorder, affective or bipolar disorder, anxiety disorder, and substance use disorder); (b) possible family interventions including parent guidance and family therapy to identify and work with parental strengths, and training parents to establish consistent positive and negative consequences and well-defined expectations and rules. In this case, the clinician decided to work to eliminate harsh, excessively permissive, and inconsistent behavior management practices. The clinician arranged for the father to receive individual substance abuse counseling and for Charlie to receive individual, peer support, and family group psychotherapy. Therapy focused on supportive, explorative, cognitive, and other behavioral techniques due to the client's age, processing style, and ability to engage in treatment. The combination of behavioral and explorative approaches is indicated because of internalizing and externalizing comorbidities (e.g., attention-deficit/hyperactivity disorder, specific developmental disabilities, intermittent explosive disorder, affective or bipolar disorder, anxiety disorder, and substance use disorder). Psychosocial skill-building training is used to supplement therapy as well as other psychosocial interventions. The use of a peer intervention was chosen to discourage deviant peer association and promote a socially appropriate peer network.

It also was important to establish and use a school intervention for appropriate placement, to promote an alliance between parents and school, and to promote prosocial peer group contact. Coordination and assistance in the juvenile justice system interventions may require the inclusion of court supervision and limit setting, as well as other special programs when available. Social services referrals were needed to help the family to obtain benefits and service providers (e.g., case managers). As discharge nears there may be a need to consider other community resources, such as Big Brother and Big Sister programs, Friends Outside, and/or Planned Parenthood. There may come a time when it may be appropriate to use out-of-home placement (e.g., crisis shelters, group homes, or residential treatment). As Charlie becomes older, he may require job and independent-living skills training. Psychopharmacology treatment using the medication Risperdal (risperidone) is recommended for a short-term treatment of aggressive behaviors (Findling, 2000). Antidepressants that could be used for therapy include lithium carbonate, carbamazepine, and popranolol and are currently used clinically for conduct disorder, but rigorous scientific studies to demonstrate their efficacy have not been performed. The risks of neuroleptics may outweigh their usefulness in the treatment of aggression in conduct disorder and require careful consideration before use.

Determining the best level of care and the criteria for hospitalization of this client can be complex although the practitioner will choose the least restrictive level of intervention that fulfills both the short- and long-term needs of the client. When or if there is an imminent risk to self or others, such as suicidal, self-injurious, homicidal, or aggressive behavior, or imminent deterioration in the individual's medical status after completing juvenile detention, clear indications of the need for hospitalization exist. Inpatient, partial-hospitalization, and residential treatment were considered as follows: (1) therapeutic milieu, including community processes and structure (e.g., level system, behavior modification); (2) significant family involvement tailored to the needs of the client (conjoint or without patient present), including parent training and family therapy. Because this is a young client, it is even more critical that the family be involved in the treatment process (Braithwaite et al., 1999; Brunk, 1999; Dziegielewski, 1998; First et al., 1995; Lewinsohn, 2000; Maxmen & Ward, 1996; Thyer & Wodarski, 1998).

SAMPLE TREATMENT PLAN

CHARLIE

Client Data:

Age: 11   Gender: Male
Race: Caucasian   Marital Status: Single
Admission Date: 8/7/2000   Discharge Date: 1/8/2001

Client Strengths: Intelligent, clear thinking, expressive/articulate, excellent manipulative abilities, excellent problem-solving abilities, and motivated for change, physically healthy, supportive family, and varied interests.

Assessments Completed:

- Children's Depression Inventory (CDI): 32 depression and 10 positive.
- Neuropsychological questionnaire for children conducted by internal medicine physician: General health is good. Other testing pending.

Presenting Problems: Client reports that a judge has ordered him to get a mental health evaluation due to his involvement in thefts and fire setting.

Primary Problem: Conduct disorder/Childhood-onset type, severe.

Mental Status Description

Presentation	Mental Functioning	Higher Order Abilities	Thought Form/Content
Appearance: Unkempt	Simple Calculations: Mostly accurate	Judgment: Impulsive	Thought Process: Logical and organized
Mood: Anxious		Insight: Intact	
Attitude: Guarded	Serial Sevens: Accurate	Intelligence: Low	Delusions: None
Affect: Appropriate	Immediate Memory: Intact		Hallucinations: None
Speech: Normal	Remote Memory: Intact		
Motor Activity: Restless	General Knowledge: Mostly accurate		
Orientation: Fully oriented	Proverb Interpretation: Mostly accurate		
	Similarities/Differences: Mostly accurate		

Risk Assessment:

Suicide risk:	None
Violence risk:	Slight
Child abuse risk:	Slight

SAMPLE TREATMENT PLAN *(Continued)*

Treatment Modalities and Approaches:

The following treatment approaches are being implemented:

- Individual: Cognitive restructuring and insight oriented.
- Group: Family, functional family, and peer group therapy.
- Behavioral: Token economy, behavioral techniques, relaxation training, and solution-oriented brief therapy.
- Social interventions: Supportive maintenance, Parent education, Social skills training, and Social skills building.
- Biological: Pharmacotherapy and medication management therapy.

Medication	Dosage	Frequency	Start Date	End Date
Risperdol	.50 mg	1 x in AM	7/5/2001	12/13/2001

Multiaxial System (DSM-IV-TR)

Axis I: 312.82 Conduct disorder/Childhood-onset type, severe.
 309.0 Adjustment disorder, with depressed mood.

Axis II: V71.09 No diagnosis.
 A. Current defenses of coping styles:
  1. Omnipotence.
  2. Devaluation.
  3. Idealization.
  4. Projection identification.
  5. Acting out.
  6. Denial.
  7. Rationalization.
 B. Predominant current defense level: Minor image-distorting level.

Axis III: Lacerations of left wrist.

Axis IV: Recent arrest for setting a fire and school fights.
 Family move six-months ago.
 Educational deficits due to truancy and school change.
 Harsh discipline by father.
 Relationship conflicts with peers due to aggressive and annoying behaviors.
 Expulsion from home by parents and court.
 Social environment pressures of low income and poor environment.
 Support group deficient of few family or friends and lack of access to social services.
 Stress Severity Rating: 3 (Severe).

Axis V: GAF = 30 (current).
 GAF = 45 (past six months).
 GAF = 50 (past year).

(continued)

SAMPLE TREATMENT PLAN *(Continued)*

Treatment Plan:

Behavioral Definitions

- Persistent failure to comply with rules or expectations in the home, school, and community.
- Excessive fighting, intimidation of others, cruelty and violence toward people, and deliberate fire setting with intention of causing damage and destruction of school property.
- History of breaking and entering and stealing from family, classmates, and neighbors.
- School adjustment characterized by repeated truancy, disrespectful attitude, and suspensions for misbehavior.
- Repeated conflict and confrontations with authority figures at home, school, and in the community.
- Failure to consider the consequences of actions, taking inappropriate risks, and engaging in thrill-seeking behaviors.
- Numerous attempts to deceive others through lying, conning, or manipulating.
- Consistent failure to accept responsibility for misbehavior, accompanied by a pattern of blaming others.
- Little or no remorse for past misbehavior.
- Lack of sensitivity to the thoughts, feelings, and needs of other people.

Long-Term Goals *(Target dates must be given for each objective)*

- The client will demonstrate increased honesty, compliance with rules, sensitivity to the feelings and rights of others, develop control over impulses, and acceptance of responsibility for his behavior.
- The client will comply with rules and expectations in the home, school, and community on a consistent basis.
- The client will eliminate all illegal and antisocial behaviors.
- The client will terminate all acts of violence and cruelty toward people and the destruction of property.
- The client will express anger through appropriate verbalizations and healthy physical outlets on a consistent basis.
- The client will demonstrate marked improvement in impulse control.
- The client will resolve the core conflicts that contribute to the emergence of conduct problems.
- The parents will establish and maintain appropriate parent-child boundaries, setting firm consistent limits when the client acts out in an aggressive or rebellious manner.
- The client will demonstrate empathy, concern, and sensitivity for the thoughts, feelings, and needs of others on a regular basis.

Short-Term Objectives *(Target dates must be given for each objective)*

- The client will complete psychological testing.
- The client will complete a psychoeducational evaluation.
- The client will complete a substance abuse evaluation and comply with the recommendations offered by the evaluation findings.
- The client and his parents will cooperate with the recommendations or requirements mandated by the criminal justice system.

SAMPLE TREATMENT PLAN *(Continued)*

- The client will remain in the juvenile detention facility for the remainder of his probation term.
- The client will recognize and verbalize how feelings are connected to misbehavior.
- The client will increase the number of statements that reflect the acceptance of responsibility for misbehavior.
- The client will decrease the frequency of verbalizations that project the blame for the problems onto other people.
- The client will express anger through appropriate verbalization and healthy physical outlets.
- The client will reduce the frequency and severity of aggressive, destructive, and antisocial behaviors.
- The client will increase compliance with rules at home and at the alternative school.
- The parents will postpone recreational activity (e.g., playing basketball with friends) until after completing homework or chores when Charlie is at home.
- The parents will establish appropriate boundaries, develop clear rules, and follow through consistently with consequences for misbehavior when Charlie returns to home.
- The client and his parents agree to and follow through with the implementation of a reward system or contingency contract.
- The parents will increase the frequency of praise and positive reinforcement to the client.
- The client will increase the time spent with the parents in leisure and school activities.
- The parents will verbalize appropriate boundaries for discipline to prevent further occurrences of abuse and ensure the safety of the client and his siblings.
- The parents will watch the video, *Toughlove* (1985) and share their understandings.
- The client will verbalize an understanding of how current acting-out and aggressive behaviors are associated with past neglect and harsh physical punishment.
- The client will identify and verbally express feelings associated with harsh physical abuse.
- The client will increase participation in extracurricular activities and positive peer group activities.
- The client will identify and verbalize how acting out behaviors negatively affects others.
- The client will increase verbalizations of empathy and concern for other people.
- The client will increase communication, intimacy, and consistency between parents.
- The client will take medication as prescribed by the physician.

Therapeutic Interventions (Target dates must be given for each objective)

- The therapist will give a directive to parents to spend more time with the client in leisure, school, or work activities.
- The therapist will explore the client's family background for a history of physical, sexual, or substance abuse, which may contribute to his behavioral problems.
- The therapist will conduct a family therapy session in which the client's family members are given a task or problem to solve together (e.g., build a craft); observe family interactions and process the experience with them afterward.
- The therapist will assist the client's parents to cease physically abusive or overly punitive methods of discipline.
- Charlie will remain in juvenile detention for the protection of siblings from further abuse until deemed unnecessary.

(continued)

SAMPLE TREATMENT PLAN *(Continued)*

- The therapist will encourage and support the client in expressing feelings associated with neglect and harsh punishment.
- The therapist will utilize the family sculpting technique in which the client defines the roles and behaviors of each family member in a scene of his choosing to assess the family dynamics.
- The therapist will conduct family therapy sessions to explore the dynamics that contribute to the emergence of the client's behavioral problems.
- The therapist will assign the client's parents reading material and relevant books.
- The therapist will encourage the parents to provide frequent praise and positive reinforcement for the client's positive social behaviors and good impulse control.
- The therapist will design and implement a token economy to increase the client's positive social behaviors and deter impulsive, acting-out behaviors.
- The therapist will utilize the therapeutic game, Talking, Feeling, Doing to increase the client's awareness of his thoughts and feelings.
- The therapist will arrange for the client to participate in group therapy to improve his social judgment and interpersonal skills.
- The therapist will assign the client the task of showing empathy, kindness, and sensitivity to the needs of others (e.g., read a bedtime story to a sibling, mow the lawn for the grandmother) after removal from juvenile detention.
- The therapist will encourage the client to participate in extracurricular or positive peer group activities to provide a healthy outlet for anger, improve social skills, and increase self-esteem.
- The therapist will provide the client with sex education and discuss the risks involved with sexually promiscuous behaviors.
- The therapist will explore the client's feelings, irrational beliefs, and unmet needs that contribute to the emergence of sexually promiscuous behaviors.
- The therapist will arrange for a medication evaluation of the client to improve his impulse control and stabilize moods.
- The therapist will arrange for a psychoeducational evaluation of the client to rule out the presence of a learning disability that may be contributing to the impulsivity and acting out behaviors in the school setting.
- The therapist will firmly confront the client's antisocial behavior and attitude, pointing out consequences for him and others.
- The therapist will arrange for psychological testing of the client to assess whether emotional factors or attention-deficit/hyperactivity disorder is contributing to his impulsivity and acting-out behaviors.
- The therapist will provide feedback to the client, his parents, school officials, and criminal justice officials regarding psychological and/or psychoeducational testing.
- The therapist will arrange for substance abuse evaluation for the client.
- The therapist will consult with criminal justice officials about the appropriate consequences for the client's antisocial behaviors (e.g., pay restitution, community service, probation).
- The therapist will encourage and challenge the parents not to protect the client from the legal consequences of his antisocial behaviors.
- The therapist will assist the client's parents in establishing clearly defined rules, boundaries, and consequences for misbehavior.

SAMPLE TREATMENT PLAN *(Continued)*

- The therapist will actively build the level of trust with the client in therapy sessions through consistent eye contact, active listening, unconditional positive regard, and warm acceptance to help increase his ability to identify and express feelings.
- The therapist will design a reward system and/or contingency contract for the client to reinforce identified positive behaviors and deter impulsive behaviors.
- The therapist will assist the client in making a connection between feelings and reactive behaviors.
- The therapist will confront statements in which the client blames others for his misbehavior and fails to accept responsibility for his actions.
- The therapist will explore and process the factors that contribute to the client's pattern of blaming others.
- The therapist will teach mediational and self-control strategies (e.g., relaxation, stop, look, listen, and think) to help the client express anger through appropriate verbalizations and healthy physical outlets.
- The therapist will encourage the client to use self-monitoring checklists at home and in the alternative school to develop more effective anger and impulse control.
- The therapist will teach the client effective communication and assertiveness skills to express feelings in a controlled fashion and meet his needs through more constructive actions.
- The therapist will assist the parents in increasing structure to help the client learn to delay gratification for longer-term goals (e.g., complete homework or chores before playing basketball).
- The therapist will establish clear rules for the client in home and school; ask him to repeat the rules to demonstrate an understanding of the expectations.

Prognosis:

The probability of successful achievement of treatment goals is fair. The rationale for this probability rating is due to a poor family economic situation and a limited means of family support. Increased use of parental support and assistance treatment that are at no cost to the family will be required and necessary. Perhaps about 30 percent of conduct disorder children continue with similar problems in adulthood. It is more common for males with conduct disorder to continue on into adulthood with these types of problems than females. Substance abuse is very high. About 50 to 70 percent of 10-year-olds with conduct disorder will be abusing substances four years later.

Discharge Criteria/Plan:

Aftercare plan: The client will continue attending peer support groups every two weeks and will continue with established extracurriculum activities. The client will return to the clinic in six months for follow-up or when needed. He also states he will continue attending after school programs so that he is not by himself.

Projected total number of sessions required for completion of treatment: Charlie will successfully achieve 100 percent of those short-term objectives that have been marked with an asterisk before being considered for discharge from treatment.

(continued)

SAMPLE TREATMENT PLAN *(Continued)*

Discharge Criteria:

- The client must attend school consistently without resistance.
- The client will comply with limits set by authority figures.
- The client will consistently abstain from mood-altering illicit drugs or alcohol.
- The client will demonstrate age-appropriate social skills.
- The client will demonstrate responsible, consistent medication-taking behavior.
- The client will engage in social interaction with appropriate eye contact and assertiveness.
- The client will have home visits completed without serious maladjustment.
- The client's mood, behavior, and thought will be stabilized sufficiently to independently carry out basic self-care.
- The client will have no exhibition of sexually inappropriate behavior.
- The client will have no expression of suicidal ideation.
- The client will have no expressions of a threat of physical aggression toward self or others.
- The client will have no violent outbursts of temper.
- The client will resolve conflicts peaceably and without aggression.
- The client will verbalize names of supportive resources that can be contacted if feeling suicidal.
- The client will verbalize plans for seeking continued emotional support after discharge.
- The client will verbalize positive plans for the future.

Client Response to Plan:

Patient response to treatment plan presentation: Client states that he wants to do whatever is needed to be a better child. He also understands that he needs to continue with extracurricular activities, support groups, and medication even after discharge from this facility.

Significant other response to treatment plan presentation: Mother and Father state that they are willing to try anything for their son's sake. Both parents report that they will be fully compliant with any and all requirements to get their son Charlie back into the family and home.

SUMMARY AND FUTURE DIRECTIONS

Conduct disorder is a complex problem with many forms. As previously mentioned, no one intervention can be used for every case. This continues to make intervention research perplexing but very crucial.

Practitioners must look carefully at the factors related to the diagnostic assessment because the identification of these factors is a critical aspect of the therapeutic process. Instead of narrowing the assessment it might be necessary to use computer technology to assist professionals in making more expedient and thorough assessments. Practitioners should utilize the Person in Environment (PIE) Classification System (see Appendix A) since it recognizes social considerations and the effects of the person-in-environment functioning which is very important for individuals who suffer from conduct disorder. Tools such as the PIE could improve the understanding of a client's case by providing a common language to describe the client's problems. All aspects of the case could be shared by various professionals involved in the client's case, including practitioners, administrators, and researchers. A person-in-environment focus helps to attend to several interrelated dimensions of the client who suffers from conduct disorder thereby focusing on the biological, intellectual, emotional, social, familial, spiritual, economic, communal, and so on, recognizing the client in relation to the immediate and distant environment.

All mental health practitioners need to stay informed of the most up-to-date research on the interventions that can be used to treat clients who suffer from conduct disorder. With the increase in managed care it is imperative that mental health practitioners develop research that will clearly identify which treatment or combination of treatments is most cost effective to ensure that clients continue to receive coverage for the necessary treatments.

7 Substance Disorders: Alcoholism

Julie Wenglinsky and Sophia F. Dziegielewski

Mental health is a field of great diversity and scope and practitioners come into contact with a multitude of client populations. Most mental health practitioners work for agencies that either directly or indirectly service the person with an alcohol disorder through assessment, clinical intervention, and/or referral (Gassman, Demone, & Abilal, 2001). Since many mental health practitioners will confront substance abuse as either their primary or secondary field of practice, it is essential to be skilled in completing the alcohol diagnostic assessment as well as intervention planning and strategy.

This chapter describes the adult alcoholic and the multiple problems that can result. Furthermore, this chapter provides a brief overview of the different treatments utilized to assist alcoholics while supporting the need for an integrated approach. The social problem of alcoholism is discussed, including the definition and description of the adult alcoholic, gender differences, the impact on society, and causes of alcoholism. Factors in the diagnostic assessment and treatment strategy are presented exploring the use of the biopsychosocial approach, behavior therapy, cognitive therapy, cognitive-behavioral therapy, systems, and the traditional self-help approach. An integrated approach is suggested that takes into account the individual and his or her support system, and the chapter concludes with suggestions and practice implications.

INTRODUCTION TO ALCOHOLISM

To start the process of gaining a common understanding of alcoholism, agreement on a common definition must be established. Unfortunately, definitions of alcoholism and alcohol use disorders are as numerous as the researchers themselves. Alcoholism, as it is commonly known, is considered to be a chronic illness with recognizable symptoms and signs proportionate to severity. Consumption of large amounts of alcohol usually causes physiologic damage, dependence, and withdrawal that can be life threatening. The desired effect requires any where from a glassful, a bottleful, or a case, depending on the type of beverage consumed.

Severe dependence or addiction and a cumulative pattern of behaviors including frequent intoxication and interference with socialization, relationships, and work identify an alcoholic. Alcoholics may incur physical injury or experience legal consequences if they drive while intoxicated, or are arrested for drunkenness. Some will seek medical treatment and, eventually, they may be hospitalized for delirium, tremors, or cirrhosis of the liver. The earlier in life these behaviors are evident, the more crippling the disorder.

DSM-IV-TR: DEFINITION OF ALCOHOL AS A SUBSTANCE ABUSE DISORDER

The definition most accepted by clinicians is outlined in the *DSM IV-TR* (American Psychiatric Association [APA], 2000). The 11 classes of substances that are abused include alcohol, amphetamines, caffeine, hallucinogens, inhalants, nicotine, opioids, phencyclidine (PCP), sedatives, hypnotics, and anxiolytics. (See the Quick Reference box.) If a client uses more than one substance and the criteria for abuse or dependence for any one substance is not met, or when the client

---

QUICK REFERENCE

SUBSTANCE-RELATED DISORDERS

Eleven classes of substances are abused:

Alcohol.	Sedatives.	Nicotine.
Caffeine.	Anxiolytics.	Phencyclidine (PCP).
Inhalants.	Amphetamines.	Hypnotics.
Opioids.	Hallucinogens.	

All substances are generally associated with:

Substance Use Disorders

Abuse: These are viewed as less severe, continue use knowing it is causing harm (does not apply to caffeine and nicotine).

Dependence: Needs to take larger amounts with unsuccessful attempts to quit.

Substance Induced Disorders

Intoxication: The development of a substance specific (reversible) syndrome, condition related to recent ingestion of psychoactive substance.

Withdrawal: Maladaptive cognitive and behavioral declines due to reduction of a substance; generally, this category is usually associated with dependence.

Source: Summarized criteria from the *Diagnostic and Statistical Manual of Mental Disorders, Fourth Edition, Text Revision.* Copyright 2000. American Psychiatric Association.

abuses more than one substance and takes them together, the designation of *poly-substance abuse* can be used. When the practitioner knows what substances are being abused as part of the complete diagnostic assessment, each substance should be listed accordingly.

The mental health practitioner is first expected to identify the substance and later relate it to the category where the symptoms fit the best. Substances are generally associated with abuse, dependence, intoxication, or withdrawal.

Alcohol use disorders are earmarked by consumption of alcohol that exceeds the limits of what the individual's culture considers acceptable and appropriate or the intake of alcohol becomes so excessive that health or social relationships are impaired. In addition, there are varied classifications of alcohol abuse, dependence, and alcohol-induced disorders. As shown in the Quick Reference of the Criteria for Alcohol Use Disorders, the primary disorders of abuse and dependence have their own differentiating criteria, symptomatology, and duration. The *DSM–IV-TR* describes two primary alcohol use disorders: alcohol abuse and alcohol dependence. A person receives a diagnosis of alcohol abuse if he or she experiences at least one of four abuse symptoms (i.e., role impairment, hazardous use, legal problems, or social problems) that lead to "clinically significant impairment or distress." These symptoms reflect either pathological patterns of alcohol use, psychosocial consequences, or both (APA, 2000).

Alcohol dependence is defined as a constellation of symptoms related to physical dependence as well as compulsive and pathological patterns of alcohol use. To qualify for a *DSM–IV-TR* diagnosis of alcohol dependence, a person must exhibit within a 12-month period at least three of the following seven dependence symptoms: (1) tolerance, (2) withdrawal or drinking to avoid or relieve withdrawal, (3) drinking larger amounts or for a longer period than intended, (4) unsuccessful attempts or a repeated desire to quit or to cut down on drinking, (5) much time spent using alcohol, and (6) reduced social or recreational activities in favor of alcohol use (APA, 2000).

In addition, to the delineation of abuse and dependency, the practitioner must also identify the differences between two common disorders: intoxication and withdrawal. Intoxication is reversible and occurs when over ingestion of the substance occurs. This may be accompanied by a lower threshold for anger and violence but usually results in generalized disinhibition. Withdrawal is defined as the biophysical reaction to the reduction of a chemical stimulus in the body. Often withdrawal is accompanied by tremors, mood instability, physical illness, and in severe cases seizures and possible death (APA, 1994, 2000; Maxmen & Ward, 1995, Zuckerman, 1995). It is not uncommon that in relation to withdrawal avoidance, many alcoholics and drug addicts are cross-addicted, naming either alcohol or street/pharmaceutical drugs as their drug of choice. For these individuals, it is not uncommon to have varied and multiple diagnoses.

QUICK REFERENCE

CRITERIA FOR ALCOHOL USE DISORDERS

Alcohol Abuse	Alcohol Dependence

Role impairment
Frequent intoxication leading to failure to fulfill major role obligations (e.g., at school, work, or home).

Legal problems
Recurrent alcohol-related legal problems.

Social problems
Continued drinking despite knowledge of persistent or recurrent social or interpersonal problems caused or exacerbated by alcohol use.

Hazardous use
Recurrent use when it is physically hazardous (e.g., driving while intoxicated).

No diagnosis of dependence in the past 12 months.

Tolerance
Need to increase consumption by 50 percent or more to achieve the same effects.

Markedly reduced effects when drinking the same amount.

Withdrawal
Signs of alcohol withdrawal.

Drinking to avoid or relieve withdrawal.

Recurrent drinking of larger amounts or for a longer period of time than intended.

Desire to quit
Unsuccessful attempts or a persistent desire to quit or cut down on drinking.

Reduced activities and social problems
Much time spent using, obtaining, or recovering from the effects of alcohol.

Important social or recreational activities given up or reduced in favor of alcohol use.

Psychological/physical problems
Continued drinking despite knowledge of a recurrent or persistent psychological or physical problem caused or exacerbated by alcohol use.

Source: Summarized criteria from the *Diagnostic and Statistical Manual of Mental Disorders, Fourth Edition, Text Revision.* Copyright 2000. American Psychiatric Association.

TYPES AND PHASES OF ALCOHOLISM

Descriptions of an alcoholic are as varied as the definitions of alcoholism, and come from various sociological, physiological, and psychological perspectives. People with alcohol problems are found in all walks of life and consist of clients, family members, and children. Alcoholics are also found at every social level, culture, race, age, and can be religious or atheist. S. Brown (1985) states that all treatment providers have known alcoholics as extremely difficult clients, although none of them understand why (p. 3). As early as 1969, theorists regarded alcoholics as sick persons, rather than weak or sinful people (K. Jones, 1969). A typical characteristic of the alcoholic includes the feeling of incompleteness and imperfection, and the need to find a sense of wholeness and completion in external sources, like a person or an object. Guilt becomes a primary emotion and the alcohol fills the person's emptiness. To cope, it is felt that alcoholics utilize a variety of defense mechanisms. The strongest of which is denial, followed by rationalization and intellectualization (Modesto-Lowe & Kranzler, 1999). Wallace (1989) states that alcoholism is not unlike coronary artery disease, in that it involves a genetic predisposition, self-destructive behaviors, and a culture and society that encourage unhealthy patterns of consumption of alcohol.

In understanding the characteristics and phases of alcoholism, research has supported the premise that alcoholic's progress through definite stages and the time in each stage is different in each individual. In addition, the degree of tolerance to alcohol increases with the progression of stages, beginning with the pre-alcoholic phases of social, cultural controlled drinking, occasional escape drinking, then frequent or constant escape drinking. During these phases, the consumption of alcohol is for the specific purpose of easing tensions and everyday cares. As time lapses, the need to consume more alcohol to achieve the same effect increases as increased tolerance. Advanced alcoholic phases begin with the first "blackout" (temporary amnesia), in which the person is conscious of activities, but when they come out of the blackout they have no memory of their actions. While anyone who drinks too much will pass out, only an alcoholic blacks out (Maxmen & Ward, 1995).

The next phase of alcoholism is loss of control of the amount of alcohol consumed. Other signs of alcoholism include secret drinking, preoccupation with alcohol, gulping the first few drinks, and guilt feelings about drinking. The guilt and effects of alcohol consumption are manifested in various ways. The alcoholic may avoid talking about alcohol or rationalize the drinking behavior. He or she may exhibit grandiose behavior, periods of remorse or periods of abstinence. Behavior change may occur that results in a change in drinking patterns.

Developments that increase alcohol-centered behavior can create negative effects on family and unreasonable resentments. The alcoholic may begin to hide bottles, neglect proper nutrition, experience a decrease in sexual drive and begin regular morning drinking. Intoxication during working hours, loss of tolerance, and mental impairment, including delirium tremens, also may result (Maxmen & Ward, 1995).

There is another delineation worth noting and that is of the Type I and Type II and Types A and B alcoholic. Type A alcoholics have later onsets and fewer disturbance of psychosocial functioning. Type B alcoholics have an earlier onset (>25 years old) and have increased psychosocial interference. According to Zuckerman (1995), the preferred mode of treatment is matched to the typology (p. 160). In the Type I alcoholic, there is a later onset of drinking, there is a strong genetic effect, and low probability of risk-taking behavior such as fighting or arrest. Type II, however, matches the Type B alcoholic in that there is earlier onset with a gender differentiation (higher in males); and, frequent risk-taking behaviors. Based on this definition, there appears to be ongoing dispute as to the ability to ensure patterns of behavior and outcome. Neither typology appears to be statistically linked on etiology and observed behavioral outcomes (Dawson, 2000; Kirst-Ashman, 1999).

Etiology of the Problem

As for the actual cause of alcoholism, Dawson (2000) emphasizes that there probably is no single cause of alcoholism, but rather it is a combination of many different factors. For the most part, the factors that result in someone becoming an alcoholic remain unique to the individual; however, there are some commonalties. According to Van den Bergh (1991):

> The setup for addiction development, then, is a generalized sense of inadequacy, insecurity, and alienation. Additionally, an external locus of control or belief that one's happiness and success is more dependent on other people, situations, and events than one's own also sets the stage for addiction onset. It has been shown that experiences of abuse, neglect, and abandonment are highly related to addiction's development. A common denominator . . . is that individuals had childhood, family, or marital experiences with neglect and abuse. (p. 7)

In addition, certain personality traits, including isolation, loneliness, shyness, depression, dependency, hostile and self-destructive impulsivity, and sexual immaturity are common among alcoholics. Alcoholics frequently have a disturbed familial pattern with poor parental relations and broken homes. Attitudes from the familial culture and environment subsequently have an effect on alcohol consumption behaviors (Duncan, Duncan, & Hops, 1998). While genetic predisposition or linkage has not been substantiated, there are studies reflecting a higher incidence of alcohol use in biologic children of alcoholics than in adopted children of alcoholics

(Dawson, 2000). Regarding biological causes and genetics, Wallace (1989) demonstrated that studies of adoptees show a three- to fourfold increase in tendency of children of at least one alcoholic biological parent to develop alcoholic or other addictive tendencies.

Social Indices and Demographic Characteristics

"Alcoholism is notoriously the world's most significant problem" (Harvard Medical School, 2000a, p. 11). An estimated 75 percent of American adults drink alcoholic beverages, and about 10 percent of them experience a problem with alcoholism or alcohol misuse at some time (Merck, 2000). According to data tabulated by the Substance Abuse and Mental Health Association (SAMHA), from 1993 to 1998, there was a decrease in the number of substance abuse admissions in the United States from 889,653 to 738,542. However, this data does not include those who have not presented to an identified treatment system and is thus an underestimation of the total alcohol and other drug abuse in the nation. Fuller and Hiller-Sturmhofel (1999) note that approximately 7.5 percent of the U.S. population engage in abuse of or dependence on alcohol. Furthermore, it is estimated that alcoholism accounts for 15 percent of our medical costs, over 100,000 deaths per year, and is in some way involved in one-third of child abuse cases (Harvard Medical School, 2000a).

When examining the specific data sets, we found that alcohol rates were highest in the northern United States. Of all admissions, 70 percent of patients were male. The age distribution from 1993 to 1998 indicates an increase in underage treatment seeking, a decrease in age group 25 to 34 and conversely an increase in ages 35 to 44. Racial dispersion shows a drastic differentiation with the number of whites being greater than all other ethnic groups combined. The majority of those treated had a high school education or GED (44 percent) and employment data reflects the majority, 49.3 percent were not in the labor force, indicating a high incidence of disability or dual diagnosis of some type.

Men versus Women: Is There a Difference?

The ratio of men to women alcoholics is 2 to 1 in the community, but only 3 to 1 in Alcoholics Anonymous, and 4 to 1 in treatment (Milkman & Sederer, 1990). The National Council on Alcoholism (1998) reports that women constitute less than 25 percent of all treatment center clients nationally, and there is a significant gender disparity between prevalence of the problem and access to care (SAMSHA, 1998; Van den Bergh, 1991). Milkman and Sederer (1990) explain that information regarding drug and alcohol problems in women reveals that women are still affected by intense stigma fostered by old attitudes. Women are also often victims of aggression and abuse (National Clearinghouse for Alcohol and Drug Information

[NCADI], 1995a, 1995b). They face special barriers that limit their access to care, but if they can be reached, and provided with appropriate services, they do well despite their high incidence of dual diagnosis (Reiss, 1995). A potential resource for the practitioner should include *The Alcohol, Tobacco, and Other Drug Resource Guide for Women,* produced by the center for substance abuse and prevention's National Clearinghouse for Alcohol and Drug Information. This comprehensive listing of groups and resources includes sections on prevention, research, and groups, organizations, and programs (NCADI, 1994).

The Social Problem of Alcoholism

Alcohol is a legal substance, but the effects on society are extensive. Divorce, child and adult abuse, unemployment, accidents, crimes, hospitalization, loss of production, and many other economic costs can be attributed to alcohol consumption. Social disorders are usually the earliest and most frequent complications of alcohol misuse. A complete range of these can be produced by, or associated with, alcohol misuse. (See the Quick Reference on page 200.) The implications and effects can be engulfing and substantially impair not only alcoholics but also their families, their communities, and society at large.

The problems related to alcoholism and its cost to society remains great. Carroll (1997) states that "each dollar spent on the treatment of alcohol and other drug use disorders saves between $4 and $12 in long-term societal, economic, and medical costs" (p. 352).

COMPLETION OF THE DIAGNOSTIC ASSESSMENT

The benefits of alcohol treatment are cost efficient in the larger view. Therefore, a clear understanding of the diagnostic assessment that will lead to the treatment process is essential. Although treatment can be initiated at any stage because of the severe medical complications that can result from this illness, the goal is to intervene in the progression of the disease, hopefully early enough to prevent severe brain damage or death.

The first stage in any treatment process is always completion of the diagnostic assessment. Since diversity is found in both clients and treatments, a complete understanding of the biological, psychological, and sociocultural perspectives is important in assessment efforts. In the treatment of alcoholism, there are a variety of factors to consider, and a number of tools to assist the mental health practitioner in this endeavor. As with any disorder, there are some basic facts to obtain and consider. Age, culture, gender, socioeconomic status, marital status, family history, developmental or childhood history, incidence of abuse or neglect (including

QUICK REFERENCE

Early Recognition of Alcohol-Related Problems

Early Indicators

- Heavy drinking (more than six drinks per day, i.e., greater than 60 grams per day of ethanol for men, and more than four drinks per day for women, i.e., greater than 40 grams of ethanol).
- Concern about drinking by self or family or both.
- Intellectual impairment, especially in the abstracting, planning, organizing, and adaptive skills.
- Eating lightly or skipping meals.
- Drinking alcohol rapidly.
- Increased tolerance to alcohol.

Psychosocial Factors

- Accidents related to drinking.
- Absence from work related to drinking.
- Majority of friends and acquaintances are heavy drinkers; most leisure activities and sports relate to drinking.
- Attempts to cut down on drinking have had limited success.
- Frequent use of alcohol to deal with stressful situations.
- Frequent drinking during the working day, especially at lunch break.
- Heavy smoking.

Investigation Factors

- Macrocytosis (MCV of red cells more than 100) in the absence of anemia.
- An elevated GGT (gamma-glut amyl transpeptidase).

- Elevated serum uric acid level.
- Elevated high density lipoprotein.
- Random blood alcohol level greater than BAC 0.05 g %.

Clinical Symptoms and Signs

- Trauma.
- Scars unrelated to surgery.
- Hand tremor and sweating.
- Alcohol smell on the breath during the day.
- Dyspepsia.
- Morning nausea and vomiting.
- Recurring diarrhea.

- Pancreatitis.
- Hepatomegaly.
- Impotence.
- Palpitations.
- Hypertension.
- Insomnia.
- Nightmares.

domestic violence), and educational status are core factors to be considered. The National Institute of Health's Substance Abuse and Mental Health Administration can help the practitioner recognize what information is the most important to gather in the diagnostic assessment resources. The following factors need to be gathered from the client in the substance and alcohol abuse/dependence diagnostic assessment: honesty about usage, social functioning while using the substance, amount used, frequency of use, and duration of use, changes in use over time, attitudes of family and others in their lives, recreational activities and with whom, composition of social circle, availability of the substance, issues of depression, anxiety, or delirium (such as orientation to person, place, and time), drug of choice, secondary drugs, and last, age when first used alcohol. (See Quick Reference for identification of general concerns.)

To obtain this crucial data, the client and the family need to be interviewed, and there are many standardized and proven measures to utilize to support this process as well.

There are numerous assessment tools for alcohol and other drugs. Several of these resources are available online or for free. The most commonly used scales are the AUDIT (Alcohol use disorder identification test), MAST (Michigan Alcoholism Screening Test) and Hudson Inventory of Alcohol Involvement (M. Bloom et al., 1999, Blow et al., 1998; Hepworth et al., 1997). Without adequate assessment, the ability to understand the client's attitudes and needs is lost and the effective practitioner cannot develop a sound treatment plan (Deitch et al., 1998).

Linking Information from the Diagnostic Assessment to Treatment

To add empirical weight to the process of treatment selection, medicine and varied social science professionals collaborated in the Project MATCH Research Group. The findings of this study identified three treatment approaches that are commonly used with alcoholics, cognitive-behavioral, motivation, and AA. They

---

QUICK REFERENCE

GENERAL CONCERNS

- Isolation from family and community activities.
- Life revolving around drinking activities.
- Increased frequency of driving accidents.

- Increase in acts of violence and crime.
- Financial problems.
- Legal problems.

At Work

- Frequent absenteeism, especially Monday and Friday and after pay day.
- Frequent and varied medical reasons for absence from work.
- Promotion failure, impaired job performance.

- A history of gaps in work, frequent changes of employment, and the threat of job loss.
- Industrial accidents.
- Early retirement.

QUICK REFERENCE

COMMON EFFECTS OF EXCESSIVE
ALCOHOL CONSUMPTION WITHIN THE FAMILY

The alcohol-dependent person:

- Denies the alcohol problem, blames others, forgets, and tells stories for self-defense and protection against humiliation; receives criticism from others in the family.
- Spends money needed by the family on alcohol.
- Ignores bills, debts pile up.
- Is unpredictable and impulsive.
- Resorts to verbal and physical abuse in place of honest, open talk.
- Loses the trust of family, relatives, and friends.
- Experiences increased sexual arousal but reduced function.
- Has unpredictable mood swings—Jekyll-and-Hyde personality.
- Uses devious and manipulative behavior to divert attention from drinking problem.
- Suffers from depression, guilt, shame.

The spouse or partner:

- Often tries to hide and deny the problem of the partner.
- Takes on the other person's responsibilities, carrying the load of two and perpetuating the spouse/partner dependence.
- Takes a job to get away from the problem and/or to maintain financial security.
- Finds it difficult to be open and honest because of resentment, anger, hurt, and shame.
- Avoids sexual contact and may seek separation or divorce.
- May overprotect the children, neglect, and/or use them for emotional support.
- Shows gradual social withdrawal and isolation.
- May lose feelings of self-respect and self-worth.
- May use alcohol or prescription drugs in an effort to cope.
- May present to the doctor with anxiety, depression, psychosomatic symptoms, or evidence of domestic violence.

The children have an increased risk of developing alcohol dependency themselves. They may:

- Be victims of birth defects (from maternal alcohol use).
- Be torn between two parents.
- Be deprived of emotional and physical support and lack trust in anyone.
- Avoid peer group activities, especially in the home, out of fear and shame.
- Learn destructive and negative ways of dealing with problems and getting attention.
- Lose sight of values, standards and goals because of a lack of consistent, strong parenting.
- Be a failure in school and indulge in petty crime.
- Suffer a diminishing sense of self-worth as a significant member of the family.
- Present with learning difficulties, school refusal, enuresis, or sleep disorders.

assessed each subject and assigned patients to one of the three treatment interventions. The study lasted eight years and the findings showed that while there appeared to be effectiveness by each model, none appears significantly more effective then the other. The goal is to develop a process and identified efficacy by treatment that will be most effective for the individual patient and most efficient in today's managed care era (Allen, 1998; Fuller & Hiller-Sturmhofel, 1999; Morey, 1996; NIAAA, 1996, 1997; Schneider, Hyer, & Luptak, 2000).

THE CASE OF ROBERT

Robert is a 56-year-old Caucasian male admitted to the psychiatric hospital on a voluntary basis as he reported he is not "handling things well" and was feeling suicidal with plans of driving truck into a tree or using a gun. Robert was intoxicated at time of admission with a BAL of .436, which was 5 times the legal limit. He reported precipitating factors to the hospitalization include loss of residence, marital separation, financial stressors, and loss of occupation. Within 49 hours prior to admission, Robert reported that he moved out of his daughter's home, and attempted to move in with a friend unsuccessfully. He reported he had been feeling depressed, was using cocaine and marijuana to excess, and had been sleeping a great deal. He reported that he has been drinking all day long from the time he wakes up until he goes to sleep.

Robert reported a long history of outpatient psychiatric treatment in three states and has never been hospitalized for depression but has multiple detox admissions by his report. He reported multiple attempts at sobriety and AA attendance but none have been successful. His diagnosis by self-report is depression but reported a history of depression and alcoholism. He reported he sees a doctor on an outpatient basis for medication to treat his depression and anxiety. He reported a history of treatment with medications such as Prozac and Paxil. Robert denied any history of suicide attempts but admits to a history of suicidal ideation. He reported he has been drinking and using drugs then driving recklessly of late with thoughts of how to kill himself. He denies having auditory or visual hallucinations or intent to act on suicidal thinking at present. Robert reported current and history of illicit drug use with cocaine and marijuana. He smokes 2 joints a day and he spends $200 to $300 a day on cocaine. He reported this has historically been intermittent but has been "a regular occurrence" for the past year.

He admitted to recurrent alcohol consumption at admission. He reported that he has been drinking a case of beer and a bottle or two of liquor a day. He reported that this has increased over the past year to "get a good buzz." He reported he has no problems when he stops using the marijuana or cocaine but gets "the shakes, sweats, and vomits" when he stops drinking. He reported he has had two seizures in the past when he quit drinking three years ago. He denied other issues of addiction such as gambling or food. He denied issues of pain or need for pain management. Robert reported medical history positive for cirrhosis of the liver and allergies to sulfa drugs.

(continued)

THE CASE OF ROBERT *(Continued)*

Robert was born in 1944 to intact parents who divorced days after his birth. Robert's birth father was not involved in his life and is now deceased from liver failure secondary to alcoholism. Robert reported his mother remarried within a few years of Robert's birth and stayed married to his stepfather for 20 years before they divorced. Robert's mother and stepfather are alive but have no contact with each other. Robert reported his mother, maternal aunt, and maternal grandmother are undiagnosed but "looney." Robert reported "they are definitely depressed or something" and reports no recent contact with his parents. Robert has two half brothers from his mother and stepfather's union and two half brothers from his birth father's second marriage. Robert denied any contact with his father's sons. He reported that of his mother's sons his youngest brother died of cancer, and his other brother, George, is "not very social." He reported George has had problems with drugs, mostly marijuana. Robert reported his stepfather was in the Navy and the family traveled quite often. Robert reported that his childhood was unproblematic and denied any abuse issues during his lifetime. Robert has been married two times and separated from his second wife a year ago. Robert has three daughters, two from his first marriage and one from what he terms a "a minor indiscretion." All are grown. Robert's second wife has three children of her own from a prior marriage, two boys and one girl (two are minors).

Robert reported he completed his education through his bachelor's degree and went on to medical school. He reported he graduated as a chiropractor in 1990. Robert denied problems in school. Robert's vocational history is varied beginning with military service as an engineer for nine years. He has worked as an assembler, a manager, and as a seaman and director of operations. Robert reported there are other jobs as well but did not supply details. Robert's spirituality or religious system is as a "spiritualist." Robert believes in a higher power and forces that guide us in all we do. He believes in reincarnation and describes his focus as an "Eastern influence." Robert's legal history is positive for multiple DUIs, charges of reckless driving, reckless endangerment, malpractice, loss of medical license, bankruptcy related to a failed business, divorce, child support issues, and default of a medical school student loan. Significant events include death of brother, separation from second wife, bankruptcy and student loan default, multiple DUIs, loss of medical license, and his house burning down last year.

Robert moved one year ago when his home had burned down mysteriously. He reported his second wife left him around this time as he "could not feed them" because he had lost his medical license for his drinking and malpractice. Robert moved into his daughter's home with his son-in-law and grandson. Within three months, Robert's first wife moved into the home as well. Robert reported that his first wife reminds him "every day how worthless" he is. Robert reported that this tension has become unbearable and he decided to move out two weeks ago. On the date of his move, Robert learned that the daughter he lived with was getting a divorce. He reported that he had planned to move into the "shed" at a female friend's home. Robert reported that the friend's boyfriend found out and therefore he is homeless. Robert currently has no source of income. He reported he has spent all of his savings, and he cannot find employment in his current state. He reported he worked at Kmart for a while but left after Christmas. He reported he may have $100 in the bank but he is unsure. Robert reported that he has been denied

──────────── **THE CASE OF ROBERT *(Continued)*** ────────────

social security or veteran's benefits due to his student loan status and his history of drinking. Robert denied involvement with vocational rehabilitation services. Robert reported he has made some drinking friends or acquaintances since he has come to Florida but denied many friendships. He reported he enjoys few things of late but does enjoy sleep as an activity. Current legal issues include the unresolved financial aid default and last DUI. Culturally, Robert has gone from small town to larger area. He has gone from an area where he had many sources of extended support to an area with few supports. Also he has gone from being a doctor to being unemployable in his trade. The loss of status related to this is significant. Legal consequences from his drinking and driving and the resultant of loss of his medical license are some of the numerous significant losses of home, career, marriage, children's involvement, social supports, and finances he has suffered.

Mental Status Description

Presentation	Mental Functioning	Higher Order Abilities	Thought Form/Content
Appearance: Unkempt	Simple Calculations: Accurate but slowed	Similarities/Differences: Accurate	Judgment: Fair to poor
Mood: Anxious and depressed	Serial Sevens: Accurate		Insight: Poor
Attitude: Cooperative	Immediate Memory: Needed prompts to remain on task, some vagueness to detail		Intelligence: High
Affect: Congruent, sad, blunted			Thought Process: Logical but some slowness noted Difficulty with concentration noted
Speech: Normal	Remote Memory: Intact		Delusions: None
Motor Activity: retarded	General Knowledge: Accurate yet slow to respond		Hallucinations: None
Orientation: Oriented X 4	Proverb Interpretation: Accurate yet slow processing		

APPLICATION OF MULTIAXIAL ASSESSMENT

Based on the data accumulated on the above case summary and on the further assessment tools of laboratory findings, and completion of the MAST, the client is diagnosed on Axis I with alcohol dependence with physiologic dependence, cocaine abuse, cannabis abuse, and major depression recurrent without psychotic features.

The justification for each listing is as follows. Alcohol dependence with physiologic dependence is diagnosed as Robert has ingested a pathologic amount of alcohol with resultant BAL of .436 percent, reported daily use of large quantities of alcohol, reported increased tolerance to achieve the desired effect, and voices a history of and current manifestation of withdrawal symptoms of elevated pulse, sweating, vomiting, tremors, and seizures. Additionally, he has had multiple attempts at sobriety with detoxification, counseling, and AA as unsuccessful methods of treatment. He is unable to sustain employment or maintain or initiate social relationships (excluding those "drinking" acquaintances). Robert has a diagnosis of cirrhosis of the liver as substantiated by abnormal laboratory findings and past medical records. This condition which is caused primarily by chronic use of alcohol can be life threatening and in spite of his medical knowledge, Robert continues to drink.

Second to alcohol dependence is the issue of cocaine and cannabis abuse. Robert reported he has used these substances for a 12-month period, he has been unable to maintain work, relationships, and has demonstrated poor performance issues with professional functioning, decision-making, and coping skills. He used these substances while driving and he reported he used them while practicing medicine. He continues to use them despite his dire financial state and legal issues. While it is difficult to show these singularly are effecting functioning as required in the diagnostic criterion the lack of physiologic signs or reports by Robert of withdrawal excludes the conditions of polysubstance dependence, cocaine dependence, and cannabis dependence.

Comorbidity with substance use disorders is prevalent for mood disorders. Depression and bipolar disorder are occurring most frequently. In this case, the diagnosis of major depression recurrent, severe without psychotic features is made with information of observation, history, and prior record review. Independent use of tools such as Beck's Inventory for Depression may also supplement data collected. As the patient clearly exhibits the history and severity of depression without report of signs of mania or mood swings, bipolar disorder is eliminated on initial evaluation. Psychological testing and use of the Minnesota Multiphasal Personality Inventory may be useful if conflicting presentation is found through the course of treatment. However, Robert clearly denied any experience of psychosis throughout the interview process. His thought was clear, intact, and he was oriented to person, place, time, and circumstance. He reported he has been depressed all the time for the past three months and reported episodic periods of such depression in the past. He reported loss of interest and increased sleep. He reported recurrent suicidal ideation with somewhat of a plan to harm himself when he was driving. He voiced feelings of hopelessness, worthlessness, and fatigue. He reported lack of concentration. In this case, the significant question to observe is the possibility of a mood disorder secondary to alcohol intoxication. However, the patient does report episodes of feeling depressed even when he has been sober. Therefore, the final diagnosis remains major depression, recurrent, severe without psychotic features.

Axis II for Robert will reflect the V Code of 71.09 as he has no retardation or personality disorders that are present at this evaluation. He does have some avoidant and antisocial traits however. These are evidenced by his report that he left his home when it burned down despite supports in that area and his continuation of illegal activity despite consequences known to him in that he is continuing to drink and drive and he is driving without a license. He appears to avoid consequences, relationships, and conflicts toward resolution of issues to the detriment of his own welfare. He appears to consistently lack a regard for persons or public safety yet this has not been a lifelong issue. He appears to fail to plan ahead and fails to adhere to societal norms.

On Axis III, the diagnosis is cirrhosis of the liver, history of withdrawal seizure, and allergy to sulfa drugs. The importance of this is twofold. When looking at potential medications for this patient, it will be important to avoid those with the potential for increased liver dysfunction. Second, drug interactions may affect the use of antidepressants that appear indicated for this patient. The presence of cirrhosis is an additionally conclusive sign that the patient has been accurately diagnosed. The inclusion of the seizure history is critical for the monitoring physicians, nurses, and social workers as protocols to prevent any present seizures must be implemented to protect the patient.

Axis IV is far more complex. Robert demonstrates issues in almost all of the psychosocial domains. Hence, based on the details of the assessment, the diagnosis reads: Problems with the primary support group: problems with child, problems with spouse (separation and divorce). Problems with the social environment: inadequate support system, no friends, inability to establish relationships, adjustment to life situation; problems with occupation: loss of career, inability to maintain or obtain employment; problems with housing, homelessness; economic problems: inadequate finances, no source of income; problems with access to health care: no transportation, no insurance, poor follow through with treatment needs. Chronic illness, legal problems: multiple DUIs, outstanding cases, loss of medical license.

Axis V looks at the clients global functioning which in this case is greatly impaired on the psychosocial domains although cognitive functioning remains fairly intact. The practitioner may be tempted to rate the functioning high based on the intelligence and cognition of the patient, however, in looking at the scale the patient actually falls in two categories. He fits the category of 30 to 40 in that he has major impairments to several areas of judgment, mood, occupation, avoidance of friends, and neglect of family, but he really does not have the severe cognitive loss or problems with reality testing. He does also fit in the category of 50 to 41 with

---

ROBERT'S MULTIAXIAL ASSESSMENT

Axis I: Alcohol dependence with physiological dependence 303.90.

Cocaine abuse 305.60.

Cannabis abuse 305.20.

Major depressive disorder, recurrent, severe without psychotic features 296.33.

Axis II: V71.09 No diagnosis.

Avoidant and antisocial traits.

Axis III: Cirrhosis of the liver, history of withdrawal seizure, allergy to sulfa drugs.

Axis IV: Problems with the primary support group: problems with child, problems with spouse (separation and divorce). Problems with the social environment: inadequate support system, no friends, inability to establish relationships, adjustment to life situation. Problems with occupation: loss of career, inability to maintain or obtain employment. Problems with housing: homelessness. Economic problems: inadequate finances, no source of income. Problems with access to health care: no transportation. No Insurance, poor follow through with treatment needs by history, chronic illness; legal problems: multiple DUIs, outstanding cases, loss of medical license.

Axis V: 40 (current).

---

suicidal ideation, in addition to the lack of friends and unemployment. In this case, due to the multiple areas of social functioning loss the best practice is to err on the side of caution. By giving the patient a score of 40, he is close to each range and hence this is the most representative of his functioning.

TREATMENT PLANNING, IMPLEMENTATION, AND EVALUATION

Considering the debates within the industry, the varied attitudes of patient populations, cultural considerations, and variety of intervention models to choose from, treatment planning for the mental health practitioner and his or her client can be a complicated process. The most effective treatment planning must take into account environmental planning and all of the information already discussed. There are new pathways for developing the most effective plan with your client. Some noted resources to achieve this means are the clinical guidelines set forth by the U.S. Department of Health and Human Resources in their Technical Assistance Manual #21, "Addiction Counseling Competencies" (1998).

In formulating the intervention plan, some sample treatment goals may include for the client to maintain abstinence, obtain and maintain sobriety, controlled drinking, resolution of legal issues, improve social and coping skills, and enhance self-esteem. Furthermore, it is important to assure that the goals match the assessment and desires of the patient. Additionally, factors such as strengths, support systems, dual diagnoses, and culture must be incorporated into the treatment planning process.

Objectives for the alcohol-related client should be clear and concise. The inherent factor of relapse and resistance should be addressed so the client is not set up for failure. It would be helpful for the practitioner to discuss this with the client initially during the diagnostic assessment and throughout treatment planning and strategy regardless of the intervention technique (George &Tucker, 1996). Ascertaining the attitude of the client about treatment is essential in developing a successful plan. Upon the initial formulation of the treatment plan, the first stage of implementation is generally detoxification.

Detoxification and Withdrawal

Detoxification is the process during which the client removes the alcohol from his system. This is generally done through abstinence or "going Cold Turkey." Most clients will complete this phase on an inpatient basis (Henderson, Landry, Phillips, & Shuman, 1994). In this disorder a medical exam is crucial. The risk here is the potential dangers of withdrawal and, consequently, withdrawal syndromes, which can leave the client in critical need of immediate medical attention (Fuller & Hiller-Sturmhofel, 1999; Wesson, 1995). These withdrawal syndromes are characterized by a continuum of signs and symptoms usually beginning 12 to 48 hours after cessation of intake that accompany alcohol withdrawal. The mild withdrawal syndrome includes tremor, weakness, sweating, hyper-reflexia, and GI symptoms. Some patients have generalized tonic-clonic seizures (alcoholic epilepsy or rum fits), usually not more than two in short succession (APA, 1994, 2000; Wesson, 1995).

The more severe withdrawal syndromes include alcoholic hallucinosis (auditory illusions and hallucinations, frequently accusatory and threatening but usually transient), and delirium tremens (anxiety attacks, increasing confusion, poor sleep with frightening dreams or nocturnal illusions), marked sweating, and profound depression, fleeting hallucinations that arouse restlessness, fear, and terror, and serious physical distress. All of which should begin to resolve within 12 to 24 hours. Known complications of these severe withdrawal syndromes are Korsakoff's syndrome, Wernicke's encephalopathy, and cerebellar degeneration may occur in alcoholics. More serious, Marchiafava-Bignami disease is a rare demyelination of the corpus callosum that occurs in chronic alcoholics, predominantly men (Wesson et al., 1995). Pathologic intoxication is another rare syndrome characterized by repetitive, automatic movements, and extreme excitement with aggressive, uncontrolled, and irrational behavior that occurs after ingesting a relatively small amount of alcohol (Miller & Gold, 1998).

SAMPLE TREATMENT PLAN

ALCOHOL USE DISORDER

Definition of Alcohol Use Disorder:

A physiological dependence on alcohol. Individuals with this disorder have severe impairment in social and physical functioning.

Signs and Symptoms of Alcohol Use Disorder:

1. Blackouts.
2. Neglected responsibilities.
3. Absences from school or work.
4. Legal difficulties.
5. Relationship problems.
6. Slurred speech.
7. Lack of coordination.
8. Impairment in memory.
9. Tremors.
10. Anxiety.
11. Insomnia.
12. Self-hatred.
13. Financial difficulties.

Goals for Alcohol Use Disorder:

1. Abstinence of substance.
2. Medical Assessment.
3. Introduce new coping skills and/or build on existing coping skills.

Objectives	Interventions
Evaluate how much and how often client drinks.	Obtain self-report from client regarding his substance history.
Client will establish a support system he can utilize and depend on during recovery.	Contact friends/relatives and ask for input on client's substance use.
	Have client list all supportive friends and family members in his life.
	Contact these members and attempt to meet or speak to them about the importance of recovery for client.
Client will have an assessment completed by a physician.	Refer client to his primary physician for evaluation. If client does not have one and does have insurance, obtain information regarding financial assistance eligibility.

ALCOHOL DEPENDENCE

Definition: Substance dependence on alcohol is indicated by the individual's continued use of the substance despite significant substance-related problems. There is a pattern of repeated self-administration that can result in tolerance, withdrawal, and compulsive drug-taking behavior. Evidence of tolerance or symptoms of withdrawal indicate physiological dependence on alcohol. The individuals who are alcohol dependent may continue to use alcohol despite evidence of adverse psychological or physical consequences (i.e., depression, blackouts, liver disease). Individuals may often continue to consume alcohol to avoid or relieve the symptoms of withdrawal. A minority of individuals who have alcohol dependence never experience clinically relevant levels of alcohol withdrawal (withdrawal symptoms that develop 4 to 12 hours after the reduction of intake following prolonged, heavy, alcohol ingestion); only about 5 percent of individuals with alcohol dependence ever experience severe complications of withdrawal (i.e., delirium, grand mal seizures).

Signs and Symptoms to Note and Document in the Record:

1. Experience of withdrawal symptoms such as sleep problems.
2. Substantial periods of time devoted to obtaining and consuming alcoholic beverages.
3. School or job performance may deteriorate.
4. Neglect of child care or household responsibilities.
5. Alcohol-related absences from school or job.
6. Legal difficulties arising from alcohol-related use.

Goals:

1. Assist client in abstaining from alcohol.
2. Help link client to socially appropriate AA chapter in the community.
3. Assist client's family in dealing with their alcoholic dependent relative.
4. Address underlying issues of alcohol dependency.

Objectives	Interventions
1. Client will discuss alcohol dependency issues responsible for self-destructive behavior.	A. Assist client in becoming fully aware of how behavior affects him and other people around him. Client and therapist will identify specific reasons why client will need to stop drinking.
2. Help client deal with symptoms of alcohol withdrawal and effects of the body.	A. Educate client as to effects of alcohol dependency and future problems that may arise later on if client continues to drink.
3. Client will discuss experience he has had while attending AA meetings and how it has helped him to become abstinent.	A. Client will keep journal of experience in AA meetings.
4. Address the needs of the alcohol dependent client's family. Encourage clients family throughout treatment.	A. Therapist will arrange for relatives to attend Alanon as well as having sessions to help client's family to deal with the alcoholism.
5. Client will take medications as prescribed for withdrawal/dependency/depression.	A. Monitor for medication use or misuse.

Medical evaluation is needed initially to detect coexisting illness that might complicate withdrawal and to rule out brain injury that might mask or mimic the withdrawal syndrome. Some drugs frequently used to treat alcohol withdrawal are CNS-depressants. Benzodiazepines are the mainstay of therapy. Compared with shorter-acting benzodiazepines (e.g., lorazepam, oxazepam), long-acting benzodiazepines (e.g., chlordiazepoxide, diazepam) provide less frequent dosing and, when the dose is tapered, an easier transition. The main problem with benzodiazepines is they may cause intoxication, physical dependence, and withdrawal in alcoholics and hence, a secondary addiction problem at times (Miller & Gold, 1998; Myrick & Anton, 1998; Wesson et al., 1995).

INTERVENTION STRATEGY FOR THE ALCOHOLIC

The alcohol use disorders are varied and treatment planning methods are diverse and can be complex. For example, late-stage alcoholics need proper attention when terminating drinking, and the degree in severity of addiction will determine the choice of intensity of intervention and treatment setting. In general, more sheltered settings are needed for people with weak social supports (J. Mendelson & Mello, 1992; Myrick & Anton, 1998). Milkman and Sederer (1990) offer six conclusions regarding treatment, based on research available to them: (1) alcoholism treatment can be quite effective; (2) there is no one superior approach; (3) not all treatment approaches are equal in effectiveness; (4) optimal treatment varies with client characteristics; (5) length, intensity, and setting of treatment do not appear to be powerful determinants of overall effectiveness; and (6) therapist characteristics seem to have an important influence on treatment impact (p. 261).

Alcoholics also experience difficulty managing stress reactions, including anxiety, tension, panic, and feeling worried, pressured, and overwhelmed. Considering the principle that a person's emotional and behavioral reactions are at least partially determined by a person's cognitions and subsequent behaviors, it makes sense that cognitive-behavioral approach to treatment continues to be utilized as the primary intervention model. The intervention palette, however, is full of alternatives to suit the patient as their needs indicate. A brief look at each will help the social work interventionist in assisting his or her clients.

Biopsychosocial Model Approach

Alcoholism is a psychological, sociocultural, and physical problem (Morales & Scheafor, 1998). The biopsychosocial approach incorporates the physical with the psychosocial to understand the person as a whole. Of all the approaches used to assist the alcoholic, the idea classifying it as a medical condition related to biomedical factors beyond the control of the individual remains an essential one (Yalisove, 1998). In studies to observe these factors, the possibility of a deficiency in natural body chemicals, like serotonin, in some alcoholics was revealed. In addition to the neurobiological changes in the patient's functioning, the theory proposes to effect change in perceptive functions of the client. Wild and Cunningham (2001) investigated the determinants of perceived vulnerability and found that there is a statistical link between a person's perception of potential harm and potential social implications for potential harm. "The biopsychosocial model for understanding and treatment of alcohol problems is a concept with much utility in primary care settings. This approach takes into account the interaction of physiological, behavioral, social, and environmental factors in the etiology of disease. It is a concept with relevance to interventions as well, since behavioral and medical management techniques are closely interrelated" (J. Mendelson & Mello, 1992, p. 481).

Pharmacotherapy

The use of medications in the detoxification and ongoing treatment of the alcoholic has continued to emerge as a prominent treatment approach. While the mental health practitioner cannot prescribe medications, it would be a noticeable deficit if they were uneducated in this approach (Dziegielewski & Leon, 2001). The brain consists of multiple neurotransmitter systems that modulate various bodily functions. These include opioids, glutamate, serotonin (5HT), and dopamine (B. A. Johnson & Ait-Daud, 1999).

Opioids are pain blockers and have the similar effect as morphine or heroin. In alcohol use, these peptides appear to increase the sense of rewarding effects when alcohol is consumed. There additionally appears to be some interaction with dopamine in the creation of this effect. Glutamate is an excitatory transmitter that appears to work with brain receptor cites to increase the effects of intoxication, cognitive impairment, and some symptoms of withdrawal in alcohol consumption. Serotonin effects bodily functioning in varied physiological, cognitive, mood, sleep, and appetite areas. Dopamine is linked to higher brain functioning and organization of thought and perception (B. A. Johnson & Ait-Daud, 1999).

The longest standing medication treatment continues to be that of the aversive medication, Antabuse or disulfiram. The effect of the medication is negative physiological reactions including nausea, vomiting, and increased blood pressure and heart rate. However, the problems with poor compliance decrease the medication's effectiveness. Supervised administration does improve results but the outcomes are still lower than originally anticipated (Fuller & Hiller-Sturmhofel, 1999). Two newer drugs being used in alcohol dependency are Naltrexone and Acamprosate.

Naltrexone is an opiate blocking agent and Acamprosate modulates GABBA/Gluta-mate (Bonn, 1999, Petrakis & Krystal, 1997). GABBA is also being effected with gamma-hydroxybutyric acid (GHB) (Addolorato et al., 1998).

While this field is developing rapidly, the clinical trials and new developments discussed above are far from being a part of common treatment regimes. The research is promising and shows that most of the drugs have at least some clinical efficacy for reductions in cravings, and biochemical impulsivity related to dependence. However, as noted in Bonn's 1999 review of new drugs, these treatments are not cures. They do not eliminate the problem of alcohol dependence. Many of those studied continued to drink while on the medications but with decreased frequency and quantity. The studies reviewed indicated that the possibility of increased efficacy may be linked to combination therapies involving more than one of these medications coupled with behavioral, cognitive, motivational, or self-help intervention.

Cognitive Behavior Therapy

This very popular intervention for addictions rests in the premise that addiction like all other behavior is learned and, therefore, is subject to modification and eventual extinction (Harvard Medical School, 2000b). Studies of alcoholics and the long-term effects of insight-oriented versus behavioral treatment further resulted in support for the behavioral approach. Milkman and Sederer (1990) declare that a person's behavioral repertoire determines the choices regarding alcohol use, which supports the use of the cognitive-behavioral approach to problem drinking. Behavior therapy has been proven effective in numerous outcome research studies in problems such as anxiety disorders, sexual problems, psychosis, gerontology, depression, obesity, and alcohol and drug addiction. Treatment rests with education, supportive therapy, and cognitive-behavioral techniques that teach coping skills, and give individuals a confident attitude (Anthenelli & Schucket, 1993; Turner, 1996; Watson, 1991).

According to Turner (1996), cognitive therapy methods utilized by practitioners must:

1. Relate to the client on the basis of behavior and his stated thoughts, emotions, and goals, without postulating unconscious forces.
2. Makes a diagnosis in terms of the distortions or limitations in the client's thinking.
3. Look for the client's strengths rather than his pathology and puts those strengths to use.
4. Guide the client into trying selected experiences that may alter his inaccurate perceptions.

5. Recognize that each client's behavior is shaped by his personal goals rather than by universal biological drives.
6. Work to achieve changes the client wants by expanding this consciousness of self, others, and the world around him.
7. Require the client to take responsibility for his behavior, not allowing the past or the "unconscious" to excuse present conduct (p. 102).

In utilizing these basic practice principles with the alcoholic individual, the first step toward intervention is to help him recognize that he is experiencing a loss of control and confront the denial common to the condition. The second goal of treatment could be assisting the alcoholic to recognize the circumstances that render him or her vulnerable to loss of control and conquer them. Some clients will be successful when integrating lifestyle changes, others will need to gain mastery over internal drives, and maturity by developing tolerance of affect (Larimer, Palmer, & Marlatt, 1999). Behavior modification and changes in cognitive processes are effective in achieving the above goals. What the client must accept is the fact that these are really guided self-help steps. The client must work actively to achieve these, and success will be determined by the degree to which the client accepts responsibility for helping him or herself. Thus, taking charge of his or her recovery.

The client must identify negative self-statements, private thoughts, or negative self-talk that in some manner inhibit the client's performance. These thoughts can then be cognitively restructured into positive, constructive statements, and combined with a perceptual redefinition of the client's reality in the inhibiting situation. The client then must learn to use the positive self-statements to reinforce himself, as new behaviors and goals are achieved (Turner, 1996).

Expectancies play an important role in the use of cognitive-behavioral therapy. The theory proposes that people act in accordance with expected outcomes, and expectancies can be positive or negative when used as an intervention in alcohol treatment. First, the stimuli that have been associated with the effects of drinking may, through classical conditioning, become cues for seeking out anticipated rewards from alcohol or for avoiding the negative consequences of drinking. Second, physiological withdrawal symptoms may, with repeated episodes of heavy drinking, become cues for the belief that more drinking will lead to a temporary reduction in aversive physical symptoms. A third influence in developing outcome expectancies regarding alcohol consists of physical and social environmental factors. For instance, an individual may develop alcohol outcome expectations that are specific to a particular setting. A fourth source of alcohol outcome expectancies consists of the beliefs an individual holds about the effects of alcohol. Cognitive-behavior theory suggests that people are more likely to abuse alcohol if they lack a sense of self-efficacy in a situation where they expect alcohol to enable them to achieve the desired outcome. The use of social skills training and redevelopment of problem-solving pathways such as in the model of cognitive-behavioral coping skills therapy used by the Veterans' Administration and a number of teaching hospitals throughout the United States, is a primary example of how expectancy modification has evolved in practice with clients who have alcohol use disorders (Longabaugh & Morganstern, 1999). The interactions of the adult alcoholic in the social environment involve friends and family. Understanding the role of these supports is particularly helpful in eliciting a successful treatment outcome.

The Family System Approach

According to this perspective successful treatment of alcoholism requires a multidimensional approach involving the abuser, his or her family, and the environment. The alcoholic is viewed as a human system, which requires more than one, and often a combination of intervention approaches. The family is viewed as a set of interconnected individuals acting together to maintain a homeostatic balance. The basic premise of this model is to allow each member of the family to achieve a higher level of functioning and emotional security (Curtis, 1999). The view of the family as a system is essential to accomplish the intended outcome. The alcoholic does not exist in a vacuum. Rather the person and his addiction are living, breathing, interacting elements of their environment, their family's environment, and the exclusionary observation of the person without these factors is impossible in this model.

Studying a single variable in isolation could not reveal the information needed about the system as a whole, because the nature of the relationships between components of a system was interactional (Kilpatrick & Holland, 1999). Duncan, Duncan, and Hops (1999) agreed with this and stated that a thorough analysis of the cognitive, social, and behavioral aspects of the abuser's drinking behavior has been shown through research to be essential before intervention can be undertaken. The observation of the system in the environment and the use of homeostasis in perpetuating addiction are of special consideration to the practitioner utilizing this approach.

Motivational Therapies

DiClemente, Bellino, and Neavens (1999) state "Motivation is an important step toward changing any action or behavior" (p. 86). They identify five stages of the decision-making process a person goes through when contemplating any change. These are (1) precontemplation, (2) contemplation, (3) preparation, (4) action, and (5) maintenance. Due to the inherent problem of denial and rationalization, this approach of enhancing motivation is well indicated. "Motivation appears to be a critical dimension in influencing patients to seek, comply with, and complete treatment as well as to make successful long term changes in their drinking" (p. 87). Determining level of motivation involves assessment for internal and external motivation. These are differentiated by the source of the desire to effect change from within the person or from external or environmental sources.

Once the baseline for level of motivation is established through assessment, intervention begins; there are several intervention approaches to utilize. First, brief motivational intervention consists of educating the patient about the negative effects of alcohol abuse to motivate the patient to stop or reduce her drinking. This approach is indicated for the nondependent alcohol use disorders. The course is generally 1 to 4 sessions lasting 10 to 40 minutes each. The setting is generally substance abuse outpatient or primary care offices (DiClemente et al., 1999).

The second motivational intervention approach is that of *motivational interviewing*. The application involves educating the patient on the stages of change, the role of denial and ambivalence as natural components of these stages, and assisting the patient to work through ambivalence toward sobriety. Techniques used include reflective listening, examination of the pros and cons of change, support of patient self-efficacy and ability to change, assessment and feedback on problem behavior (i.e., abc charting, behavioral counts), and last, eliciting self-motivational statements or affirmations from the patient. The length of treatment is undefined and can be as long as needed to effect change. Sessions last from 30 to 60 minutes and are generally one time a week (DiClemente et al., 1999).

The third approach in motivational therapy is motivational enhancement therapy (MET), which was developed specifically for the PROJECT MATCH study and combines motivational interviewing with a less intensive setting. The four sessions occur over 12 weeks and are initiated upon completion of an intensive assessment process. The use of standardized measures occurs at session one and clear, concise feedback about the patient's addiction behavior is relayed to the patient in each session. Session two is intended for the purpose of developing a change plan. Session three is used for reinforcement and enhancing commitment to motivation and change. Session four is termination (DiClemente et al., 1999).

In assessing the model, research indicates that each intervention approach is successful for a variety of patients of alcohol abuse. The research is unclear as to the efficacy against other models, but to note that as in PROJECT MATCH, motivational interventions appear no less effective than other approaches reviewed. There was no data available at this time on the potential effect of combination therapies such as cognitive and motivation techniques. It appears that an integrated approach for the treatment of alcohol use disorders is indicated based on these efficacy data sets.

The Traditional Self-Help Approach

There is one approach that is most often considered a primary intervention strategy for those who suffer from alcohol abuse and dependence. This approach, referred to as the traditional approach or the disease model, is provided through Alcoholics Anonymous (AA) and is the major nonmedical support system available to alcoholics. Others offer emotional support and practical advice in similar circumstances and many, but not all, alcoholics can be helped by the mutual/self-help fellowship of Alcoholics Anonymous (J. Mendelson & Mello, 1992; Tonigan, Connors, & Miller, 1998).

The Twelve Steps model (see box) forbids promotion and anonymity is of paramount importance. AA differentiates religion from spirituality, and bases beliefs in a "higher power of one's own understanding." Despite criticisms, there are many followers of this model and most professionals agree that for millions of people this model of intervention does work.

QUICK REFERENCE

THE TWELVE STEPS TO RECOVERY

1. We admitted we were powerless over alcohol—that our lives had become unmanageable.
2. Came to believe that a power greater than ourselves could restore us to sanity.
3. Made a decision to turn our will, and our lives, over to the care of God *as we understood Him.*
4. Made a searching and fearless moral inventory of ourselves.
5. Admitted to God, to ourselves, and to another human being the exact nature of our wrongs.
6. Were entirely ready to have God remove all these defects of character.
7. Humbly asked Him to remove our shortcomings.
8. Made a list of all persons we had harmed, and became willing to make amends to them all.
9. Made direct amends to such people wherever possible, except when to do so would injure them or others.
10. Continued to take personal inventory and when we were wrong promptly admitted it.
11. Sought through prayer and meditation to improve our conscious contact with God, as we understood Him, praying only for knowledge of His will for us and the power to carry that out.
12. Having had a spiritual awakening as the result of these steps, we tried to carry this message to alcoholics and to practice these principles in all our affairs.

Source: National Institute on Alcohol Abuse and Alcoholism, No. 30 PH 359, October 1995.

TOWARD AN INTEGRATED APPROACH:
IMPLICATIONS FOR PRACTICE

Alcoholism is a multifaceted problem that results from elements of conditioning and learning, and also from neurobiological processes, genetics, cognitive processes, family systems, society, and culture (Latorre, 2000; Wallace, 1989). Turner (1996) explains that "too long we have labored under an impression that adherence to one approach to practice by definition excluded others; there was some component of disloyalty or some quality of machiavellian manipulation to attempt to move from one approach to another depending on the situation" (p. 709).

Therefore, when separating these perspectives for practice, each intervention strategy has its own strengths and limitations. For example, the best plan of cognitive/behavioral intervention can easily go astray if environmental and family supports are ignored. Incorporating the ideas from systems theory as part of the intervention process allows the social worker to acknowledge the importance of taking into account the whole situation. Intervention needs to include more than just individual and family behavior change strategy. It involves the sociological, psychological, biological, and environmental elements of the client.

The challenge for the mental health practitioner is to approach the client's entire system in unison with a multidimensional treatment strategy. This involves more than just using the principles inherent in cognitive-behavior therapy where the role of the practitioner is primarily that of an educator who expects clients to set their own standards, monitor their own performance, and reward or reinforce themselves appropriately. In this respect, the counselor strives to help the client become his or her own therapist (Milkman & Sederer, 1990). According to Watson (1991), the preferable strategy is empowerment of people who feel spiritually and personally empty and giving this area ample attention. Latorre (2000) concurs with this approach stating, "We are dealing with a system, not just a collection of parts, a system that continually strives to balance itself using symptoms as a way to self heal" (p. 67).

Furthermore, although easily forgotten, effective treatment must include the client's family. Westermeyer (1990) explains that as drug and alcohol addicts recover they "have need for both (1) involvement with their own special social identity groups and (2) involvement with others broadly representative of the communities in which they will live and function." Cultural competency and the primary understanding of the ethnocentrensic factors in the alcohol disorders are needed and are added components in this approach (Arredondo, 1998).

An integrated approach that involves family education and support, combined with self-help groups are particularly important to the patients in treatment. Alcoholism is a family disease. The significant others and any other persons close to the alcoholic typically also benefit from treatment. Milkman and Sederer (1990) relate the possible need to restructure the family, and need to adjust to the recovery of the family member. The alcoholic's family and his or her support system is a vital and powerful aspect of the client's ability for recovery. If the intervention strategy does not include the client's family system, the prognosis for long-term recovery from the illness is greatly decreased. A further understanding of familial stages and elderly families or patients must also be included in further interventions (Zimberg, 1996). From the traditional perspective, Alcoholics Anonymous urges participation in Al-Anon for family members. In addition to the need for counselors treating alcoholics to include the family, the social worker who specializes in family therapy needs training in the awareness of, and diagnosis of, addiction problems in families (Steinglass, 1976).

Medelsor and Mello (1992) believe that the diagnosis of the disease is complicated by the intense denial evidenced by the alcoholic, by his or her family, and by society. The use of a genogram is suggested when working with a troubled family. Though the family denies the possibility of a chemical abuse problem, a genogram that reports chemical abuse in previous generations is at least an indicator of the strong possibility of prevalence of this condition in this family.

Among the tasks of the worker are (1) helping the alcoholic and the family accept that alcoholism is the primary problem, (2) recommending treatment options, and (3) instilling a sense of hope for recovery. Therapeutic alternatives are the use of antabuse, individual therapy, family therapy, and Alcoholics Anonymous. Relapses, when properly handled, can help the alcoholic to accept his or her powerlessness over alcohol.

SUMMARY

Alcoholism is a social, psychological, and physical affliction that is difficult to define yet has a profound impact on individuals, their families, and society. Causes of alcoholism are as diverse as those afflicted. Alcoholics can be difficult clients, but can be treated if intervention is initiated early enough to arrest cognitive and biological deterioration. Successful intervention is possible using a number of treatments. The focus has been on the cognitive-behavioral treatment, which teaches new behaviors and thinking processes. A look at treatment matching studies and efforts and at special considerations of treatment planning was included to examine these facts. Also addressed was the efficacy of Alcoholics Anonymous for the client and family, the importance of biopsychosocial considerations, and the need for a systems approach. To provide the best care possible, it is imperative that social workers possess knowledge about addictions, and the addictive process.

8 Eating Disorders: Anorexia Nervosa

Sophia F. Dziegielewski and Janet D. Murray

Eating disorders are prevalent in today's society. The pressure to be thin can be so strong that many individuals, primarily women, do not eat enough, or practice fanatical eating or binging and purging in order to meet a state of thinness that for most is unachievable. Furthermore, the exact definition of what constitutes thin can be elusive. This leaves food, weight, and body image an almost unavoidable preoccupation for many individuals. On any given day, 50 percent of American women are said to be on diets (Wilson & Blackhurst, 1999). Since approximately two-thirds of women are dissatisfied with their weight and the way they look (Rabak-Wagener & Eickhoff-Shemek, 1998), the development of eating disorders for women has become a widespread problem that requires attention.

Today, eating disorders appear gender related, and women are most at risk for developing these disorders. Sobal (1995) stated that messages about body shape are "transmitted by mass media and oral traditions within societies and are reinforced in everyday social interactions that express social norms about weight and apply sanctions against people who deviate from accepted weight standards" (p. 74). While the average body weight in the United States has been increasing over the past few decades, the ideals for beauty, especially for women, have increasingly emphasized slimness (Byely, Archibald, Graber, & Brookes-Dunn, 2000; Sobal, 1995). Biological and genetic factors tell us that the current "thin is beautiful" ideal describes a body weight for most women that is unrealistically low and unhealthy (Wilfley & Rodin, 1995). Women constantly confronted with the media's slender and beautiful ideals thus aspire to a standard that is impossible for most to achieve (Pliner, Chaikin, & Flett, 1990).

Attention to the psychological and physiological development of eating disorders is critical because eating disorders are associated with serious and even fatal medical complications. Two common types of eating disorders are bulimia nervosa and anorexia nervosa. Bulimia nervosa is a widespread eating disorder with symptom behaviors such as characteristic bouts of over eating and subsequent troublesome methods of controlling weight (i.e., self-induced vomiting, laxative abuse, and overexercise). In anorexia nervosa, the essential feature is refusal to maintain a minimum body weight. Death from starvation is a realistic concern for individuals who suffer from anorexia nervosa—mortality rates range from 6 percent to 20 percent (Pomeroy, 1996). However, since many clients strongly deny that they are having a problem and that anything needs to be done about it, practitioners experience difficulty in effectively treating eating disorders. Treating these conditions can be problematic even with active participation from the client. Only one-half of the individuals who suffer from anorexia nervosa recover, and of those who do recover, up to 25 percent experience severe disabilities from the chronic nature and severity of the disease (Pomeroy, 1996).

Our societal definition of what is "desirable and attractive" plays an important role in the development of body image and self-worth (Wilfley & Rodin, 1995, p. 80). Feelings and attitudes toward the body constitute an important aspect of a woman's feelings regarding her self-esteem (McAllister & Caltabiano, 1994) and these feelings and attitudes begin to impact an individual early in life. For example, as reported by Wilfley and Rodin, "adolescent girls who perceive themselves to be less attractive have lower self-esteem scores than do girls who are more satisfied with their appearance" (p. 80). It has been suggested that the "thin ideal" has been internalized by many women and negative perceptions of their own weight and appearance are associated with negative affective states such as anxiety and depression (McAllister & Caltabiano, 1994; V. Thomas, 1989).

"Body image refers to a person's mental image and evaluation of his or her physical appearance and the influence of these perceptions and attitudes on behavior." An essential feature of eating disorders, body image is ". . . the most consistent predictor of improvement and relapse after treatment" (Rosen, 1995, p. 369). Although all individuals are exposed to mass media and cultural messages about physical appearance, some will actually develop eating disorders or could have serious body image problems, or both. Negative or traumatic experiences associated with appearance or development can trigger negative assumptions about body shape. These assumptions impact self-esteem, personality, and behavior. Over time, an individual may rehearse negative and distorted self-statements about her appearance until she becomes unconsciously held beliefs. This sets up behavior patterns that maintain the preoccupation with appearance.

When an individual is diagnosed with an eating disorder, there are numerous things that must be taken into account and intervention options can vary. This chapter discusses one of the most common forms of eating disorders, anorexia nervosa, and addresses related issues from a community and societal perspective. To reduce the magnitude of disturbances this disorder can have on the individual, the family, and society, it is critical that practitioners complete a thorough diagnostic assessment, treatment plan, and practice strategy that can efficiently embrace, identify, and effectively treat individuals who suffer from anorexia nervosa.

USE OF THE *DSM-IV-TR* MULTIAXIAL SYSTEM

The essential features of anorexia nervosa (307.1) as defined in the *DSM-IV-TR* (American Psychiatric Association [APA], 2000) include the individual's refusal to maintain a minimally normal body weight. (See Quick Reference for the criterion needed to make the diagnosis.)

Individuals with this type of eating disorder look in the mirror and believe their reflection is too heavy for their body frame and height. They have a distorted body image—a significant disturbance in the perception of the shape or size of their body. This leads to adopting methods that contribute to severe weight reduction (see Criterion A). Weight loss is achieved by reduction in total food intake, although it could also occur through purging, such as self-induced vomiting, or misuse of laxatives or diuretics, and excessive exercise. Minimal body weight is reached when the individual weighs 85 percent less than what is considered normal for age and weight based on published charts such as the Metropolitan Life Insurance tables. In the diagnostic assessment, it is important that the individual's body build and weight history be considered when evaluating this criterion.

Individuals suffering from anorexia nervosa also have an intense fear of gaining weight (see Criterion B). The intense fear of gaining weight is not alleviated by the weight loss, but often increases as the individual's weight decreases, often leading to desperate measures to control weight. In addition, the self-esteem of anorexic individuals is critically tied to their body weight and size. These individuals perceive weight loss as an impressive achievement and a feat of great self-discipline and self-control. Some individuals may feel globally overweight while others recognize that they are thin but focus on certain body parts that they consider "too fat" (Criterion C). Techniques used by these individuals to monitor their weight and size include weighing themselves numerous times per day, obsessive measuring of body parts, and constant checking in the mirror for fat. In addition, they may participate in avoidance behaviors that help them maintain their

---

QUICK REFERENCE

CRITERIA FOR ANOREXIA NERVOSA

Criterion A	Maintaining a body weight that is below normal.
Criterion B	Intense fear of gaining weight.
Criterion C	Distortion of the significance of body weight and shape.
Criterion D	Amenorrhea.

QUICK REFERENCE

SUBTYPES FOR ANOREXIA

restricting type: During the current episode, the individual has not regularly engaged in binge eating or purging and weight loss is primarily accomplished through restriction of food intake.

binge-eating/purging type: During the current episode, the individual has regularly engaged in binge eating or purging (or both).

---

drive to lose weight. For example, they often avoid situations where they may be expected to eat or where others may view them eating or they wear loose-fitting clothing to disguise their diminishing shape.

The severe weight loss associated with anorexia nervosa often results in the cessation or disruption of menstrual cycles (amenorrhea) in postmenarcheal females (Criterion D). Abnormally low levels of estrogen secretion bring about amenorrhea, and the cessation of menstruation is a physical indication of significant physiological dysfunction. Many anorexic women judge success at losing and maintaining their desired weight only when their menstrual cycle stops.

In anorexia nervosa there are two primary subtypes that focus on the current or presenting symptoms or episode (see Quick Reference for brief discussion of the various subtypes). The first subtype is the *restricting type.* In this subtype, the individual does not regularly engage in binge eating or purging to maintain weight but rather focuses primary attention and efforts on restriction of food intake. In the second subtype, the *binge-eating/purging type,* the individual regularly engages in binge eating or purging (or both). Generally, a binge is defined as eating in a discrete period of time (usually less than 2 hours) an amount of food that is definitely larger than most individuals would eat under similar circumstances. If the individual binges, she will also purge by self-induced vomiting or the misuse of laxatives, diuretics, or enemas. Many will purge without binge eating, doing so after eating even small amounts of food.

ASSOCIATED CONDITIONS AND FEATURES

The associated conditions and features of anorexia include information that is frequently associated with the disorder but, unlike the criteria elements, are not considered essential to making the diagnosis. These may include associated laboratory findings, physical examination findings, and associated general medical conditions. For many individuals who suffer from this disorder, depressive features such as depressed mood, social withdrawal, irritability, insomnia, and diminished interest in sex may coexist. This is why in the diagnostic assessment it is important to assess symptoms of depression and whether the criteria for a comorbid diagnosis of major depressive disorder may be met. In addition, the client may be so consumed with the thought of controlling food intake that obsessive-compulsive features may also exist. Furthermore, the need to control may be so strong that at times, these behaviors may also be unrelated to food. Since the client is preoccupied with thoughts of food it is not uncommon for some of them to collect or hoard food. Other features of the disorder include concerns about eating in public, feelings of ineffectiveness, a strong need to control one's environment, inflexible thinking, limited social spontaneity, and overly restrained initiative and emotional expression.

One important aspect of completing the diagnostic assessment is looking carefully at the general medical conditions coded on Axis III. Assessment and documentation on this axis is important because the semi-starvation state can effect most major organs and produce a variety of serious medical disturbances. Induced vomiting and use of laxatives, diuretics, and enemas associated with anorexia nervosa can also cause a number of physical disturbances. These physical disorders include severe anemia, hepatic, thyroid, cardiovascular, dental, and hormone disturbances. Every possible attempt should be made to include information in the diagnostic assessment from associated laboratory and medical findings. Furthermore, a physical exam should always be the first referral if one has not already been completed.

SPECIFIC CULTURE, AGE, AND GENDER FEATURES

Prevalence studies show that 0.5 percent to 1.0 percent of the population meets the full criteria and many more are on the threshold for the disorder. Although often body image concerns may begin in late childhood or early adolescence, anorexia nervosa symptoms rarely begin before puberty. Although men also suffer from this disorder, more than 90 percent of the cases occur in females (APA, 2000). Generally, anorexia nervosa appears more frequently in industrialized societies where there is an abundance of food and where being considered attractive is linked to being extremely thin.

For most individuals who suffer from this disorder the mean (average) age at onset is approximately 17 years, although some individuals start earlier. Peaks in the disorder occur at ages 14 and 18. The course and outcome of this disorder are variable with some individuals experiencing only one episode while others experience a chronically deteriorating course over many years. It is not uncommon for hospitalization to be required in order to maintain weight and restore body functioning. The long-term mortality rate is 10 percent and death commonly results from starvation, suicide, or electrolyte imbalance. In terms of familial pattern, there is an increased risk of anorexia nervosa among the first-degree biological relatives of individuals with the disorder.

Probably one of the biggest factors to consider when first meeting with a client who suffers from this disorder is that most times individuals do not generally seek treatment on their own. Instead, individuals with anorexia nervosa are often brought to treatment by a concerned family member or a friend. Individuals with anorexia will rarely seek help on their own because they fear that getting help will lead to weight gain. In addition, they frequently lack insight into their problem and the overriding characteristic is denial. In completing the diagnostic assessment, accurate information regarding symptoms and duration should be collected from family members or other outside sources in addition to what is stated by the client.

HISTORICAL ASPECTS AND
INTERVENTION WITH ANOREXIA

Cash (1996) discussed social, cultural, and developmental theories and personality factors that contribute to body image disturbance and the development of eating disorders. From childhood, individuals have a tendency to evaluate their appearance in relation to ideal physical standards set by society. Self-worth is often based on how closely these standards are met. Socialization, particularly influences from parents, peers, and the media, contributes to the acquisition of values and attitudes about appearance. Messages that convey the importance of appearance contribute to ongoing social comparison and beliefs that looks and body shape and size symbolize a person's worth.

Normal developmental changes brought about by puberty can also bring on an intense preoccupation with changes in the body and concern about how one will be perceived by others. Normal changes in the body such as menstruation and increases in body fat in the breast or hips as a girl matures often precipitates persistent negative body-image disturbances (Byely et al., 2000; Cash, 1996).

Personality traits also provide a moderating influence on body image development. Individuals may define themselves in terms of their physical attributes, which contributes to a substantial negative impact on self-esteem and social confidence. These individuals have developed negative perceptions or schema and are more vulnerable to societal "shoulds" which define their physical acceptability.

Cognitive-behavioral therapy formats are effective interventions for avoiding negative thinking patterns. Changes such as fewer cognitive body image errors, less frequent negative body image thoughts, and less preoccupation with weight are addressed. Cognitive-behavioral therapy appears to be effective in improving cognitive, evaluative, effective, perceptual, and self-reported behavioral aspects of body image. Many of these improvements were found to generalize to self-esteem, social-evaluative anxiety, and eating disturbance (Grant & Cash, 1995).

To further understand the development of this condition, current research has examined the relationship of familial influences on the development of one's body image and dieting patterns. Byely et al. (2000) reported a substantial relationship between both family relationships and young girls' eating behavior. Both the girl's perception of the quality of her family relationships and the mother's perceptions of her daughter's weight were related to that girl's eating behavior one year later. Often, a girl will perceive that the only aspect of her life that she can control is her own weight. Thus, family involvement in treatment of the anorexic individual is often an essential component in recovery and prevention of relapse.

─────────────── **THE CASE OF M** ───────────────

M is a 19-year-old Caucasian female college sophomore who came to the University Counseling Clinic because of the urging of her friends. At first M was resistant and stated that her only reason for coming in to "talk to someone" was to please her friends and family. However, during the initial session, she also admitted feeling frustrated with herself and her physical appearance. She stated that she was experiencing problems with eating and had lost her appetite. She stated that she realized that she was having "some problems" but denied that they were as severe as her family and friends thought. She said, "They're just making a big deal out of this." She expressed an interest in wanting to learn how to "lose weight in a healthy way." M also reported that at times she has "anger at food" and cannot stop thinking about eating. M reported that she lost 18 pounds in the past 4 weeks, and, although she wishes to lose more weight, she is beginning to be concerned (along with her family and friends) that she may be losing weight too fast. She stated, "It's really easy for me to lose weight. It's easy for me to just not eat."

COMPLETION OF THE DIAGNOSTIC ASSESSMENT

The first step in starting the diagnostic assessment is to identify the presenting problem. To complete this information, the initial assessment includes factual information about the client and her behaviors.

Once the primary and presenting problems have been identified the first task of the mental health practitioner, especially with the concern for the client's desire to stop eating and continue losing weight, is to complete a risk assessment. Key questions will identify if there is a potential for self-harm or suicide. These questions are always asked in a straightforward and direct manner. Once identified, this information should be clearly recorded in the client's file. In this case, while assessing lethality, M reported having thoughts of suicide while in high school. She

---

QUICK REFERENCE

IDENTIFY PRIMARY AND PRESENTING PROBLEM

Primary problem: Anorexia nervosa.

Presenting problems: Preoccupation with eating and weight reduction, anger at food. Recent extensive and quick loss of weight.

---

stated that although she never attempted to harm herself, she thought about it seriously for a long time. However, currently, she denied any suicidal or homicidal thoughts and stated, "I have too much to live for and don't want to end my life."

The mental status exam report described M as slightly overweight to normal weight for her height, well groomed, neatly and appropriately dressed. She was cooperative and spoke willingly and openly. Her thought processes and speech were logical and coherent, with occasional tangential drifts when giving details. Her mood fluctuated between moderate calmness, anxiety, and anger as she described her concerns. Her affect fluctuated between appropriate and dramatic, particularly when speaking about her anger regarding food and eating. Motor movement was within expected limits and there was no evidence of delusions or hallucinations; however, she exhibited pronounced preoccupation with food and the eating behaviors of herself and others. M appeared to have above average intellectual functioning, however, her insight and judgment appeared somewhat limited, particularly concerning eating and weight.

In gathering history information, M stated that she grew up in a small town, with still-married parents and has a brother 6 years younger. Her mother is a registered nurse and her father is an engineer. She voiced a strong sense of obligation to please her parents and stated that her biggest fear was disappointing them. M reported that she was not fat as a child, but always felt that she was. By high school, she described herself as significantly overweight, weighing approximately 180

QUICK REFERENCE

RISK ASSESSMENT

Document and assess suicide risk: Previous history of ideation, no previous attempts, no current ideation, no evidence of current attempts.

Document and assess violence risk: None.

pounds with a height of 5'3". Although she stated that she was not teased as a child and had many friends, she began to experience strong anger, resentment, hurt, and a sense of unfairness when she compared herself to her peers during her first years in high school. M reported that when she was a sophomore in high school she hated herself and had thoughts of suicide. Nevertheless, she did not make an attempt, and then felt even more anger at herself that she couldn't follow through with it. She wrote of her anger at herself and her wish for death in journals, and after 2 years, stated that she "let go" of the anger. M reported that at that time she also developed an aversion to using public bathrooms and reported that she was able to control her bowel habits and could refrain from having a bowel movement for several weeks if she wished. She admitted that she felt powerful controlling her body in this way and also in her ability to limit her food intake.

By the end of her junior year in high school, her concerns about food led her to consult with a practitioner of alternative medicine who focused on the unhealthy additives and chemicals in foods. Using this information as rationale, she began eliminating more and more foods from her diet. When she did this, she began to lose weight. She stated that she set a goal of attaining a size 12 or 14, which she selected because "it represented the size of the average female." Throughout her senior year in high school and by the end of her freshman year at college, she had lost 90 pounds. She stated that she did this by limiting her intake of food, exercising every day, and occasionally purging by vomiting. She became a vegetarian 5 months ago, further restricting the foods she "allows" herself to eat.

She reported that she has not told her parents that she is having any difficulties at this time. Although she occasionally goes to her hometown for a weekend, she stays with friends and often she does not let her parents know that she is in town.

Family history of psychopathology reveals that her mother has experienced depressive symptoms for more than 10 years; however, it is unknown if she was ever diagnosed with a mental health condition or has taken psychotropic medication. She stated that her father's psychiatric history is unremarkable.

Based on the chronic nature and negative effects that can result from limiting food intake, a complete medical and dental history is suggested. M denied any significant medical history. She reported a dislike and distrust for traditional medicine and medical providers and prefers alternate methods such as herbs, vitamins, and meditation. M reported that she has a strong aversion to menstruation. She stated that this aversion was so great in high school, that she would constantly clean herself, changing clothes and bathing frequently. She reported that in the past, she has had amenorrhea for a period of time (unknown duration), and currently has very irregular periods. She stated that she thinks she may be infertile because of this. Although she denied having allergies, she voiced a strong aversion to preservatives, dyes, and other chemical additives to foods, and is fearful of eating foods containing them. For example, she stated she could eat white rice that she has prepared, but worried that it contained additives if she purchased it from a restaurant and would not eat it. Although she denied purging behavior at this time, her front teeth appear uneven and have moderate calcification. M denied any psychiatric treatment in the past. She stated that she has not had a physical examination recently but would be willing to get one if it would help her family and friends feel better about her.

When assessing her daily functioning ability, the client stated she felt a great deal of anger and this anger is directed primarily at food. M reported feeling angry when watching others eat or when others watch her eat, and is also angry and resentful that others can eat "bad" things and not have a "problem" as she does. She reported feelings of guilt if she eats something "unhealthy" and maintains rigid rules for what she considers healthy or okay to eat. M reported that she refuses to eat food that she hasn't prepared herself or hasn't watched as others prepared it, voicing a fear that there may be "bad" things in the food. She identified these bad things as additives, chemicals, fat, or animal products. Currently, she stated that it is easier for her to fast than it is to eat and that she has difficulty keeping food down when she does try to eat. M reported feeling uncomfortably full and very guilty when she eats even small amounts (e.g., ½ cup plain pasta or white rice). She stated that she consumes vitamins and herbs. She admitted that she stores food in her room, but that she rarely eats it because she feels it is "old." M reported that she weighs herself 3 to 5 times a day and that she now wishes to attain a dress size of 7 to 8 within two months. M reported that she drinks large amount of liquids, primarily water, sugar-free caffeine drinks, and coffee, and that she smokes cigarettes. She reported having good grades in high school, taking many advanced placement classes, and currently has a 3.2 college grade point average.

She reported that at this time, she feels happier with herself and her life and attributes this to the weight loss. Although she reported that she belongs to a sorority and has many caring friends, she also spoke of a sense of not belonging or fitting in. Although she reported dating occasionally, she stated that she has never had a boyfriend or serious dating experience.

At this time, M reported a general feeling of tiredness and concern that her grades are slipping. She admitted that she is extremely concerned about her appearance and will not go out of her room if her clothing, hair, and makeup are not exactly the way she wants. Although, she attends classes most days, she stated that she skips class if she does not have enough time to dress and groom properly. Although she voiced an extreme concern for health, this does not generalize to concern about smoking or drinking caffeine. She reported that she has no difficulty falling asleep, however, feels that she is getting less sleep than she would like. M reported that she rarely gets to bed before 2 A.M. and admitted that much of her time is spent doing favors for her friends and listening to their problems and counseling them. She denies problems with dreams or nightmares.

Although she stated that she does not have an eating disorder, she mentioned that some of her behaviors are "similar to those of a person with an eating disorder" and she voiced concern that she may be losing control of eating. She also stated that she is so focused on food and dieting that she worries that she will not be able to stop losing weight and is concerned that she may become unhealthy from her current eating habits.

When asked what M would like to achieve from mental health intervention she stated that her goal is to "decrease her weight in a way that is healthy and to understand more about her anger at food."

APPLICATION OF THE MULTIAXIAL FORMAT

After compiling the information for the diagnostic assessment it appears as though M disguises and justifies her extreme fear of weight gain and her extreme restriction of foods into more acceptable terms that she refers to as "maintaining health consciousness." She constantly attempts to rationalize systematically (uses the defense mechanism, rationalization) by limiting her range of allowable foods in the name of good health. She displays many of the classic symptomatic behaviors of anorexia nervosa such as hoarding but not eating food; avoiding eating when others can observe her; feelings of power only when she controls her body; feelings of guilt about eating; feeling overfull after eating tiny amounts of food; as well as many monitoring, restricting, and purging behaviors. Although M is not below normal weight at this time, her eating disordered behaviors appear to be escalating. Since M does not meet all the *DSM-IV* criteria for anorexia nervosa at this time, this diagnosis will not be recorded on Axis I. However, since there is strong evidence of anorexia-like symptoms which should be monitored closely, the most appropriate AXIS I diagnosis appears to be eating disorder not otherwise specified. The reason for this diagnosis opposed to anorexia nervosa is that all of the criteria for anorexia nervosa are met except that, despite significant weight loss, the individual's current weight is in the normal range. If her weight falls below 85 percent of normal weight, she would then fit the criteria for anorexia nervosa. It is important to note, however, that in actual practice, it may be possible that the diagnosis of anorexia nervosa might be given regardless of whether the full criteria are met or not. Clinical practice justification for this may include: (1) the symptoms are progressing so rapidly that it is possible all criteria will be met shortly; and (2) insurance reimbursement or hospital admission may be complicated by an NOS diagnosis since the criteria are often screened very thoroughly because of the flexibility allowed in establishing the criteria. Regardless of the billing or system concerns, however, good practice would lend itself to starting out with the NOS diagnosis and later when the criteria are met changing to the subsequent diagnosis of anorexia nervosa.

Furthermore, M's recent decision to become a vegetarian also appears to be of concern because it contributes to the compilation of increasing evidence of an eating disorder. Although there is not evidence of causation, Lindeman, Stark, and Latvala (2000) have provided evidence regarding an interrelationship between vegetarianism and eating pathology. Special caution should be raised as individuals with anorexia nervosa may turn to vegetarianism as part of their symptomolgy. Although many vegetarians clearly do not have an eating disorder, the literature reports that between 2.5 percent and 4.5 percent of individuals with clinical eating disorders also reported being vegetarian (Gilbody, Kirk, & Hill, 1999). Vegetarianism may provide anorexic individuals with more "valid" or more easily defended reasons to support a food-centered lifestyle, avoidance of social eating situations, and general dietary restraint.

QUICK REFERENCE

MULTIAXIAL DIAGNOSIS

Axis I: Clinical Disorders

307.50 Eating disorder not otherwise specified, with obsessive/compulsive features rule out 307.4 anorexia nervosa, restricting type.

Axis II: Personality Disorders Deferred

Current defense mechanisms:

> Displacement.
>
> Intellectualization.
>
> Idealization.
>
> Rationalization.
>
> Denial.

Axis III: General Medical Conditions

Rule out 625.3 dysmenorrhea.

Axis IV: Psychosocial and Environmental Problems

Stressors: Self-inflicted maintenance of high standards; fear of disappointing parents; over-involvement with problem solving for friends; living in sorority house, no food preparation site available to her, forced to eat in a communal setting.

Axis V: Global Assessment of Functioning

GAF on service admission = 61 (current).

The diagnosis on Axis II is deferred. Although the client has obsessive compulsive personality disorder traits, there is not enough to substantiate a diagnosis. Also, often these types of traits can accompany or result from the primary diagnosis. Based on lack of information, this axis will be deferred rather than placing "no diagnosis" on this axis at this time. In addition, the client also appears to practice several defense mechanisms that can directly affect her daily level of functioning. The use of defense mechanisms represents mental processes or coping styles that result in automatic psychological responses that are exhibited as a means of protecting her against anxiety. Since the behaviors are automatic, she is having difficulty identifying when these defenses are being used and how to control them. It is believed that in this case identification of these defense mechanisms is essential because either

---

QUICK REFERENCE

DEFENSE MECHANISMS EXHIBITED

displacement: M often deals with emotional conflict or internal or external stressors by transferring a feeling about food or a response to food, to her distaste for food or anger in regard to food.

intellectualization: M often deals with emotional conflict or internal or external stressors by the excessive use of abstract thinking or the making of generalizations to control or minimize disturbing feelings. She reports that so much of food is not healthy and she tries to make eating into a "science" ensuring her own protection from unhealthy things.

idealization: Is a defense mechanism that is considered to be minor image distorting. Her behaviors are often characterized by distortions in self-image, in terms of self-worth and self-esteem as well as body image. She often tries to regulate her eating behaviors and relates eating patterns directly to her own self-esteem. She also deals with internal or external stressors by attributing exaggerated positive qualities to the ability to control her eating habits and other body functions and feelings that by doing this, her problems will also resolve.

rationalization: M deals with internal or external stressors by concealing the true motivations of her own actions or feelings through the elaboration of reassuring or self-serving but incorrect explanations in regard to her eating behavior and her concern for good health.

denial: M deals with emotional conflict or internal or external stressors by refusing to acknowledge that she may have a serious problem surrounding her eating behaviors. Although it is apparent to friends and family that she has a problem the client does not believe she "really" has one and is seeking treatment primarily to appease family and friends.

Source: Reprinted with permission from the *Diagnostic and Statistical Manual of Mental Disorders, Fourth Edition, Text Revision.* Copyright 2000. American Psychiatric Association.

consciously or unconsciously developed defense mechanisms can influence the diagnostic condition and impede intervention progress. Current defense mechanisms for this client include: displacement, intellectualization, idealization, rationalization, and denial. (See box for definitions and application of these defense mechanisms.)

On Axis III, a careful review of medical conditions is critical given the seriousness of the physical complications that can occur from depriving the body of adequate nutrition. Assurance of a recent physical should be verified and if absent a referral should be made. For M, a diagnosis on Axis III to rule out dysmenorrhea (625.3) seems most appropriate. Medical attention is necessary as problems with menstruation can stem from multiple causes.

On Axis IV, the client's psychosocial and environmental problems and stressors are identified. For M, one of her primary stressors appears to be her own self-inflicted maintenance of high standards and her fear that she will disappoint those she loves if she does not maintain these unrealistic standards. M also seems to involve herself actively in the life problems of her friends and places a great deal of her energy toward solving the problems of others thus avoiding addressing issues in her own life that are causing her distress. Another significant stressor for M is that she now lives in a communal setting where she does not have complete control over meal preparation. She reported she cannot control the way the food is prepared and uses this to rationalize her food intake avoidance behaviors.

Axis V describes the client's psychosocial and occupational functioning for the past year. In the diagnostic assessment this requires that M's behaviors and coping styles be identified and compared to the severity of the behaviors that are rated on the Generalized Assessment of Functioning (GAF) scale. Assessment of Axis V for M is particularly important because it will later be used to support concrete measurement of the increase or decline of problem behaviors. In *DSM-IV* and *DSM-IV-TR,* the GAF scale has a maximum of 100 points and the lower the number the lower the level of functioning (1 = minimal functioning, 100 = highest level of functioning). Using the GAF scale, the number 61 is assigned to represent the current severity of M's behaviors. Although it is not clear, it appears that M has had a higher level of functioning in the past (possibly an 81) but it is difficult to tell as the historical information has only been obtained from the client and not family members or other collateral supports.

Standardized Assessments: Self-Report Measures

To facilitate the diagnostic assessment, standardized measurements to assess problem behaviors in individuals who suffer from eating disorders is recommended (Garner & Garfinkel, 1997). A self-report measure that may be of help is the Eating Disorder

> ## QUICK REFERENCE
>
> ### CASE APPLICATION OF THE GAF
>
> M's possible range for past behaviors. Score of 81.
>
> 80–71 If symptoms are present, they are transient and expectable reactions to psychosocial stressors (e.g., difficulty concentrating after family argument); no more than slight impairment in social, occupational, and school functioning (e.g., temporarily falling behind in schoolwork).
>
> M's current range for current behaviors. Score of 61.
>
> 70–61 Some mild symptoms (e.g., depressed mood and mild insomnia) OR some difficulty in social, occupational, and school functioning.

Inventory-2 (EDI-2) (Garner, 1991; Garner, Olmsted, & Polivy, 1983). This measure may be particularly relevant for differentiating severity as well as subtypes of the disorder. Another relevant measure is the Mizes Anorectic Cognitions Scale, which measures cognitions associated with anorexia nervosa and bulimia nervosa.

Another measure that can be utilized is the Self-Esteem Rating Scale (SERS) developed by Nugent and Thomas (1993). This may be particularly helpful as a pretest and posttest measure for self-esteem. The SERS provides scores ranging for −120 to +120; the more positive the score the more positive the self-esteem and the more negative the score the more negative the self-esteem. The SERS has an excellent reliability rating. Its internal consistency has an alpha of 0.97. The SERS correlates significantly with the Index of Self-Esteem and the Generalized Contentment Scale for good construct validity. This 40-item instrument is said to "indicate not only problems in self-esteem but also positive or nonproblematic levels" (Fischer & Corcoran, 1994).

The Body Image Avoidance Questionnaire (BIAQ) developed by Rosen, Srebnik, Saltzberg, and Wendt (1991) is another instrument that can be used to measure behaviors that often accompany body image disturbance. The BIAQ contains 19 items that deal with "avoidance of situations that provoke concern about physical appearance." Totaling the points on each of the six items scores the questionnaire. The possible range is 0 to 94. The higher the score the more avoidance behaviors are used. The internal consistency for the BIAQ is excellent, with a Cronbach's alpha of 0.89. It has a stable two-week, test-retest reliability coefficient of 0.87. Further, the BIAQ has fair to good concurrent validity, with a low but significant correlation of 0.22 with body size estimation, and a correlation of 0.78 with the Body Shape Questionnaire. The scale also has good known-groups validity, significantly distinguishing between clinical (bulimia nervosa) and nonclinical populations and has been shown to be sensitive to changes in clients with body-image disturbance (Fischer & Corcoran, 1994).

Daily Body Satisfaction Logs

In addition, to aid in data collection and self-monitoring of behaviors, a computer supported data collection system known as the Self-Monitoring Analysis System (SMAS; Schlundt, 1989) may be used. When a computerized system is not available, Dziegielewski and Wolfe (2000) suggest the creation of a Daily Body Satisfaction Log (see Figure 8.1). This log can be used to record baseline data regarding personal body satisfaction. Body satisfaction is rated on a scale of 1 to 10 (1 = "very satisfied with my body," 10 = "totally dissatisfied with my body"). Individuals are instructed to rate body satisfaction three times a day; after breakfast, lunch, and dinner. This log should be kept throughout the course of the study. Overall, concrete and standardized measures such as these can help support the diagnostic assessment, lead to more successful treatment planning and strategy, and provide measurement of progress during treatment.

Figure 8.1 Daily Body Satisfaction Log

Instructions: Please circle a number from 1–10 that best represents how you feel about the appearance of your body after each mealtime. 1 = "very satisfied with my body" and 10 = "totally dissatisfied with my body." Use a separate log for each day.

DAY # _____

Breakfast

                                 1 2 3 4 5 6 7 8 9 10

"Very *satisfied* with how my body looks"   "Totally *dissatisfied* with how my body looks"

Lunch

                                   1 2 3 4 5 6 7 8 9 10

"Very *satisfied* with how my body looks"   "Totally *dissatisfied* with how my body looks"

Dinner

                                   1 2 3 4 5 6 7 8 9 10

"Very *satisfied* with how my body looks"   "Totally *dissatisfied* with how my body looks"

TREATMENT PLAN AND INTERVENTION

A complete treatment plan with M's goals and objectives and practice strategy is included at the end of this section. Treatment should be provided in a continuum of care that allows flexible application of modalities by a cohesive treatment plan. In developing the treatment plan for M, it is important for the practitioner to gather a comprehensive history that includes information about medical conditions and if possible additional information from family and friends. On some occasions, lab tests and X-rays are needed to rule out biological complications that can occur from the nutritional deprivation that is a symptom of anorexia nervosa. Referral for a blood test should be considered to detect use or abuse of drugs or hormonal problems. In addition, a referral to a dentist should be made to evaluate the possibility of dental damage due to purging techniques.

Problem behaviors must be clearly identified, and related directly to the stated goals of the client as this relationship is critical to formulation of the intervention process.

When working with an individual suffering from anorexia nervosa, intervention time can vary. However, it is rarely brief, since breaking ritualistic patterns of behavior and establishing new attitudes and behavior patterns take time. Planned and early intervention, however, can offer the client a better chance for considerable improvement. Often, intervention with individuals diagnosed with this mental disorder requires a comprehensive approach that combines individual therapy and family supports.

The connection between body image and self-esteem has been well established in the research and clearly needs to be linked in the intervention plan (McAllister & Caltabiano, 1994; McCaulay, Mintz, & Glenn, 1988; Rosen, 1995). Thus, accurate assessment of self-esteem, depression, and body image is an important ingredient for establishing the best intervention efforts possible. Body image, weight, and dieting habits can be examined by using a variety of self-report or standard measures. The treatment plan for M should include interventions to

---

QUICK REFERENCE

M's IDENTIFIED GOALS

1. Diminish feelings of anger and guilt, particularly regarding food and eating.
2. Establish healthy eating patterns.
3. Change beliefs related to food and weight.
4. Establish a sense of self-worth that is not paired with weight and body image.

improve both self-esteem and body image. Also important is continued assessment for depression and the effects it could have on the intervention plan.

Another factor to be considered in treating individuals with eating disorders is whether the symptoms such as amenorrhea, exhibited in severe cases of anorexia nervosa, serve as a method of avoiding development as a sexually mature individual (Ghizzani & Montomoli, 2000). Since these women often feel they have little or no control over external events and their own lives, the resultant changes in sexual characteristics brought on by decreased body fat, and thus decreased estrogen, are often a desperate attempt to achieve bodily control. This has led to the psychosexual attitudes of women with anorexia nervosa that endorse ambivalence toward menstruation, pregnancy, and seeking and maintaining mature sexual relationships. Since these women often consider their sexual experiences in a negative way or experience extreme guilt feelings, individual intervention strategy can be geared toward helping the client to identify and address these issues as well.

Last, to facilitate the initiation of treatment strategy, it must be determined whether the client will benefit most from assistance from either inpatient or outpatient admission. Since anorexia nervosa and bulimia nervosa are complex and almost always chronic disorders, an assessment as to whether the physical problems that result from nutritional deprivation must be stabilized in the inpatient setting must be made. Furthermore, considering that there is the potential for death due to starvation in as many as 10 percent of the cases, the decision for inpatient versus outpatient treatment remains a critical one. Although determining the best level of care and the criteria for hospitalization of a client can be complex, the practitioner should consider the least restrictive level of intervention that can fulfill both the short- and long-term needs of the client. When or if there is an imminent risk to the client, such as suicidal or self-injurious behavior, or extreme weight loss leading to possible starvation, the practitioner is justified in limiting intervention to the inpatient setting where the client can be monitored closely by a medical team.

Whether it is implemented in an inpatient or outpatient setting, the intervention strategy will follow a similar path. All efforts for intervention strategy should include: (1) education about the condition of anorexia nervosa; (2) individual therapy to address issues of self-esteem, body image, dysfunctional eating attitudes and patterns of behavior, and teaching healthy patterns for eating; and (3) significant family involvement tailored to the needs of the client (conjoint or without the client present), including education on eating disorders, how to recognize signs and symptoms of increased severity, and supportive family therapy.

A sample treatment plan follows. Although specific dates to complete goals are required in an actual treatment plan, the authors provide the treatment plan as a sample of suggestions for inclusion in treatment. If it were an actual treatment plan goals and dates for completion would have been indicated.

SAMPLE TREATMENT PLAN

Goals:

1. Diminish feelings of anger and guilt, particularly regarding food and eating.
2. Establish healthy eating patterns.
3. Change beliefs related to food and weight.
4. Establish a sense of self-worth that is not paired with weight and body image.

Objectives	Interventions
Support and increase motivation to change; heighten awareness of the disadvantages of eating disorders.	Share and discuss educational information regarding disadvantages of disordered eating (physical problems such as skin tone and color, hair loss, halitosis, low energy, lack of concentration, etc.)
Analyze the pros and cons of maintaining the disordered eating patterns—identifying functional higher-order goals of behavioral patterns and beliefs.	Develop a detailed list of the pros and cons of maintaining the disordered eating habits at this time—recognizing the adaptive nature of the symptoms.
Introduce a consideration of irrational beliefs.	Begin to introduce doubt about the practicality and utility of eating habits as a means of meeting her goals—examining the evidence of the nonadaptive factors of the disorder.
Identify specific targets of anger—increase awareness of the antecedents to her feelings of anger. Pair anger and pleasure with non-eating activities.	Keep lists of all the possible targets of anger (which foods, when, what other than food, how angry did you feel, how long did the anger last) throughout the day.
Increase understanding of the development of her body image disturbance and eating disorder.	Write a developmental history of her body image—include physical appearance and important events that influenced her body image as she developed.
Change beliefs regarding body image perceptions.	Keep record of negative "body talk" and create a positive or neutral statement to counter each negative statement.

Psychopharmacology

It is common for those who plan to implement psychosocial strategies for treating eating disorders to initially consider starting a course of medication therapy. Unfortunately, however, psychopharmacological treatment of eating disorders has not met with widespread success (B. T. Walsh, 1995). The medications that are often utilized are not designed specifically for treating eating disorders but rather for the symptoms that often accompany them. For example, antidepressants, such as specific serotonin reuptake inhibitors (SSRI) or the tricyclics, designed to address the depressive symptoms that often are comorbid to eating disorders, are often used. (See Quick Reference for list of SSRIs and tricyclics that can be used.)

In addition, recently, a few successful cases have been reported using the antipsychotic medicine Olanzapine (Zyprexa). For example, Ridley-Siegert (2000) discussed three cases of chronic anorexia nervosa that were successfully treated after 2 to 9 months of a trial with this medication. In summary, it appears that further research is needed before conclusions can be drawn regarding the possibility for successful pharmacological treatment with individuals who suffer from anorexia nervosa. Furthermore, once a medication is started mental health practitioners still need to encourage the client to supplement this intervention with psychosocial strategies that are designed to address problem behaviors. Therefore, while medication may be an important component of treating this eating disorder, medications generally are prescribed to address the behaviors that are manifested by the condition as opposed to the condition itself, making medications most effective when utilized as an adjunct to psychotherapy.

QUICK REFERENCE

SSRIs AND TRICYCLICS

Selective Serotonin Reuptake Inhibitors

Drug	Maximum Daily Dosage
Fluoxetine (Prozac)	80 mg
Paroxetine hydrochloride (Paxil)	50 mg
Sertraline (Zoloft)	200 mg
Fluvoxamine (Luvox)	200–300 mg
Citalopram (Celexa)	40 mg

Examples of Tricyclics include:

Drug	Sedative Effect	Dosage Range
Elavil (Amitriptyline)	Strong	150–300 mg a day
Tofranil (Imipramine)	Moderate	150–300 mg a day
Pamelor/Aventyl (Nortriptyline)	Mild	50–150 mg a day
Norpramine/Pertofrane (Desipramine)	Mild	100–300 mg a day

Note: The manufacturer's brand name is listed in parentheses. Dosage information is verified with PDR, 2000.

Strategies for Individual Therapy and Intervention

Individual therapy may help our client M gain greater insight into her dysfunctional behaviors and develop more thoughtful and efficient problem-solving strategies. But perhaps most important, it gives M the opportunity to better understand and express her feelings with words instead of avoidance behaviors such as denying herself food. At this time, cognitive behavioral approaches to individual therapy appear to have the best track record for control of the disorder and return to normal weight and eating behaviors (Garner & Garfinkel, 1997). Therefore, to help M achieve success, a cognitive-behavioral approach such as that developed by Cash (1996) may be helpful to address low self-esteem, locus of control, shape and weight concerns, and fears.

To begin the cognitive behavioral strategy the client will be assisted to identify her negative self-thoughts, and apply behavioral-change talk to social situations allowing her to adjust her problem behaviors accordingly. In addition, she will use self-monitoring and tracking techniques and problem-solving skills to clearly identify triggers and resulting problem behaviors. She will be assisted in learning alternate behaviors and identifying clearly and preparing for any negative or devastating consequences that can result if certain behaviors continue to occur.

Cognitive Restructuring and EMDR with Eating Disorders

"Eye movement desensitization and reprocessing (EMDR) is an intervention tool that combines elements of the major modalities such as cognitive restructuring. Although eye movement, or other forms of dual stimulation, has garnered the most attention, the method actually consists of eight phases and numerous procedural elements that all contribute to its efficacy" (F. Shapiro, 1997, p. 1). EMDR is being widely used and tested as an effective brief therapy for clinically challenging issues such as posttraumatic stress disorders, anxiety disorders, and phobias. In addition, K. W. Brown, McGoldrick, and Buchanan (1997) used EMDR with seven cases of body dysmorphic disorder. These authors used between one and three EMDR sessions, and reported improvements in six of the seven clients. Five of the seven clients reported complete resolution of symptoms. Although the symptoms of body dysmorphic disorder should not be confused with a diagnosed eating disorder, its similarity of interest is in the "preoccupation with an imagined defect in appearance" (APA, 1994, p. 468).

In practice with individuals who suffer from an eating disorder, the relationship between body image, weight, and dieting is pronounced. However, most studies attempted measurement but not treatment or improvement of either body image or self-esteem even though both factors are targeted in treatment plans and research related to eating disorder symptoms (McAllister & Caltabiano, 1994; McCaulay et al, 1988; Rosen, 1995).

According to Dziegielewski and Wolf (2000), however, the EMDR method of brief therapy can also be used with clients who suffer from problems related to distorted body image and low self-esteem. Their study emphasized a single subject design for improvement of both self-esteem and body image in a noneating disordered subject who reported eating disorder symptoms. EMDR with cognitive restructuring was introduced as the treatment intervention. Body image and self-esteem were pre- and posttested using standardized scales. Weight and dieting habits were not the focus of this study. The EMDR intervention consisted of an eight-phase treatment plan. The eight phases were as follows: (1) Client history and treatment planning; (2) preparation (for EMDR, includes explanation of the procedure, relaxation training); (3) assessment (identifying a target negative and positive cognition and establishing a baseline response on the Subjective Units of Disturbance and Validity of Cognition Scales before processing); (4) desensitization (eye movements or other bilateral stimulation); (5) installation (strengthening of identified positive cognition to replace negative cognition); (6) body scan (target residual tension in the form of body sensations); (7) closure; and (8) reevaluation (F. Shapiro, 1995).

In addition, Dziegielewski and Wolfe (2000) utilized the SUD (Subjective Units of Disturbance) and the VOC (Validity of Cognition) scales to rate emotional and cognitive functioning related to the treatment target. The subject selected an image or picture as the disturbing or target event, and rated the level of disturbance on the 10 point SUDs scale. (See Quick Reference for SUDS scale.)

In addition, after identifying the negative statement the client will be asked to change it to a positive statement. This can be formed as an "I statement" and represents what the client would like to believe. All statements must be realistic and obtainable. In turn, positive cognitions can be rated on a seven point VOC scale which constitutes a baseline before processing begins (see Quick Reference for VOC scale).

QUICK REFERENCE

SUDS SCALE DEVELOPMENT

To develop a SUDS scale, the client is asked to focus directly on a recent event that is believed to be "tantrum-like." For example, if the client identifies the statement "I hate the way my body looks now." This statement would be rated prior to processing on the SUD scale, with 0 = No disturbance, and 10 = The highest disturbance imaginable. This way negative cognitions are identified and scaled throughout the intervention process.

QUICK REFERENCE

VOC SCALE

To develop a VOC scale, the client is asked to take a negative cognition related to body image such as *"I'm ugly / I have no control"* and turn it into a positive statement. The positive cognition now becomes *"I have control over my feelings about how I look"* and this statement is rated on the VOC scale. On the VOC scale, 1 = Completely false, and 7 = Completely true.

For a sample EMDR Session Worksheet, which includes the VOC and SUD scales see page 244. A more thorough explanation of EMDR protocols and procedures can be found in F. Shapiro (1995) and Dziegielewski and Wolfe (2000).

The use of EMDR as a treatment intervention for eating disorder symptoms as seen in this presentation merits consideration for future practice intervention. According to Dziegielewski and Wolfe (2000), when using this method, the subject's increase in self-esteem and decrease in body-image avoidance behaviors indicated positive progress after only two scheduled sessions. The combination of cognitive restructuring and EMDR may be of particular importance to practitioners who are constantly challenged to do more, with less time, for less money, and at the same time asked to provide concrete indications of their effectiveness (Dziegielewski, 1996, 1997). By using standardized scales along with clear treatment protocols, clinicians can document this effectiveness in a way that is acceptable to the managed care milieu. It is further recommended that only practitioners trained by the EMDR International Institute use the EMDR protocols in treatment or research.

Environmental Considerations

When working with an individual who suffers from an eating disorder the factors in the environmental context that can influence intervention whether positive or negative must be identified. This can be accomplished by identifying the assets or strengths the client has in her support system and potential barriers that may exist. (See quick reference for strengths/assets and barriers.)

In terms of assets or strengths, M has her parents as well as several friends who are concerned for her and have encouraged her to seek help. She has also acknowledged that her parents and friends care for her and considers that the input of her parents and peers is a very important part of her life. This makes it essential to consider the impact of her peer social support at school and the influence of her family as treatment progresses. Sociocultural factors contribute substantially to the development of body image disturbance and eating disorders. To facilitate a more

SAMPLE TREATMENT PLAN

SAMPLE EMDR SESSION WORKSHEET

EMDR Session # _____   Client

Name: _____

Date: _____

"What we will be doing often is a check on what you are experiencing. I need to know from you exactly what is going on with as clear feedback as possible. Sometimes things will change and sometime they won't. There are no 'supposed tos.' Just give as accurate feedback as you can as to what is happening without judging whether it should be happening or not. Just let what ever happens happen." Remember the **STOP** signal. Choose a metaphor. Remember a safe place.

Presenting Issue or Memory:

Picture:

Negative Cognition: "What words go best with that picture/incident that express your negative belief about yourself now?"

Positive Cognition: "When you bring up that picture/incident, what would you like to believe about yourself now?"

VOC (Validity of Cognition): "When you think of that picture/incident, how true does that (repeat PC) feel to you now on a scale of 1–7, where 1 feels completely false and 7 feels completely true?"

1	2	3	4	5	6	7
completely false					completely true	

Emotions/Feelings: "When you bring up that picture/incident and those words (previous NC), what emotion(s) do you feel now?"

SUDs: "On a scale of 0–10, where 0 is no disturbance or neutral and 10 is the highest disturbance you can imagine, how disturbing does the incident feel to you now?"

0	1	2	3	4	5	6	7	8	9	10
no disturbance/neutral										highest disturbance

Location of Body Sensation: "Where do you feel the disturbance in your body?"

Desensitize: Check SUDs—should be down to 0 or 1 before doing installation.

Installation: Link positive cognition with initial target—EM—take VOC: should be 6 or 7—EM.

Body Scan: Access any material from original target—hold with PC—if residual discomfort—reprocess until discomfort subsides.

Closure: Debrief. Explain there may be after-session processing; ask to keep a log. New material will be targets for future sessions.

Source: Sample Form Adapted from Dziegielewski and Wolfe (2000).

QUICK REFERENCE

ENVIRONMENTAL CONSIDERATIONS

Client strengths and assets for intervention include:

- M has several friends who are concerned about her who have encouraged her to seek help.
- M acknowledges their caring and values their continued concern and support.
- M voices a desire to meet her weight goals in a healthy way.
- M recognizes that she is demonstrating behaviors that could be ultimately dangerous.

Barriers to intervention include:

- M believes with strong conviction she can only have a sense of control when she controls her body.
- M pairs food restriction and food rituals with healthfulness.
- M uses food as a focus for her feelings of anger and frustration related to internal and external life stressors.
- M avoids trying to identify and focus her attention on other factors that may be contributing to her anger.

global treatment of M, it would be valuable to have more information regarding her relationships with her family and peers.

When addressing issues with her family, special attention needs to be given to her relationship with her mother. M has reported that she often avoids visiting with her parents and that she is afraid of their reaction and refuses to share her current eating difficulties with them. Her relationship with her parents may be a significant factor in her eating disorder. Working with the whole family (i.e., family therapy) is essential to facilitate a more positive prognosis. Family therapy and behavioral therapies, such as parent training programs, will address the family stress normally generated by living with an individual who suffers from an eating disorder. These treatment modalities will provide strategies for managing M's behavior, and may help the parents identify and encourage appropriate behaviors for their daughter. By involving the entire family, this treatment will foster mutual support, positive reinforcement, direct communication, and more effective problem solving within the family (Braithwaite, Duff, & Westworth, 1999; Brunk, 1999). Since peer support is also a critical factor, outreach programs to educate social groups such as sororities may help to alert women to the signs and symptoms of eating disorders. Education would heighten awareness and may contribute to identification of eating difficulties before they become disorders.

Since M is a student, several university resources are recommended. Upon evaluation, M initially refused to use her own family physician for a medical consultation and physical exam, which is not uncommon with individuals who suffer from this type of eating disorder because there is such strong denial that a problem exists. Keeping this in mind, special attention was given to finding an acceptable medical referral for M. After discussion of the options, she agreed to go to the student health services clinic for a checkup with a nurse practitioner. She also could benefit from a program that encourages healthy eating and weight reduction. An example of such a program for this client was available on campus. This particular program monitors weight and exercise, provides consultation with a dietitian, and encourages peer-to-peer "buddies" who are available to address a wide range of typical student problems or concerns. Programs like this can be invaluable to the client who is obsessed with food and is prone to unhealthy eating patterns.

SUMMARY

Since the media and societal expectations continue to remain prominent in the promotion of "thin is beautiful, perfect, and desirable," mental health practitioners must be prepared to intervene in the predictable increase in chronic eating disorders. This requires a through diagnostic assessment, documented clearly in the multiaxial system as well as supplemented with standardized assessment measures. Intervention plans and strategy must incorporate evidence-based practice principles and techniques especially when working with self-esteem, body image disturbance, and other eating disorder symptoms. More research in this area is needed to anchor and support the treatment strategies that are being employed. Medications, although considered an essential intervention strategy with many mental disorders, clearly fall short in this area. By using the ideas presented in this chapter and incorporating these suggestions with evidence-based efforts supported by client-reported gain, mental health practitioners can have an impact on the development and subsequent treatment of the mental health problems experienced by the individual who suffers from an eating disorder.

Schizophrenia and the Psychotic Disorders

SOPHIA F. DZIEGIELEWSKI AND CHERYL E. GREEN

Of all the psychotic disorders, receiving a diagnosis of schizophrenia can be one of the most devastating experiences for an individual and his or her family; unfortunately, no known prevention or cure exists for this disorder (Jacob, 1995). The behaviors and coping styles characteristic of psychotic disorders such as schizophrenia, which include symptoms such as hallucinations, delusions, and bizarre or inappropriate behavior, can be problematic. The individual who suffers from schizophrenia has difficulty performing daily tasks, particularly those that involve interpersonal relationships. Schizophrenic symptoms appear as a thought disorder, with poor reality testing, social isolation, poor self-image, problems in relating with family, and problems at work (S. Shapiro, 1981). According to Whitaker (1992), the individual who suffers from schizophrenia experiences numerous and repeated states of terror that cause changes in behavior and hinders daily interactions with others. As a result, the individual develops an inability to distinguish fantasy from reality.

This resulting separation from reality makes the symptoms that an individual client suffers extend far beyond personal discomfort; the individual's schizophrenia affects all of the other people who come into contact with him or her. This disorder has far-reaching effects, not only disrupting the life of the individual, but tearing apart support systems and alienating the client from his or her daily contacts with family and friends. Not knowing the actual cause of schizophrenia and misrepresenting its signs and symptoms may frustrate both family and friends. Therefore, it is not surprising that the mental disorder of schizophrenia has been documented as a leading, worldwide public health problem.

The potential severity of schizophrenia and its associated problems make the information gathered in the diagnostic assessment and treatment plan crucial, especially as it relates to the identification of environmental factors that are important in the prevention, early identification, and treatment of this disorder. Individuals who suffer from schizophrenia and members of their support systems can all benefit from educational interventions as well as other types of intervention programs.

Since first being introduced in the earliest versions of the *Diagnostic and Statistical Manual of Mental Disorders* (American Psychiatric Association [APA], 1952), the diagnosis of schizophrenia continues to raise many questions for practitioners. Concerns center on its validity and application of criteria, as well as the detrimental and negative impact that this diagnosis can have on the future life of the individual. In addition, many mental health practitioners and other helping professionals remain leery of working with these individuals because of the unpredictability and uncertainty of their behavior. For many individuals who suffer from this disorder, complete or total remission is rare, and a chronic yet variable course of the illness is to be expected. Furthermore, schizophrenia appears to be an equal opportunity illness that affects the rich and poor alike. In terms of treatment, individuals with schizophrenia constitute over 2.5 million in the United States and more cases of this condition beginning in childhood are being diagnosed (Jaffe, 1998).

The often negative reaction by both lay individuals and professionals to individuals who suffer from schizophrenia and other psychotic disorders is much more extreme than what might be experienced by individuals who suffer from depression. Once diagnosed, clients with schizophrenia often need extensive monitoring and support that most primary care physicians and other practitioners are not able to or interested in providing. Furthermore, although they might not openly admit it, few professionals actually seek out this type of client to work with, unless they are working in a mental health setting. Many professionals simply prefer not to work with clients with schizophrenia because the monitoring problems and the unpredictability of the client's responses make it difficult to provide the support and supervision required in a nonspecialized treatment environment. On the more optimistic side, it does appear that the views of practitioners toward this population are changing somewhat, although the process of professionals developing a greater interest in working with these clients will continue to be a slow one. Psychopharmacology is one area in which changes have been made for many clients who suffer from this chronic and debilitating condition (Dziegielewski & Leon, 2001).

To better understand the condition of schizophrenia, it is necessary to examine the risk factors and symptoms, the diagnostic criteria, the problems identifying the disorder, and the different interventions that have been used for treatment of this population. This chapter discusses the condition of schizophrenia from a personal, community, and societal perspective. To reduce the magnitude of disturbances and impairment that this disorder can have on the individual, his or her family, society, or a combination of these, it is critical that practitioners complete a thorough diagnostic assessment. Based on this information, a treatment plan and practice strategy will be developed that can efficiently embrace, identify, and effectively treat individuals who suffer from psychotic disorders such as schizophrenia.

OVERVIEW OF SCHIZOPHRENIA AND THE PRIMARY PSYCHOTIC DISORDERS

The primary psychotic disorders include *brief psychotic disorder, schizophreniform disorder, delusional disorder, schizoaffective disorder, shared psychotic disorder, psychotic disorder due to a general medical condition, substance-induced psychotic disorder, psychotic disorder not otherwise specified* (NOS), and the five subtypes of *schizophrenia.* Each of these disorders is generally characterized by symptoms such as delusions, hallucinations, and disorganized speech and behavior, as well as numerous negative symptoms. (See the Quick Reference for a general listing of the positive and negative signs and symptoms often present in these disorders.)

Although it is beyond the scope of this chapter to define all psychotic disorders, a brief definition of criteria for each is included in the Quick Reference on page 251.

Since so many mental health practitioners confuse brief psychotic disorder, schizophreniform disorder, and schizophrenia, these disorders will be differentiated with a brief case example. The most important thing to remember when approaching a client who may suffer from one of these disorders is to look carefully at the time frame for the active problematic symptoms for each disorder:

- Brief psychotic disorder less than one month.
- Schizophreniform disorder less than six months.
- Schizophrenia more than six months.

In brief psychotic disorder, the symptoms are often severe but generally are brief in nature, lasting at least 24 hours (one day) but less than a month. When the symptoms subside the client generally returns to the premorbid level of functioning. In addition to the time frame criteria, in brief psychotic disorder there may or not be a stressor, although if there is a precipitating stressor it should be clearly identified. In brief psychotic disorder the onset is sudden and accompanied by positive

---

QUICK REFERENCE

DEFINITION OF PSYCHOTIC

The word *psychotic* can easily be misinterpreted. In these disorders, individual criteria must be met, and the definition and meaning of what constitutes a psychotic symptom can change based on the diagnosis being considered. Further, the disorders in this category do not always stem from a common etiology.

QUICK REFERENCE

PSYCHOTIC CHARACTERISTICS AND SYMPTOMS

Positive Symptoms

Delusions—strong beliefs held in spite of strong evidence to the contrary.

Hallucinations—misperceptions.

Disorganized speech.

Disorganized or catatonic behavior.

Negative Symptoms

Blunted affect.

Poor rapport.

Apathy.

Difficulty in abstract thinking.

Stereotyped thinking patterns.

Avolition—the lack of goal directed behavior.

*Alogia—deals primarily with the fluency and productivity of speech.

* Volition—relates directly to goal directed behavior and drive.

Emotional withdrawal.

Passivity.

Social withdrawal.

Lack of spontaneity.

---

*These are two new negative symptoms that have been included in the *DSM-IV-TR* (APA, 2000).

---

symptoms such as hallucinations, delusions, or disorganized speech. In schizophreniform disorder, the symptoms are very similar to schizophrenia; however, this provisional diagnosis is usually applied to the first psychotic break. In a diagnosis of schizophreniform disorder, the criterion of one month has been met, but the six-month time frame has not. In addition, there is no requirement in schizophreniform disorder, as in the criteria for schizophrenia, that there be a decline in either social or occupational functioning during some point in the illness. Schizophreniform disorder is considered primarily a provisional diagnosis because if the criteria and the time frame of six months are met, the diagnosis will be changed to schizophrenia. (See the Quick Reference box for the signs, symptoms, and comparison of these different types of psychotic disorders.)

To further highlight the relationship of these three psychotic disorders, a brief clinical case example is provided of a military recruit. It is not uncommon for a recruit to experience his or her first psychotic breakdown during Basic Training. In this six-week, intensive training experience, the new recruit is placed under considerable stress and extreme pressure is applied to change his or her usual style of

TYPES OF PSYCHOTIC DISORDERS

Types of Disorders

schizophrenia: In this condition, individuals suffer from characteristic psychotic symptoms and deterioration in adaptive functioning. The active phase of the disorder must last at least one month with a time frame of at least six months in duration.
There are five subtypes:

- *Disorganized type:* Marked incoherence, lack of systematized delusions, and blunted, disturbed, or inappropriate affect?
- *Catatonic type:* Stupor, negativism, rigidity, bizarre posturing, and excessive motor activity.
- *Paranoid type:* One or more systematized delusions or auditory hallucinations with a similar theme.
- *Undifferentiated type:* "Garbage can" bits of other types.
- *Residual type:* Not currently displaying symptoms displayed in the past.

brief psychotic disorder: A disorder in which a symptom generally lasts at least one day (24 hours) but no longer than a month. Sudden onset is generally linked to some type of psychosocial stressor.

schizophreniform disorder: In this disorder, the diagnosis is usually considered provisional because it generally relates to the first episode of psychosis that has lasted at least one month, with the absence of the requirement that there be a decline in functioning. When the active phase of the episode extends beyond six months, the diagnosis will be changed to schizophrenia.

delusional disorder: A disorder in which an individual suffers from non-bizarre delusions that last approximately one month; however, many of the other active-phase symptoms of schizophrenia are not present.

schizoaffective disorder: A disorder in which the individual suffers from the signs and symptoms prevalent in both the schizophrenic disorder and the mood disorder, with the schizophrenic symptoms being prevalent.

shared psychotic disorder (induced psychotic disorder): In this condition, delusions are present in an individual who is clearly influenced by someone else who has a longer-standing delusional system.

psychotic disorder due to a general medical condition: Disorder in which the psychotic symptoms an individual is experiencing are related directly to a medical condition.

substance-induced psychotic disorder: In this condition, the psychotic symptoms an individual is experiencing are related directly to drug abuse, a medication or toxin exposure.

psychotic disorder not otherwise specified (NOS): In this condition, the psychotic symptoms and client's presentation of the psychotic symptoms do not meet all the criteria for any of the specific psychotic disorders, or information is either inadequate or contradictory to confirm a clear diagnosis.

Source: Summarized criteria from the *Diagnostic and Statistical Manual of Mental Disorders, Fourth Edition, Text Revision.* Copyright 2000. American Psychiatric Association.

coping and patterns of behavior. Recruits are forced to abruptly learn and adopt an entirely new lifestyle. Emphasis on the individual is negated in an effort to have recruits form a group identity. For new recruits, this pressure to conform is so intense that it is not uncommon for some of them to experience what would appear to be a psychotic break. In this case, a female recruit became hysterical and actively delusional. When told that she would have to take a shower in a communal setting with the other female recruits, she experienced auditory hallucinations that told her that others were plotting against her. The recruit was so uncontrollable and volatile that she was immediately referred for inpatient admission and evaluation. After completing the initial evaluation, it was clear that the client met the criteria for schizophrenia except that there was no documented history of this disorder and the six-month time frame had not been met. Thus, the diagnosis of either schizophreniform or brief reactive psychosis seemed more appropriate.

In looking at the recruit's symptoms, there was clearly a severe stressor related to the incident; within several hours and after problem solving the situation the positive symptoms resided and within one week all previous discomfort was resolved. This would make the diagnosis of schizophrenia or schizophreniform inappropriate because of the short time frame. The recruit's symptoms supported neither diagnosis. In addition to duration of symptoms, cultural factors should always be taken into account when making a diagnosis. This particular client, during an interview, stated that she was always taught that the naked body was sacred and should only be viewed by her mate. The recruit believed that by taking a communal shower she would be violating this sacred trust and tainting her physical body, which she was saving for marriage.

If the client had been diagnosed with schizophrenia (at that time it was military policy to do so), the recruit would have immediately been processed for discharge. However, by carefully looking at her symptoms, and taking into account environmental and cultural factors, it was determined that the diagnosis of schizophrenia was inappropriate. This is an excellent example of how the mental health practitioner's clinical judgment will always need to include a mixture of both *art* and *science* when completing an assessment.

In taking into account all of the above mentioned factors, the client was allowed to shower independently, resulting in the full resolution of all previous signs of psychosis. In this case, it appears that no mental health diagnosis at all would be appropriate as the time frame for brief psychotic disorder was not met (symptoms lasted less than one day). Nevertheless, perhaps one of the additional conditions that may be the focus of clinical attention, such as acculturation problem (coded V62.4), should be considered for this recruit.

Other mental disorders listed in the category of psychotic disorders are schizoaffective disorder, shared psychotic disorder, delusional disorder, psychotic disorder due to a general medical condition, substance-induced psychotic disorder,

---

QUICK REFERENCE

ACCULTURATION PROBLEM

According to the *DSM-IV-TR* (APA, 2000), this category can be used when the focus of clinical attention is adjustment to a different culture. In the example, the recruit's difficulties occurred because of adjustment problems related to rapid integration into the military culture.

---

and psychotic disorder not otherwise specified (NOS). In schizoaffective disorder, the individual suffers from the signs and symptoms prevalent in both the schizophrenic disorder and the mood disorder (for at least a two-week period). At first it is expected that these symptoms will continue to occur together, although later (in a subsequent two-week period) the schizophrenic symptoms (such as hallucinations and delusions) are prevalent without prominent mood symptoms.

In the shared psychotic disorder (folie a duex), two individuals generally share the same delusional system. When looking at individuals who share this disorder, one individual's (the "leader") delusional system influences the other party, such that the other person grows to share the primary individual's delusional beliefs. Individuals who suffer from this type of disorder often live in isolated or rural settings where the belief system can remain undisturbed for a period of time by outside influences. In these settings, outside influences are not present to question or directly challenge the delusional beliefs, thereby allowing these patterns of coping and behavior to grow and strengthen.

In delusional disorder, the individual often suffers from nonbizarre delusions that last approximately one month, although many of the other active-phase symptoms of schizophrenia are not present. These individuals often perform well at work or in certain situations where the delusional beliefs can be controlled. However, when something happens to change this situation or disturb the usual coping styles of the individual, problems with social or occupational functioning often result.

In psychotic disorder due to a general medical condition, the psychotic symptoms an individual is experiencing are related directly to a medical condition. In substance-induced psychotic disorder, the psychotic symptoms an individual is experiencing are related directly to abuse of a drug, a medication, or toxin exposure.

Psychotic disorder not otherwise specified (NOS) is what many mental health professionals refer to as the "catch-all" diagnosis for psychotic disorders. In this condition, the psychotic symptoms and client's presentation of the psychotic symptoms do not meet the full criteria for any of the specific psychotic disorders or information is either inadequate or contradictory to confirm a clear diagnosis in this category.

INTRODUCTION TO SCHIZOPHRENIA

Currently, those who suffer from schizophrenia in the United States are estimated to be approximately one out of every 100 people, or 1 percent of the population; this is roughly equivalent to 2.5 million individuals (Abbott Health Care Worldwide, 1997). The condition of schizophrenia was first identified and described by Kraepelin in 1899 and since then many theories about the causes of this mental health condition have evolved (Lehmann & Ban, 1997). Some theories of causation include: oxygen deficiency, biological causes related to the biological similarity of epilepsy and schizophrenia, and an imbalance with natural neurochemical balances within the brain, such as serotonin or dopamine disturbance or both (Hong, Lee, Sim, & Hwu, 1997; Lehmann & Ban, 1997). Most researchers agree that schizophrenia is an illness with a complex and heterogeneous nature (Gottesman, 1991; Kendler & Diehl, 1993; Lieberman & Koreen, 1993; NIMH, 1999).

Biology and Etiology of Schizophrenia

Support for the belief that there is a biological component to schizophrenia increased substantially when psychotropic medication showed a decrease in schizophrenic symptoms (Dziegielewski & Leon, 2001; Lehmann & Ban, 1997). Subsequently, the medications that had an affect on these symptoms also opened the window for further understanding of the biological dynamics of schizophrenia (Lehmann & Ban, 1997). Researchers took great interest in the role that neurotransmitters, such as serotonin and dopamine, had related to establishing a biological basis for schizophrenia. For example, when the brains of individuals who suffered from schizophrenia were examined during autopsy, it was found that the D-4 (dopamine) receptors (which are members of the G-protein family that bind with antipsychotic medications) were six times denser than the brains of nondisordered individuals (Hong et al., 1997). In turn, this discovery led to the biological or dopamine D-4 hypothesis of schizophrenia (Lehman & Ban, 1997).

Studies on the structure and function in the temporal lobe, subcortical structures, and prefrontal structures have noted differences in schizophrenic individuals (Buchanan, Stevens, & Carpenter, 1997). Specifically indicated are decreased hippocampal volume, hypofrontality, and larger ventricles (Buchanan & Carpenter, 1997; Keshavan et al., 1997).

Neuroendocrinology studies have offered another perspective on the etiology of schizophrenia. These studies focus on the relationship of the workings of the pituitary gland to the hypothalamus and the central nervous system (CNS). In these studies, the growth hormone (GH) and thyroid-releasing hormone (TRH) have been examined, but results linked directly to a causal interpretation have been mixed (Keshavan et al., 1988; Lieberman et al., 1992).

Neuro-imaging studies, first introduced in the 1970s, have also been helpful in identifying the possible causative factors related to schizophrenia (Raz & Raz, 1990). These studies are helpful in exploring both the functional and structural changes that can occur in the brains of individuals who suffer from schizophrenia. Through these studies, specific areas of the brain can be identified and studied (e.g., Magnetic Resonance Imaging [MRI], or Cerebral Blood Flow [CBF]; Gur & Pearlson, 1993; Keshavan, Montrase, Pierri, Dick, Rosenberg, Talagala, & Sweeny, 1997).

There have also been some researchers who believe there is a genetic link that contributes to the subsequent risk of developing schizophrenia (Brzustowicz, Hodgkinson, Chow, Honer, & Bassett, 2000). This is based on research studies where it has been found that the risk for schizophrenia in a first-degree relative of a person with schizophrenia is 9.7 times as great as a relative in a matched control group (Kendler & Diehl, 1993). Furthermore, other researchers conducting studies in the United States, Germany, Greece, and Ireland affirm findings that schizophrenia strongly runs in families (Baron et al.,1985; Kendler et al., 1993; Kendler, Gruenberg, & Tsuang, 1985; Maier, Hallmayer, Minges, & Lichtermann, 1990).

In addition, twin studies also appear to support a link toward genetic transmission of schizophrenia; however, not all individuals who possess a genetic predisposition will experience symptoms of schizophrenia (Kendler & Diehl, 1993; Kessler, 1979). Several accounts for this discrepancy have been posited, including the interplay of genetic and environmental considerations where a biological child of an individual with schizophrenia has a similar risk for developing the disorder whether or not the child grows up in a home with that parent (Altshule et al., 1976; Gottesman, 1991; Tiernari et al., 1991). Brzustowicz, Hodgkinson, Chow, Honer, and Bassett (2000) found that there is a susceptibility point on a particular gene for schizophrenia, which lends support to the theory that schizophrenia is related to genetic as well as environmental factors.

Furthermore, environmental issues are highlighted by family response to a person diagnosed with schizophrenia and how soon the person relapses following hospitalization. It appears that relapse occurs most quickly if the family environment is "critical, hostile or emotionally over involved" (Weisman, 1997). Nonetheless, it is

---

QUICK REFERENCE

SCHIZOPHRENIA SPECTRUM

The term *schizophrenia spectrum* was added to the *DSM-IV-TR* (APA, 2000) familial pattern section. Schizophrenia spectrum represents the range of mental disorders that are more likely to occur in family members of individuals with schizophrenia (schizoaffective disorder, schizotypal personality disorder, etc.).

fairly well accepted that genetics may be a necessary, but not a sufficient, cause for schizophrenia (Kendler & Diehl, 1993).

Concerns Regarding Misdiagnosis and Treatment

Over the years, misunderstandings surrounding schizophrenia have resulted in individuals being treated primarily by trial and error with a variety of supposed remedies to alter body states. Some examples include substances such as cocaine, castor oil, turpentine oil, sulfur oil, and barbiturates; the injection of animal blood; and carbon dioxide inhalation and various methods designed to induce convulsions (Lehmann & Ban, 1997).

Schizophrenia has a lifelong course for approximately 95 percent of those with the diagnosis (Abbott Health Care Worldwide, 1997). It is estimated that 50 percent of individuals with this diagnosis will suffer from relapse within the first year of their most recent episode, regardless of whether they are taking medication. In fact, relapse occurs so often that sufferers can expect to be in the hospital 15 percent to 20 percent of their life. If a person with schizophrenia stops taking his or her medication, relapse tends to be longer, and most do not return to previous baseline functioning (Ayuso-Gutierrez & del Rio Vega, 1997).

The chronic course of treatment and the high relapse rate make care for the individual who suffers from schizophrenia extremely costly within the healthcare system (Ayuso-Gutierrez & del Rio Vega, 1997). In the United States, it is estimated that $33 billion is spent yearly by families, by welfare officials, and by law enforcement agents fighting crime in relation to schizophrenia. Furthermore, "more than 75 percent of taxpayer dollars spent on treatment of mental illness are used for people with schizophrenia. People with schizophrenia occupy 25 percent of inpatient hospital beds, and an estimated one-third to one-half of homeless people in the United States suffer from schizophrenia" (Abbott Health Care Worldwide, 1997, p. 6).

In summary, clients who suffer from schizophrenia and other psychotic disorders are usually thought to be "out of touch" with reality and to have an impaired ability to evaluate the environment around them. Often these clients are not receptive to the intervention that the mental health practitioner may try to provide, even though they require help. Schizophrenia remains a very complex disease that can manifest itself in numerous ways. Overall, a general understanding of schizophrenia and the related psychotic disorders has improved; however, it still remains a significant challenge for those who try to provide therapeutic treatment. To achieve a current, ethical, and efficacious practice, a general understanding of the condition of schizophrenia and the resulting behaviors must be achieved for mental health practitioners to accurately complete or facilitate the diagnostic assessment.

DSM-IV-TR AND THE DEFINITION OF SCHIZOPHRENIA

Since schizophrenia was first introduced in the *DSM,* many changes have occurred in practice related to this disorder, requiring revisions in the *DSM.* The *DSM-IV* and the *DSM-IV-TR* combine three sections (e.g., schizophrenia, delusional disorder, and psychotic disorder not elsewhere classified) that were listed separately in the *DSM-III-R* (1987).

The essential features of schizophrenia are a mixture of characteristic signs and symptoms (Criterion A). The magnitude of the symptoms must be significant enough to impair occupational and social functioning (Criterion B). Furthermore, the duration of the symptoms must be at least six months, and include a period of one month with active phase symptoms. This period can be less than a month if successfully treated with medication and may include periods of prodromal or residual symptoms (Criterion C). It is important to note that the one-month criterion is different from older versions of the *DSM,* which listed it as one week. Other conditions such as schizoaffective and mood disorder must be ruled out (Criterion D), and what the client is experiencing cannot be related to a substance abuse problem or a general medical condition (Criterion E). Last, the relationship between the pervasive developmental disorder known as autism must be clearly identified, and in schizophrenia it must be determined that the client is experiencing hallucinations and delusions (Criterion F).

To diagnose the individual who suffers from schizophrenia, the characteristic signs and symptoms (Criterion A) must be identified. Since these signs and symptoms are often multifaceted, careful identification is required. In schizophrenia, different positive and negative symptoms will always occur. Basically, a *positive* symptom involves the development of delusions (distortions of thought content), conceptual disorganization (grossly disorganized speech or grossly disorganized or catatonic behavior), hallucinatory behavior (distortions of perception), excitement, grandiosity, suspiciousness/persecution, and hostility. (Negative symptoms are discussed later in this chapter.)

Positive symptoms are further divided into two categories: the *psychotic* and the *disorganized*. The psychotic dimension relates directly to positive symptoms such as hallucinations and delusions. Delusions often contain ideas of reference, which are delusions having a theme or involving one certain idea. A variety of themes may occur such as religious, persecutory, or grandiose.

Hallucinations are usually auditory (70 percent), but can more rarely be visual, olfactory (related to smell), gustatory (related to taste), or tactile (related to touch). Visual hallucinations may exist but are less common than auditory. When a client is experiencing visual hallucinations, an assessment to rule out potential organic brain damage is warranted. Less common forms of hallucinations in schizophrenia include tactile (touch), taste, and smell (olfactory) sensations.

These may also be indicative of an organic problem. In some cases, clients may report feeling tactile misperceptions, such as bugs crawling on them. In this case, a simple rule that may be helpful to remember is that clients' reporting of "bugs" on them may be related to substance use and abuse. In these cases, a client should immediately be referred for a drug screen, physical examination, or both to determine if the resulting psychosis is possibly related to drug abuse or a related type of delirium.

The *disorganized* dimension of a client's behavior can be seen in his or her disordered patterns of speech. Disordered speech can be expressed in a variety of ways. For example, clients may make loose associations and jump from one topic to another, or their speech may be tangential or even incoherent. The disorganized dimension of a client's thought process relates to the primary symptoms most relevant to problematic behaviors that occur through speech and behavior. For the mental health practitioner, these symptoms are often very obvious and easy to detect in the diagnostic assessment process.

In contrast, *negative* symptoms, which are often more common than the positive symptoms, remain harder to detect. This is because negative symptoms involve behaviors that should be present but are absent. For example, one symptom may be flat or blunted affect, which involves restrictions in the range or intensity of facial expressions. Additional negative symptoms include avolition (lack of goal-directed behavior), emotional withdrawal, poor rapport, passivity, apathy, social withdrawal, difficulty in abstract thinking, lack of spontaneity, and stereotyped thinking patterns. In addition, the *DSM-IV-TR* has included two new negative symptoms (APA, 2000). The first is alogia, which deals primarily with the fluency and productivity of speech, and the second is volition, which relates directly to goal-directed behavior and drive. Since the negative symptoms commonly occur, but are often subtler than the positive symptoms, controlling these symptoms can often block clients from leading fruitful and productive lives (Malhotra, Pinsky, & Breier, 1996). Often, the negative symptoms overlap with symptoms that also occur in individuals who are depressed, such as reduced appetite, lack of energy, lack of pleasure, and inattention. Medications appear to be most helpful in controlling the positive symptoms but less effective in controlling the negative ones.

In the *DSM-IV-TR*, there are five identified subtypes of schizophrenia. These include paranoid type (Coded 295.30), disorganized type (Coded 295.10), catatonic type (Coded 295.20), undifferentiated type (Coded 295.90), and residual type (Coded 295.60). It is suspected, however, that in the modifications that will occur in the *DSM-V*, these subtypes will either be revised or discontinued. Current research used to support the diagnostic categories does not appear to find these subtypes as stable, nor do they appear to have clear diagnostic value.

In the paranoid type, individuals have a preoccupation with one or more delusions or frequent auditory hallucinations; however, these individuals do not have prominent symptoms related to disorganized speech or behavior, or flat or inappropriate affect. Many times, clients of the paranoid type will present with numerous complaints in regard to being watched, plotted against, or both. In the disorganized type, disorganized speech and behavior are apparent, as is flat or inappropriate affect. Catatonic behaviors, however, should not be present. The catatonic subtype presents with at least two of the following symptoms: extreme negativism or mutism; excessive, purposeless motor activity; peculiarities of involuntary movement; and catalepsy, stupor, or motoric immobility. The client can also present with echolalia (parrot-like representation of someone's speech) and/or echopraxia (parrot-like repetition of someone's speech and movements). In the undifferentiated type, delusions and hallucinations are present, but the criteria are not met for the other types. Finally, the residual type is diagnosed when the active phase symptoms are not present, but there is continuing evidence of the disturbance.

DIFFERENTIAL DIAGNOSTIC CONSIDERATIONS

The diagnosis of schizophrenia is often complicated by the fact that symptoms remain susceptible to change during subsequent assessment. Depression and the symptoms relevant to it occur in 25 percent of the cases in which there is clear documentation of schizophrenia (Siris, 2000). To provide the best care, mental health practitioners need to realize that negative symptoms can overlap with, and therefore can be easily confused with, other mental health conditions such as depression.

Generally, most individuals who suffer from schizophrenia experience a characteristic deterioration in adaptive functioning that accompanies the psychotic symptoms. The first psychosis or "break with reality" usually occurs between age 17 and 30 in men, and 20 and 40 in women (Carpenter, Conley, & Buchanan, 1998). Because the course and variation of schizophrenia remain extremely variable, the first episode of this illness should always be assessed carefully because after a first episode, some individuals may not become psychotic again. The majority of individuals with schizophrenia improve after the first episode but continue to manifest symptoms and remain unpredictable with future occurrences.

Schizophrenia can have either a gradual and insidious onset or a rapid and sudden onset. As noted earlier, in order for a diagnosis of schizophrenia to be given, the active phase must last approximately six months and the person must present with psychotic symptoms for a significant portion of time during a one month period or less if the client responds to treatment. If the time period is less, the individual should be diagnosed with schizophreniform disorder or brief psychotic disorder.

Mood disorders, substance abuse, and medical conditions can imitate schizophrenia and must be ruled out. It is possible for individuals who suffer from schizophrenia to also abuse alcohol and other drugs. In addition, since substance abuse can reduce effectiveness of treatment, a clear and comprehensive assessment to rule out co-occurring conditions and complicating factors must be conducted (National Institute of Mental Health, 1999).

Factors for Consideration in the Diagnostic Assessment

When starting the diagnostic assessment for this disorder, there are two factors that must be clearly understood. First, schizophrenia is probably not a single disorder (Flaum, 1995; MacKeen, 1999). In professional practice, mental health practitioners quickly realize that the single problem client does not exist, nor does the client who clearly and concisely fits perfectly into an identified diagnostic category. Clients often have multiple problems that require a multifaceted approach to intervention. The same can be said for the client with schizophrenia who has multiple mental health problems and difficulties (Dziegielewski & Leon, 2001). Some of these problems can easily overlap with other mental health conditions such as the affective disorders (bipolar and depression) or the dementia- or delirium-based disorders. Since the etiology of schizophrenia is not yet fully understood, the use of medications to control the little we do understand is essential. As understanding of the causes and origins of schizophrenia and the psychotic disorders increases, so will the ability of mental health professionals to better treat this illness.

Cultural Considerations

Since the diagnostic assessment will serve as the foundation for intervention with an individual who has schizophrenia, it is imperative to consider the cultural background and experiences of the client, and how the client's culture may influence or affect subsequent behavior (Brekke & Barrio, 1997). In developing societies, it is indicated that there is a better prognosis for schizophrenia than in societies that are more industrial (Weisman, 1997). Furthermore, some theorists have posed that cultural factors can be directly involved with the expression of positive symptoms (Weisman, 1997) and negative symptoms (Dassori et al., 1998).

Ethnic group identity, religion, and spirituality can help to establish culturally sanctioned behaviors that appear to be different than behaviors demonstrated in the dominant culture. For example, for those who practice Catholicism in the

Latino culture, mental health difficulties are often explained via "God's will" (Lefley & Pederson, 1986; Weisman, 1997). Typically, Latinos first confer with indigenous healers, curanderos or espiritistas, or Catholic leaders, or both before discussing mental health symptoms with mental health practitioners (Weaver & Wodarski, 1996). For Mexican-Americans who suffer from schizophrenia, there appears to be a greater manifestation of cognitive negative symptoms when compared to their Caucasian-American counterparts (Dassori et al., 1998).

For people who are African American, controversy continues about the relevance of culture as related to the diagnosis of schizophrenia. It is believed that African Americans are more likely to be incorrectly diagnosed as suffering from schizophrenia than other minority groups (Weaver & Wodarski, 1996). Although the actual reason for this is not known, it may be influenced by misperceptions of African American clients as having limited abilities or being excessively suspicious and hostile (Wodarski & Meggett, 1996). Samoan culture tends to view mental health disturbances as spiritual; Somoans thus often attribute symptoms to possession by spirits (Weisman, 1997). Vietnamese and Chinese cultures tend to view expressions of psychotic symptomology as uncontrollable, linking it to supernatural causes (Hong et al., 1997; Weisman, 1997).

It is important to note that a study by Brekke and Barrio (1997) did not find any racial differences among individuals who suffered from schizophrenia. Regardless of this study's conclusions, the authors found that cultural factors are important in both the diagnostic assessment and the intervention plan. Cultural factors always need to be identified and taken into account when working with individuals. The ways in which cultural factors can affect or contribute to problematic behavior should not be underestimated.

THE CASE OF JOHN

John is a 48-year-old divorced, Caucasian man. He is of large build and tall, with brown hair and brown eyes. He is unshaven, with long greasy hair, and appears to care little about his personal hygiene, as evidenced by his dirty and disheveled appearance and layers of sloppy clothing. John was recently released from jail after being arrested for vagrancy and resisting arrest. Currently, John states he was evicted from his apartment by his landlord several weeks ago and has been homeless and living on the streets for weeks. Upon interviewing John, he appeared guarded and suspicious of the police and his previous landlord. While in jail, John had gotten into a fight with another inmate and suffered a black eye and two broken ribs. Officers in the jail referred him for an evaluation, as he appeared to have limited insight and judgment.

Upon arrival at the Crisis Stabilization Unit, John displayed suspiciousness and refused to answer any questions that could reveal any personal information about himself or his behaviors.

(continued)

THE CASE OF JOHN *(Continued)*

He appeared agitated, showed bizarre posturing, and appeared unpredictable in terms of his re-actions and movement. When left alone for a few moments, John was observed talking to him self. When he was finally able to talk, John told the practitioner that he played backup music for Dylan in the sixties. John stated that his being locked up in jail was a plot to keep him away from his real brother, Elvis, who really was not dead like everyone thought.

After obtaining permission from John to call his family, his father related that John had a long history of mental illness since age 25 and had been previously diagnosed with schizophrenia, paranoid type, chronic. John had reportedly been in and out of the state mental hospital, the VA hospital, his parent's house, and various assisted living facilities for the past 15 years. Recently, John had been doing so much better that he was discharged from an assisted living facility and moved into his own apartment. According to his father, it was around this time that John started hanging around with the wrong crowd, drinking wine, and smoking marijuana. His new friends would help him cash his disability check; they would then visit John to drink the wine and smoke cigarettes that he would buy. According to his father, John constantly reported that he could not sleep, as he often had nightmares of bombs exploding. John's father suspected that John had stopped taking his antipsychotic medication shortly after he got into his apartment, but he could not be sure of exactly when. After John failed to pay his rent, his landlord threw him out. This led to John being on the street and his subsequent arrest for vagrancy. According to his father, John had become quite paranoid and frightened in jail. John had never had any legal problems prior to being arrested for vagrancy.

John is a Vietnam veteran who did not have direct combat time but spent a great deal of time on tactical training maneuvers. His father insists that John was fine until he was discharged from the military at age 21. After leaving the military, John had gradually increasing symptoms, particularly hearing voices. John told family and friends that he was discharged from the military because he was caught trying to help the North Vietnamese people. After the military discharge, he began to stay in his room all of the time and his hygiene became very poor. John began to ex-press bizarre and paranoid thoughts. The family tried to ignore John's behavior until one night when he had a psychotic episode; John tried to stab his mother with a kitchen knife while alter-nating between cries for help and fiendish ranting. After this incident, John was hospitalized nu-merous times with delusions and hallucinations.

John was married for six months to another patient whom he met during one of his hos-pitalizations. Between his times in the hospital, John has usually lived with his parents or alone. He has no children. John's last hospitalization was one year ago. His father states that John feels overwhelmed and doesn't know what to do. John's father is elderly, legally blind, and feels that he cannot handle John anymore. He asked if permanent placement in the state hospital could be an option for John because, if it was, then he would know that John was safe. After a three-day course of antipsychotic medication, John presents as more friendly and cooperative, al-though his affect is flat and he complains of being sleepy. John says that he knows that he is a worry to his father but begs not to be put back in the state hospital. He asserts that he goes off his medication because it has such terrible side effects, and then he smokes and drinks in an attempt to self-medicate.

APPLICATION OF THE MULTIAXIAL DIAGNOSTIC SYSTEM

Given the behaviors that John has exhibited and his past history, as well as the symptoms that he is now experiencing, John's diagnosis, diagnosed according to the *DSM-IV-R,* is shown in the box.

John is given the Axis I diagnosis schizophrenia, paranoid type. The diagnosis of posttraumatic stress disorder (PTSD) is given provisionally, as there is not enough information to determine whether some of his behaviors may be related to stressors that originally surfaced from his military experiences. In speaking with the client, John said that he had never been diagnosed with or treated for PTSD. It is possible, however, that although the client presents with the symptoms that seem indicative of schizophrenia, John could also being experiencing PTSD based on his military experiences. The medications for schizophrenia and PTSD differ, and if the client does also suffer from PTSD, he might benefit from an antianxiety medication along with his antipsychotics.

On Axis II and Axis III, no diagnosis (V71.09) is recorded since there are no apparent personality disorders, borderline intellectual functioning, or mental retardation present. On Axis IV, the psychosocial stressors include problems with primary support (strained family relations); problems related to the social environment (recent arrest for vagrancy, fighting, and resisting arrest); housing

---

QUICK REFERENCE

MULTIAXIAL ASSESSMENT

Axis I:	295.30	Schizophrenia, paranoid type, chronic.
	309.81	Posttraumatic stress disorder, provisional.
Axis II:	No Diagnosis.	
Axis III:	No Diagnosis.	
Axis IV:	Problems with primary support.	
	Strained family relations.	
	Problems related to the social environment.	
	Recent arrest for vagrancy, fighting, and resisting arrest.	
	Housing problems.	
	Recent eviction.	
	Economic problems.	
	Inability to manage disability income.	
Axis V:	GAF = 35 (current).	

problems (recent eviction); and economic problems (inability to manage disability income). On Axis V, the Global Assessment of Functioning (GAF) rating for current = 35 is noted.

The assignment of the Axis I diagnosis (schizophrenia, paranoid, chronic) is supported by the long chronic history of positive and negative symptoms. These symptoms have clearly lasted for a period of at least six months and have continued for approximately one month unless he was given antipsychotic medication (APA, 2000).

In terms of addressing John's symptoms, his condition seems consistent with what many clinicians refer to as the four As that determine and influence the intervention process. The first consideration is that many of these individuals suffer from *associative disturbances*. For John, his associative disturbances were related directly to how he interacted within the environmental context. Very often he was unsure of the best way to relate with others, as evidenced by his behaviors with his new friends when he would either try to "buy" their allegiance or withdraw from all social contact. After talking with John's family, it is understandable how disturbing these behaviors seem. John's behaviors have become so dysfunctional that they clearly disturb his social and occupational functioning and have resulted in his isolation from others within his environmental context.

The second associated feature relative to the assessment of John is related to *affective disturbances*. John often exhibits unpredictable moods and emotions, and at times he appears to have a *splitting of mood*. In this type of splitting, John exhibits polarities in emotions, becoming angry one minute and laughing the next. The incongruence between the emotions John is exhibiting and the actual situation is very alarming to his family and friends. This unpredictability of mood led to John's immediate hospitalization and his parent's reluctance to let him live with them at their home.

In addition to associative and affective disturbances, John also suffered from *autistic-like symptoms,* which involve a separation or lack of responsiveness to the reality surrounding him. This makes it difficult to communicate with John and to

---

QUICK REFERENCE

GAF SCORE RANGE 40–35

40–35 Some impairment in reality testing or communication (e.g., speech is at times illogical, obscure, or irrelevant) or major impairment in several areas, such as work or school, family relations, judgment, thinking, or mood (e.g., depressed man avoids friends, neglects family, and is unable to work; child frequently beats up younger children, is defiant at home, and is failing at school).

QUICK REFERENCE

PRIMARY SYMPTOMS: FOUR AS—JOHN

There are generally four "As" that represents the primary symptoms relevant to schizophrenia:

associative disturbances: John experienced numerous incidences that involved disturbances in his ability to respond to and relate to others. As noted, his greatest difficulty was in relating to his family and friends.

affective disturbances: John had repeated disturbances in mood.

autism: John often would isolate himself. He had difficulty understanding his environment and in communicating with others in his environment.

ambivalence: John could not make decisions related to his own welfare and self-care.

---

determine exactly how much John is actually able to comprehend. John also appeared extremely ambivalent, having a great deal of difficulty in making decisions or adhering to structure in terms of completing his own activities of daily living. John would consistently express willingness to do something but moments later change his mind and refuse to go somewhere or participate in an activity. For John, simple tasks, such as dressing himself or deciding whether to go outside or not, may be daunting activities.

For John, the secondary symptoms included delusions. John had many beliefs that he felt were true despite evidence to the contrary. John was so convinced that "people" were out to get him that this belief clearly disturbed his daily functioning ability. John believed that the police, his family, and his friends were out to get him.

John also appeared to be having auditory hallucinations as evidenced by his talking to himself. Most often medications are used to help clients gain control of this aspect of the illness, and it is important to determine how long John had not been taking his antipsychotic medications. In schizophrenia, it appears that auditory hallucinations (e.g., inaccurately hearing spoken speech or voices) are the most common types of hallucinations experienced by clients, making up almost 70 percent of all reported hallucinatory symptoms (Hoffman, 2000). This means that John will often struggle with addressing these auditory hallucinations and how the voices relate to what he is experiencing. John did not report being commanded by these voices to engage in certain behaviors, but this area needs further assessment.

When working with clients such as John, it is important to realize that many of these clients can experience disturbances in motor behavior such as bizarre

---

QUICK REFERENCE

DELUSIONS OF REFERENCE VERSUS IDEAS OF REFERENCE

It is important to differentiate the delusions of reference, so common in schizophrenic conditions, from ideas of reference as experienced in some of the personality disorders. For example, in the schizotypal personality disorder, there is often social withdrawal from family and friends accompanied by *ideas of reference*.

An *idea of reference* is different from a *delusion of reference* in that the idea of reference is much more individualized.

An idea of reference often refers to a specific, individual event or item that can be surrounded by magical thinking or involve a certain degree of exaggerated importance. An example of an idea of reference is the client who believes that because his father had a heart attack, he will also have one, regardless of his state of health. However, other areas of the client's life are not affected by such beliefs.

This is very different from the more extensive condition known as schizophrenia where the client can exhibit *delusions of reference*. John, in the case example, suffered from delusions of reference where "police, family, and friends were all out to get him." Delusions of reference are much more pervasive and affect almost every part of the client's life.

---

posturing, catalepsy (a state of stupor), and waxy flexibility. For example, in *waxy flexibility,* a client may appear somewhat rigid and may seem to get stuck in certain positions or stay frozen in these positions for a long period of time. Waxy flexibility and catalepsy are both characterized by a state of continual and unusual muscle tension (Moore & Jefferson, 1997). If you view a client in this state, he or she appears to be stuck, soldered in place, and unable to move on his or her own. For the inexperienced mental health practitioner, family, or friend who sees this type of behavior, it can be very frightening. The bizarre nature of the behavior can often result in the client posturing and having an inability to respond. This can cause family members to withdraw support from the client. Therefore, if this does occur in a client being served, it is essential to educate the client, his or her family, and professionals about the condition of schizophrenia, the possible signs and symptoms, and the interventions that work best to address them.

For John and so many other individuals who suffer from schizophrenia, the symptoms tend to be so arbitrary and susceptible to change that the course of the illness can remain unpredictable. The mental health practitioner must be aware of current and past symptoms and anticipate changes in symptoms that may develop during the intervention process as well as in the future course of the illness. This understanding of schizophrenia becomes particularly important when gaining an increased knowledge about the disease process and the mechanisms that lead to development of difficulties (Flaum, 1995).

Mental Status Description

Presentation	Mental Functioning	Higher Order Abilities	Thought Form/Content
Appearance: Unkempt	Simple Calculations: Mostly accurate	Judgment: Impulsive	Thought Process: Disorganized and tangential
Mood: Anxious		Insight: Poor	
Attitude: Guarded	Serial Sevens: Accurate	Intelligence: Low to average	Delusions: Paranoid
Affect: Blunted/Flat	Immediate Memory: Intact		Hallucinations: Auditory
Speech: Guarded	Remote Memory: Intact		
Motor Activity: Restless	General Knowledge: Mostly accurate		
Orientation: Fully oriented	Proverb Interpretation: Refused		
	Similarities/Differences: Refused		

TREATMENT PLANNING AND INTERVENTION STRATEGY

A complete treatment plan with John's goals, objectives, and practice strategy is included at the end of this section. With the information gathered during the diagnostic assessment as the basis of treatment, the intervention plan allows for application. As part of the intervention process, problem behaviors must be clearly identified and related directly to the stated goals and objectives.

Treatment should be provided in a continuum of care that allows flexible application of modalities based on a cohesive treatment plan. In developing the treatment plan for John, it is important for the practitioner to gather a comprehensive history, which includes information about medical conditions. Since John has difficulty

---

QUICK REFERENCE

JOHN'S IDENTIFIED GOALS

Goal:

To help John stabilize and to create a plan for him that allows him to return to the most appropriate and least restrictive environment possible.

Objectives:

- To help John reduce agitation and paranoia.
- To help John get control of his behaviors and activities of daily living (ADL).
- To help John find an appropriate place to live upon discharge.

recalling his treatment history, supplemental information is needed from family and others in his immediate support system. Information about whether John has had a recent medical exam is important, especially since he does not appear motivated for self-care. It is not known whether he is eating and sleeping; John's overall nutritional status is questionable. In addition, a referral for a blood test should be considered to detect use or abuse of drugs or hormonal problems.

In schizophrenia, planned and early intervention can offer the client a better chance for considerable improvement. Often intervention with individuals diagnosed with this mental disorder requires a comprehensive approach that will primarily combine individual therapy, case management, and family supports.

ACUTE TREATMENT PLAN AND INTERVENTION

To best assist a client with schizophrenia, two treatment plans are recommended. The first is an *acute care plan* and the second is to assist with *transitional* or *continued care needs* of the client. In the acute care plan, the primary goal is stabilization. The initial acute care plan will serve as the transitional plan for the client when he or she is discharged. Some type of long-term supervised care or community case management to assist the client with necessary linkage to successfully live in the community should follow this. At discharge, the decrease in or elimination of the client's agitation, paranoia, and incoherence needs to be documented. Also, as the client stabilizes (before discharge), the mental health practitioner will need to meet with the client to discuss his or her discharge plans and to plan the transition care part of the treatment plan.

TRANSITION CARE TREATMENT PLANNING
AND STRATEGY

With his permission, while John was still hospitalized, the mental health practitioner began to make telephone calls to family members and various assisted-living facilities. After an honest and comprehensive presentation of John's case with the potential representative of the services, John was accepted into a community-based program provided by the mental health center in his area. This program offered a stepwise approach designed to assist individuals with chronic mental health problems, allowing the client to return to the community. In this program, clients such as John start out in a more restrictive atmosphere and go through stages of training that allow for less restrictive facilities until they end up in apartments, either alone or with a roommate, operated by the center. If John fails to meet the goals for a particular level of care, he will remain at the highest level that he can achieve until

SAMPLE TREATMENT PLAN

SAMPLE ACUTE CARE GOALS AND INTERVENTION PROVIDED

Goal:

To stabilize John and discharge him to the least restrictive environment.

Objectives:

1. To help John reduce agitation and paranoia.
2. To help John get control of his behaviors and activities of daily living (ADL).
3. To help John find an appropriate place to live upon discharge.

Treatment provided:

Psychiatric evaluation and consultation.
Prescribed medication and monitoring for mental status and side effects.
Nursing assessment and ongoing nursing care.
Contacts with clinician for counseling.
Participation in therapeutic and psycho-educational group meetings as scheduled.
Observation and, as needed, other care by the treatment team.

SAMPLE APPLICATION OF ACUTE PLAN

- Medication compliance.
  Objective: Monitor and evaluate medication effectiveness, side effects, and compliance and report observations to social worker once a month.

- Stabilization of schizophrenia.
  Objective: As client moves up the levels in the program, he will take progressively more responsibility for making sure that he takes his medication.

- Linkage with community resources.
  Objective: During the next month, the client will phone a self-help group for schizophrenics in the area and inquire about meetings. He will report back to the worker on this task when they meet.

- Development of a support system.
  Objective: During the next month, the client will phone and inquire about a day treatment program run by the facility and decide if he wants to participate in the program.

- Education about medications.
  Objective: The client will attend all psycho-educational group meetings at the facility and meet with his social worker once a month for counseling.
  Objective: The client will be prepared to discuss with the worker the above objectives and the progress he has made during the month.

he is ready to progress further. It is highly recommended that the client and his family make arrangements to visit the program. John's father agreed to visit him and to lend support while John is in the program.

CHRONIC CARE TREATMENT PLANNING AND STRATEGY

As the client continues to move up the placement levels of the various facilities, a case manager will monitor the client once a month. By the time that the client is on the last level, the case manager will only be helping with minimal problems such as medication monitoring and facilitating community linkage. If medication compliance by John were still a problem, an injectable medication with a longer lasting effect would be suggested. In addition, medication monitoring would include suggesting adjustments or changes if the client was not receiving the desired effect. The client would be monitored for conditions such as tardive dyskinesia and agranulocytosis, as well as side effects such as dystonia and akathisia. If these conditions were present, newer antipsychotic medications would be considered and an evaluation for PTSD would be recommended. A referral to attend Alcoholic Anonymous (AA) or Narcotics Anonymous (NA) is also given. Continual assessment for suicidal thoughts and ideation is conducted, since about 10 percent of individuals with schizophrenia commit suicide, while 20 percent attempt it (Maxmen & Ward, 1995).

Generally, the individual treatment provided for people who suffer from schizophrenia is supportive in nature. Other methods, however, are being tried and explored. For example, Lukoff, Wallace, Liberman, and Burke (1986) empirically tested a holistic program to treat schizophrenia. The program utilized stress reduction through exercise, meditation, yoga, and stress management education. Although the sample size in this study was small, the results indicated that there were significant decreases in symptoms; this finding did not change over time in a two-year follow-up. It should be noted, however, that this program utilized both a token economy and medications, which might have confused the results as to which brought about the desired changes. Other alternative therapies suggested to treat schizophrenia include acupuncture, magnetic field therapy, naturopathic medicine, sound therapy, and traditional Chinese medicine (Chopra, 1994). None of the alternative therapy methods described should be attempted without the supervision and specification of a licensed health practitioner.

Family and Support Systems

Special attention and emphasis should always be given to building the client's family and community support systems. Schizophrenia is a disease that makes its victims feel lonely and isolated, and this chronic illness due to its unpredictable course can alienate family and friends. It is important to ensure that the family does not burn out or withdraw support from the client. Support groups can help the family members to see that they are not alone and that others are also struggling. In addition, family members need to be educated that the condition of schizophrenia is real and that their loved one is not "just making it up for attention." Learning to identify the unusual behaviors associated with this condition may help family members to better understand and accept their loved one's behaviors (National Institute of Mental Health, 1999). In addition, myths about schizophrenia in which clients with this illness are portrayed as menacing figures also need to be addressed because these depictions are often violent and may lead to the belief that all individuals suffering from schizophrenia are violent (Long, 2000).

Family members must also be encouraged to remain part of the support system, and strategies need to be used to keep the family involved (e.g., case management support, community residential placement). Most of the therapeutic interventions used with individuals suffering from schizophrenia are intended to be supportive in nature. For instance, in the case of John, most of the practitioner's goals for this client were directed toward helping him to develop and sustain his social support system. Supportive therapy may provide the client with friendship and encouragement; it may also give the client practical advice about how to access community resources, information on how to develop a more active social life, vocational counseling, suggestions for minimizing friction with family members, and, above all, hope that the individual's life circumstance will improve (Long, 2000).

Medication as a Treatment Modality

Over the years, the treatment for the individual who has suffered from schizophrenia has involved primarily supportive therapy, family and community supports, and psychopharmacology. In schizophrenia, the mystery surrounding what the disease is has led to its being treated by trial and error with a variety of supposed remedies to alter body states (Lehmann & Ban, 1997). For the most part, medications used with the individual who suffers from schizophrenia focus on altering the positive and negative psychodynamic symptoms of schizophrenia.

Medications in this area were first introduced in 1952, with the first antipsychotic (neuroleptic) medication, chlorpromazine, a combination of narcotic, sedative, and hypnotic drugs that was used with a patient suffering from schizophrenia in Paris (Lehmann & Ban, 1997). Over the years, many derivatives of chlorpromazine have been synthesized and differ in dosage and side effects.

Today, there are several classes of neuroleptic medications used to block dopamine receptors (thioxanthemes, azaphenothiazines, benzoquinolizines, diphenylbutylpiperidines, dibenzoxipine, and indole), and these medications are most commonly referred to as typical antipsychotics (Lehmann & Ban, 1997). These medications affect positive and negative symptoms with minimal side effects (Lehmann & Ban, 1997). Unfortunately, it has been estimated that 25 percent of individuals diagnosed with schizophrenia generally do not respond adequately to traditional antipsychotic medication (Abbott Health Care Worldwide, 1997; Lehmann & Ban, 1997). In addition, unpleasant conditions and side effects such as tardive dyskinesia (that occur in 15 percent to 20 percent of clients) and akathisia, dystonia, and Parkinsonism (that occur in 50 percent to 90 percent) can occur. With such side effects, it is understandable why approximately 60 percent of individuals diagnosed with schizophrenia are noncompliant with medication within the first six weeks of treatment (Lehmann & Ban, 1997).

The second group of antipsychotic agents used to treat schizophrenia is the atypical antipsychotics or nontraditional antipsychotic medications. This group of medications has fewer or little movement symptoms similar to the typical antipsychotics (Lambert, 1998). Examples of these medications include: clozapine (Clozaril), risperidone (Risperdal), sertindole (Serlect), olanzapine (Zyprexa), and quentiapine (Seroquel). These medications have gained increased popularity because their use can help individuals to think more clearly, follow directions better, learn new facts, master new skills, and interpret emotions more accurately. Although there are several medications that fall into this category, special attention needs to be given to the use of clozapine because of the potential problems that can result in monitoring this medication's use.

For mental health practitioners who have clients on clozapine (Clozaril), an atypical antipsychotic medication, there are two factors related to its use that need to be considered (Dziegielewski & Leon, 2001). First, this medication is usually dosed one week at a time to ensure client compliance with the medical regime. Second, clients must have a blood count drawn every week to ensure that the development of the potentially fatal condition called agranulocytosis does not occur. Agranulocytosis causes a severe depression in the number of granulocytes, a particular type of white blood cell (WBC) manufactured in the body. Without these granulocytes available, the human body becomes unable to fight life-threatening infections. While the percentage of the population in which agranulocytosis occurs is rare (1 percent to 2 percent), all clients taking this medication need to be monitored closely for potential complications. Once this side effect occurs, the drug must be promptly discontinued, and the medicine is excluded from future use. However, on the positive side, the effectiveness of this medication and its side effect profile (when monitored correctly) make it very frequently prescribed. Nevertheless, the expense and inconvenience of this drug can limit the number of clients who take it.

Other newer antipsychotic medications include risperidone, olanzipine, and quetiapine. Risperidone (Risperdal) was introduced as the first official atypical antipsychotic medication in 1992 (Schulz, 2000). Risperdone is often more widely

QUICK REFERENCE

ANTIPSYCHOTIC MEDICATIONS IN SCHIZOPHRENIA

Medications Used with the Psychotic Disorders:

Antipsychotic Drugs (Neuroleptic Drugs):

Used to treat severe psychotic disorders (i.e., schizophrenia). Generally, symptoms include: hallucinations, delusions, and a depressed flat affect. Peak concentrations occur between 2–4 hours. Should not prescribe two antipsychotics at the same time. After discharge, wait 3–6 months before you consider changing medication.

Old or Typical Antipsychotic Medications:

- Chlorpromazine/Thorazine.
- Thioridazine/Mellaril.
- Trifluoperazine/Stelazine.
- Phenazine/Prolixin.
- Haloperidol/Haldol.
- Loxapine/Loxitane.
- Thiothixene/Navane.

General Side Effects with Antipsychotic Medications:

Most common side effect is DROWSINESS or SLEEPINESS.

Parkinsonian or extra-pyramidal (EPS) side effects include:

Dystonia—Acute contractions of the tongue (stiff or thick tongue).

Akathisia—Most common form of EPS (e.g., inner restlessness).

Some Anti-Parkinsonian Medications Used to Decrease EPS Side Effects:

- Cogentin/benzotrpine.
- Akineton/biperiden.
- Artane/trihexyphenidyl.
- Benadryl/diphenhydramine.

Tardive Dyskinesia:

A permanent neurological condition that can result from using the older antipsychotic medications and not taking anything to help control the EPS side effects.

New or Atypical Antipsychotic Medications:

- Clozapine/Clozaril.*
- Risperdone/Risperdal.
- Olanzapine/Zyprexa.

---

*Side effect for Clozaril is *Agranulocytosis*, which affects WBCs (white blood cells) and requires weekly monitoring.

SAMPLE TREATMENT PLAN

TREATMENT PLAN DEVELOPMENT TOPIC: SCHIZOPHRENIA

Definition:

Two or more characteristic symptoms (delusions, hallucinations, disorganized speech, grossly disorganized or catatonic behavior, or negative symptoms) that persist for at least six months, one month of which must include the characteristic symptoms, and the person must experience a decline in two or more areas of functioning. Symptoms may not be associated with a general medical condition, schizoaffective, mood disorder, substance abuse, or withdrawal. If a pervasive developmental disorder exists, a diagnosis of schizophrenia can only be made if the symptoms are prominent and are present for at least a month (and last over six months).

Signs and Symptoms:

 1. Delusions.
 2. Hallucinations.
 3. Disorganized speech.
 4. Disorganized behavior.
 5. Catatonic behavior.
 6. Negative symptoms (flatted affect, alogia, avolition).
 7. One or more areas of functioning are disturbed (self-care activities, work, social, and academic).
 8. Persists continuously for six months (can shift between symptoms).
 9. At least one month of symptoms from Criterion A (delusions, hallucinations, etc.).
10. Inappropriate affect.

Goals:

1. Client will not pose danger to self or others.
2. Client will independently perform self-care activities.
3. Client will maintain prescribed medication regimen after discharge.
4. Client will increase adaptive functioning.

Objectives	Interventions
1. Client will not exhibit symptoms of psychosis (hallucinations and delusions), as measured by observations of psychiatric staff and self-reports by client, during the course of treatment and after release.	Psychiatric staff to record behaviors associated with hallucinations or delusions in chart, every day.
2. Client will increase cooperation (with taking prescribed medications) from zero compliance before hospitalization (self and family reported) to full cooperation (taking medications as prescribed), as reported by hospital staff in client's chart.	Client will take his medication as prescribed each day.

SAMPLE TREATMENT PLAN *(Continued)*

Objectives	Interventions
3. Client will increase his performance of self-care activities from 0 per day to 5 per day, as measured by staff behavior count, by the end of treatment.	a. Clinician to contract with client specific self-care behaviors to be learned and performed daily. b. Clinician to apply a cognitive/behavioral approach to teach/train client to perform self-care activities (teeth-brushing, combing hair, bathing, dressing, etc.) c. Clinician will work with client and family of client to reinforce, maintain, and expand on self-care activities, when released from the hospital.
4. Client will maintain taking prescribed meds after discharge, as evidenced by record of full compliance in case management record and family reports (indefinitely).	Case manager will monitor client's compliance with medication protocol through 2 times/week contact with client and family members.
5. Client to increase social functioning from a score of 15 at pretest to a score of 55 by the end of treatment on the Social Adjustment Scale for Schizophrenics (SASE-II).	a. Client will receive positive reinforcement from family members and clinician for behaving in a socially positive way. b. Client will participate in at least 12 weeks of social skills classes.
6. Client's family members will increase in adaptive functioning, as measured by a score of 55 to a posttest score of 250 by the end of treatment on the Social Behavior and Adjustment Scale (SBAS).	a. Client's family will participate in a six-week educational program about schizophrenia. b. Client's family will network with other families who share similar stressors.
7. Family of client will increase existing household income by $500/month through SS Disability to help care for client in the home, within six months.	Family of client will be assisted in filing for SS Disability for client's special needs.

used than clozapine and accounts for over a quarter of all prescriptions written for antipsychotic medications (Schulz, 2000). Studies on this medication have supported its reduction of both positive and negative symptoms when compared with the older, more traditional medications such as Haldol (Armenteros, 1997). Risperidone has also been utilized with schizotypal personality disorder to help decrease the psychotic–like or positive symptoms of the condition, as well as negative symptoms such as cognitive impairment (Saklad, 2000).

Another atypical antipsychotic, olanzipine (Zyprexa), followed risperdone because neither had been associated with the condition of agranulocytosis.

Zyprexa appears to be well tolerated and readily accepted by clients, especially considering its low incidence of movement-based side effects and its ability to address the negative symptoms found in schizophrenia when given at higher doses (Harvard Medical School, 1999). Finally, quetiapine (Seroquel) is the most recently developed atypical antipsychotic medication, having been introduced in this country only two years ago. Seroquel has fewer side effects, but does cause considerable sedation in the early stages of treatment (PDR, 2000; Schulz, 2000).

For mental health practitioners, it is critical to educate clients and their family members that taking these medicines will not result in a "quick fix." Depending on the specific medication, peak concentrations in the system can vary, resulting in varied time periods before therapeutic affects can be detected. Also, the relief gained based on the use of antipsychotic medications does not cure but only helps to control the symptoms. Further, although the side effect profiles associated with these medications show a lower incidence of EPS, there can be other disturbing side effects.

Medications play such an important role in management of this condition that it is impossible to cover all the newer medications and side effect profiles. Therefore, it is recommended that the reader refer to Dziegielewski and Leon (2001), which presents psychopharmacological information to the nonmedically trained practitioner. In addition, companies such as Janssen Pharmaceutics have established programs, such as "Pathways to Change," to offer support and assistance to those diagnosed with psychosis, their families, caregivers, and mental health providers. In these programs, particular attention is given to medication compliance, relapse prevention, remaining in mental health treatment, and return to the community (Easing the Emotional Cost of Schizophrenia, 1997).

SUMMARY

Despite 50 years of knowledge and treatment of schizophrenia, insight into what causes the disease and the best course of intervention remains unknown (Jacobs, 1995). Although great strides are being made in the field of research in understanding the mental disorder of schizophrenia, we are only standing at the forefront of what can be learned. Since 2.5 million Americans have schizophrenia, this mental disorder either directly or indirectly costs taxpayers $65 billion a year, or 2.5 percent of all U.S. health care costs (Walker, 2000).

Schizophrenia remains a chronic disabling illness without any known cure. Management of clients with this disease includes psychopharmacological and psychosocial approaches, as well as a broad array of services to address housing and social support needs (Awad & Lakshmi, 1999, Mohandle & Duffy, 1999). Furthermore, many clients with this disorder who receive both medication and counseling to address the difficulties they are having only experience minimal relief. Often we refer to these individuals as *partial responders*. Unfortunately, this leaves many individuals who are not substantially helped by the traditional courses of supportive therapy or medication intervention.

In mental health practice, the debate continues as to what constitutes relief or good outcomes for the client who suffers from this disorder. In schizophrenia, the ultimate goal of intervention is to help the client to be free from the usual debilitating problems that can accompany the disorder, as well as help the client to feel better and be more productive in dealing with his or her life expectations and tasks. The skills of the mental health practitioner can assist the individual who suffers from schizophrenia by helping the client to gain some semblance of control over life events and tasks. Furthermore, in addition to improvements in medication use, recent developments in the treatment of this disorder have led to a sincere interest in using diagnostic information to assist both professionals and family members in understanding this often devastating condition. However, despite the advent of new medications and the greater understanding of how this disorder works, there is still much to be learned. The role of the mental health practitioner is essential in ensuring that quality of life issues are considered, rather than just a role focused on how to measure and cut costs (Walker, 2000). In addition, when working with individuals who have schizophrenia, mental health practitioners play an important role in helping to address the stigma often associated with this illness. Practitioners can help clients and their families avoid the negative stereotypes associated with schizophrenia that often result in them being blamed for this illness.

CHAPTER

10 Anxiety Disorders: Obsessive-Compulsive Disorder

JENNIFER LOFLIN, CAROL (JAN) VAUGHN,
AND SOPHIA F. DZIEGIELEWSKI

The percentage of individuals who present with symptoms severe enough to constitute an anxiety-related mental disorder is small when compared to the claim that more than a third of all clients coming for mental health services suffer from anxiety-related problems. To complicate this further, it is estimated that only one in four people who actually present with symptoms so severe that an anxiety disorder is present are correctly diagnosed and treated (R. Hales, 1995). This is particularly alarming because anxiety disorders are treatable with some studies reporting a short-term success rates in excess of 70 percent (Roth & Fonagy, 1996).

To skillfully serve clients with anxiety disorders, mental health practitioners need to be knowledgeable of anxiety conditions, diagnostic assessments, and specific models and techniques that have been shown to be effective in treating these disorders. This chapter briefly introduces the anxiety disorders, focusing on obsessive-compulsive disorder (OCD), along with guidelines for completing the diagnostic assessment and intervention aspects consistent with current literature about effective treatment for assisting persons suffering from anxiety disorders such as OCD.

ANXIETY DISORDERS

Anxiety is a normal reaction to stress. In life there will always be situations that involve pressured responses that may seem unavoidable, hence feelings of anxiety are expected. Anxiety is generally reflective of a response to a threat and can alert individuals to danger or help prepare them for the challenges that need to be addressed. In this sense, anxiety can create feelings of uneasiness and tension thereby helping individuals to prepare for changes, danger, or conflicts. The symptoms indicative of anxiety can involve a combination of cognitive, behavioral, and somatic responses such as nervousness, sweating, irritability, sleeplessness, fear, muscular tension, obsessive thoughts, poor concentration, compulsive actions, feelings of depression, and other types of general discomfort. Often these feelings can be handled adequately with minimal if any intervention. Anxiety only becomes characteristic of a disorder when it interferes with an individual's daily functioning or in relation to social and emotional functioning with family and friends.

According to Bentley and Walsh (1996), anxiety becomes problematic when (1) it creates a sense of powerlessness in the client; (2) the anxiety forces the client to prepare for a threat or danger that is not realistic; (3) the person becomes exhausted as if constantly preparing to face a danger that does not exist; (4) it produces a level of self-absorption that stops the client from responding to his or her situation; and (5) creates doubt in the client about the perceived threat. Frightening symptoms occur that often accompany the anxiety disorders such as intense fear or discomfort; palpitations; heart pounding; sweating; trembling; shaking; feelings of choking, nausea, or abdominal distress; feeling faint; and derealization (feelings that what is occurring is not real). When these panic-like symptoms are combined with desperate attempts to avoid a specific anxiety-producing stimulus *agoraphobia* can result. In agoraphobia, without or with a history of *panic disorder,* avoidance behavior can characterize and cluster around situations such as being outside of the home, being in a crowd, or being selected out as standing alone, being in an automobile or other mode of transportation, as well as being on a bridge (American Psychiatric Association [APA], 2000). Generally, agoraphobia is not coded alone, but is a building block used to help define other *DSM-IV-TR* diagnoses, although agoraphobia without history of panic disorder is codable (300.22). Intervention effectiveness for individuals who suffer from panic disorder with agoraphobia is guarded, as some studies report that fewer than half achieve symptom-free status (Burns, Thorpe, & Cavallaro, 1986; Munby & Johnston, 1980).

A second type of anxiety condition often involves phobias, which are defined as intense and unrealistic fears of an object, an event, or feeling. Although it is estimated that 18 percent of the U.S. adult population suffers from some type

---

QUICK REFERENCE

PRESENTATION OF ANXIETY

- Many clients who are anxious often seek the help of a primary care physician before seeing a mental health practitioner.
- During the diagnostic assessment, few clients say that the actual problem is related to anxiety or nervous problems or both, and often initially attribute what signs and symptoms are experienced to medical factors.
- Many clients present with physical or mental symptoms or both (e.g., tremors, dyspnea, dizziness, sweating, irritablility, restlessness, hyperventilation, pain, heartburn), and the symptoms seem unrelated or involve two or more organ symptoms (e.g., headache and back pain).

of phobia, exactly how phobias develop or what specifically triggers a phobic response remains a mystery (Hall, 1997). There are three primary types of phobias: *agoraphobia* (fear of being unable to escape when leaving a safe place), *social phobia* (fear, embarrassment, and avoidance of social situations), and *specific* or *simple phobia* (fear of an object or situation—other than social situations).

According to the *Diagnostic and Statistical Manual of Mental Disorders* (*DSM-IV-TR;* APA, 2000), when an individual suffering from a phobia is exposed to an anxiety-provoking stimulus an immediate anxiety response almost always develops. If possible, the individual will attempt to avoid the stimulus. If it cannot be avoided, it is endured with discomfort and dread. In order to be diagnosed with a phobic disorder, the avoidance fear or anxiety experienced must be severe enough to interfere with an individual's daily functioning and routine, or social and occupational functioning. Generally, individuals seek treatment when their fear is severe enough to interfere with their lives (Hall, 1997).

In posttraumatic stress disorder (PTSD), the person generally has either directly experienced or witnessed a traumatic event. Symptoms of intense fear, helplessness, or horror must last more than a month and the reported discomfort will often persist creating difficulties in falling asleep and temper control (e.g., irritability or outbursts of anger). Individuals who suffer from this condition often want to avoid thoughts and feelings or conversing in association with the stressful event.

In the *DSM-IV* and *DSM-IV-TR,* a new category, similar to PTSD, addresses acute reactions to extreme stress. The name of this newly established condition is acute stress disorder (ASD). The onset of the stress reaction is expected to occur within four weeks of exposure to the stressor and the experience will generally last from two days to four weeks. Many professionals believe that the development of this condition can provide a foundation for the development of heightened symptoms relative to the development of PTSD.

Another type of anxiety disorder is generalized anxiety disorder (GAD). In GAD, there is undue persistent worry about two or more life circumstances that last for at least six months. Some professionals believe that the pattern for GAD is extremely difficult to treat because in spite of marked fluctuations, the pattern of illness is considered lifelong that might be better classified as a personality disorder.

In summary, it appears that regardless of what anxiety disorder is being experienced, all anxiety conditions share a misinterpretation that results in unrealistic fear(s), a dread of common life situations, or both. Since the specific symptoms experienced and the range of discomfort can differ, the diagnostic criteria as outlined in the *DSM-IV-TR* delineate the different types of disorders that fall in this category. (See Quick Reference.) It is beyond the scope of this chapter to describe each of these disorders in detail; rather, the focus will be on the diagnostic assessment and intervention related to obsessive–compulsive disorder.

OVERVIEW OF OBSESSIVE-COMPULSIVE DISORDER

According to the *DSM-IV-TR,* obsessive-compulsive disorder (OCD) is an anxiety disorder featuring "recurrent obsessions or compulsions that are severe enough to be time consuming or cause marked distress or significant impairment" (APA, 2000, p. 456). This impairment must be severe enough to interfere with an individual's performing of daily activities. Often the individual's normal routine, occupational and academic functioning, and social activities or relationships are disrupted. According to Eddy and Walbroehl (1998), obsessions are defined as recurring and distressing thoughts, images, and impulses that are perceived as inappropriate, anxiety provoking, and contrary to the patient's will. Some of the most common obsessions are a fear of contamination, a fear of being harmed or harming others, disturbing visions of a sexual or aggressive content, doubting, and unacceptable impulses (Cooper, 1999).

Compulsions are defined as "repetitive behaviors (e.g., hand washing, ordering, checking) or mental acts (e.g., praying, counting, repeating words silently) that the person feels driven to perform in response to an obsession, or according to rules that must be applied rigidly" (APA, 2000, p. 462). Common compulsions include cleaning (or avoidance of contaminated objects), checking, counting, repeating, hoarding, and putting things in order (Cooper, 1999). The goal of performing these compulsions is to help the individual alleviate the anxiety caused by the mental obsessions. Therefore, there is a relationship between compulsive behaviors and the obsession that causes them. Although this relationship exists there is no realistic connection between performing the compulsions and the relief of the obsessive thought(s) (Eddy & Walbroehl, 1998). Compulsive acts that are performed to relieve anxiety are also seen to be excessive. In almost all individuals who suffer from OCD both obsessions and compulsions are present. While the occurrence of one without the other is rare, it is possible (Pato, Pato, & Gun, 1998).

OCD has a number of suspected causes, these include genetic, biological, personality development, and environmental. Biological components are thought to include an imbalance in the neurotransmitter, serotonin. Research is ongoing to identify genes linked to OCD by exploring family trends of OCD and related disorders. A person's placing an inordinate emphasis on cleanliness is evidence of strong environmental influences. The lifetime prevalence of OCD in adults has been estimated to be between 2 percent and 4 percent of the population whereas the lifetime prevalence in children is between 1 percent and 2.3 percent (O'Connor, Todorov, Robillard, Borgeat, & Brault, 1999). The average age of onset in boys is between 6 and 16 years of age and between 20 and 29 years of age in women. Although OCD is more common in boys during childhood, it is equally common in both genders in adulthood (APA, 2000). Associated disorders (often referred to as the obsessive-compulsive spectrum disorders) in adults include major depression, anxiety disorders, eating disorders, and personality disorders. In children, OCD is often associated with learning disorders and disruptive behavior disorders (APA, 2000).

QUICK REFERENCE

obsessions: include recurring and distressing thoughts, images, and impulses that are perceived as inappropriate, anxiety provoking, and contrary to the individual's free will.

compulsions: include repetitive behaviors (e.g., checking and rechecking) or mental acts (e.g., counting) that an individual feels driven to perform in response to an obsession, or according to rules that must be applied rigidly.

Source: Modified from *DSM-IV-TR* (APA, 2000) p. 462.

According to Cooper (1999), alcohol abuse, Tourette's syndrome, epilepsy, and Syderham's chorea have frequently been found to be comorbid with OCD.

CONSIDERATIONS IN THE DIAGNOSTIC ASSESSMENT

Multiple issues need to be addressed by the treating mental health practitioner when working with an individual with OCD. First, it is important that the practitioner not diagnose OCD in cases where the obsession or compulsion arises from another mental disorder (APA, 2000). For example, a client with anxiety disorders may present with excessive worries that resemble obsessive thinking, but usually considers these worries to be realistic and appropriate, rather than absurd. Also, practitioners often note that clients' fear and embarrassment regarding their behaviors often cause reluctance in disclosing their symptoms. This problem may cause the client to complain only of depression and anxiety and not represent the true spectrum of the problems that he or she is experiencing. Therefore, the disorder might not come to the practitioner's attention until the client presents with a secondary physical symptom such as dry hands due to excessive washing.

When symptoms are not overt or openly presented the practitioner may suspect OCD and can explore this possible diagnosis by asking nonthreatening questions and having the client complete some type of rapid assessment instrument (RAI) to determine symptoms of OCD. Scales such as that created by Schwartz, Davidson, and Goleman (1978) may be helpful in starting this process. Furthermore, accurate assessment of the pressure and stress this may be causing the family is critical since many times family members may become frustrated because they cannot understand why the individual who suffers from OCD cannot simply stop the behaviors. Family education is a necessity when working with individuals who suffer from OCD (Mental Health Net, 2000).

THE CASE OF K

K, a 45-year-old Caucasian male, who had been referred by his family physician, presented at the office with his wife of 20 years, Mrs. K, and their two teenage daughters S and R. The wife reported K had been threatening to kill himself, and that he had lost 10 pounds in the past month. K explained that he felt worthless because he could not hold down a job and was causing his family too much stress. He stated that he sleeps all day, was tired of everything, and wanted to die. Further discussion revealed that Mr. and Mrs. K, along with their two-teenage daughters, recently had moved across the country looking for work for K.

According to K, he was able to get a job but could not keep it because of his problems. He described his problems as, "worrying about everything and not being able to relax." When

(continued)

THE CASE OF K *(Continued)*

prompted to disclose more information about what he was worrying about, he explained that everything was always such a mess and he was always left cleaning and securing things. K disclosed that he constantly had to check and recheck everything after his family. He reported having to make sure that the house was secure and often locked and relocked the door just to verify that it had been done correctly. K also reported that he could not get up out of bed until the family (Mrs. K and his two daughters R and S) was dressed and ready to leave the house. He then had to clean the bathrooms, bedrooms, and kitchen, which family members had used. The family was allowed to sit in the living room and watch television while he did this. K reported how this could be extremely frustrating. For example, just yesterday after the rooms had been cleaned his daughter had to go back and use the bathroom. This meant that K had to re-clean the bathroom and retrace her path to ensure it was cleaned. Once all the rooms were cleaned and checked, except for the living room, the family moved outside to wait for him. K then cleaned and made sure the living room was also ready. He then proceeded outside and allowed the family to sit in the car while he locked and relocked the front door.

Afterward, he joined his family in the car and once seated he reviewed the contents of the car. When he was satisfied that things were in place, he would put his hand cream on his hands and wait for it to dry before he would turn the car's ignition to start. Only if this routine was followed could he allow himself to pull out of the driveway. He also described how on this morning when he pulled out of the driveway he noticed a piece of litter on the curb. He pulled back into the driveway, picked up the litter and went into the house to throw it away. Therefore, he had to clean his pathway in the kitchen and lock and relock the front door again. Variations in his routine are not well tolerated. This process took over three hours and was described as a typical example of what it took for the K family to leave the house.

When asked about his childhood, K reported that he could remember washing and rewashing his hands and clothes numerous times a day as early as eight years old. He stated that he began to organize his closet after watching a movie on military training postulated that each hanger in his closet should always be exactly one inch apart. While growing up he realized that other children were not doing things to the extreme he was, so he tried to stop. He stated he was unable to stop his behaviors so he worked on hiding them from others to avoid being teased.

Mrs. K stated she first noticed something was different in the second week of their marriage. She explained that before coming to bed K would turn the light switch on and off numerous times and when asked why, his response was "I have to." According to Mrs. K when they bought their first home these behaviors escalated. K insisted that everything be in a specific place: for example, he super-glued the VCR to the TV and the clock to the VCR. Mrs. K confirmed the behaviors described by K, elaborating that when he owned something his anxiety and behaviors increased. Reportedly, the family has owned over 50 cars. Whenever the smallest problem arose with a car such as a small scratch K would trade the car in for a new "perfect" one, promising each time that this would be the last car. This added to the financial strain on the family and recently K filed for bankruptcy. Mrs. K stated she convinced her husband to finally come in for help because of his desire to kill himself. She felt his desperation was a result of him not feeling he could provide for the family, and she realized his inability to hold down a job was a result of his strange behaviors.

THE CASE OF K *(Continued)*

Both daughters agreed with the descriptions of the behaviors. They added that they felt they could not take anything out of its place at home without getting in trouble. As children, they remembered S began to copy her father's behavior. She would not play with her toys, rather she organized them in such a way that they were not to be disturbed. S explained she would get upset if anyone played with her toys or moved anything in her room. On the other hand, R had no issues regarding playing with her toys as a child. R explained that S would leave her own toys in her room and come and play with R's toys instead. S stated she was annoyed at her father for the problems he was causing the family and for the fact that she had picked up some of his perfectionist behaviors. She wanted him to stop his behaviors and engaged in harassing behaviors regarding his perfectionism. For instance, she described going into her parents' room and moving one object an inch out of place. When her father noticed he would then have to check and recheck the entire room. This caused extreme conflict between S and her father. This continues to be an ongoing problem in the family as R and Mrs. K try to mediate between the two. Mrs. K added that S appears to have developed some of her own repetitive behaviors and that although his daughter harasses K about his behaviors, she appears unable to stop her own repetitive behaviors.

Completion of the Diagnostic Assessment

To ascertain information for the diagnostic assessment the practitioner asked K what thoughts preceded his repetitive behaviors. K stated that he felt an impending feeling of doom that things would fall apart if he did not make everything perfect. Based on this information, the clinician had K complete the Cognitive-Somatic Anxiety Questionnaire (CSAQ) created by Schwartz et al. (1978). The CSAQ is a 14-item instrument that focuses on a general tendency toward defining thoughts and somatic responses. The CSAQ has a score ranging between 7 and 35; the higher the score the higher the degree of cognitive and somatic complaints. K scored a 30 on this scale. The practitioner also implemented the Hudson's (1990) Generalized Contentment Scale (GCS). The GCS is a 25-item scale that measures the severity of nonpsychotic depression. It produces a score range of zero to 100 with higher scores indicating greater magnitude of depression. The GCS has three cutoff points: 30, 50, and 70 (all plus or minus 5). Scores below 30 indicate the absence of a clinically significant depression, scores above 50 indicate some suicidal ideation, and scores above 70 nearly always indicate severe stress and suicidal tendencies. Mr. K received a score of 75 on the GCS.

QUICK REFERENCE

IDENTIFY PRIMARY AND PRESENTING PROBLEM

Primary problem:	Obsessive-compulsive thoughts and behaviors.
Presenting problems:	Unemployment and strained personal and family relations. Difficulty completing activities of daily living.

QUICK REFERENCE

RISK ASSESSMENT

Document and assess suicide risk: Ideation with no plan.

Assess violence risk toward family: None noted.

Once the primary and presenting problems have been identified the first task of the mental health practitioner, especially with the client's history of depression, is to complete a risk assessment. Key questions need to identify the potential for suicide risk. These questions are asked in a straightforward and direct manner. Once identified this information needs to be clearly recorded in the record.

The second step for the mental health practitioner is identification of client strengths and behaviors that contribute to impairment in daily functioning. The clinician should also consider the client's presentation in terms of appearance, mood, attitude, affect, speech, motor activity, and orientation in assessing mental status. Mental functioning should be assessed in terms of the client's ability to complete simple calculations, serial sevens, immediate memory, remote memory, general knowledge, proverb interpretation, and recognition of similarities and differences. In addition, questions in regard to K's higher order abilities and thought form and content need to be processed.

Mental Status Description

Presentation	Mental Functioning	Higher Order Abilities	Thought Form/Content
Appearance: Well groomed	Simple Calculations: Accurate	Judgment: Impaired	Thought Process: Logical yet overorganized
Mood: Anxious	Serial Sevens: Accurate	Insight: Intact	Delusions: None
Attitude: Guarded	Immediate Memory: Intact	Intelligence: Average	Hallucinations: None
Affect: Appropriate			
Speech: Normal	Remote Memory: Intact		
Motor Activity: Restless	General Knowledge: Mostly accurate		
Orientation: Fully oriented	Proverb Interpretation: Accurate		
	Similarities/Differences Accurate		

APPLICATION OF THE *DSM-IV-TR*, MULTIAXIAL ASSESSMENT SYSTEM

On Axis I, K is diagnosed with OCD and major depressive episode. The OCD is evidenced by the presence of obsessions and compulsions. K's obsessions are recurrent persistent thoughts of impending doom, which cause him severe stress. Furthermore, his thoughts are not excessive worries about real life problems. Upon further examination, K revealed that he recognized that these thoughts were his own and stated he had tried to suppress the thoughts with his repetitive behavior. K's compulsions include intense rituals and repetitive behaviors the purpose of which is to impede the thoughts of impending doom. In this case, the client openly stated that his behaviors were abnormal and excessive. K also reported that his obsessions and compulsions take over seven hours a day, and was the reason for his present state of unemployment. These behaviors also significantly disturbed his family relationships. Since the obsessions and compulsions the client is experiencing are not caused by another Axis I disorder, nor are they the result of substance abuse or a medical problem, the diagnosis of OCD is supported.

K's reporting of depressed mood that lasts most of the day, every day, evidences the major depressive episode. He also reports diminished pleasure in daily activities, significant weight loss, fatigue, and feelings of worthlessness and suicidal ideation. This client does not appear appropriate for a diagnosis of mixed episode because he is not experiencing any manic phases. There is no evidence to suspect the client suffers from symptoms due to substance abuse; medical problems; bereavement; or the schizoaffective, delusional, or psychotic disorders.

On Axis II, there is no evidence of mental retardation, a personality disorder, or the frequent use of a defense mechanism. K does suffer from hypertension as reported by himself and confirmed by the family doctor and this medical condition is therefore noted on Axis III. Axis IV explores the psychosocial stressors K

QUICK REFERENCE

MULTIAXIAL DIAGNOSTIC SYSTEM

Axis I: Obsessive-compulsive disorder (300.3).

Axis I: Major depressive disorder, single episode, moderate (296.22).

Axis II: No diagnosis (V799.9).

Axis III: Hypertension, essential (401.9).

Axis IV: Unemployed, family problems, economic problems.

Axis V: GAF 39, SOFAS 38, GARF 30.

is experiencing. K self-reported that he was unemployed and having family and economic problems. On Axis V, K's Global Assessment of Functioning (GAF) score is 39 as evidenced by major impairment in work, family relationships, thinking, and mood. His Social and Occupational Functioning Assessment Scale (SOFAS) revealed a score of 38 as evidenced by major impairment in work and family relationships. This corresponded closely with his score on the Global Assessment of Relational Functioning (GARF), which showed a score of 30 as evidenced by serious dysfunction in family relations such as routines being firmly adhered to, ineffective decision making, and family members' strict behavior adherence to father's obsessions at the price of their individuality.

TREATMENT PLANNING

In establishing the treatment plan, special attention needs to be given to the fact that anxiety such as that experienced by K involves cognitive, behavioral, and somatic (body) responses. It is critical for the mental health practitioner to note these behaviors and clearly document the experiences reported by the client. Record keeping needs to be "problem oriented" and as specific as possible. First, the practitioner needs to ask the question, does the client seem to worry excessively about certain life circumstances? If so, what specific things is he worried about? It is important to be specific and give examples of how these anxious thoughts lead to the behaviors that are exhibited. Making a connection between the thought and the resulting behavior is critical. The thoughts, as evidenced through the behaviors, can be addressed in the treatment contract and the intervention plan. In addition to the cognitive/behavioral responses a connection to the bodily (somatic) responses should also be made.

The mental health practitioner needs to document concrete examples of symptoms such as motor tension (restlessness, tiredness, shakiness, or muscle tension), autonomic hyperactivity (palpitations, shortness of breath [SOB], dry mouth, trouble swallowing, nausea, or diarrhea), or symptoms of hypervigilance. As in the case example, K was constantly checking and rechecking rooms in his home. Once this behavior is identified and outlined clearly, a plan can be established to address it. Later, K can be encouraged to use cognitive restructuring to assure himself that it is complete along with deep breathing to relax him. A contract can be made that after checking two times he must breathe deeply and after reassuring himself it is done, simply contract to walk away and begin another project. Although this may sound simple, in reality for the client changing a behavior that has been ritualized into habit is never easy and will take a sincere effort to reinstitute another more constructive pattern of behavior in its place. Furthermore, anxious individuals have trouble with eating and sleeping. They may have no appetite or they may have

SAMPLE TREATMENT PLAN

Long-Term Goals

1. Stabilize anxiety level while increasing ability to complete own activities of daily living.
2. Assist to reduce overall frequency, intensity, and duration of anxiety symptoms.

Short-Term Objectives	Plan or Intervention
Take medications responsibly as prescribed by the physician and report any side effects experienced from the medications.	Assess needs for antianxiety medications and arrange for prescription if needed.
	Monitor and evaluate medication compliance and the effectiveness of the medications in regard to level of functioning, refer for re-evaluation if needed.
Assess for suicide potential.	Carefully monitor for suicidal tendencies related to client's depression.
	Contract at beginning of medication treatment to continue treatment regime while taking medication.
Verbally identify, the source of the anxiety.	Client to make a list of what he is anxious about in past and present (complete in session with worker).
	Encourage client to share feelings of anxiety and develop healthy self-talk as a means of handling anxiety.
	Assign participation in recreational activities and reinforce social activities and verbalizations.
	Train in guided imagery and CBT as means of stress reduction.
	Write at least one positive affirmative statement each day.
	Identify at least one irrational thought and one way to address it.
Identify cognitive self-talk that supports irrational thoughts and fears.	Educate client and support system about anxiety.
	Assist in developing awareness of cognitive messages that reinforce control and address irrational fears.
Complete assessments of functioning. Depression and anxiety scales, as well as scales such as GAF, GARF, SOFAS.	Arrange or complete administration of the tests.

trouble falling asleep because of excessive worry. These behaviors should be documented and identified as part of the treatment component. The medications that
are being taken should also be monitored. Do the medications appear to be helping
the client to relax and address treatment issues, is there a history of substance abuse?
Since addiction and suicide potential are high with many of these medications, assessing for suicidal ideation and intent is a must. Be sure to document any history of
current suicidal thoughts or gestures. This is particularly important for the client
who has a history of previous gestures.

INTERVENTION STRATEGY

When working with the individual who suffers from OCD one popular treatment
is cognitive-behavioral therapy (Taylor, 1996). The basis of cognitive therapy
(often referred to today as cognitive-behavioral therapy [CBT]) is that the client's
mistaken appraisal of the situation results in inappropriate behaviors (Ellis, 1971).
From a cognitive-behavioral perspective, the assumption that "maladaptive behaviors are learned and maintained in accordance with principles of conditioning" is
emphasized (Getz, Wiesen, Sue, & Ayers, 1974, p. 7). In anxiety, the relationship
between thinking, feeling, and behaving as well as the belief that people experience emotional distress as a result of faulty thinking, is highlighted (Wilhelm &
Margraf, 1992). Individuals who suffer from compulsive thoughts and behaviors
often have distorted beliefs about themselves and their behaviors. In practice many
of these individuals, similar to K, usually realize that their fears are unrealistic or
exaggerated.

   One model of CBT intervention is that of Ellis' Rational Emotive Therapy
(RET) model (Ellis & Grieger, 1977). This model is particularly helpful when the
client "catastrophizes" or imagines the worst event that could possibly happen if the
behavior cannot be completed. In treatment, the client's irrational, unrealistic
thoughts are identified, and these thoughts are replaced with more competent and
successful alternatives (Ellis & Grieger, 1977). RET employs active-directive techniques, such as role playing, assertiveness training and conditioning, and counter-
conditioning procedures (Ellis, 1971). In this model, the "ABCDE" format provides
structure for the analysis of cognitions. The A is defined as the activating experience, B is the belief about A, C is the consequence (emotional, behavioral, or both),
D is the disputation of the distorted beliefs, and E is the new effect or philosophy
that evolves out of the rational belief that replaced the faulty belief (Ellis & Grieger,
1977). The client is taught that an irrational or faulty belief causes C, not the activating experience. The client is also instructed that everyone has "irrational"
thoughts. This model is ideal for working with anxiety problems because it allows
the mental health practitioner to be relatively confrontive, yet respectful, of the

---

QUICK REFERENCE

SAMPLE SCALE FOR MEASURING
FEELINGS OF ANXIETY AND SELF-CONTROL

Date: _____   Session #

Feelings of Self-Control

On the scale below how do you rate your level of self-control to deal with anxiety in regard to your program objectives.

7	6	5	4	3	2	0
No Control	Some Control		Moderate	Very Much		Total

What percentage of the time do you feel you have control over your behavior?

0 ____ 0% none of the time	6 ____ 51–60%
1 ____ 1–10%	7 ____ 61–70%
2 ____ 11–20%	8 ____ 71–80%
3 ____ 21–30%	9 ____ 81–90%
4 ____ 31–40%	10 ____ 91–100%
5 ____ 41–50%	

---

client. This relationship is essential for promoting client independence and positive self-regard. Clients are than asked to rate feelings of anxiety in regard to problematic behaviors.

The majority of the literature recommends a combination of cognitive-behavioral therapy (CBT) and medication for individuals suffering from OCD. However, some studies are showing that there are no differences in success rates between individuals getting just CBT, just medication, or both (Van Balkom & Van Dyck, 1998; Van Balkom, Van Oppen, Wermeulen, Van Dyck, & Nauta, 1994). A second approach in CBT is exposure related directly to response prevention (EX/RP) (O'Connor et al., 1999). According to Abramowitz (1998), "Exposure involves systematic and prolonged confrontation with feared stimuli until anxiety levels decrease. Ritual prevention entails abstinence or postponement of compulsive rituals" (p. 340).

The study by O'Connor et al. (1999) clearly states that,

Medication and CBT can complement each other and the specific effect of CBT may be to help focus on and dislodge obsessional beliefs. . . . Further improvement of the medication only group after

CBT suggests that administering CBT after a period of medication may be more advantageous then providing both at the same time. (p. 69)

There are many medications that can be used to supplement the treatment of OCD. One of the first medications found to have a significant effect on OCD was Clomipramine, which is a tricyclic antidepressant. However, tricyclic antidepressants have severe side effects, which make them a poor drug of choice if others are available. The selective serotonin reuptake inhibitors (SSRIs) appear to have less side effects then Clomipramine and have gained in popularity making these medications a better choice as an antiobsessional medication (O'Connor et al., 1999). There are multiple SSRIs available including, Prozac (Fluoxetine), Paxil (Paroxetine), Zoloft (Sertraline), and Luvox (Fluvxamine). Although, these are the same medications used to treat major depression, when given for OCD the dosages are usually higher (Eddy & Walbroehl, 1998). With this multitude of medications, it is possible to try different medications in succession if one is not successful or has intolerable side effects. The general consensus is that medication needs to be continued throughout life to prevent relapse. However, according to O'Connor et al. (1999), "a gradual decrease of 30 percent to 50 percent of the effective treatment dosage is still effective as a long-term maintenance pharmacotherapy" (p. 65).

In developing a treatment plan for K, the concern for his immediate safety due to his depression and suicidal ideations must be addressed. In the first session, a suicide agreement was made between mental health practitioner and client, ensuring that if K felt like hurting himself he would contact the therapist immediately. He was provided with the office phone number and a pager number for after hours and weekend emergencies. Mrs. K was also educated about suicide, the early warning signs, and interventions. During this session, an appointment was made for K to meet with the psychiatrist the following day to investigate starting medication. When K met with the psychiatrist and the therapist the following day he was prescribed 20 mg of Prozac to begin treatment of the depression and OCD. The medication dosage was congruent with the necessary dosage to treat depression rather then the 40 to 80 mg that is congruent with treating OCD. The lower dosage was given to test for and safeguard against serious side effects (Van Balkom & Van Dyck, 1998). Another appointment with the mental health practitioner was set for the following week.

As part of the intervention plan education about the condition of OCD is essential. To support this K and his wife attended the second session, which was primarily an educational session about OCD. They were informed about OCD, including its causes and possible treatments. This set a framework for discussion to begin for developing a treatment plan for Mr. K. During this session the family's financial problems were also addressed. With a clearer understanding of the disorder, and the struggle that lay ahead, K asked what options were available to financially maintain his family. The mental health practitioner gave K a referral source for financial planning advice and also explained that application for Social Security due to a mental disability could also be an option. In providing this information, however, the client was reminded that applying for disability would take time and that he needed to prepare for this as it would not provide immediate relief. Since K decided he wanted to pursue this option, the mental health practitioner referred him to the proper agency to fill out the necessary paperwork.

At the third session, it was decided between the family and mental health practitioner that a combination treatment of CBT and medication would be utilized with an added counseling component to address family issues. At the fourth session, no bothersome side effects from the medication had been reported and no improvement in obsessions or compulsions had been seen. It was therefore agreed that K would make an appointment with the psychiatrist who prescribed the medication and request a reevaluation to consider increased dosage. After this appointment the medication was increased to 60 mg. During this session CBT was also started. As suggested by Van Balkom and Van Dyck (1998), when the disturbing behaviors do not decrease within three weeks of initiation of the medication the dosage should be increased and CBT should be started in the second phase of treatment.

To facilitate a complete diagnostic assessment O'Connor et al. (1999) recommend the following: ". . . it is necessary to complete an evaluation over at least three sessions to establish, in order of priority, a hierarchy of subjects' obsessional beliefs and their compulsions" (p. 67). This hierarchy enabled graded exposure to proceed from the least troubling rituals to the more difficult rituals.

Sessions four, five, and six focused on establishing this hierarchy. During the sixth session the family attended the meeting to discuss what they viewed as the most troubling compulsions. From these two sources of information, the hierarchy of obsessions and compulsions was established. In this session, supportive, educational therapy was introduced as an option for the family members. The family was receptive to this suggestion and referrals were made to available educational and support agencies.

The hierarchy of compulsions from least to worse was excessive cleaning, repetitive checking, and ritualistic procedures. The hierarchy of obsessions from least to worst was fear of contamination, thoughts of harming self and others, thoughts of impending doom. Medication alone does not have a significant effect on lessening the strength of primary obsessional beliefs and CBT is utilized to dislodge obsessional beliefs (O'Connor et al., 1999). In session seven, K was taught appropriate relaxation techniques such as imagery, breathing skills, and muscle relaxation and demonstrated their appropriate use to the therapist. According to Van Balkom and Van Dyke (1998):

A commonly used form of behavioral therapy is gradual self-controlled exposure *in vivo* with response prevention. The patient is encouraged to conduct exposure to fearful situations and to endure the anxiety that is evoked by these exercises. It is agreed with the patient that he . . . will attempt to refrain from carrying out compulsions. Once a fear hierarchy has been established the first homework exercise is chosen. Each day the patient should register the frequency and severity of the obsessive-compulsive symptoms. Homework should be discussed in each session and new homework should be assigned. (p. 363)

In preparation for in vivo techniques of extinction, K was instructed to practice the relaxation techniques at home for at least three hours in the following week. In session eight, the first homework assignment involved excessive cleaning and fear of contamination (the client's stated lowest hierarchical problem). In session nine and all following sessions, homework was discussed, reviewed, and modified where needed. The goal is to successfully deal with each of the hierarchical problems before moving on to the next level of severity. A total of 30 sessions were completed with K. At the conclusion of his therapy he reported a marked decrease in obsessions and compulsions. A decreased score on the OCS from 19 to 9 and the decrease on the GCS from 75 to 40 supported this analysis. As with most individuals with OCD, treatment alone did not alleviate all the obsessions and compulsions, but it did decrease them to a level that allowed K to regain control of his life. He continues on medication and has bimonthly appointments with the psychiatrist to monitor his medication.

BUILDING SUPPORT SYSTEMS

Cooper (1998) addresses the specific problems family members experience when a loved one suffers from OCD. For this family these losses include: loss of income, loss of privacy, loss of normal family activities, loss of pleasure, loss of freedom for caregivers, loss of self-esteem, loss of control, and loss of security and certainty. The family members are brought into the illness as they are expected to comply with the ritualized behaviors. When a family member opposes the rituals, violence can occur. In this family S rebelled against expected behaviors and faced verbal and physical aggression from the father. Codependency is often seen in families with OCD, where family members neglect their personal needs, have extremely high tolerance for inappropriate behavior, and feel hopeless in regard to making life manageable. Mrs. K exhibits signs of codependency in that she has given up her outside friendships, often misses work, worries about others' feelings at the expense of her own, and neglects her own health.

Families that Cooper (1998) worked with describe a need for classes and support groups where they can learn how to cope with OCD behaviors and receive help in understanding why their loved one behaves this way. The K family currently attends monthly psycho-educational groups for family members. Cooper recommends, ". . . developing a time-limited, 12 session group where families can learn about the illness, receive mutual aid, and also have the opportunity to talk about feelings . . ." (p. 34). Treatment for OCD needs to include family support for the suffering client. It is also important that the family, as a whole, receive assistance in strengthening their own support systems. Part of the support system for this family includes OCD groups, extended family, friends, and other agencies. The extended family (maternal grandparents and maternal aunt) needed to be educated about OCD because they misinterpreted K's inability to hold a job as laziness. Extended family members were included in the educational groups where they received a better understanding of OCD, and became a valuable asset to the family. The extended family now provides financial and emotional support to the K family. In some families education about OCD and support groups may not be enough. For instance, with this family, there appears to be an ongoing conflict between the father and one daughter. Family therapy, directed at improving the relationship, may be necessary.

SUMMARY

Some degree of anxiety is considered normal; however, when these feelings impair occupational or social functioning or both, attention and concern is warranted. Knowledge of the different anxiety conditions, completion of a complete diagnostic assessment, and awareness of the related intervention in today's practice environment is essential. Since many clients who suffer from anxiety disorders are prescribed medications, knowledge of how these medications can affect intervention planning, regime, and protocol is essential. In addition, service provision must also include assistance with improved communication, coordination, and referral among all treatment professionals and primary health care providers, as well as, mental health and community-based programs.

Regardless of the anxiety-related condition under treatment, mental health practitioners need to complete an accurate diagnostic assessment and referral process for all clients served. This requires that they take an active role in advocating for their clients, particularly when medications are used to supplement time-limited intervention strategy. The confounding nature of the anxiety condition requires that mental health practitioners become proficient in many areas of psychological, sociological, and physiological practice implications. This does not mean that they must become ultimate experts in all these areas, however, they must have some basis of

information to assist clients to obtain and maintain the most therapeutically productive treatment possible. Simply stated, they must be able to recognize potential
problem areas in order to refer the client for adequate or revised treatment.

While controlled studies have documented statistically significant improvements in the clients who suffer from anxiety, there is concern that these improvements may not be clinically significant or that they will not provide enduring
effects. Literature suggests that while clients improve over the course of treatment,
most remain below the mean of the general population on fear measures, or when
asked if they are completely improved (Marks & Mathews, 1979; Mattick & Newman, 1991; Mattick & Peters, 1988). This requires that professionals accept the fact
that regardless of treatment modality there are no guarantees that clients will be
cured. The ultimate therapeutic outcome rests in helping clients to regain previous
levels of functioning. Just as physicians providing concrete medical services are not
distressed when clients return for additional services, mental health professionals
also must not be disturbed by the thought of clients returning for "checkups"or
booster sessions (either in the office or over the phone). This type of follow-up
should be expected.

All mental health practitioners need to stay informed of the most up-to-date
research on the intervention strategy that can be used to treat clients who suffer
from this type of anxiety disorder. Research supports the importance of involving
the family in treatment, which has often been overlooked in traditional methods
of helping. With OCD, more research is needed to address whether CBT alone,
medication alone, or combining the two, produces more effective results. It is already known that these are the effective treatments for OCD, but which is more
effective or in what combination is unknown. With the increase in managed care
it is imperative that mental health practitioners develop research that will clearly
identify which treatment or combination of treatments is most cost effective to
ensure that clients continue to receive coverage for the necessary treatments.

11

Mood Disorders: Bipolar Disorders

SHIRLEYANN AMOS, JENNIFER LOFLIN,
KAREN SIMONS, AND SOPHIA F. DZIEGIELEWSKI

Families and communities pay a heavy toll when a disorder involving an individual's mood is not recognized and treated. For so many individuals who suffer from these disorders, problems with family relations and support systems are common as well as the potential for suicide. In adults, adolescents, and children who suffer from a mood disorder, legal difficulties can develop along with employment and school difficulties that can have devastating affects on the client, his or her family, and the eventual involvement of the judicial system. Promptly recognizing a mood disorder in children, adolescents, and adults is imperative. Furthermore, no single medicine, treatment, or therapy holds the key to success and *all* options should be used to assist this population.

This chapter presents a brief overview of the mood disorders listed in the *DSM-IV-TR,* focusing primarily on the bipolar disorders. Specific application is made to the application of the bipolar disorders in regard to adults. In addition, since the diagnosis of bipolar disorder is becoming increasingly more common with children and adolescents, a case example in this area has been included as well. Discussion of the bipolar disorders from a community and societal perspective will identify how critical it is for practitioners to complete a thorough diagnostic assessment, treatment plan, and practice strategy. It is important to identify and effectively treat the bipolar disorders in adults and children while attempting to reduce the magnitude of disturbances these disorders can have on the individual and his or her support system.

OVERVIEW OF MOOD DISORDERS

According to the *DSM-IV-TR,* there are several disorders that fall into this category. The most prominent characteristic that all share is a disturbance of mood (American Psychiatric Association [APA], 2000). For the mental health practitioner these clients may be seen as especially frustrating to deal with as these complaints (generally somatic in nature) usually result in negative medical workups.

Addressing these multifaceted disorders gives way to fertile ground for misunderstandings and frustration on the part of both health care providers and the clients served (NIMH, 2000). To further complicate this scenario, about 70 percent of the individuals who have suffered from a mood disorder related to depression once can expect a reoccurrence (W. M. Resnick & Carson, 1996).

In the diagnostic assessment of an individual who suffers from any type of mood disorder depression is a primary symptom, yet when clients report the symptoms of depression the lack of clarity and problems in semantics related to defining what the terms such as "depression" mean can be problematic. These feelings of depression can frequently be overstated or understated, as reflecting the definition and normalcy standards set within an individual's unique social and environmental context. For many individuals depression can mean feeling sad, blue, or down in the dumps, whereas for others it constitutes clearly established criteria that reflect consistent patterns, signs, and symptoms relative to a mood disorder. Furthermore, some form of depression (also referred to as *dysphoric mood*) is characteristic of the mood disorders and is also present in almost all other mental health conditions, with the only possible exceptions being some forms of mania, schizophrenia, and dementia (Gitlin, 1996).

Therefore, when first approaching the individual who is suffering from a mood disorder, the first step is to be aware of the different *mood episodes* that can characterize this disorder. In the *DSM-IV* and the *DSM-IV-TR* mood episodes are not considered diagnostic conditions. The mood episodes are considered the basic ingredients or the building blocks for the disorders that follow (see Quick Reference). The types of mood episodes that clients who suffer from the bipolar disorders may manifest are *manic, hypomanic, major depressive,* or *mixed episodes* (APA, 2000).

In the first type of mood episode, referred to formally as the manic episode, the client's mood is persistently elevated. Along with elevated mood, the client must also be exhibiting at least three of the following symptoms: increased psychomotor agitation, distractibility, flight of ideas, decreased need for sleep, and grandiosity. These symptoms should last for at least a week, and if less than a week the need for hospitalization should be indicated.

In a hypomanic episode the symptoms may initially appear similar to the manic episode as it involves persistently elevated, expansive, or irritable mood. The time frame for this mood episode is approximately four days, and it is clear that the individual is exhibiting signs that remain uncharacteristic of previous levels of functioning. Individuals experiencing a hypomanic mood episode rarely need to be hospitalized, because although the symptoms may impair functioning, marked impairment is not noted. Furthermore, these individuals also do not show evidence of psychotic features even though others are aware that the behaviors they are exhibiting are uncharacteristic.

The third type of mood episode involves the major depressive episode and it generally involves at least five or more characteristic signs. Often these individuals will report having appetite disturbances that occur on almost a daily basis. At times these eating patterns when consuming too much food will result in weight gain (5 percent of the body weight in one month), or if eating too little may result in weight loss. A second common symptom is sleep disturbance: either too much sleep (hypersomnia), an inability to sleep, or disturbance in sleep (insomnia). Other signs and symptoms include: daily bouts of depressed mood, markedly diminished interest or pleasure in activities that usually are pleasurable (anhedonia), psychomotor agitation or psychomotor retardation nearly every day, fatigue or loss of energy, and other related symptoms. Furthermore, it is not uncommon for individuals experiencing these symptoms to consider suicide. In addition, the symptoms experienced must be significant enough to impair occupational and social functioning and last for a period of at least two weeks and involve either depressed mood or loss of interest or pleasure.

The last type of mood episode is referred to as the mixed episode. This episode is referred to as mixed because it generally meets the criteria for the manic and the depressive episodes. The major difference is that it does not last for two weeks; rather, it only lasts for approximately one week. In this type of episode the individual frequently experiences rapidly alternating moods such as feelings of sadness, irritability, and euphoria.

QUICK REFERENCE

MOOD EPISODES

Types of Mood Episode:

manic episode: Present mood is persistently elevated and must also have at least three of these symptoms: increased psychomotor agitation, flight of ideas, decreased need for sleep, inflated self-esteem or grandiosity, and so on, last at least *one week*.

hypomanic episode: Similar to manic, but all psychotic features and symptoms are severe enough to interfere with functioning. Criteria for hypomanic include a distinct period of persistently expansive, irritable, and elevated mood that lasts at least *four days*, but less than one week.

major depressive episode: Depressed mood for at least *two weeks*, plus five other associated features (e.g., appetite disturbance, fatigue, reduced ability to concentrate). In children and adolescents, can be irritable mood.

mixed episode: Alternating moods that last at least *one week*, must meet criteria for both manic and depressive.

Source: Summarized criteria from the *Diagnostic and Statistical Manual of Mental Disorders, Fourth Edition, Text Revision.* Copyright 2000. American Psychiatric Association.

Although it is beyond the scope of this chapter to discuss all the signs and characteristic symptoms of the mood disorders, a brief overview of the most common ones are presented. No discussion of the mood disorders would be complete without the mention of depression. Each year, it is estimated that 1.5 million individuals receive treatment for unipolar illness and still another 4.5 to 7.5 million people go untreated. *Unipolar* illness refers to a client who suffers from only one type of mood and that mood is characterized by depressive symptoms. In the clinical setting, it is estimated that approximately 25 percent of individuals who suffer from a depressive disorder present for treatment in inpatient mental health settings and about 50 percent in outpatient and private practice settings (*Merck Manual,* 1992). Of the clients who seek treatment to address their depression, it is further noted that 50 to 80 percent go unrecognized or misdiagnosed (Higgins, 1994). Unfortunately, about 70 percent of the individuals who have suffered from depression once can expect to suffer from it again (W. M. Resnick & Carson, 1996). The episodes, as stated earlier, are classified as depressive, manic, or mixed, coinciding to its predominant features. In the depressive disorders these individuals all experience some degree of depressive symptoms that are characteristic of the depressive episode. (See Quick Reference for a brief description of the depressive disorders.)

A number of treatment methods exist for mood disorders and several are discussed throughout this chapter. It is important to understand that not any one method works for all clients and it may take several different methods to assist them. Making an individualized treatment plan to work with the client is essential in successfully assisting them in improving their functioning in society and enjoying life.

QUICK REFERENCE

DEPRESSIVE DISORDERS

depression disorders: These disorders have the presence of one or more *depressive episodes* without history of manic or hypomanic episodes.

major depressive disorder: This disorder is characterized by one or more major depressive episodes, episodes that must last at least *two* weeks.

dysthymia: This disorder is characterized by a *two-year history* of depressed mood, and the individual must not be without symptoms for two months. This disorder is considered less sever than the symptoms noted in major depressive disorder.

depressive disorder NOS: This disorder is similar to the other NOS categories as individuals in this area do not meet the full criteria for one of the other mood disorders listed above.

Source: Summarized criteria from the *Diagnostic and Statistical Manual of Mental Disorders, Fourth Edition, Text Revision.* Copyright 2000. American Psychiatric Association.

Also, this chapter covers some information about electroconvulsive therapy (ECT) and its uses for depression and mania.

DSM-IV-TR *and the Definition of Bipolar Disorders*

All of the bipolar disorders are distinguished from the depressive or unipolar disorders because individuals who suffer from these disorders have at least one or some degree of symptoms related to mania. The episodes, as stated earlier, are classified as depressive, manic, or mixed, coinciding with its predominant features. Even when a client initially presents with only manic symptoms, it is assumed that a bipolar disorder exists and that a depressive episode will eventually occur.

The symptoms of the depressive form of bipolar disorder are usually clinically indistinguishable from those exhibited in the major depressive disorders, although psychomotor retardation and hypersomnia may also occur in the depressed phase of bipolar disorder. The essential difference between the major depressive disorders and the bipolar disorders is that the depressive episodes do not stand alone and alternate with manic phases. Manic episodes either immediately precede or immediately follow a depressive episode and in some cases the manic and depressive episodes are separated by intervals of relatively normal functioning (APA, 2000).

QUICK REFERENCE

DESCRIPTION OF BIPOLAR MOOD DISORDERS

bipolar disorders: These disorders have the presence of at least one or more manic or hypomanic episodes with a history of depressive symptoms.

bipolar disorders: Mixed, manic, and depressed.

Bipolar I disorder: This disorder is considered the most severe and it is characterized by one or more manic episodes and also consists of a history of depressive episodes. Psychosis as evidenced by psychotic features may also be present in the manic stage.

Bipolar II disorder: This disorder is characterized by one or more depressive episodes with at least one hypomanic episode.

cyclothymic disorder: This disorder is characterized by a persistent mood disturbance lasting at least two years, and the individual must not be without the symptoms for two months. This disorder although considered more chronic because of the duration of the symptoms is considered less severe because the symptoms are not nearly as intense as Bipolar I or Bipolar II.

bipolar disorder NOS: This disorder is similar to the other NOS categories as individuals in this area do not meet the full criteria for one of the other mood disorders listed above.

Source: Summarized criteria from the *Diagnostic and Statistical Manual of Mental Disorders, Fourth Edition, Text Revision.* Copyright 2000. American Psychiatric Association.

According to the *DSM-IV-TR*, there are four primary types of bipolar disorders; *bipolar I, bipolar II, cyclothymia,* and *bipolar disorder NOS.* (See Quick Reference for brief definitions of each.)

There are six subgroups of bipolar I disorders identified in the *DSM-IV-TR.* Five of these subgroups include criteria to determine if a client is experiencing a single manic episode and the other five describe the most recent episode. In addition, there are specifiers that mental health practitioners can use to describe the episode recurrence. Badger and Rand (1998) identify these specifiers as "rapid cycling, which indicates at least four episodes in a year; the presence or absence of inter-episode recovery; and the emergence of a seasonal pattern in the depressed episodes"(p. 83). (See Quick Reference for subgroupings.)

When working with the bipolar I disorders, it appears that either depressive episodes, manic episodes, or mixed episodes can be involved (Maxmen & Ward,

---

QUICK REFERENCE

SIX SUBGROUPS OF BIPOLAR I DISORDER

Bipolar I Disorder, Single Manic Episode-296.0x

- Presence of only one manic episode and no past major depressive episodes.

Bipolar I Disorder, Most Recent Episode Hypomanic-296.40

- Currently (or most recently) in a hypomanic episode.
- There has previously been at least one manic episode or mixed episode.

Bipolar I Disorder, Most Recent Episode Manic-296.4x

- Currently (or most recently) in a manic episode.
- There has previously been at least one major depressive episode.

Bipolar I Disorder, Most Recent Episode Mixed-296.6x

- Currently (or most recently) in a mixed episode.
- There has previously been at least one major depressive episode.

Bipolar I Disorder, Most Recent Episode Depressed-296.5x

- Currently (or most recently) in a major depressive episode.
- There has previously been at least one manic episode or mixed episode.

Bipolar I Disorder, Most Recent Episode Unspecified-296.7

- Criteria, except for duration, are currently (or most recently) met for a manic, a hypomanic, or a major depressive episode.
- There has previously been at least one manic episode or mixed episode.

Source: Summarized criteria from the *Diagnostic and Statistical Manual of Mental Disorders, Fourth Edition, Text Revision.* Copyright 2000. American Psychiatric Association.

1995). Practitioners should keep in mind that clients with bipolar I disorders frequently report depressive episodes, as well as symptoms such as agitation and hyperactivity that often are associated with it. In this condition a full depressive episode is also reported and between episodes 20 percent to 30 percent of clients may continue to have mood *lability* (fluctuations) that is significant enough to disturb interpersonal or occupational relations. In some cases the development of psychotic features may occur. When this happens subsequent manic episodes are more likely to also have psychotic features.

The manic episodes characteristic of bipolar I disorder tend to be extreme, and there is a significant impairment of occupational and social functioning. A person who experiences a manic episode has a marked elevated, euphoric, and expansive mood, frequently interrupted by outbursts of irritability or even violence, particularly when others refuse to go along with the manic person's antics and schemes. For a manic episode to exist, the mood must persist for at least a week. In addition the following symptoms must also occur in the same time period. First there is a notable increase in goal-directed activity, which sometimes may appear to be a nonrelievable restlessness. Second, thoughts and mental activity may appear to speed up, so that the individual appears to exhibit a "flight of ideas" or thoughts that "race" through the brain. Other features include: distractibility, high levels of verbal output in speech or in writing, and a severely decreased need for sleep may also occur. Additionally, inflated self-esteem is common and when severe becomes delusional, so that the person harbors feelings of enormous grandeur and power. Finally, personal and cultural inhibitions loosen, and the person may indulge in foolish ventures with a high potential for painful consequences, such as foolish business ventures, major spending sprees, and sexual indiscretions (APA, 2000).

In bipolar II, a clinical course is characterized by the occurrence of one or more major depressive episodes accompanied by at least one hypomanic episode. Furthermore, the presence of a manic or mixed episode precludes the diagnosis of bipolar II disorder. The presence of the hypomanic episode as opposed to the manic episode is a critical factor for differentiating between these two conditions. In bipolar II, the symptoms must cause clinically significant distress or impairment in social, educational, or occupational functioning, although in some cases the hypomanic episodes themselves do not cause the impairment. Often this impairment can result from major depressive episodes or from a chronic pattern of unpredictable mood episodes that result in unreliable interpersonal or occupational functioning. Furthermore, according to the *DSM-IV-TR,* bipolar II disorder may be gender related. This disorder occurs more commonly in women than in men; and, it is also noted in the *DSM-IV-TR* that women with bipolar II disorder may be at risk of developing subsequent episodes in the immediate postpartum period. (See Quick Reference for diagnostic criteria for bipolar II.)

> ## QUICK REFERENCE
>
> ### DIAGNOSTIC CRITERIA FOR BIPOLAR II DISORDER
>
> Diagnostic Criteria for 296.89 Bipolar II Disorder:
>
> - Presence (or history) of one or more major depressive episodes.
> - Presence (or history) of at least one hypomanic episode.
> - There has never been an episode or a mixed episode.
> - The mood symptoms in Criteria A and B are not better accounted for by scizoaffective disorder and are not superimposed on schizophrenia, schizophreniform disorder, delusional disorder, or psychotic disorder not otherwise specified.
> - The symptoms cause clinically significant distress or impairment in social, occupational, or other important areas of functioning.
>
> ---
>
> Source: Summarized criteria from the Diagnostic and Statistical Manual of Mental Disorders, Fourth Edition, Text Revision. Copyright 2000. American Psychiatric Association.

In both bipolar I and bipolar II disorders, symptoms of persistent depressed mood, loss of interest in activities, poor concentration, feelings of hopelessness, and changes in eating and sleeping patterns characterize the depressive phase. In contrast, the hypomanic client usually exhibits increased levels of energy, irritability, decreased need for sleep, and changes in eating patterns, increases in activities (including spending), and increases in pressured verbalization. Because of the increase in energy and activities, many individuals become quite creative during these spurts and later experience the depressive trend. Bipolar II individuals are at higher risk for suicide and usually have a strong family history of Bipolar or depressive disorders (McElroy, Strakowski, West, & Keck, 1997).

According to the *DSM-IV-TR,* clients with the diagnosis of cyclothymic disorder appear to have milder experiences than individuals who suffer from bipolar disorder, although the symptoms are more chronic, lasting for approximately two years. In order to be diagnosed with cyclothymia disorder, the client's history has to indicate that he or she has not been without hypomanic and depressive symptoms for a period of two months (APA, 2000); however, a client with only a major depressive episode should not be diagnosed with cyclothymia. Remember, that although this is a milder form of mood disorder, individuals with this disorder are *not* free of symptoms for more than two months over a two-year period. It is commonly referred to as a chronic disorder (Austrian, 1995).

In the last bipolar disorder, known as bipolar disorder not otherwise specified (NOS), caution should always be exercised when utilizing this diagnosis because of the variety of symptoms that can be included. In clinical practice, this diagnosis is generally used with clients who do not meet all of the criteria described for the bipolar disorders, yet still exhibit some of the basic symptoms evident in manic, major depressive, or mixed episodes (APA, 1994).

Summary of Bipolar Disorders

For adults with bipolar disorder, these individuals seem in some ways to be even more unfortunate than those who suffer from recurrent major depression because more than 90 percent of those who have one manic episode will go on to have further episodes (APA, 2000). Overall, the probabilities of "full recovery" for bipolar and unipolar disorder are equally discouraging and about 40 percent experienced another manic episode within one to two years following hospitalization and lithium therapy (Harrow, Goldberg, Grossman, & Meltzer, 1990; APA, 2000).

DIAGNOSTIC ASSESSMENT IN ADULTS WITH BIPOLAR DISORDER

To facilitate and provide direct application of the diagnostic assessment with an adult, an in-depth biopsychosocial analysis of a case involving a woman with bipolar disorder is presented. Issues critical for the diagnostic assessment are outlined, including how to elicit important factors that affect treatment planning and intervention strategy.

THE CASE OF D

D, a 36-year-old Caucasian woman, was admitted to the inpatient psychiatric unit and reports a long complicated history of social and behavioral problems, which have manifested themselves at home, work, school, and in the community. This has resulted in one voluntary hospitalization and ongoing attempts at psychiatric treatment, none of which has been successful in stabilizing her mood swings. According to the client, treatment modalities utilized with her in the past include numerous antidepressants, mood stabilizers, counseling, and therapy. D reports that she does not take her medications regularly due to various side effects and an inability to tolerate many of the medications prescribed. According to D, it appears that many of the antipsychotics and mood stabilizers sedate her to the point that she cannot get out of bed, while most of the antidepressants tried stimulate her episodes of mania. The mania has manifested itself with delusions, compulsions, argumentative behavior, paranoia, dissociation, anxiety, and obsessions. D reports that the first severe symptoms presented at age 16, immediately following a second trimester abortion. She reports the manic symptoms increased with the use of oral birth control. According to medical records, D first received a mental health diagnosis of clinical depression at the age of 30 from a primary physician. Approximately two years later, at a mental health clinic in Georgia, D received mental health counseling and medication. She does not recall the name of the medication prescribed at that time. During this treatment, D was living with an abusive partner, which

(continued)

—————————— **THE CASE OF D** *(Continued)* ——————————

added the stress of domestic violence. D miscarried during her first trimester as a direct result of domestic violence from her partner. D firmly believes that her partner buried the remains of the fetus in the backyard, but this would be illegal and is highly unlikely. D moved to Florida two years ago and started receiving counseling and medication at a local mental health facility at the age of 34. At that time, she states she was diagnosed with bipolar disorder. Medications that have been prescribed but which have not stabilized her include numerous medications such as Lithium, Valproic Acid, Elavil, Seroquel, Trazadone, Celexa, Prozac, Paxil, Zoloft, Serzone, Remeron, Well-butrin, Neurotin, Zanax, and Ambien.

According to D's biological sister, D has struggled with depression, low self-esteem, and attachment issues since childhood. D was molested at age 8 by a family member and again at age 13 by a brother-in-law. D's biological father abandoned the family numerous times but would later return. The divorce of her parents during her senior year of high school reportedly had a profound effect on D. D isolated from her father and discontinued her relationship with him. D reports that she was married at age 16, and she also states that two men raped her at age 17. D has been married three times and states that during the marriages she experienced violent mood swings and deep depressions. She states that she did not understand why she was behaving in this manner. She attributed her symptoms to PMS. D reports that she self-medicated daily with marijuana from the age of 16 to the age of 36.

Completion of the Diagnostic Assessment

Once the initial information about the client's symptoms has been obtained, it is important to guide the remainder of the interview to yield the information that will facilitate the diagnostic assessment process. When completing an assessment with clients who suffer from a mood disorder, special attention needs to be given to identifying the mood episodes that are being exhibited. Once the mood episode is established, the criteria is later applied to the existence of a mood disorder. When determining whether the criteria for a mood episode are met, it is important to realize that the disturbance in mood must be severe enough to affect many areas of an individual's functioning. When identifying a mood episode current and past behaviors must be considered.

While the *DSM-IV-TR* provides technical definitions of what constitutes the manic and the hypomanic episodes, it is helpful for the practitioner to know the kinds of symptoms such clients regularly present. During the assessment process, to confirm the presence of a manic or hypomanic episode, the mental health practitioner should elicit information about changes in the following areas:

- Sleeping and eating habits/patterns.
- Levels of energy.
- Levels of restlessness.
- Increase in activities, especially in those that are considered risk taking or destructive.
- Problems concentrating, easily distracted.
- Instances of extreme feelings of happiness.
- Laughing inappropriately, usually accompanied with agitation.
- Increase in talking.
- Talking takes on a pressured quality.

──────────── **THE CASE OF D** *(Continued)* ────────────

- Thoughts are racing—the client may report he or she cannot keep up with the influx of thoughts.
- Impaired judgment.
- Grandiose thinking.
- Inflated self-esteem.
- Increased irritability and impatience with others.
- Easily excitable.
- Indications of violent behavior.
- Disorientation.
- Incoherent speech.
- Bizarre hallucinations.
- Lack of interest in personal relationships.

For clients with a poor history of treatment compliance it is important early on to assess whether there is a substance abuse history that may be complicating the diagnostic or intervention process. Always ask the client what substances are used, and the date of first and most recent use. In this case, D denied any and all other substance use or experimentation besides marijuana, alcohol, and tobacco.

Substance Use/Abuse

Drug Substance	Age of First Use	Frequency	Usual Amount	Date of Last Use
Marijuana	13	2 times per week	1 to 2 joints	2/2001
Alcohol	12	1 to 2 times per week	1 to 2 wine coolers/beer	1/27/2001
Hallucinogens	17			1983
Amphetamine	19			1985
Cocaine	Spring 1999			Summer 1999
Ecstasy	January 2001			2/2001
Nicotine	12			8/30/2001

In the diagnostic assessment, it is critical to get a complete medical and medication history asking the client questions about health conditions, as well as using medical records and previous history and physicals to substantiate information received. When gathering the medical history for D she reported that she has seasonal allergies but any specific allergies are unknown. She describes her general health as good. She states that she has continuous sore throats and sinus infections. D reports she uses over-the-counter medications prior to each visit to see her physician. D states that she has arthritis and many times has pain in the pelvic area, her feet, shoulders, and hands. According to previous records, D had a tubal ligation a couple of years ago and has had her gallbladder removed. D reports having carried two children to term, Justin,

(continued)

THE CASE OF D *(Continued)*

18 years old and Savannah, 4 years old. D has had 3 abortions and 2 miscarriages. D's pelvic bone was broken during the birth of Savannah and this was not detected for approximately seven weeks after she had given birth. D used a walker until the bones healed. D is currently taking multiple psychotrophic medications. She is taking Celexa, Neurotin, Zanax, and Ambien. D's sister reports that she has four living siblings: two sisters and two brothers. D is the youngest woman in the family. It is reported that D had two older brothers who died in early infancy due to a rare blood disorder. It is unknown whether D is a carrier of this disorder. D's sister did not know of any other significant medical history, nor could any additional information be obtained from medical records.

In assessing D's personal history and recent life stressors and events the following information was gathered. D was born in Florida. She states that her father and mother were living together at the time of her birth. D's parents were separated numerous times during her childhood. The primary caretakers were D's maternal grandmother and her mother.

From collateral reports and interviews with the family, D was described as a quiet child who sought the attention of her father. It is reported that D was well bonded to her mother. D reports that she always felt inferior to her classmates and peers during school. She reports feeling that she was "looked down on" by classmates and teachers. She felt this was because of the way she dressed, the neighborhood she lived in, and because she was not as smart as the other children. Corporal punishment was used as discipline in D's family. D reports that she skipped school frequently. She states that she was sexually active at age 11. D states that her brother-in-law molested her at age 13 and that she was gang raped at the age of 17. It is reported that D's mother and father divorced in her senior year of high school. Although many years have passed, the tension is still strong between D's mother and father. D feels she must validate her need to interact with her father. D harbors anger and resentment toward her father and her mother. It is reported that D's father sexually molested her oldest sister. D denies sexual abuse by her father. However, she explained that she remembers little of her childhood. Her second husband is the father of her oldest child. She and her son Justin (oldest child) have an ongoing relational struggle and they quarrel frequently. D reports she has a deep sense of guilt over leaving Justin with his father after their divorce. Justin has been in the juvenile system since early adolescence and is currently in jail. D's third marriage ended in divorce after approximately five years of domestic violence. D is currently unmarried, but has lived with her paramour Calvin for five years. Calvin is her youngest child Savannah's father. It is reported that D fears Calvin will get custody of Savannah because of D's mental health issues. Calvin is reported to be an alcoholic and he has been physically, emotionally, and psychologically abusive toward her. She said that in the past several weeks they argue on a daily basis. Collateral sources and family reports indicate that there is an ongoing struggle with domestic violence in this relationship. D states that there is a "no contact clause" in a court order due to physical and verbal violence in front of the four-year-old child. Repeatedly, family members and police reports indicate Calvin violates this order and often D encourages the violation. Results show that as recent as February 5, 2001, Savannah witnessed her father hitting D and D retaliating. The Department of Children and Families currently has an open case on D's child Savannah.

THE CASE OF D *(Continued)*

In assessing her socialization and support system resources, D states she has very few friends currently, but that 95 percent of those she does associate with are involved in substance use, promiscuous sex, and have questionable integrity. She reports numerous relationships with men. D states that at the beginning of each relationship she feels that this is "Mr. Right." It is reported that she is deceitful and misleading. As a result, she has difficulty keeping and maintaining relationships with others. D reports that she feels "dumped" by her last four relationships. D is unable to identify any social or recreational interests. She stated that she is religious in the fact that she believes in a God, but she is not currently affiliated with a particular church or organization. In reviewing one of D's psychological evaluations, there were observations that she can be worked with easily on a one-on-one basis. However, when discussing sociable manners and involvement with others, it became visible that D frequently feels inferior when socializing with people outside her current circle of friends. She states there are several reasons: her low self-esteem, her inability to get beyond a high school education, and her feelings of embarrassment surrounding her need for public assistance. It is further indicated that D's manic episodes and depression create stressors in social situations. D appears very suspicious of different social circumstances and is unwilling to enter into situations (college, support groups) that may require her academic performance to be tested.

D started in the public school system at the age of 5 years. It is reported that D's problems such as poor attentiveness, poor concentration, poor social skills, and poor retention started as early as the first grade. She said that she excelled in school when she applied herself but overall her grades were poor. D dropped out of school in the eleventh grade for six months and then returned to finish high school. It is reported that D has attempted junior college, but due to her social suspicions and unstable momentum, she has been unable to complete her degree.

Various types of employment characterize D's vocational history. She has been employed as a daycare worker, cashier, teacher's assistant, driver for auto parts company, assembly line worker in a clothing factory, fast food worker, telemarketer, light office/receptionist, and retail sales clerk. A doctor issued her a leave of absence due to mental instability, but her time ran out and she is no longer employed. Both D's psychiatrist and her attorney suggested that she apply for social security disability. Currently, D is receiving unemployment social security benefits. D states she will seek vocational rehabilitation during the time she is not working. However, her self-doubting and her social fears keep her from following through on any final career decision.

D reports that she compulsively goes on shopping binges, which frequently prevent her from paying her bills. Currently, D and Savannah are living in low-income housing. She owns and drives a 1988 Pontiac automobile. D's sister has concerns about the costs of repairs and maintenance of the car and because D frequently borrows money from her mother for gas and repairs for her automobile.

D's legal history involves being arrested once for writing a check with insufficient funds. It is reported that there have been no other incidents involving bad checks. Law enforcement has been called numerous times due to domestic violence issues.

(continued)

——————————— **THE CASE OF D** *(Continued)* ———————————

Due to the instability of the client and her moods a clear risk assessment is needed. D reports that she is not currently suicidal. Yet according to her biological sister, D has made statements that she was going to kill herself. When asked about the statements, D minimizes the incident stating that it was no big deal; she was merely making her point. According to her sister, D had stated that she was going to "blow my brains out." D does own a handgun but reports it is used for home protection only. Immediate attempts by the mental health practitioner are needed to ensure that this weapon is no longer available to the client. As a result the client agrees to give the weapon to a trusted family member or friend prior to her returning home. Since D has a very good relationship with her two sisters, with permission of D, the sisters will be invited to participate in any family group support sessions that are available. The strongest support appears to be her oldest sister. The relationship with her biological mother is tenuous and the mother states she "is very worried about D and what is going to happen to her." D's relationship with her biological father is strained and D does not get along with her stepmother.

In completing the mental status D reports that her appetite has increased and she has gained 30 pounds in the past three months. She states she has had problems with insomnia for years. The mental status exam revealed that the client is aware of her name (orientation to person), where she is (orientation to place: city, state, name of the facility), what day and time it is (orientation to time: time, day, day of week, month, year), and spatial (her current situation, serial sevens, spell *world* backward, medications taken, age, year born, last meal, count backward from ten, three object recall, etc.). She was thus oriented times four (Oriented x4). Her eye contact strayed often and was fair. Twice she just got up and walked out but returned several minutes later with no reason given on her return. She reports her mood is depressed. Affect appeared dramatized. She was cooperative with this assessment. Her motor activity was normal. Speech was pressured and non-goal directed. D appeared very talkative. There was no abnormality of thought content, ideas of reference, or obsessions/compulsions. D reports a history of delusions. She denies any phobias. Her judgment has been inappropriate in the past. Her intellectual capability is undetermined and she should be referred for further testing. Her concentration is poor. She was alert during this session. Her general level of insight appears to be poor. Her motivation for treatment is good, based on her desire to do what is necessary to retain custody of her daughter.

Bipolar Disorder in Childhood and Adolescence

In terms of adolescents, between 10 percent and 15 percent of adolescents with recurrent major depressive episodes also later develop bipolar disorder. With the average age of 20 for the onset for bipolar disorder, a client can have a differential diagnosis of attention-deficit/hyperactivity disorder, conduct disorder, and schizophrenia. Also, bipolar symptoms may be easily misunderstood if there are no distinguishing symptoms of risk-taking behavior from the reckless nature of manic symptoms of the adolescent. If *agitation* is prominent in bipolar disorder, hypomanic symptoms may be misunderstood as reflecting an anxiety state (APA, 2000).

QUICK REFERENCE

APPLICATION OF *DSM-IV-TR* MULTIAXIAL SYSTEM

Diagnostic Impressions:

AXIS I: 296.89   Bipolar II disorder.

          304.30   Cannabis dependence (provisional).*

AXIS II: None.

AXIS III: Deferred.

AXIS IV: Inability to control moods and manage money and spending.

          Relationship issues and domestic violence.

          Poor decision making for self and children.

AXIS V: GAF (current/highest in past year) = 45/75.

---

*Provisional diagnosis of cannabis dependency based on clients reported history.

In children, the existence of the mania episode of bipolar remains controversial. In the data that is available, bipolar disorder resembling the adult form of the illness is rare in prepubertal children, yet if an expanded *phenotype* is accepted this disorder may be more common. Until these questions are answered or resolved, identifying bipolar in children will remain controversial (Keltner & Folks, 2001).

Recent research on bipolar disorders in children and adolescents appears to support an increased prevalence of this disorder. In several studies, it appears that most adults diagnosed with bipolar disorders in the United States experienced the onset of illness in their teen years or before. Bipolar disorder has frequently been misdiagnosed as attention-deficit/hyperactivity disorder (ADHD) or oppositional defiant disorder (ODD), conduct disorder (CD), or depression. Until recently, it was rare that a diagnosis of bipolar disorder was made in childhood yet the best chance for children with emerging bipolar symptoms is early identification and intervention (National Institute of Mental Health, 2000).

DIAGNOSTIC ASSESSMENT

In this case example, J has hyperactive and distractible actions that resulted in bad judgment that led to social impairment resulting in the Department of Juvenile Justice probation and care at a mental health facility. These behaviors provide rationale and supportive information for the manic episode. A major depressive episode is supported as the client attempted to cut his wrist due to depression,

THE CASE OF J

J, a 12-year-old overweight boy, arrived at the clinic with his head down and a refusal to look up for the first 10 minutes of the session. Over the past two years, he explained that he was afraid that people were out to hurt or harm him and he did not like looking at people. After the mental health practitioner explained that looking at a person that was speaking was a way of showing courtesy and that the individual was listening, he eventually lifted his head and began to talk. J reported that people are watching him and talking about him out on the streets and when he becomes depressed he feels sad and empty. In the past two years, he indicated that when he gets depressed the feelings can last several weeks. Since his appetite has increased he has gained weight, sleeps excessively, and because he is fatigued he stays in bed the majority of the day. J reports that he has difficulty concentrating, is bored, and has a loss of interest in most of his usual activities. Although J does not admit directly to suicidal thoughts, he states openly he does not like himself or others and many times wishes he were dead. His mother and his sister confirm J's self-statements. Fifteen minutes into the session, the client excused himself for a drink of water and took a bathroom break for 10 minutes. His mother explained that in the past two years he has had bouts of unresponsiveness and that he appears to feel worse in the evening and better in the morning. She also explained in the past year, that he has been cruel to animals and has killed several cats and birds in the neighborhood in the past couple of years. Six months ago, he was hospitalized for an attempted suicide because he slit his wrist with a kitchen knife and was hospitalized a year ago for a similar attempt. Shortly after J returned to the session, he left again for another drink of water and a walk down the hallway. His mother stated that during the past two years her son can be fine one month and totally depressed the next. Additionally, the mother says that he can also rapidly cycle through episodes of irritability, depression, disruptive behaviors, and temper tantrums.

J's mother states that his behavior scares her because he often engages in unexpected reckless behaviors. To support this statement, she describes several incidents that frightened her. The first occurred when her son jumped on the back of her vehicle for a ride as she was pulling out of the driveway. Another occurred when he was caught walking on the ledge of a building two stories high. She explained that at times he seems very excited, however, irritability surfaces quickly when what he wants is refused and he can become unpredictable with changing moods. Some days she says he can go on a few hours of sleep, and there are days he does not sleep at all. A problem the family is having difficulty with is when he will not stop talking, he will jump from one topic to another and what he says can be unorganized and difficult to understand. At times during the past two years, he has been unable to complete something because he is unable to concentrate or stay with it long enough, while at other times he will not stop what he is doing until completion. He has had to change schools twice in the past year due to behavioral problems with his teachers and classmates. His mother reports that over the past year and a half, he has called total strangers, which has resulted in expensive telephone bills. In the past two years, he has had bouts where he is outrageously excitable, intrusive, and demanding. During this session, he stated that he was currently seeking a girlfriend with whom he could have a sexual relationship.

Six months ago, he was arrested for simple assault for chasing his mother and sister around the house with a fork. His family members have lost patience with his habitual moaning

――――――――― **THE CASE OF J** *(Continued)* ―――――――――

and complaining, as well as his becoming upset by what family members consider trivial matters. His sister and mother say he will argue, make verbal threats, and rage for hours over a glass of milk, a sandwich, a television program, or some other unimportant matter. Two weeks ago, he got on a city bus, put on headphones and listened to music at top volume, but when he was asked to turn his music down, he became irritable, nasty, and cruel to the passengers. This resulted in another arrest and he was placed in an inpatient mental health facility for several days. The mother now involves the police in transporting her son to a hospital or residential treatment when there have been physical threats or he becomes irrational. The mother has petitioned the court for her son's admission to a psychiatric unit or into residential treatment for his protection and the protection of others.

weight gain, marked appetite increase, excessive sleep, fatigue, difficulty concentrating, and low self-worth. (See Quick reference for the multiaxial diagnostic assessment.)

Since it is unusual for a child or adolescent to be given this diagnosis, it is critical that clear justification occurs for the use of this diagnostic category. Therefore, in completing the diagnostic assessment the problematic behaviors the client is exhibiting need to be identified and clearly documented. J clearly meets the criteria for bipolar I disorder by exhibiting distinct behavioral periods of mood swings (at least six) from profound depression to extreme euphoria and irritability (mania) with intervening periods of normalcy in the past three years. During these periods of mood disturbance, he has shown the following symptoms:

1. Inflated self-esteem as evidenced by his demanding others to do things for him, and his inability to express or understand shame/guilt. At times he experiences euphoria and elation, however, irritability surfaces rapidly when his wishes and desires go unfulfilled, and he becomes very volatile as his mood fluctuates.
2. Periods where he has a decreased need for sleep, difficulty falling asleep, and an inexhaustible energy as evidenced by his feeling rested after only two or three hours of sleep. He also has periods where he goes without sleep for several days.
3. Periods of being more talkative than usual with a need to keep talking.
4. During communications with others he demonstrates flight of ideas and his speech becomes disorganized and incoherent.
5. Easily distracted and frequently leaves those who are around him to tend to become unimportant or irrelevant external stimuli. Becomes paranoid and states that he hears voices. Goal-directed activities become difficult.

6. Increase in goal-directed activities at home/school as evidenced by extensive computer use and playing video games.

7. Excessive involvement in pleasurable activities that have a high potential for painful consequences as evidenced by unrestrained listening to music at extreme levels in public. He seldom accepts responsibility for his own behaviors. Excessive sexual interest is increasing. Poor impulse control resulting in becoming socially uninhibited.

Overall, these problematic behaviors are severe enough to cause marked impairment in usual social activities and relationships at home and school. For example, he has been arrested for assault, disturbing the peace, and was hospitalized to prevent harm to others. In the past three years he has made two suicide attempts and the most recent six months ago required hospitalization. He displays impaired social interaction related to narcissistic behavior evidenced by inability to develop satisfying relationships. He also displays impaired social interactions because he manipulates others to carry out his wishes, and if things go wrong, he is skillful at projecting the responsibility for the failure onto them (APA, 2000).

QUICK REFERENCE

MULTIAXIAL ASSESSMENT

Axis I: 296.44 Bipolar I disorder, most recent episode manic, severe with psychotic features.

Axis II: None.

Axis III: None.

Axis IV: Psychosocial and environmental problems.

A problem with primary support is evident by his not being able to get along with and making threats to his sibling and his mother.

Problems related to the social environment as evidenced by being removed from a city bus, and having no friends.

Educational problems as evidenced by poor performance, being expelled from school, and inability to follow directions and rules.

Problems related to interaction with the legal system as evidenced by recent arrest and a charge of simple assault, Department of Juvenile Justice resulting in probation, and his inability to comply with probationary stipulations.

Mother is working toward expulsion from home.

Axis V: Global Assessment of Functioning Scale (GAF) = 30 (current).

In addition, he clearly meets the criteria for major depressive episodes where he exhibits many symptoms during depressive episodes that are present during three- to two-week periods and a change from previous function due to depressed mood.

1. Depressed all day, nearly every day, as evidenced by reports of feelings of sadness and observed by family members, schoolmates, and teachers.
2. Marked diminished interest or pleasure in all, or almost all, activities most of the day as evidenced by family members, schoolmates, and teachers.
3. He has had a significant weight gain with an increase in appetite daily.
4. Insomnia or hypersomnia nearly every day.
5. Psychomotor agitation exists whereas he and his family report that he is restless and slow to accomplish assigned tasks.
6. During these periods he experiences fatigue and loss of energy every day.
7. He experiences feeling of worhtlessness nearly every day with hypersensitivity to criticism.
8. Client and family members state that he has a diminished ability to think or concentrate and that he is indecisive.
9. Recurrent suicidal attempts and threats as evidenced by his attempts to stab himself with a knife on several occasions resulting in hospitalization.

(See Quick Reference on page 316 for a detailed description of J's symptoms that support the multiaxial diagnostic assessment.)

TREATMENT PLANNING AND DOCUMENTATION

A treatment plan with the client's goals and objectives needs to be formulated. With the information gathered during the diagnostic assessment as the basis for treatment, the intervention plan allows for application. In the diagnostic assessment, information given by the client is supplemented with other resources to confirm history and check out all other possible contradictory information and comorbid conditions. Clients should undergo a complete physical examination, complete blood count and general chemistry screening, a thyroid function test, and if substance abuse is suspected a test of urine toxicology is recommended. In addition, the referral of a blood test should be considered to detect use or abuse of drugs or hormonal problems (APA, 2000). If the client is taking or will be taking medications serum levels should be considered especially if the medications include valproic acid (Depakene), carbamazepine (Tegretol), or venlafaxine (Effexor). If the client is treatment resistant the practitioner can use the results from more standardized radiological tests such as computed tomography or magnetic resonance

---

QUICK REFERENCE

CHARACTERIZATIONS, SYMPTOMS, AND BEHAVIORS

During periods of manic episodes he has shown the following symptoms:

- Inflated self-esteem and very volatile and this mood fluctuates.
- Periods of decreased need for sleep, difficulty falling asleep, and other times has inexhaustible energy and goes without sleep for several days.
- Periods of being more talkative than usual with a need to keep talking.
- During communications with others there is flight of ideas and speech becomes disorganized and incoherent.
- Easily distracted and frequently leaves those who are around him to tend to become unimportant or irrelevant external stimuli.
- Increase in goal-directed activities at home/school as evidenced by extensive computer use and playing video games.
- Excessive involvement in pleasurable activities with high potential for painful consequences.
- Frequently does not accept responsibility for his behaviors.
- Sexual interest is excessive with poor impulse control resulting in becoming socially uninhibited.

During depressive episodes he has shown the following symptoms:

- Depressed all day, nearly every day, as evidenced by reports of feelings of sadness and observed by others.
- Marked diminished interest or pleasure in all, or almost all, activities most of the day as evidenced others.
- Significant weight gain with an increase in appetite daily.
- Insomnia or hypersomnia nearly every day.
- Experiences fatigue and loss of energy every day.
- Experiences feeling worthless nearly every day with hypersensitivity to criticism.
- Diminished ability to think or concentrate and is indecisive.
- Recurrent suicidal attempts and threats.

---

imaging and electroencephalography as second-line options in the evaluation (Griswold & Pessar, 2000).

Problem behaviors must be clearly identified, as these are the behaviors that will be reflected in terms of the intervention efforts. While a clinical interview is often an adequate method to assess the treatment needs of a bipolar patient, other instruments may assist the therapist in arriving at a more careful and comprehensive easement and a treatment plan. The Mood Disorder Questionnaire developed by Hirschfeld, Williams, Spitzer, Calabrese, et al. (2000) offers an overall assessment of the client's symptoms and functioning. Semantic Differential and Mood Scales

SAMPLE TREATMENT PLAN

BIPOLAR I DISORDER, MOST RECENT EPISODE MANIC

Definition: Bipolar I disorder, most recent episode manic, is characterized by the presence of a manic episode. There has previously been at least one major depressive episode, manic episode or mixed episode but the client is presently in a manic episode. A manic episode consists of a period of elevated, expansive, and irritable mood that lasts at least one week.

Signs and Symptoms to Note in the Record:

- Inflated self-esteem or grandiosity.
- Decreased need for sleep.
- Pressured speech.
- Flight of ideas or racing thoughts.
- Distractibility.
- Psychomotor agitation.
- Excessive involvement in pleasurable activities that may have harmful consequences, such as sexual promiscuity or impulse buying.

Goals:

1. Reduce uncontrollable energy, return to a normal activity level, and increase good judgment.
2. Reduce agitation, impulsive behaviors, and pressured speech and increase sensitivity to consequences of behaviors.
3. Cope with underlying feelings of low self-esteem and fears of rejection or abandonment.
4. Increase controlled behavior, achieve a more stable mood, and develop more deliberate speech and thought processes.

Objectives	Interventions
Client will cooperate with a psychiatric evaluation and take medications as prescribed.	Arrange for a psychiatric evaluation for psychotropic medications and monitor patient's reaction to the medication.
Client will reduce impulsive behaviors.	Psychotherapy to address consequences of behaviors.
Client will decrease grandiosity and express self more realistically.	Confront the client's grandiosity through psychotherapy and reinforce more realistic self-statements.
Client will be able to sit calmly for 30 minutes without agitation or distractibility.	Reinforce client's increased control over his energy and help the client set attainable goals and limits on his agitation and distractibility.
Client will speak more slowly and maintain focus on one subject at a time.	Provide structure for the client's thought processes and actions by directing the course of the conversation and developing plans for the client's behaviors.
Client will acknowledge the low self-esteem and fear or rejection that underlies his grandiosity.	Psychotherapy to explore the psychosocial stressors that are precipitating the client's manic behaviors, such as rejection by peers or past traumas.

(SDFMS) developed by Lorr and Wunderlich (1998) permits a therapist to measure changes on various dimensions of symptoms relevant to depression and mania. The Mood Related Pleasant Events Schedule (MRPES) developed by MacPhillamy and Lewinsohn (1982) can be used to measure changes in the client's perception of life events and provide the clinician with quantifiable data in making modifications to treatment plans. The Family Sense of Coherence (FSOC) and Family Adaption Scales (FAS) used together designed by Antonovsky and Sourani (1988) can be used to evaluate the family's sense of coherence and adaption helping the therapist to better understand family dynamics and functioning.

TREATMENT STRATEGY

Medications are frequently utilized as either the sole treatment strategy or a supplemental treatment strategy for the bipolar disorders in adults and adolescents and children. The same medications may be used for the disorder regardless of a client's age. Currently, several medications are used to treat bipolar disorder, yet not many are completely effective long term (Young, Macritchie, & Calabrese, 2000). Many of these medications were originally designed to control and prevent epileptic seizures, but now are primarily used to stabilize moods. Most medications used to treat bipolar disorder are effective in treating the manic episode, but few medications are available to treat the depressive phase. Lithium remains the most common medication used for bipolar disorder despite the lack of knowledge of how lithium achieves its normalizing effects. In a January 2001, *Psychopharmacology Update,* a new study of venlafaxine extended-release (Effexor XR) is showing promise for being effective for bipolar depression, but it recommends that therapists use mood stabilizers in combination with bupropion, venlafaxine, or any selective serotonin reuptake inhibitor (Manisses Communication Group Incorporated, 2001). At present, many therapists use lithium (Cibalith-S, Eskalith, Lithane, Lithium Citrate, Lithobid, Lithonate, Lithonate-S, Lithotabs), valproate (Depakote, Depacon, Depakene), and carbamazepine (Carbatrol, Mazepine, or Tegretol) as an adjunctive therapy for acute mania. These are prescribed to lessen the severity of manic and depressive symptoms and reduce the likelihood of a reemergence of symptoms. Professionals are cautioned to start low and go up slowly when dosing venlafaxine for clients with bipolar depression. Because every client is unique it may be necessary to change medications (Keltner & Folks, 2001). For a more detailed review of medications and the relationship psychopharmacology can have to mental health practice the reader is referred to Dziegielewski and Leon (2001).

In terms of applying medication as a treatment modality for children and adolescents, there are very few medication studies available. The studies conducted are limited in that there are few follow-up studies on medications over the long-term effects and it is difficult and dangerous to test children because they are still developing. In a March 1999 *Brown University Child & Adolescent Behavior Letter,* the researchers assessed lithium (Eskalith and others), valproic acid (Depakote and others), carbamazepine (Tegretol and others) antidepressants, antipsychotics, and stimulates in 59 patients. There were significant improvements of manic-like symptoms using lithium as indicated by 39 of the 59 (66 percent) of the children. There were no significant improvements with antidepressants, antipsychotic and stimulant medications. Researchers indicated that additional research is needed to look at individual mood stabilizers in single and combined treatment of juvenile mania. A more recent placebo-controlled study of 50 children that were on average 10 years old demonstrated that lithium was effective in reducing severe aggressive behaviors. New antidepressants have not been well studied in children or adolescents (Keltner & Folks, 2001).

Lithium is not recommended for use in children younger than age 12. Nonetheless, several published studies (Keltner & Folks, 2001) document its use in prepubertal children with bipolar illness. Valproate is an anticonvulsant medication that has been effective in treating clients with acute mania. There have been very small sample size testing on adolescents, yet the studies indicate that there is evidence that the medication is useful for core symptoms of bipolar disorder. Carbamazepine (Tegretol) has had very few studies to demonstrate the efficacy of this medication with adolescents with bipolar disorder. The studies that have been done have shown bipolar disorder, conduct disorder, paranoid thinking, seizure disorder, and aggressive behavior were improved in a substantial percentage of children and adolescents tested. Very few studies have been placebo controlled for prepubertal children. Buspirone (BuSpar) studies have shown some improvement in anxiety and aggressive behaviors, but if there is no improvement after six weeks, it should be discontinued. The benefit of buspirone is that it does not cause physical dependence and does not cover benzodiazepine withdrawal.

Although medications are many times used with both adults and children, caution in regard to children, based on the limited studies and empirical findings appears prudent. For the mental health practitioner, knowledge of medications is a practice necessity. The practitioner also provides assistance to the client and family in understanding how medication reduces the impact of the bipolar symptoms. Education is needed to help clients realize that medication can also reduce the likelihood of a recurrence of the disorder once symptoms are reduced. Education can help the support system to understand that continuity of care is essential when combined with psychotherapy. They also need to understand the power and the limitations of medications as a treatment modality. In addition, it is important to review psychosocial variables that mediate medication compliance and effectiveness while emphasizing the goal of strengthening understanding of and cooperation in the treatment plan (Griswold & Pessar, 2000; Thyer & Wodarski, 1998).

Counseling Strategy

There are several different types of counseling that are frequently considered when working with individuals who suffer from the mood disorders. A complete diagnostic assessment can help the mental health practitioner decide what problem behaviors are most prominent and how to best address what is identified. The Quick Reference highlights the goals that can be addressed in counseling strategies including cognitive therapy, peer support group therapy, and family therapy, and family support group therapy.

Electroconvulsive Therapy (ECT) for Depression and Mania

Electroconvulsive therapy (ECT) is a form of treatment for depression and other mental illnesses that involves the introduction of a series of brain seizures in the patient (West, Prado, & Krystal, 1999). To date there is no definitive explanation as to how or why ECT works. Yet, there are numerous neurochemical, neuroendocrine, and neurophysiologic hypotheses concerning this matter (Willoughby, Hradek, & Richards, 1997). What is known is that it is not the electrical shock that causes the therapeutic effect, but rather the resulting seizure, which is a rapid firing of neurons in the brain (Fischer, 2000).

Unfortunately, there are no nationwide figures that show the true frequency of ECT usage. Yet, it is probable that ECT usage has increased during the past two decades due to its efficiency and resulting shorter hospital stay (Willoughby et al., 1997). A study by Reid, Keller, Leatherman, and Mason (1998) showed that between September of 1993 and April of 1995 more than 2,500 people received ECT in state psychiatric hospitals in Texas. With this information and other statistics, Fischer (2000) concluded that more than 100,000 patients receive ECT every year. Society's stigma against ECT has inhibited its use because not only do many public and rural hospitals not offer it as a treatment, but also many doctors are never taught how to perform the procedure. As a result, ECT is considered a treatment of last resort.

ECT is not without its risks and, similar to medications, side effects are possible. According to Willoughby et al. (1997) "Adverse effects of ECT may include apprehension or fear, headache, muscle soreness, nausea, cardiovascular dysfunction, prolonged apnea, prolonged seizures, and emergent mania" (p. 11). The most troubling of these affects is cognitive dysfunction, which many times entail memory loss for a period of time before and after the procedure. This memory loss frequently lasts several weeks but can extend up to six months. In

QUICK REFERENCE

COUNSELING STRATEGIES FOR COGNITIVE THERAPY

- Look at distortions that are factors in the development and maintenance of mood disorders. Look at mania characteristics of self that are seen as power or overly valued regarding abilities.
- Discuss negative distortions related to expectations of the environment, self, and future that contribute to depression.
- Examine the client's perceptions of the environment and activities that are seen as unsatisfying or unrealistic.
- Identify dysfunctional patterns of thinking and behaving and guide the client to evidence and logic that test the validity of the dysfunctional thinking.
- Assist in understanding "automatic" thoughts that occur spontaneously and contribute to the distorted affect (e.g., personalizing, all or nothing, mind reading, discounting negatives). Looking specifically at situations, thoughts, and consequences. If this technique is not helpful or does work for the client, help them to understand and explore other possibilities.
- Help the client use "I" statements in identifying feelings and reactions.

PEER SUPPORT GROUP THERAPY

- Provides the client with a feeling of security when discussing troublesome or embarrassing issues. Also, this group will help the client in discussing medication-related issues and serve as an avenue for promoting education related to the affective disorder and its treatment.
- This group will help the client gain a sense of perspective on his condition and tangibly encourage him to link up with others who have common problems. A sense of hope is conveyed when the individual is able to see that he is not alone or unique in experiencing affective illness.

FAMILY THERAPY FOR DEPRESSION AND MANIA

- Working with families to formulate a therapeutic plan to resolve symptoms and restore or create adaptive family function.
- Build an alliance with the client and the family members. It is important to establish a positive working relationship between the client and his family.
- Combining psychotherapeutic and pharmocotherapeutic treatment education.
- Obtain each family member's view of the situation and specify problems, clarify each individual's needs and desires using his preferred vocabulary, and accepting his perceptions at this time. Be nonblaming and accepting of the client and the family. Assure the family members that they did not cause the condition. Allow the family members to ventilate about the chronic burden they have experienced.

(continued)

QUICK REFERENCE (Continued)

- Review ambient family stress. Examine any objective and subjective burdens the family is experiencing due to observable aspects of the illness and the need to provide care giving. Look for criticism or emotional over involvement of family members in response to the client's illness.
- Help to redefine the nature of the family's difficulties.
- Encourage recognition of each member's contribution to the discord.
- Recognize and modify communication patterns, rules, and interactional patterns.
- Increase reciprocity through mutual exchange of privileges.
- Decrease the use of coercion and blaming.
- Increase cooperative problem solving.
- Increase each member's ability to express feeling clearly and directly, and to *hear* others accurately.

FAMILY SUPPORT GROUP THERAPY

- Provides therapeutic benefits for the family and support. Enhance knowledge in complying with the medication regimen.
- Provide the family members with a feeling of security when discussing troublesome or embarrassing issues. Also, this group will help the family members in discussing medication-related issues and serve as an avenue for promoting education related to the affective disorder and its treatment.
- This group will help the family members gain a sense of perspective on his condition and tangibly encourage the family members to link up with others who have common problems. A sense of hope is conveyed when the family members are able to see that they are not alone or unique in experiencing affective illness.

Source: Griswold & Pessar, 2000; Thyer & Wodarski, 1998.

---

some cases, the memory loss persists longer. Research has shown that the cognitive dysfunction caused by ECT does not adversely affect functions not associated with memory, such as intelligence and judgment, in any lasting way. According to Johnstone (1999), approximately 80 percent of patients report some side effects, with memory impairment being the most frequent with a range of responses including fear, humiliation, increased compliance, failure, worthlessness, betrayal, lack of confidence, and degradation, as well as a sense of having been abused and assaulted.

According to Willoughby and coworkers (1997), despite all the controversy surrounding ECT, the APA has determined that ECT is an affective treatment option for people with "major depressive disorder, bipolar affective disorder, schizophrenia, and related psychotic disorders" (p. 2). ECT can also be used with affective disorders and psychotic depression, which is seldom responsive to medications. In addition, ECT can lead to significant improvement of the patients with severe affective disorders. Reid and coworkers (1998) found that 90 percent of all patients they reviewed who had undergone ECT had been diagnosed with a severe mood disorder and the remaining 10 percent had schizophrenia. With the research supporting the effectiveness of ECT with mood disorders, specifically bipolar disorder and depression, ECT can be viewed as an appropriate treatment option (Fischer, 2000).

ECT is effective with clients who are acutely suicidal and in the treatment of severe depression, particularly in those clients who are also experiencing psychotic symptoms and those with psychomotor retardation in sleep, appetite, and energy. It is often considered for treatment only after a trial of therapy with antidepressant medication has proved ineffective (Griswold & Pessar, 2000; Thyer & Wodarski, 1998).

Episodes of acute mania are occasionally treated with ECT, particularly when the client does not tolerate or fails to respond to lithium or other drug treatment, or when dangerous behavior or exhaustion threatens life. For example, although this treatment is a viable option for the first case of D, the adult with bipolar III disorder, it is not recommended for case example J, the child with bipolar I disorder. Due to the extensive history of unsuccessful treatments for D with medication, therapy, and counseling, a recommendation for electroconvulsive therapy seems viable. The extensive history and present abuse of substances complicate her case. Although many of the medications the client attempted resulted in unbearable side effects, including inducing mania, it is unknown how many of these reactions were attributable to the client's substance abuse. Likewise, many of the medications that have been attempted resulted in no improvement in D's depression. What affects the client's alcohol and drug usage, while on these medications, is unknown. Given her substance abuse history, ECT will not be affected and likewise the dangerous side effects of combining alcohol and drugs with ECT is nonexistent compared to the dangerous effects of combining alcohol and drugs with psychotropic medications. This therapy is not recommended for J because he is not currently experiencing any extreme depressive episodes (Griswold & Pessar, 2000; Harvard Medical School, 2001; Moise, 1996; Thyer & Wodarski, 1998).

SUMMARY

Regardless of the type of bipolar disorder a client is suffering from, during assessment it is important to remember the variability that can result in the client's behaviors and actions that is indicative of the mental disorder. Mental health practitioners need to be well versed in the signs and symptoms identified in the

DSM-IV-TR and capable of using this manual to facilitate the diagnostic assessment, treatment planning, and intervention that will follow.

If a mental health practitioner suspects that any client, regardless of age, may suffer from bipolar disorder, it is critical to confirm this diagnosis using the *DSM-IV-TR* criteria (APA, 2000; Meeks, 1999). This requires a determination that the client meets the criteria for one of the mood states of bipolar disorder. In other words, does the client meet criteria for depressive, manic, hypomanic, or mixed episodes? In addition, every practitioner should also assess for critical symptoms reflective of other mental health problems that a client can exhibit (Cassano, Pini, Saettoni, & Dell'Osso, 1999).

There are limitations because every individual is unique. Mood disorders, and the bipolar disorders in particular, can be complex and more research is needed to establish the best evidence-based practices as well as more research in the area of children and adolescents. Accurate measurements of problem behaviors and social problems provide fuel for starting the most comprehensive approaches to quality client care.

Mental health practitioners are in a unique position not only to provide services to those with bipolar disorders, but they are also in a position of advocating for the needs of the client that are going unmet. There are a number of families struggling with someone with bipolar disorder who need the support of the community, physicians, and mental health organizations. As a mental health practitioner, it may be necessary to develop support groups for both family and client because it will provide low-cost assistance. In addition, the legal justice system and the medical society red tape must be removed or simplified to expedite the aid and assistance for clients with bipolar and the assistance needed by their families. Finally, in the diagnostic assessment, mood variability makes it imperative to teach individuals in the client's support system to be aware of suicidal indications. According to the U.S. Surgeon General David Satcher, suicide prevention is critical as 31,000 people who end their lives each year, along with 775,000 who attempt suicide (90 percent to 95 percent) are associated with one of several major illnesses, including depression, bipolar illness, schizophrenia, drug and alcohol abuse, and personality disorders (NIMH, 2000).

12 Borderline Personality Disorder

ANGELA S. MAGEE AND SOPHIA F. DZIEGIELEWSKI

Borderline personality disorder is a mental illness with a chronic, fluctuating course. It affects an estimated five million Americans or approximately 2 percent of the population (D. Hales & Hales, 1996). Individuals who suffer from borderline personality disorder make up 20 percent of psychiatric inpatients and 10 percent of psychiatric outpatients, and the diagnosis is five times more common among close relatives of the borderline patient than in the general population (Grim, 2000). This disorder is severe, as approximately 5 percent of borderline individuals will eventually kill themselves (D. Hales & Hales, 1996).

Personality disorders are generally considered to be indicative of a lifelong pattern of behavior. Therefore, when an individual is diagnosed with a personality disorder such as this one, numerous things must be considered and intervention options can vary. This chapter discusses one of the most common and severe forms of personality disorders known. In order to reduce the magnitude of disturbances this disorder can have on the individual, the family, and society, it is critical that practitioners complete a thorough diagnostic assessment, treatment plan, and practice strategy that can efficiently embrace, identify, and effectively treat individuals who suffer from borderline personality disorder.

OVERVIEW OF BORDERLINE PERSONALITY DISORDER

Borderline personality disorder was first diagnosed in 1938, describing individuals who straddled the border between neurosis and psychosis (Maxmen & Ward, 1995). Generally, personality disorders develop in childhood or adolescence and become apparent by young adulthood (Grim, 2000). In borderline personality disorder, individuals suffer with numerous problem behaviors that impair current occupational and social functioning. The exact cause of this problem, however, remains unknown. Some professionals believe a history of early abandonment, physical and sexual abuse, sustained neglect, or a lack of stability makes it difficult for individuals to maintain a firm sense of themselves or others later in life (D. Hales & Hales, 1996). Borderline personality disorder is a chronic mental illness that historically has not responded well to therapeutic or medicinal interventions.

DSM-IV-TR MULTIAXIAL SYSTEM

According to the *DSM-IV-TR,* individuals with borderline personality disorder have a pervasive pattern of instability of interpersonal relationships, self-image, and affects, and marked impulsivity beginning by early adulthood (American Psychiatric Association [APA], 2000). These individuals make frantic efforts to avoid real or imagined abandonment, sometimes resulting in a suicide attempt or self-mutilation. Additional characteristics of borderline personality disorder include frequent mood changes, recurrent suicidal or self-mutilating behavior or both, chronic feelings of emptiness, and difficulty controlling inappropriate anger (D. Hales & Hales, 1996).

For individuals who suffer from borderline personality disorder, the following criteria are prominent with at least five of the following symptoms being exhibited (APA, 2000). First, individuals often make frantic efforts to avoid real or imagined abandonment. When this happens regularly, it can become difficult for family and friends to maintain long-term relationships as often everyday relationship fluctuations or upsets are thought of as catastrophic. Second, relationship patterns often become unstable because the intense responses and constant demands the individual places on these relationships are often characterized by unstable and intense moods that alternate between the client expressing idealization for the individual and devaluation. When utilizing the defense mechanism of *idealization,* the individual deals with emotional conflict or internal or external stressors by attributing exaggerated positive qualities to others. In *devaluation,* the individual deals with emotional conflict or internal or external stressors by attributing exaggerated negative qualities to self or others. Constant use of these types of defense mechanisms can easily strain the most caring of relationships.

These individuals often experience identity disturbances in which they are markedly unable to understand the relationship of the self to others. Patterns of behavior remain persistently unstable and self-image or the sense of self is often impaired. To try and take control of these ambivalent feelings, the individual is often seen as compulsive in at least two areas and the impulsivity is often unpredictable and self-damaging. It is not uncommon for these individuals to have recurrent suicidal behavior, gestures, or threats, as well as self-mutilating behavior. Moods are often unstable and individuals often complain of chronic feelings of emptiness that are reflected in inappropriate episodes of intense anger or difficulty controlling their actions based on the fear of abandonment. At times, the fears and desperation to control the situation may become so severe that these individuals report transient, stress–related paranoid ideation or severe dissociative symptoms. When this occurs, the individual believes people are plotting to destroy his or her relationships (e.g., paranoid ideation) or that he or she is mentally separated from the relationship when reality testing remains intact (e.g., dissociative symptoms).

QUICK REFERENCE

CRITERIA FOR BORDERLINE PERSONALITY DISORDER

The diagnostic criteria as outlined for this disorder have at least five or more of the following symptoms:

- Frantic efforts to avoid real or imagined abandonment.
- A pattern of unstable and intense interpersonal relationships characterized by alternating between extremes of idealization and devaluation.
- Identity disturbance: markedly and persistently unstable self-image or sense of self.
- Impulsivity in at least two areas that are potentially self-damaging.
- Recurrent suicidal behavior, gestures, or threats, or self-mutilating behavior.
- Affective instability due to a marked reactivity of mood.
- Chronic feelings of emptiness.
- Inappropriate, intense anger or difficulty controlling anger.
- Transient, stress-related paranoid ideation or severe dissociative symptoms.

Source: Summarized criteria reprinted with permission from the *Diagnostic and Statistical Manual of Mental Disorders, Fourth Edition, Text Revision.* Copyright 2000. American Psychiatric Association.

Up to 75 percent of individuals with borderline personality disorder have experienced some sort of sexual abuse in childhood. Yet, it is unclear whether the abuse itself facilitates the development of the disorder or whether the abuse and development of borderline personality disorder both result from the extent of invalidation and familial dysfunction (Linehan, 1993).

Basically, the core symptom evidenced by the individual who suffers from borderline personality disorder is emotion dysregulation, which constitutes a combination of an emotional response system that is oversensitive and overreactive. In these cases the individual is unable to modulate the resulting strong emotions and actions associated with the feelings that are experienced. In addition, the developmental circumstance that produces emotional dysregulation is an invalidating environment in which individuals fail to label and modulate arousal, tolerate distress, and trust emotional responses as valid interpretations of what is happening around them (Linehan, 1993). Overall, those who suffer from borderline personality disorder often have a chronic, fluctuating course that significantly impairs social and occupational functioning (Maxmen & Ward, 1995).

The chronic nature of progression of borderline personality disorder mandates that alternative forms of treatment be explored. This population has a high rate of use of psychiatric services and emergency room visits. For these individuals, mental health utilization costs are great, treatment dropouts are high, and estimated rates of completed suicide average about 9 percent (Simpson et al., 1998). In addition, for individuals with borderline personality disorder, medication noncompliance is common, and the rate of substance abuse is great (Koerner & Linehan, 1999).

MEASUREMENT INSTRUMENTS AND DIAGNOSTIC ASSESSMENT

To facilitate the diagnostic assessment when working with individuals suffering from borderline personality disorder, several clinical scales can be utilized. The overall assumption for using these scales in the self-harm risk assessment is the assumption that many negative thoughts coupled with few positive thoughts indicate a risk of suicide (Fischer, 1999). Furthermore, these measurement scales help to identify symptoms, evaluate client progress, and help to determine the direction of the therapeutic intervention. To facilitate the immediate risk assessment, scales used with individuals with borderline personality disorder should address parasuicidal behavior, depression, and anxiety. In addition, scales that focus on sexual abuse can help the clinician to determine a possible history and the impact of the event on the client's current level of functioning.

One such scale, Reasons for Living Inventory (RFL), is designed to assist with measuring suicide potential by looking at the adaptive characteristics of suicide (Linehan, Goldstein, Nielsen, & Chiles, 1983). The Reasons for Living Inventory is based on cognitive-behavioral theory, which asserts that cognitive patterns influence suicidal behavior. The scale looks at the topic of suicide from the absent adaptive coping skills in the client. See Fischer (1999) for a more complete list of scales that could be of benefit in this area.

Numerous scales are available that measure one's level of depression. The Self-Rating Scale can provide the practitioner with an easy to complete short scale (Zung, 1965). The items on the measurement scale were selected to look at the three areas stated above and include cognitive, affective, psychomotor, somatic, and social-interpersonal items. As many individuals with borderline personality disorder suffer from anxiety, appropriate scales that address this symptom are imperative. Zung also developed the Self-Rating Anxiety Scale (SAS). This measurement assesses anxiety as a clinical disorder and quantifies the symptoms of anxiety.

The majority of individuals diagnosed with borderline personality disorder may have been victims of child abuse (Linehan et al., 1999). To measure a client's beliefs associated with sexual abuse, the Beliefs Associated with Childhood Sexual Abuse (BACSA) was developed (Jehu, Klassen, & Gazan, 1986) to help to depict changes in clients who are receiving cognitive therapy to help restructure distorted beliefs.

THE CASE OF C

C is a 27-year-old Caucasian woman who currently lives with her husband and three children in their owned home in Florida. The client was recently approved for Social Security Disability and receives $488.00 a month. She has no insurance but will be eligible for Medicare in two years

——————————— **THE CASE OF C *(Continued)*** ———————————

Her husband is employed in the retail business. C reports a history of emotional problems in the form of anxiety and depression. She reports that she has excessive worry about a number of events in her life. She worries about her children, her mother, her husband, and her self. She often finds these symptoms hard to control and reports restlessness or feeling on edge, irritability, difficulty concentrating, but most of all fears that she will do something wrong and "everyone" close to her will leave her.

She stated that she first had these problems with feelings of anxiety and abandonment when she was a child, with a recurrence of more pronounced symptoms approximately three years ago. C first received mental health services at age 12. She also received outpatient psychiatric treatment when 19 or 20 years old. She participated in a two-month partial hospitalization program three months ago. She is currently receiving outpatient treatment, occasionally attends a weekly anxiety support group and sees a psychiatrist every two months and a case manager monthly. The psychiatrist currently prescribes C the medication Paxil and she takes it daily.

C was born in a rural town and is one of a pair of twin sisters. They were born two and a half months premature and had to stay in an incubator for 4 to 6 months following delivery. C's sister died soon after birth and C believes much of her problems in infancy are related to the fact that her mother took drugs and smoked during her pregnancy. The client has eight older biological siblings. Her mother left her family when the client was two years old. C subsequently lived with grandparents, her father, mother, and in several foster group homes. She stated that she keeps in contact with her mother who has also suffered from several emotional breakdowns. C also reported extensive physical, emotional, and sexual abuse during her childhood. She has addressed the abuse in individual therapy, but she continues to experience nightmares, flashbacks, and problems with sexual relations.

C attended mainstream classes in school and never had to repeat any grades. She graduated high school in 1989 as an average student. She began a medical secretarial program one-year following her graduation, but quit after only six weeks. C's employment history is sporadic. She was a waitress in the past and reports she lost the job due to her panic attacks.

C was married for the first time in May of 1999. She gave birth to a healthy boy two months ago. She has another son, age two, and a daughter, age four, with the same man. She currently lives with her husband and their three children. C takes care of her personal hygiene except when very depressed. She does some household chores, such as cooking and cleaning, only when absolutely necessary. She enjoys taking care of her children, watching TV, and listening to music. She does not have any hobbies. C forces herself to walk once or twice a week for exercise. She has no friends locally despite her attempts to make some. She stated that "people must think I am boring or screwed up." C does not belong to any clubs and does not attend church. She has a valid driver's license but only drives when she has to. She is not able to shop by herself due to panic attacks.

C reported first drinking alcohol when she was 16 years old. She admitted drinking heavily on weekends for a while after high school, but she denied having a problem with alcohol abuse. She first tried illegal drugs in the form of marijuana a few times when she was 16 years old. C reported taking powder cocaine once when she was 22 years old. She has never been in

(continued)

THE CASE OF C *(Continued)*

---

any formal substance abuse or 12-step programs. C denies any current alcohol or drug use. She smokes one pack of cigarettes daily.

C reported two incidents of trouble with the law for domestic violence when she was in her early twenties, although the charges were dropped the following day. C reported her husband has become verbally and physically abusive in the past. He has refused to participate in marital therapy.

Completion of the Diagnostic Assessment

The diagnostic assessment began with the collection of biological and psychosocial information. C was born as one of a pair of twin sisters (the other twin died in infancy) and the client has eight older biological siblings. Her mother left her family when the client was two years old and C subsequently had an unstable living situation growing up having lived in several places with different people (grandparents, father, mother, foster group homes). She stated that her mother has suffered several emotional breakdowns. C also reported extensive physical, emotional, and sexual abuse during her childhood.

C's presenting problems include difficulty with relationships, reported domestic violence issues with her current husband, a history of sexual and physical abuse, and anxiety. C reports that the domestic violence is generally emotional abuse but she fears that when the fighting escalates it might turn into mutual physical abuse. Overall, C has a poor self-image, which is not uncommon for individuals who have suffered abuse. C, similar to other adult survivors who have escaped from the abusive situation, views herself with contempt, shame, and guilt. Although C states that she has escaped the abuse from her father and brothers, her present relationship with her husband has the potential to also become abusive. She states, "I escaped an abusive home life, only to fall into another abusive relationship where I have minimal power and control."

Once the primary and presenting problem have been identified the first task of the mental health practitioner, especially with the history and potential engagement in impulsive activity that could lead to self-harm or suicide attempts, is to complete a risk assessment. Key questions need to identify the potential for suicide risk, violence to others risk, and the risk of her impulsive behavior and how that might lead to current incidents of abuse toward her children. These questions are asked in a straightforward and direct manner. Once identified this information needs to be clearly recorded. C states she is not suicidal and would not harm herself because of her children but shows evidence of lacerations to her wrist from a previous attempt. She also reports that she would not harm her children in any way and although she appears impulsive to action she has no history of ever hurting them when angry or irritated. C also states that there is no

---

QUICK REFERENCE
IDENTIFY PRIMARY AND PRESENTING PROBLEM

Primary problem: Borderline personality disorder.

Presenting problems: Difficulty with relationships, poor self-image.

THE CASE OF C *(Continued)*

present physical abuse in her marriage but the relationship and the fighting gets so intense she feels there could be. She states that when they fight her husband verbally abuses her by calling her names and telling her she is crazy.

The second step for the mental health practitioner is to identify client strengths and behaviors that contribute to impairment in daily functioning. In addition, the clinician should observe the client's appearance, mood, attitude, affect, speech, motor activity, and orientation. Mental functioning should be assessed in terms of the client's ability to complete simple calculations, serial sevens, immediate memory, remote memory, general knowledge, proverb interpretation, and recognition of similarities and differences. In addition, questions in regard to higher order abilities and thought form and content need to be processed.

The primary problem for C is her difficulty in establishing and maintaining healthy relationships. Her current relationships are intense, unstable, and chaotic. She and her husband battle daily, she and her mother like each other one day and the next day they become sworn

Mental Status Description

Presentation	Mental Functioning	Higher Order Abilities	Thought Form/Content
Appearance: Appropriate	Simple Calculations: Mostly accurate	Judgment: Impulsive	Thought Process: Logical and organized
Mood: Anxious		Insight: Impaired	
Attitude: Guarded	Serial Sevens: Accurate	Intelligence: Average	Delusions: None
Affect: Appropriate	Immediate Memory: Intact		Hallucinations: None
Speech: Normal			
Motor Activity: Restless	Remote Memory: Intact		
	General Knowledge: Accurate		
Orientation: Fully oriented	Proverb Interpretation: Mostly accurate		
	Similarities/Differences Mostly accurate		

(continued)

THE CASE OF C *(Continued)*

enemies. C has no close friends and does not trust easily, always fearing abandonment. Effective interpersonal relationships depend on both a stable sense of self and appropriate emotional expression, which C seems to struggle with and with problems in this area it appears understandable that the client has chaotic relationships.

It appears that C's emotional development was stunted due to the emotional instability of her household while growing up. Unfortunately, for many survivors of abuse the development of chronic anxiety and depression may persist into adult life. C has been left with difficulty in forming stable relationships whereby ordinary interpersonal conflicts may provoke intense anxiety, depression, or rage. She has many arguments with her husband, for which she rotates between blaming herself and blaming him. According to Herman (1992), survivors of abuse have relationships that are driven by the hunger for protection and care and are haunted by the fear of abandonment. Due to her inability to protect herself from her father during her childhood, C has difficulty in protecting herself in her current relationships. A desperate longing for nurturance and care makes it difficult to establish safe and appropriate boundaries with others.

APPLICATION OF THE MULTIAXIAL SYSTEM

C is given two Axis I provisional diagnoses. The first is generalized anxiety disorder (GAD) as her behaviors are characterized by anxiety, worry, restlessness, or feeling on edge as well as difficulty concentrating and irritability. However, it is unclear if these symptoms are related to this disorder or whether the symptoms are directly related to her relationship difficulties characteristic of the diagnosis borderline personality disorder. Since she has a documented history of anxiety-related problems, that cause impairment in social and occupational functioning, previous treatment and medications, it appears prudent to list this as a possibility for further exploration. Furthermore, at this time it is difficult to tell whether the symptoms of generalized anxiety disorder are severe enough to warrant such a diagnosis.

In addition a second provisional diagnosis and the potential for posttraumatic stress disorder (PTSD) will be explored further. This diagnosis is characterized by an extremely traumatic event accompanied by symptoms of increased arousal and by avoidance of stimuli associated with the trauma, which is directly related to her history of child physical and sexual abuse. C reports that she often has an intense fear of having sexual relations with her husband and fears that he will leave her blaming her for the problems that they are having. She says that she experiences intense distress when she hears about child abuse or thinks about what has happened to her. She begins to relive the incidents in her mind and based on this experience she detaches from her husband to escape the possibility of it happening again. Although it is possible that this client meets the criteria for the disorder it remains unclear whether the symptoms she is experiencing relate directly to the diagnosis of PTSD or her primary diagnosis of borderline personality disorder.

Since C's emotional development may have been stunted due to the emotional instability of her household while growing up, it is possible her feelings of chronic anxiety and depression may be related primarily to her difficulty in forming stable relationships. For C, ordinary interpersonal conflicts may provoke intense anxiety, depression, or rage. Regardless, these two diagnoses are listed as provisional and warrant further exploration and attention in the terms of treatment planning and intervention.

C's principal or primary diagnosis of borderline personality disorder is placed on Axis II. Characteristics of borderline personality disorder include a pattern of unstable, intense relationships, unstable self-image or sense of self, impulsivity, frequent mood changes, chronic feelings of emptiness, and difficulty controlling anger or inappropriate anger. For C, this disorder is clearly related to a history of early abandonment and physical and sexual abuse. This makes it difficult for her to maintain a firm sense of who she is, or how she contributes either positively or negatively in a relationship. Individuals with personality disorders live within a system of internal defense mechanisms on which they rely to avoid or overcome feelings. Although these defense mechanisms can cause a great deal of difficulty, clients, similar to C, will utilize them as the only way to deal with problems (D. Hales & Hales, 1996).

Defense mechanisms that can be coded on this Axis include the following: idealization and devaluation. C deals with emotional conflict and internal and external stressors through idealization where she attributes exaggerated positive qualities to family members and all relationships. In turn she also practices devaluation in which she deals with emotional conflict or internal or external stressors by attributing exaggerated negative qualities to her own actions. For example, C has difficulty in establishing and maintaining healthy relationships. Effective interpersonal relationships depend on both stable sense of self and a "capacity for spontaneity in emotional expression" (Linehan, 1993). Without these capabilities, it is understandable that the client develops chaotic relationships.

On Axis III no diagnosis is noted, although there is evidence of lacerations of the right wrist noted from a previous attempted suicide years ago.

On Axis IV, stressors include: relationship conflicts due to aggressive behaviors between her and her spouse (potential for domestic violence); and social environmental pressures due to low income and a poor living environment. She has many arguments with her husband, for which she blames herself. She justifies his violent behavior by willingly faulting herself. According to Herman (1992), survivors of abuse have relationships that "are driven by the hunger for protection and care and are haunted by the fear of abandonment." Due to her inability to protect herself from her father during her childhood, C has difficulty in protecting

> ## QUICK REFERENCE
>
> ### APPLICATION OF THE MULTIAXIS SYSTEM
>
> Axis I: Generalized anxiety disorder   300.02 (provisional)
>   Posttraumatic stress disorder   309.81 (provisional)
>
> Axis II: Borderline personality disorder   301.83 (principal diagnosis)
>
>   Defense Mechanisms:
>   Idealization.
>   Devaluation.
>
> Axis III: Deferred.
>
> Axis IV: Limited social support, primary relationship problems.
>
> Axis V: 50 (current level of functioning).

herself in her current relationships. A "desperate longing for nurturance and care makes it difficult to establish safe and appropriate boundaries with others."

On Axis V the Global Assessment of Functioning (GAF) rating for current = 50 is noted since she has limited access to social support (that is, as she has few family members or friends). Current stress severity rating is moderate.

TREATMENT PLANNING CONSIDERATIONS

Treatment of borderline personality disorder is difficult and the best approaches to practice remain a subject of debate. Overall, the most important techniques revolve around developing a stable, trusting relationship with a mental health practitioner who does not respond punitively to provocative acts, who actively participates in therapy and provides assurance of the therapist's interest and concern, and who emphasizes the negative effects of self-destructive behavior (D. Hales & Hales, 1996).

Borderline personality disorder is a lifelong disorder in which a pervasive pattern of disregard for and violation of the rights of others occurs that is generally noted in adolescence. Basically, the first step of the mental health practitioner is to clearly define the behaviors that the client is experiencing and how these behaviors can be addressed in the treatment or intervention plan.

The goals in therapy are to decrease or eliminate these behaviors and improve the client's adaptation to change. Many clinicians refuse to see these patients or will limit the number of individuals with borderline personality disorder in their

---

QUICK REFERENCE

BEHAVIORAL EXAMPLES

- Identify problems related to impulse control (e.g., unsafe sex, substance use, or driving recklessly).
- Identify results or problems that result when impulses are not controlled.
- Assess for history and use of substances.
- Identify episodes when explosive temper outbursts or threats based in aggression are most likely to occur.
- Identify concrete examples of low self-esteem and unstable self-image.
- Identify feelings of abandonment and acts to diminish this feeling.
- Explore lethality or danger to self or others.

---

practice to only one or two, as borderlines are often seen as provocateurs and expert manipulators (P. Perry, 1997). Therefore, individuals with this disorder have reputations for being difficult, noncompliant with treatment, and manipulative. Despite these barriers to treatment, research indicates positive directions for the future and a good prognosis for these individuals (APA, 2000).

The diverse treatment types and duration of treatment types makes it difficult to conclude that any one form of treatment consistently demonstrates greater effects than no treatment or a comparison treatment (A. Perry, Tarrier, Morriss, McCarthy, & Limb, 1999). However, "one of the common findings has been that long-term treatment is necessary for individuals with borderline personality disorder and it has been concluded that people with this disorder have a less favorable outcome than other mental illnesses without proper intervention (Cheisa & Fonagy, 1999).

QUICK REFERENCE

GOALS

- Assess for suicide risk and stabilize.
- Develop and demonstrate coping skills to deal with mood swings.
- Develop the ability to control impulses.
- Develop and demonstrate anger management skills.
- Learn and practice interpersonal relationship skills.
- Reduce self-damaging behaviors.

BORDERLINE PERSONALITY DISORDER

Definition: A pervasive pattern of instability of interpersonal relationships, self-image, and affects, and marked impulsivity beginning by early adulthood and present in a variety of contexts.

Signs and Symptoms:

1. Frantic efforts to avoid real or imagined abandonment.
2. Pattern of unstable and intense relationships characterized by alternating between extremes of idealization and devaluation.
3. Identity disturbance—unstable self-image.
4. Impulsivity in at least two areas of functioning: spending, sex, substance abuse, reckless driving.
5. Recurrent suicidal behavior, gestures or threats, or self-mutilating behavior.
6. Affective instability due to a marked reactivity of mood.
7. Chronic feelings of emptiness.
8. Inappropriate anger, difficulty controlling anger.
9. Stress-related paranoid ideation or severe dissociative symptoms.

Goals:

1. Client will stop self-injurious behaviors.
2. Client will maintain prescribed medication regimen.
3. Client will learn to regulate her emotions.
4. Client will learn to express emotions appropriately.
5. Client's family will increase knowledge about BPD.

Objectives:	Tasks/Interventions
Client will cease self-injurious behaviors (cutting on self, suicide attempts) as measured by client's self report.	Practitioner will establish a "no harm" contract with client to prohibit her from cutting on self or attempting suicide.
	Practitioner to provide supportive counseling throughout treatment.
Client will continue taking prescribed medications as recorded by client in daily journal.	Client to take medications as prescribed.
	Client to record in daily journal each time she takes her medication.
Client to have a better ability to regulate her emotions, as measured by an average score of 5 at baseline to an average of 2 at the end of treatment on client's daily report of emotional intensity.	Practitioner to use technique called "dialectical behavior therapy" 2X per week with client.
	Practitioner to facilitate client awareness of appropriate behaviors to express emotion.
Client to express emotions appropriately, as measured by an average score of 2 at baseline to an average score of 15 at the end of treatment on clinician-developed behavior count of appropriate behaviors used during sessions.	Client to evaluate the intensity of her emotions on clinician/client-developed scale three times per day during treatment.
	Practitioners to evaluate client progress on clinician-developed behavior count of appropriate behaviors at the end of each session.
Client's family will increase knowledge borderline personality disorder, as evidenced by scores of 16 on pretest to 40 on posttest on clinician's developed questionnaire, by the end of treatment.	Client's family will participate in six-week educational program about BPD.
	Client's family will network with others who have family members in BPD.

INTERVENTION STRATEGY

It appears that the most effective interventions for individuals with borderline personality disorder include intensive outpatient individual and group psychotherapy. In addition, antipsychotic medications, including Clozapine and Naltrexone, have been proven effective in reducing severe symptoms of the disorder (Benedetti, Sforzino, Colombo, Marrei, & Smeralde, 1999; Bohus et al., 1998). Therefore, the ideal treatment modality for individuals with borderline personality disorder is most likely a combination approach that consists of extended individual and group therapy with psychiatric services available to those with more severe symptoms. In addition, best practice with clients diagnosed with borderline personality disorder addresses suicidal and self-mutilating behavior, depression, anxiety, and issues revolving around childhood sexual abuse. Involving family members if available is imperative. This helps to build a support system for the client and will help to maximize the quality of her interpersonal relationships. As individuals with borderline personality disorder have intense, chaotic, and emotional relationships, teaching them skills to help regulate their emotions is imperative (Linehan, 1993).

Strategies for Individual Therapy and Intervention

Chiesa and Fonagy (1999) reported that psychosocial intervention for individuals with chronic personality disorders can be effective. Treatment programs that consist of short hospital admissions (when behaviors are severe) followed by a period of outpatient treatment appear to be the most productive model. Although this program had a decreased length of inpatient hospitalization days, the combined hospital and community-based model helped these individuals improve their overall level of functioning and chronic maladaptive relational and behavioral patterns addressed through intense inpatient group and individual counseling. Furthermore, it was stated that a gradual discharge to a community-based program decreases the client's potential for relapse.

In addition, Bateman and Fonagy (1999) evaluated the effectiveness of partial hospitalization in the treatment of borderline personality disorder by comparing the effectiveness of a psychoanalytically oriented partial hospitalization program with standard psychiatric care for individuals diagnosed with borderline personality disorder. Group psychoanalytic psychotherapy within a structured, flexible, consistent, limit setting, and reliable partial hospitalization program was evaluated and in this study individuals with borderline personality disorder improved dramatically with their participation in a partial hospitalization program over standard psychiatric care. The number of suicide attempts, inpatient days of hospitalization, level of anxiety and depression, and self-mutilation acts all decreased following their participation in the partial hospitalization program. Since borderline personality disorder is a chronic mental illness that requires intensive psychiatric care, long-term follow-up treatment is imperative and those who received intensive group and individual treatment did better when community supports are included.

A second type of intervention for the individual with borderline personality disorder is dialectical behavior therapy. This type of therapy is a broad-based cognitive behavioral treatment developed specifically for individuals with borderline personality disorder and through controlled clinical trials has proven to be effective with this disorder. The form that has been most effective with individuals with borderline personality disorder is a combination of individual psychotherapy and skills training. The goal of skills training is the acquisition of adaptive skills and the goal of individual therapy is getting the client to use the skills in place of maladaptive behaviors (Linehan, 1993).

The dialectical perspective contains three main characteristics, each of which is important in understanding borderline personality disorder. First, dialectics directs the client's attention to the immediate and larger contexts of behavior, as well as to the interrelatedness of individual behavior patterns. Second, reality is "comprised of internal opposing forces out of whose synthesis evolves a new set of opposing forces." These include extreme thinking, behavior, and emotions that make progress difficult. The third characteristic is an assumption that the individual and environment are undergoing continuous transition. This aims to assist the client to become more comfortable with change. Since the core disorder in borderline personality disorder is emotion dysregulation, this type of therapy creates a type of emotional regulation teaching the client to label and modulate arousal, to tolerate distress, and to trust his or her own emotional responses as valid interpretations and to events (Linehan, 1993). Dialectical behavior therapy tries to reframe dysfunctional behaviors as part of the client's learned problem-solving skills and engages both the practitioner and client in active problem solving. At the same time, emphasis is placed on understanding the client's current emotional, cognitive, and behavioral responses. In this method, the mental health practitioner is expected to address all of the client's problematic behaviors in a systematic manner. This includes conducting a collaborative behavioral analysis, formulation of hypotheses about possible variables influencing the problem, generation of possible changes, and trying out/evaluating solutions. This intervention emphasizes the necessity of teaching clients to fully accept themselves and their world as they are in the moment.

Furthermore, the criteria for borderline personality disorder reflect a pattern of behavioral, emotional, and cognitive instability and dysregulation. Based on this premise, Linehan (1993) outlines four specific skills training modules aimed at treating these difficulties. In the first module, core mindfulness is taught in which the client learns emotional regulation skills. In the second module the client learns interpersonal effectiveness skills to deal with chaotic and difficult relationships.

The third module teaches the client emotion regulation skills. The fourth skills training module teaches the client distress tolerance skills helping the client to learn to consciously experience and observe surrounding events.

Dialectical behavior therapy can form the foundation of a sound practice model to follow when establishing a treatment plan for individuals with borderline personality disorder supported through controlled trials. Even if the mental health practitioner is unable to engage the client in long-term therapeutic ventures utilizing the treatment methods, dialectical behavior therapy may help by improving the client's overall level of functioning.

Psychopharmacological Interventions

When establishing a treatment plan for an individual with borderline personality disorder, the use of psychotropic medication should be addressed. The wide range of symptoms apparent in individuals with this illness mandates that every avenue of treatment be explored, including mixing therapy and medication. Although the use of medication has been shown to be effective, "even with potentially effective pharmacotherapy, some form of concomitant psychosocial intervention is generally required" (Linehan, Tutek, Heard, & Armstrong, 1994).

For individuals with borderline personality disorder, the treatment dropout rates are high, medication noncompliance is common, and the rate of substance abuse is great (Koerner & Linehan, 1999). Practitioners must stress the need for clients to comply with all aspects of treatment and to monitor for the potential of substance abuse. Linking the client to Alcoholics Anonymous groups or substance abuse treatment centers or both will help them develop a support system that revolves around abstinence.

In terms of specific medications for use with this disorder, attention has been given to Clozapine and Naltrexone. Recently, the medication Clozapine, an antipsychotic that is given to people with severe schizophrenia who have failed to respond to standard treatments, has been utilized in an attempt to reduce the episodes of severe self-mutilation and aggression in psychotic patients with borderline personality disorder (Chengappa, Elbeling, Kang, Levine, & Parepally, 1999). Psychotic symptoms in these individuals include paranoia, delusions, referential thinking, and dissociations. These symptoms generally increase when the individual is under a great deal of stress. This medication does not produce many of the disturbing side effects associated with other antipsychotic medication. However, this medication may produce agranulocytosis, which is a potentially lethal disorder of the white blood cells. Due to this risk, individuals who take Clozapine are required to have a blood test once a week (Sifton, 1998).

The medication Naltrexone has been used to address dissociative symptoms in individuals with borderline personality disorder. The symptoms related to dissociation include depersonalization, analgesia, derealization, and altered sensory perceptions and these individuals often experience flashbacks. Research supports that flashbacks in people with PTSD were reduced (Bohus et al., 1999) and the study concluded that since increased activity of the opioid system contributes to dissociative symptoms, including flashbacks, that these symptoms may respond to treatments with opiate antagonists. The one area not influenced by Naltrexone was the level of tension experienced by the subjects.

Although drug management of borderline personality disorder is controversial, it warrants further investigation due to the chronicity of the illness and the high rate of use in both health and social services. Despite the limitations of the research, it appears clear that further research is needed in the treatment of borderline personality disorder. This is a chronic personality disorder where the nature of this disorder lies in the unpredictability of behaviors and variations in symptomology. As many psychotherapeutic interventions are researched, medication treatment must also be evaluated.

SUMMARY

Borderline personality disorder is a chronic mental illness that historically has not responded to therapeutic or medicinal interventions. According to the *DSM,* the essential feature of this disorder is a "pervasive pattern of instability of interpersonal relationships, self-image, affects, and marked impulsivity" (APA, 2000). Individuals with this disorder have reputations for being difficult, noncompliant with treatment, and manipulative. Despite these barriers to treatment, research indicates positive directions for the future and a good prognosis for these individuals.

In terms of the diagnostic assessment, a careful risk assessment is needed that can support the chronic nature of borderline personality disorder. This population has a high rate of use of psychiatric services and emergency room visits. For these individuals, mental health utilization costs are great, treatment dropouts are high, and estimated rates of completed suicide average about 9 percent (Simpson et al., 1998). Individual approaches such as dialectical behavior therapy and other pyschosocial individual and group therapy can assist with improvement in a client's overall general and interpersonal adjustment.

Research evidence to date indicates that borderline personality disorder is a treatable mental illness and with the proper interventions, individuals with this disorder can improve their overall level of functioning, enhance their social relationships, and prevent self-damaging suicidal and self-mutilating behavior.

Additional research needs to be completed in several areas to assess adequate treatment interventions with borderline personality disorder. Studies that determine which components of dialectical behavior therapy contribute to the positive outcomes are needed. Also, longitudinal follow-up studies are needed to determine suicide rates and maintenance of long-term treatment gains.

In addition to a complete intervention plan the pathology common among individuals who suffer from borderline personality disorder requires the development of a treatment regimen that involves follow-up care and community support. Many individuals with this disorder are frequent consumers of inpatient psychiatric facilities. As a result, their chronic maladaptive relational and behavior patterns can initially be addressed in an inpatient setting. Outpatient follow-up treatment will help the client to reestablish his or her social network and work on behaviors that precipitated the admission. The key to best assisting the individual who suffers from borderline personality disorder is helping to prevent a relapse.

Abuse: Improper behavior that can jeopardize another or the self that results in physical, psychological, or financial harm to an individual, family, group, or community. Generally in professional helping fields, the term abuse is most often related to acts against children, elderly, mentally impaired, spouse, or in terms of a drug or other type of substance.

Activities of daily living (ADL): The general performance of basic self and family care responsibilities needed for independent living.

Acute: This is often related to a disease process where there is a marked intensity or sharpness that subsides over a short period of time.

Affect: An outward manifestation of a person's feelings or emotions. The general expression of mood (e.g., flat or blunted).

Advocacy: When professional activities are aimed at educating, informing, and/or directly defending or representing the needs and desires of individuals, families, or communities through direct intervention or empowerment.

Agoraphobia: According to the *DSM-IV-TR,* this is a type of panic disorder that arises when an individual becomes anxious about being alone generally when away from the home. The panic or fear experienced is incapacitating. In addition, the individual suffering from agoraphobia may also fear having an unexpected panic attack in a public setting where withdrawal is difficult or embarrassing.

Akathisia: A side effect of the typical or traditional antipsychotic medications that results in an extreme internal sense of restlessness.

Akinesia: A feeling of fatigue or weakness in the arms or legs.

Amenorrhea: Diagnostic criteria for anorexia nervosa defined as the absence of at least three consecutive menstrual cycles. Typically a consequence of severe weight loss that is due to abnormally low levels of estrogen.

The definitions and information in this glossary were modified from several sources including the *2000 PDR;* the *PDR Medical Dictionary* (1995); the *DSM-IV-TR;* Dziegielewski and Leon, *Psychopharmacology and Social Work Practice* (2001); and Dziegielewski, *The Changing Face of Health Care Social Work: Professional Practice in the Era of Managed Care* (1998); and *The Social Work Dictionary* (1999).

Anhedonia: Loss of interest or pleasure in everyday activities that the individual usually enjoys.

Anorexia nervosa: A severe eating disorder that is characterized by a refusal to maintain body weight at or above 85 percent of one's normal body weight, an intense fear of gaining weight even when underweight, disturbance in the way one's body weight or shape is experienced, and **amenorrhea.**

Antianxiety drugs: This includes several groups of medicines that are used to treat anxiety (nervousness). Generally, these drugs are used to treat the symptoms of anxiety and some can assist with sleep disorders as well. These medications can help to address and decrease fears and excessive worry allowing individuals to function with minimal improvement to current occupational and social functioning.

Anticonvulsants: These medications are generally used to treat seizures (fits or convulsions); however, they can also be used to address behavior problems regardless of whether the client has seizures or not. Basically, it is believed that the anticonvulsants can help to reduce anger, aggression, and severe mood swings. Examples of commonly used medications in this area include Tegretol (carbamazepine), Depakene or Depakote (valproate or valproic acid), and Clonopin (clonazepam).

Antidepressant drugs: A major class of psychotropic drugs with diverse chemical configurations including the Monoamine Oxidase Inhibitors (MAOIs), the heterocyclic drugs (composed of mono-, di-, tri- and heterocyclics), the serotonin reuptake inhibitors (fluoxetine, paroxetine, sertraline, trazodone, and venlafaxine), and bupropion are more recent innovations. Antidepressants usually must be taken for several weeks to have the desired effect and they often have a low therapeutic index, so they must be closely monitored.

Antipsychotic drugs: A major classification of drugs, most of which are dopamine receptor antagonists (with the exception of the newer antipsychotic medications) used to address disturbances in affect and mood such as psychosis, delusions, and psychotic depression.

Anxiety: This is generally related to a response that occurs without the presence of real threat; it can be differentiated from fear in that the threat is considered serious and negative enough to impair psychological, occupational, or social functioning.

Anxiety disorders: A classification of disorders often characterized by persistent worry.

Anxiolytics: Medications used to treat anxiety, agitation, or tension. Also known as **antianxiety drugs.**

Assessment: The process of determining the nature, cause, progression, and prognosis of a problem and the personalities and situations involved therein; it is the thinking process by which one reasons from the facts to tentative conclusions regarding their meaning.

Aphasia: The inability to use language skills that were present in the past.

Behavior disturbances: Marked changes in a person's behavior patterns, typical of psychotic disorders. The disturbances generally include withdrawal, apathy, and bizarre actions.

Bereavement: Loss, due to death, of someone to whom one feels close and the process of adjustment to the loss. Often mimics **depression.**

Bibliotherapeutic: Outside or supplemental readings that support a mental health practitioner in terms of the practice intervention being utilized.

Biobibliotherapy: Refers to the use of a medical intervention such as medicine, outside reading materials, and brief intervention techniques to assist in the helping process.

Binge eating: Eating, in a discrete period of time (e.g., within a two-hour period), an amount of food that is definitely larger than most people would eat during a similar period of time. In addition, experiencing a sense of lack of control over eating during the episode.

Body image: One's personal relationship with their body rather than what one actually looks like, for example, one's beliefs, perceptions, thoughts, feelings, and actions that pertain to one's own physical appearance.

Bipolar disorders: This group of mental disorders has historically been referred to as manic depression or bipolar affective disorder and is characterized by extreme fluctuations in mood. There are three major diagnoses that fall in this area: bipolar I, bipolar II, and cyclothymia.

Bipolar I disorders: There are six subgroups of this mental health disorder identified in the *DSM-IV-TR*. Basically, bipolar I involve a reoccurring illness of elevated mood that impairs psychosocial functioning (a manic episode) and depressed affect that also impairs psychosocial functioning (an episode of depression). Five of these subgroups include criteria to determine if a client is experiencing a single manic episode and the other five describe the most recent episode. The specifiers describe the episode recurrence. The six subgroups included in the *DSM-IV* are: bipolar I disorder single manic episode, bipolar I disorder, most recent episode hypomanic, bipolar I disorder, most recent episode manic, bipolar I disorder most recent episode mixed, bipolar I disorder, most recent episode depressed, bipolar I disorder, most recent episode unspecified.

Bipolar II disorders: In this mental disorder there are one or more major depressive episodes and the client has no history of either a manic or mixed episode. Bipolar II disorders are best described as the alternating experiences that a client has with episodes of major depression and periods of hypomania.

Bipolar disorder not otherwise specified (NOS): A type of bipolar disorder that does not meet all of the criteria described for the bipolar disorders, yet still exhibits some of the basic symptoms evident in manic, major depressive, or mixed episodes.

Blood level: The measure of a drug's presence in the plasma at a given time.

Cardiovascular agents: Drugs that have their action on the heart or peripheral blood vessels for the treatment of hypertension (high blood pressure), angina, heart failure, or cardiac arrhythmia (e.g., beta blockers, nitroglycerin, digoxin).

Cerebral hemorrhage: Escape of blood from an artery into the cerebrum, often referred to as a type of stroke.

Central nervous system: The system of neurons comprising the brain and the spinal cord. It serves as the body's major nerve control system, directing and regulating all parts of the body to receive stimuli from external and internal environments and interpreting the stimuli that cause the body to react.

Cerebellum: The cerebellum controls bodily functions that operate below the level of consciousness, including posture, balance, and movement through space. It receives information directly from sense organs, muscles, and joints.

Cerebral cortex: The folded, outermost region of the cerebrum. It is responsible for primary sensory functioning, visual processing, long-term memory, motor and perceptual coordination and integration, language, thinking, and problem solving. It is entirely made up of the so-called "gray matter" and four lobes (the frontal lobe, the temporal lobe, the parietal lobe, and the occipital lobe) that manage all functions.

Cerebrovascular accident (CVA): An imprecise term for cerebral stroke.

Cirrhosis: A disease of the digestive system, related specifically to the liver and its function.

Cognitive restructuring: An essential component of cognitive-behavioral therapy in which irrational beliefs, distorted thinking patterns, and faulty assumptions are identified, challenged, and replaced with realistic and adaptive thinking patterns.

Cognitive-behavioral therapy: Uses a combination of selected techniques incorporating the theories of behaviorism, social learning theory, and cognition theories to understand and address a client's behavior.

Comorbidities: The simultaneous existence of two or more diseases or dysfunctions within an individual. Each disease may or may not intensify the severity, duration, or prognosis of the other but frequently causes the diagnostician to overlook one or the other disease.

Conduct disorder: Childhood disorders marked by *persistent* acts of aggression, deceitfulness, or theft, and or serious violation of rules. Classified as "childhood onset type" if before age 10 and adolescent-onset type if after age 10.

Coping index: A coding classification within the PIE; the degree to which a client can handle a problem with his or her internal resources.

Crisis: A temporary state of upset and disequilibrium, characterized chiefly by an individual's inability to cope with a particular situation. During this period, customary methods of coping and problem solving do not work and the social worker is able to assist the client to explore and develop new values.

Crisis intervention: A practice strategy that is used to help clients in crisis regain a sense of healthy equilibrium.

Cultural bias: Tendency of psychometric tests to include questions involving content or skills more familiar to some cultural groups than to others.

Cyclothymic disorder: A form of depressive disorder typified by mood swings, hypomania, and depression. In this mental disorder, clients have milder experiences than those who suffer from bipolar disorder although the symptoms are more consistent and last for approximately two years.

Defense mechanisms: These are mental processes that help protect a person from anxiety, guilt feelings, or unacceptable thoughts. Selected defense mechanisms as described in the *DSM-IV-TR* include.

> *Acting out:* The individual deals with emotional conflict or internal or external stressors by actions rather than reflections or feelings. This definition is broader than the original concept of the acting out of transference feelings or wishes during psychotherapy and is intended to include behavior arising both within and outside the transference relationship. Defensive acting out is not synonymous with bad behavior because it requires evidence that the behavior is related to emotional conflicts.

> *Affiliation:* The individual deals with emotional conflict or internal or external stressors by turning to others for help or support. This involves sharing problems with others but does not imply trying to make someone else responsible for them.

> *Altruism:* The individual deals with emotional conflict or internal or external stressors by dedication to meeting the needs of others. Unlike the self-sacrifice

sometimes characteristic of reaction formation, the individual receives gratification either vicariously or from the response of others.

Anticipation: The individual deals with emotional conflict or internal or external stressors by experiencing emotional reactions in advance of, or anticipating consequences of, possible future events and considering realistic, alternative responses or solutions.

Autistic fantasy: The individual deals with emotional conflict or internal or external stressors by excessive daydreaming as a substitute for human relationships, more effective action, or problem solving.

Denial: The individual deals with emotional conflict or internal or external stressors by refusing to acknowledge some painful aspect of external reality or subjective experience that would be apparent to others. The term *psychotic denial* is used when there is gross impairment in reality testing.

Devaluation: The individual deals with emotional conflict or internal or external stressors by attributing exaggerated negative qualities to self or others.

Displacement: The individual deals with emotional conflict or internal or external stressors by transferring a feeling about, or a response to, one object onto another (usually less threatening) substitute object.

Dissociation: The individual deals with emotional conflict or internal or external stressors with a breakdown in the usually integrated functions of consciousness, memory, perception of self or the environment, or sensory/motor behavior.

Help-rejecting complaining: The individual deals with emotional conflict or internal or external stressors by complaining or making repetitious requests for help that disguise covert feelings of hostility or reproach toward others, which are then expressed by rejecting the suggestions, advice, or help that others offer. The complaints or requests may involve physical or psychological symptoms or life problems.

Humor: The individual deals with emotional conflict or external stressors by emphasizing the amusing or ironic aspects of the conflict or stressor.

Idealization: The individual deals with emotional conflict or internal or external stressors by attributing exaggerated positive qualities to others.

Isolation of affect: The individual deals with emotional conflict or internal or external stressors by the separation of ideas from the feelings originally associated with them. The individual loses touch with the feelings associated with a given idea (e.g., a traumatic event) while remaining aware of the cognitive elements of it (e.g., descriptive details).

Omnipotence: The individual deals with emotional conflict or internal or external stressors by feeling or acting as if he or she possesses special powers or abilities and is superior to others.

Passive aggression: The individual deals with emotional conflict or internal or external stressors by indirectly and unassertively expressing aggression toward others. There is a facade of overt compliance masking covert resistance, resentment, or hostility. Passive aggression often occurs in response to demands for independent action or performance or the lack of gratification of dependent wishes but may be adaptive for individuals in subordinate positions who have no other way to express assertiveness more overtly.

Projection: The individual deals with emotional conflict or internal or external stressors by falsely attributing to another his or her own unacceptable feelings, impulses, or thoughts.

Projective identification: As in projection, the individual deals with emotional conflict or internal or external stressors by falsely attributing to another his or her own unacceptable feelings, impulses, or thoughts. Unlike simple projection, the individual does not fully disavow what is projected. Instead, the individual remains aware of his or her own affects or impulses but misattribute them as justifiable reactions to the other person. Not infrequently, the individual induces the very feelings in others that were first mistakenly believed to be there, making it difficult to clarify who did what to whom first.

Rationalization: The individual deals with emotional conflict or internal or external stressors by concealing the true motivations for his or her own thoughts, actions, or feelings through the elaboration of reassuring or self-serving but incorrect explanations.

Reaction formation: The individual deals with emotional conflict or internal or external stressors by substituting behavior, thoughts, or feelings that are diametrically opposed to his or her own unacceptable thoughts or feelings (this usually occurs in conjunction with their repression).

Self-assertion: The individual deals with emotional conflict or stressors by reflecting on his or her own thoughts, feelings, motivation, and behavior, and responding appropriately.

Splitting: The individual deals with emotional conflict or internal or external stressors by compartmentalizing opposite affect states and failing to integrate the positive and negative qualities of the self or others into cohesive images. Because ambivalent affects cannot be experienced simultaneously, more balanced views and expectations of self or others are excluded from emotional awareness. Self and object images tend to alternate between polar opposites:

exclusively loving, powerful, worthy, nurturant, and kind—or exclusively bad, hateful, angry, destructive, rejecting, or worthless.

Sublimation: The individual deals with emotional conflict or internal or external stressors by channeling potentially maladaptive feelings or impulses into socially acceptable behavior (e.g., contact sports to channel angry impulses).

Suppression: The individual deals with emotional conflict or internal or external stressors by intentionally avoiding thinking about disturbing problems, wishes, feelings, or experiences.

Undoing: The individual deals with emotional conflict or internal or external stressors by words or behavior designed to negate or to make amends symbolically for unacceptable thoughts, feelings, or actions.

Delusion: A false belief strongly held despite contrary evidence of a different social (commonly agreed-on) reality. Common types are persecutory delusions (belief of threat/harm from others), delusions of grandeur (inflated sense of self), delusions of being controlled (external agents impose thoughts/feelings), and delusions of reference (external events are significant/reflective of self).

Dementia: Deterioration of mental processes such as memory, abstract thinking, and judgment. Personality changes may occur. There are numerous causes of dementia, including Alzheimer's disease and vascular dementia (stroke).

Depression: A state of sunken mood where an individual feels their daily living and functioning are impaired.

Diagnosis: Identifying a problem (social and mental, as well as medical) and its underlying causes and formulating a solution.

Diagnostic product: What is obtained after the health care social worker uses the information gained in the diagnostic process.

Diagnostic process: Examination of the parts of a problem to determine the relationships between them and the means to their solution.

Diabetes Mellitus (DM): A deficiency in the body results in chronic inability to create insulin, which results in too much sugar in the blood and urine.

Dissociation: The human mind's capacity to mediate complex mental activity in channels split off from or independent of conscious awareness.

DSM-IV-TR: The *DSM-IV-TR* is a manual developed by the American Psychiatric Association that presents a classification system designed to assist professionals in assigning a formal diagnostic pattern.

Axis I: The first level of coding with the *DSM-IV-TR* multiaxis diagnostic system, including major clinical syndromes, pervasive developmental disorders, learning disorders, motor skills disorders, communication disorders, and other disorders that may be the focus of clinical treatment.

Axis II: The second level of coding with the *DSM-IV-TR* multiaxis diagnostic system, including personality disorders and mental retardation.

Axis III: The third level of coding with the *DSM-IV-TR* multiaxis diagnostic system, including general medical conditions that can affect the mental health condition of the client.

Axis IV: The fourth level of coding with the *DSM-IV-TR* multiaxis diagnostic system, including psychosocial and environmental problems/stressors such as problems with primary support, problems related to social environment, educational problems, occupational problems, housing problems, economic problems, problems with access to health care services, problems related to interaction with the legal system, and other psychosocial problems.

Axis V: The fifth level of coding with the *DSM-IV-TR* multiaxis diagnostic system, records the level of functioning a client has.

Dysphoric: A state of unease or mental discomfort. Something hard to bear.

Dysthymia: A depression that is chronic (all day or most of the day) but not acute, and lasts for at least two years, according to the *DSM-IV*.

Dystonias: Uncoordinated, involuntary twisting movements of the jaw, tongue, or entire body, produced by sustained muscle spasms generally associated with the neuroleptic medications. Very often clients will complain of having a "thick" tongue.

Eating disorder: A psychological disorder characterized by severe disturbances in eating behavior (either restricting or binging) and a disturbed perception of body shape and weight. There are two primary classifications of eating disorders defined by the *DSM-IV-TR:* anorexia nervosa and bulimia nervosa.

Educative counseling: A loosely defined approach to practice that focuses on helping the client to become an educated consumer and through this information is better able to address his or her own needs.

Efficacy: The ability of a treatment or intervention to address and control an illness based on how well it works and how much is needed to make it work effectively. It measures the level to which desired goals or projected outcomes are achieved.

Electroconvulsive therapy (ECT): A procedure used in the treatment of severe depression where an electric current is briefly applied through electrodes to one or both sides of the brain. Temporary side effects may include convulsions, unconsciousness, and memory loss.

Emphysema: A disease of the respiratory system that results in continued episodes of difficult breathing and breathlessness.

Epilepsy: A chronic disorder characterized by paroxysmal neuronal brain dysfunction related to excessive activity and characterized by the development of seizures.

Ethics: A system of moral principles used in decision making in an attempt to discern right from wrong and/or to discern between two or more seemingly equal choices.

Etiology: The causation or the systematic study of the causes of a disorder.

Extrapyramidal symptoms (EPS): These include numerous negative side effects experienced by clients as a result of taking several types of medications, especially typical antipsychotic medications.

Failure to thrive (FTT): A condition in which an infant's weight gain and growth is far below what is expected for that level of development and age.

Fear: An individual's response to a real threat.

Generalized assessment of functioning (GAF): A scale using Axis V of the *DSM-IV* to incorporate measures for a client's highest level of functioning.

Global assessment of relational functioning (GARF): This measurement scale is used to address family or other ongoing relationship status on a hypothetical continuum from competent to dysfunctional.

Hallucinations: "False" sense of perceptions of "external objects" that do not exist. The most common type is auditory (hearing), followed by visual (sight), tactile (touch), somatic (internal organs), olfactory (smell), and hypersensitivity (hyperacute sight, sound, and smell).

Hypersomnia: Sleeping for significantly longer than the usual length of time.

Insomnia: Difficulty falling asleep or staying asleep.

Interdisciplinary teams: These teams consist of a variety of health care professionals who are brought together to provide effective, better coordinated, and improved quality of services for clients.

Interpersonal therapy: A form of time-limited treatment often used in a medical setting. Generally an assessment that includes a diagnostic evaluation and a psychiatric history. The focus of treatment is directed toward interpersonal problem areas such as grief, role disputes, role transitions, or deficits.

Intervention: A broad-based term used to describe treatment, services, advocacy, mediation, or any other practice action performed for or in conjunction with client systems that attempts to ameliorate problems.

Lability: Instability, particularly with regard to affect.

Mania: A psychological and emotional state where an individual is experiencing increased excitement and persistent elevated mood.

Manic episode: According to the *DSM-IV-TR,* a state of mood that features euphoria, irritability, and the lack of inhibition. It is often accompanied by substance abuse. There is a distinct period of consistently elevated or irritable mood followed by significant problems in psychosocial functioning that may require hospitalization.

Major depression: A severely depressed mood state featuring a total loss of interest and/or pleasure in life, with a significant change in the usual quality of life functioning. Characteristic symptoms include marked weight changes, daily psychomotor disturbances, sleep disturbances, loss of concentration, loss of energy, and recurring thoughts of death or suicide. The *DSM-IV* diagnosis of major depression requires two or more major depressive episodes, separated by at least two months of regular functioning.

Medications: These are medications that are used to help in treatment of mental disorders.

Alprazolam (brand name Xanax): A benzodiazepine with a rapid onset making it effective in dealing with episodic bursts of anxiety. Often used in the treatment of panic disorder.

Amitriptyline (brand name Elavil): A commonly prescribed tricyclic antidepressant drug. Also used in the treatment of bulimia.

Bupropion (brand name Wellbutrin): An antidepressant drug known to induce seizures and therefore is administered with specific recommendations on dosage ranges. It should not be administered with MAOIs.

BuSpar (Buspirone): An antianxiety drug that is not often associated with abuse because of the absence of withdrawal phenomena, cognitive impairment, and sedation. It has a short half-life and therefore must be taken several times daily. It is also said not to have the same addicting or euphoric quality that is often noted in the benzodiazepines. BuSpar is not a benzodiazepine and is referred to as a nonbenzodiazepine. BuSpar is generally prescribed for a limited time to help control the symptoms of anxiety and allow the client to be calmer while trying to learn new ways of coping with anxiety producing events.

Carbamazepine (brand name Tegretol): Originally developed as an anticonvulsant medication, it is used along with other medications such as valproic acid, depakote, or depakene to treat individuals suffering from some type of mood disorder (acute mania and bipolar disorders). It is thought to retard the electrochemical process in the nervous system that can help set off either convulsions or manic episodes. Also used to treat alcohol withdrawal, cocaine addiction, and emotional disorders.

Citalopram hydrobromide (brand name Celexa): An antidepressant used to treat major depression. It should not be taken any sooner that 14 days after discontinuing a MAO inhibitor. Some side effects may include abdominal pain, agitation, impotence, and loss of appetite and sweating.

Clomipramine (brand name Anafranil): A heterocyclic antidepressant drug that is also effective in the treatment of obsessive-compulsive disorders. This drug should not be taken with the MAOs.

Clozapine (brand name Clozaril): An atypical antipsychotic drug found to be effective in treating schizophrenia. Generally, it is not used as a first-line antipsychotic drug because it produces a small risk of Agranulocytosis, a depletion of white blood cells that can be fatal if not monitored. Clozapine has demonstrated effectiveness in treating both the positive and negative symptoms of schizophrenia. One of the most problematic aspects of this drug is the regular (generally weekly) monitoring that it requires.

Depakene or Depakote (valproate or valproic acid): Used as a mood stabilizer, for the following reasons: (1) inadequate response or intolerance to antipsychotics or lithium, (2) manic symptoms, (3) rapid cycling of the condition, (4) EEG abnormalities, and (5) head trauma. The side effects include upset stomach, increased appetite, thinning hair, tremor, drowsiness, and weight gain. Behavioral or emotional side effects involve increased aggression and irritability. Serious but rare side effects are very similar to Tegretol (Carbamazepine) except valproic acid has not been noted to decrease the number of blood cells or lead to lung irritation. If this medication is stopped suddenly, uncomfortable withdrawal symptoms may occur. A planned course for discontinuance of this medication should always be implemented.

Desipramine (brand name Norpramine): A tricyclic antidepressant sometimes prescribed because it is has the least anticholinergic effects of the heterocyclic drugs.

Diazepam (brand name Valium): A benzodiazepine used to treat anxiety, which may act as a sedative. It provides short-term relief for mild to moderate anxiety and is used to treat epileptic and alcohol withdrawal symptoms.

Doxepin (brand name Sinequan): A commonly prescribed heterocyclic antidepressant drug. It is also occasionally used for the treatment of anxiety. This medication should not be used with a MAO.

Fluphenazine (brand name Prolixin): A high-potency antipsychotic drug used for the treatment of disorganized and psychotic thinking, delusions, and hallucinations.

Fluvoxamine (brand name Luvox): An SSRI often prescribed for obsessive compulsive disorder.

Haloperidol (brand name Haldol): A high-potency antipsychotic drug used for the treatment of schizophrenia, can also be used to treat the neurological condition known as Tourette's syndrome, which involves both motor and vocal tics.

Imipramine (brand name Tofranil): The oldest tricyclic antidepressant available and has traditionally been used for the treatment of depression and panic attacks. Currently, it is sometimes used to assist those with withdrawal from cocaine addiction and obsessive compulsive disorder.

Lithium: The most commonly used mood-stabilizing medication, a derivative of lithium salts that is naturally occurring and relatively inexpensive. With a shorter half-life than most antipsychotics and antidepressants, it must generally be taken more than once a day. As a rule, it is the drug of choice for treating bipolar disorder but it can also be used to treat certain types of depression, severe mood swings, and very serious aggression. Caution should be used due to the possibility of developing toxicity. Therefore, routine checks of lithium levels are considered essential for effective and safe treatment. Lithium is available in several different forms, which includes lithium carbonate tablets (Lithotabs) or capsules (Eskalith or Lithonate), controlled-release capsules or tablets (Eskalith CR or Lithobid), and lithium citrate syrup. Lithium salts are used to treat manic episodes of bipolar disorder, a condition where a person's mood swings fluctuate severely from normal-to-elated-to-depressed. Of note is the recent use of lithium with all age groups including children and adolescents.

Mesoridazine: An antipsychotic drug with a fairly strong sedating effect that may calm persons who feel highly agitated or violent.

Mirtazapine (brand name Remeron): An antidepressant that functions as a SSNRI used for the treatment of depression.

Nefazodone hydrochloride (brand name Serzone): An antidepressant that functions as an SSNRI used in the treatment of severe depression. Some side effects include blurred or abnormal vision, dry mouth, nausea, and weakness. This medication may be considered the drug of choice for those who suffer from depression and also have difficulty with sexual interest and performance.

Paroxetine (brand name Paxil): One of the new classes of atypical antidepressant drugs, which function as a serotonin-reuptake inhibitor in producing a therapeutic effect. Also used to treat panic disorder and obsessive compulsive disorder.

Risperdone (brand name Resperdal): An atypical or nontraditional antipsychotic medication used to treat schizophrenia and other types of psychotic features.

Sertraline (brand name Zoloft): An antidepressant medication that functions as an SSRI prescribed primarily for major depression. It can also be used to treat obsessive compulsive disorder. Some side effects include difficulty with ejaculation, dry mouth, dizziness, and decreased sex drive.

Thorazine: The first antipsychotic drug that was discovered over 40 years ago.

Venlafaxine hydrochloride (brand name Effexor): An antidepressant medication that functions as an SSNRI used in the treatment of depression. Some side effects include abnormal ejaculation/orgasm, blurred vision, bruising, and impotence.

Wellbutrin (bupropion hydrochloride): Successfully used to treat depression in adults. Zyban (aka bupropion hydrocholoride) has been used to treat smoking cessation. Since both of these medications contain bupropin they should not be used together. If clients are known to have eating disorders such as bulimia or anorexia nervosa, this medication is not recommended because of the potential for the incidence of seizures.

Mental status exam: Set of simple questions aimed at gauging orientation to person, place, time, short- and long-term memory.

Metabolism: The process by which the body breaks down a drug into chemical form where it is later ready and able to be excreted from the system.

Migraine: A symptom complex occurring periodically and related to pain in the head.

Mitral Valve Proplapse (MVP): A problem related to the mitral valve in the heart.

Mood disorders: Characterized by disturbances in affect that is typical of psychotic disorders and depression. The disturbances in mood are reflected by severely flattened affect and by extreme emotional ambivalence.

Mood episodes: There are four types of mood episodes. These episodes cannot be diagnosed separately and constitute the building blocks for the mood disorders. The types of mood episodes that clients may manifest who suffer from the bipolar disorders are *manic, hypomanic, major depressive,* or *mixed* episodes.

Manic episode: A mood episode where a client's mood is persistently elevated. Along with elevated mood, other symptoms such as increased psychomotor agitation, distractibility, flight of ideas, decreased need for sleep, and grandiosity may be noted. These symptoms should last for at least a week.

Hypomanic episode: A mood episode where the symptoms may initially appear similar to the manic episode as it also involves persistently elevated, expansive, or irritable mood. The time frame is approximately four days, and it must be clear that the individual is exhibiting signs that remain uncharacteristic of previous levels of functioning. Individuals experiencing a hypomanic mood episode rarely need to be hospitalized, as although the symptoms may impair functioning, marked impairment is not noted. Furthermore, these individuals also do not show evidence of psychotic features even though others are aware that the behaviors they are exhibiting are uncharacteristic.

Major depressive episode: Mood episode involving at least five or more characteristic signs such as appetite disturbances that result in either weight gain or loss, disturbances in sleeping, (hypersomnia or sleeping too much), or insomnia (an inability or disturbance in sleep), daily bouts of depressed mood, markedly diminished interest or pleasure in activities that usually are pleasurable, psychomotor agitation or retardation nearly every day, fatigue or loss of energy, and other related symptoms.

Mixed episode: Generally meets the criteria for the manic and the depressive episode. The major difference is that it does not last for two weeks; rather, it only lasts for approximately one week. In this type of episode, the individual often experiences rapidly alternating moods.

Mood-stabilizing drugs: Drugs that feature actions aimed at keeping mood within a stable range, and lower moods from a manic state. Included in this grouping are the tricyclics, MAOIs (for depression) and lithium (for bipolar disorders). The mood stabilizers work to keep moods regular, avoiding extremes of either pole.

Multidisciplinary teams: Are composed of a mix of health and social welfare professionals, with each discipline in most part working on an independent or a referral basis.

Neuron: A basic nerve cell.

Neurotransmitters: Chemicals found in the nerve cells that act as messengers carrying electrical impulses through the cells.

Obsessive-compulsive features: Persistent ideas, thoughts, impulses, or images that are experienced as intrusive and inappropriate, for example, a preoccupation with food, hoarding food or pictures of food. In addition, repetitive or ritualistic behaviors may be used to prevent or reduce anxiety or distress, such as cutting food into precise, tiny pieces rather than eating it or exaggerated exercise rituals.

Overt behavior: Activities and/or behaviors that can be observed by an outsider.

Pharmacokinetics: The management of a drug within the body including absorption, distribution, metabolism, and excretion.

Pharmacotherapy: Medications used to help maximize the physical or mental health potential of a client. This includes education in regard to the medication and how it can interact with the counseling support that can be provided.

Phenotype: The observed structural and functional characteristics of an individual that result from an interaction between the inherited characteristics and the environment.

Phobic avoidance: When dealing with an individual who has severe anxiety and fear in regard to a particular object or stimulus, attempts will be made to avoid coming into contact with the specific object or stimulus. This type of avoidance behavior is known as stimulus avoidance.

Photosensitivity: A physical reaction to the sun.

Person–in–environment (PIE): A systematic approach to classify social functioning. Employs a four-level system to aid in the systematic collection of data to assist social workers to better understand the uniqueness of the client(s) and in designing interventions.

> *Factor I:* This is the first of the IV levels for problem classification utilized in the PIE. This constitutes a measurement of social functioning.

> Factor II: This is the second area for classification utilized in the PIE. Emphasis here is placed on the identification of environmental problems.

> *Factor III:* This is the third area for classification utilizing the PIE. This category deals with mental health problems and uses the codification of the *DSM-IV* to describe it.

> *Factor IV:* This is the fourth category of the PIE classification system. This area explores the physical problems and diagnoses that can affect the client.

Polypharmacy: The use of more than one drug for the treatment of the same ailment. This includes the concurrent administration of several psychotropic drugs.

Positive symptoms of psychosis: The presence of bizarre and frequently affect-laden experiences ordinarily absent from a person's "normal" experience. Symptoms include hallucinations, delusions, and bizarre thinking or behavior.

Postural (orthostatic) hypotension: The drop in blood pressure that occurs after suddenly sitting or standing, where the individual often feels faint or dizzy.

Psychomotor agitation: An abnormal increase in physical and emotional activity.

Psychomotor retardation: An abnormal slowing of physical and emotional responses that is commonly seen in depression.

Psychopharmacology: The study of drugs that affect cognition, behavior, and bodily responses.

Purging: Compensatory behavior typically performed after a binging episode that consists of expelling food or calories by self-induced vomiting; the misuse of laxatives, diuretics, or enemas; or extreme, compulsive exercise.

Psychotropic drugs: Alter psychological functioning and/or mood, thoughts, motor abilities, balance, movement, and coordination.

Pyramidal: These are the long nerve pathways that stretch from the cerebral cortex to the spinal cord. One of the two pathways taken by motor nerves (the other pathway is known as extrapyramidal). Pyramidal pathways carry messages to and from the central nervous system and control groups of muscles that contract simultaneously. An example might be grasping an object with the hand.

Schizoaffective disorder: Defined by the *DSM-IV-TR* as a continuous period of illness during which there are some symptoms of schizophrenia, such as delusions, hallucinations, grossly disorganized behavior, and so on, concurrent with either a major depressive episode, a manic episode, or a mixed episode.

Schizophrenia: A major mental disorder classified in the *DSM-IV-TR* as lasting more than six months and characterized in part by thought disturbances, misinterpretations of reality, mood change (including blunting and inappropriate moods), communication problems (poverty of speech and coherence), and bizarre, withdrawn, or regressive behaviors. The *DSM-IV* identifies five different subtypes: disorganized, catatonic, paranoid, undifferentiated, and residual. Symptoms in schizophrenia include:

Positive symptoms: Involves the development of delusions, conceptual disorganization, hallucinatory behavior, excitement, grandiosity, uspiciousness/persecution, and hostility. These symptoms are often very obvious and easy to detect in the assessment process.

Negative symptoms: Harder to detect than the positive symptoms. These symptoms often involve blunted affect, emotional withdrawal, and poor rapport, passive apathetic social withdrawal, difficulty in abstract thinking, lack of spontaneity, and stereotyped thinking patterns.

Social and occupational functioning assessment scale (SOFAS): A scale that can be used to address an individual's level of social and occupational functioning that is not directly influenced by overall severity of the individual's psychological symptoms.

Selective serotonin norepinephrine reuptake inhibitors (SSNRIs): The newest group of medicines that have successfully been used to treat emotional and behavioral problems such as depression, panic disorder, obsessive-compulsive disorder (OCD) similar to their counterparts the SSRIs. Some examples of the SSNRIs include Effexor, Serzone, and Remeron.

Selective serotonin reuptake inhibitors (SSRIs): SSRIs are a relatively new group of medicines that have successfully been used to treat emotional and behavioral problems such as depression, panic disorder, obsessive-compulsive disorder (OCD), bulimia, and posttraumatic stress disorder in adults. Currently, these medications are now being used to treat the same types of behaviors in children. Some examples of SSRIs include: Prozac (fluoxetine), Zoloft (sertraline), Luvox (fluvoxamine), and Paxil (paroxetine).

Serotonin: A specific type of neurotransmitter.

Side effects: Any unintentional and nontherapeutic effects of a drug on the body. Side effects, also called adverse effects, are frequently due to the interaction of the brain, drug, and the body.

Standardization: The procedures used to evaluate a measurement scale, treatment or medication.

Syndrome: A group or pattern of symptoms that occur together in a disorder and represent the typical picture of the disorder.

Tardive dyskinesia: This condition is thought to be irreversible and serious and develops as a side effect of the traditional or typical antipsychotic medications. Most professionals agree that the longer the client is on the typical antipsychotic medication, the greater the likelihood that the client may develop tardive dyskinesia. Those who suffer from this disorder often exhibit coordinated but involuntary rhythmic movements such as facial movements; grimacing and lip tremors; and involuntary movement of the fingers, hand, and trunk.

Token economy: Reinforcement technique often used whereas individuals are rewarded for socially constructive behavior with tokens that can then be exchanged for desired objects or activities.

Withdrawal symptoms: Symptoms that result when a drug or medication is discontinued.

Treatment Plans

1. Mild Mental Retardation

2. Attention-Deficit/Hyperactivity Disorder, Predominantly Inattentive Type

3. Attention-Deficit/Hyperactivity Disorder, Predominantly Hyperactive-Impulsive Type

4. Expressive Language Disorder

5. Autistic Disorder

6. Separation Anxiety Disorder

7. Bulimia Nervosa (Purging Type)

8. Schizophrenia (Paranoid Type)

9. Major Depressive Disorder, Recurrent

10. Bipolar I Disorder, Most Recent Episode Manic

11. Generalized Anxiety Disorder

12. Antisocial Personality Disorder

13. Bereavement

14. Male Erectile Disorder, Acquired Type, Generalized Type, Due to Psychological Factors

15. Posttraumatic Stress Disorder (PTSD)

16. Dementia of the Alzheimer's Type

These treatment plans were prepared by Laurel Torres, J. Erin Webb, and Sophia F. Dziegielewski.

TREATMENT PLAN

I. MILD MENTAL RETARDATION

Definition: The main feature of mental retardation is significantly subaverage intellectual functioning which is evidenced by an IQ score of below 70. Mild mental retardation occurs when the individual has an IQ between 50/55 and 70.

Signs and Symptoms to Note in the Record:

- Subaverage intelligence; specifically, an IQ of between 50/55 and 70.
- Limitations in communication, self-care, social and interpersonal skills, self-direction, and academic skills.
- Difficult in coping with everyday demands.
- Difficulty in functioning independently.

Goals:

1. Behavior will correspond to appropriate level of functioning within social contexts, such as school, home, and community settings.
2. Accept intellectual limitations, but also be able to express strengths.
3. Reduce the number of socially inappropriate behaviors.
4. Parents should develop a simple routine at home and positively reinforce compliance with the rules.

Objectives	Interventions
Client will be placed in an appropriate school setting and an appropriate residential setting.	Consult with teachers, parents, and mental health professionals to determine appropriate classroom setting depending on the client's intellectual capabilities.
	Determine appropriate residential setting, depending on the client's abilities and the level of care required.
Teachers will develop an educational plan that focuses on the child's abilities and compensates for the child's weaknesses.	Implement a reward/token system for compliant behavior and positive academic performance.
Parents will increase use of positive reinforcement at home.	Develop and implement a list of daily chores that the child is developmentally able to achieve and positively reinforce achievements.
Parents and teachers will recognize and verbally express when the child is behaving in a socially inappropriate way.	Design a reward system to reinforce the child's socially appropriate behaviors.

TREATMENT PLAN

2. ATTENTION-DEFICIT/HYPERACTIVITY DISORDER, PREDOMINANTLY INATTENTIVE TYPE

Definition: A disorder that becomes apparent in childhood, must be present before the age of seven and is characterized by an inability to maintain focus/concentration, an inability to complete tasks and poor organization skills.

Signs and Symptoms to Note in the Record:

- Inability to follow through on assignments/tasks from beginning to end.
- Inattention to detail/often makes careless mistakes.
- Loses interest in activities/frequent shifting of focus from one project to another without completion.
- Messy working space/area.
- Dislike of activities that require sustained attention.

Goals:

1. Client will take medication as prescribed by psychiatrist.
2. Client will increase attention/concentration span.
3. Client will adhere to firm limits as established by parents and teachers.
4. Client will increase self-esteem.

Objectives	Interventions
Parents will insure that medication is being taken in appropriate dosage and at specified times.	Child will adhere to a daily routine of taking medications as established by parents.
Client will maintain attention to activities for increasing intervals of time.	Assist parents and child in developing a routine, schedule child's chores and assignments to be completed each day, and the time frame in which each is to be completed.
	Make recreational activities contingent upon completion of daily assignment while systematically increasing the length of time required to complete such tasks.
Therapist will introduce and help the client utilize self-monitoring techniques to help client stay on-task.	Introduce the client to a nondisruptive, self-repeating tape of tones that regularly reminds the child to ask himself, "Am I working on my assigned task?"
Parents and teachers will establish and implement rules and consequences for the child.	Assist the parents in determining clear rules for the child and developing a system of natural consequences for inappropriate behaviors.
Parents and teachers will positively reinforce appropriate behaviors of the child.	Utilize verbal praise to reward compliance with rules.
	Utilize a reward system to reinforce on-task behaviors and completion of tasks at home and in the classroom.
Client will improve self-confidence and self-worth.	Client will list, recognize, and focus on strengths, and utilize these in interpersonal relationahips.

TREATMENT PLAN

3. ATTENTION-DEFICIT/HYPERACTIVITY DISORDER, PREDOMINANTLY HYPERACTIVE-IMPULSIVE TYPE

Definition: A disorder that becomes apparent in childhood, must be present before the age of seven, and is characterized by excessive motor activity, as well as poor impulse control of emotional and physical behaviors.

Signs and Symptoms to Note in the Record:

- Inability to remain seated for an extended period of time.
- Excessive fidgeting.
- Excessive talking/noise.
- Blurting out of answers/inability to think before speaking/inability to raise hand and wait to be called on.
- Frequent interruption of conversations, activities, and so on.
- Frequent accidents.

Goals:

1. Client will take medication as prescribed by psychiatrist.
2. Client will improve impulse control.
3. Caretakers will set firm and consistent limits and reinforce positive behaviors of the child.
4. Client will improve self-esteem.

Objectives	Interventions
Parents will insure that medication is being taken in appropriate dosage and at specified times.	Client will adhere to a daily routine of taking prescribed medications as established by parents.
Child will increase awareness of disruptive/impulsive behavior at home and in the classroom.	Parents and teachers will develop a system responsible for immediately alerting the child to impulsive or off task behaviors (i.e., attention training system) at home or in school.
Parents and teachers will establish and implement rules and limitations for child.	Assist parents and teachers in determining clear rules and boundaries for the client, and responsibilities of the client.
Parents and teachers will decide upon and implement consequences for inappropriate behaviors of the client.	Develop natural and meaningful consequences for noncompliance with rules.
Parents and teachers will positively reinforce appropriate behaviors of the client.	Utilize verbal praise to reward compliance with rules and appropriate behaviors.
Client will improve self-confidence, self-regard, and self-worth.	Increase the client's frequency of positive self-statements.
	Client will identify things which he/she does well.

TREATMENT PLAN

4. EXPRESSIVE LANGUAGE DISORDER

Definition: A disorder characterized by underdeveloped expressive language substantially below the intellectual/developmental level expected of the individual. This is often demonstrated by scores on the expressive language portion of standardized tests being substantially below scoring on the nonverbal intellectual and language reception portions.

Signs and Symptoms to Note in the Record:

- Expressive language scoring on standardized tests below normal range, while nonlinguistic and comprehensive scoring is often within or above the normal range.
- Limited speech, often the result of limited vocabulary, poor sentence structure, and improperly conjugated verbs.
- Children often begin speaking late and progress through language development stages at a lower rate.
- Difficulty introducing new vocabulary into the range of verbal expression.

Goals:

1. Parents and child will utilize the expertise of a language pathologist in determining language capabilities and assisting the child in reaching full expressive capacity.
2. Parents and child will develop an awareness/acceptance of expressive language limitations.
3. Child will utilize tools to help cope with frustrations and ridicule often associated with language deficits.
4. Child will improve self-esteem.

Objectives	Interventions
Client and parents will comply with all recommendations of language pathologist.	Consistent communication between parents, teachers, and therapist to reinforce learning techniques and language development.
Child and family will accept limitations of language deficit.	Individual therapy to eliminate denial of and encourage acceptance of language deficit in order to facilitate proper educational placement and an optimal learning environment.
	Family therapy to eliminate the denial of and encourage acceptance of child's language difficulties in order to facilitate proper educational placement and maximum language development.
Child will implement effective coping mechanisms to deal with peer ridicule due to language difficulties.	Individual therapy to introduce, practice, and encourage client use of effective coping mechanisms including: positive self-talk, deep breathing strategies, relaxation techniques.
Parents and teachers will reinforce client strengths.	Focus on client strengths (math, manual dexterity, creativity, etc.) and further the development of these to their full potential in order to compensate for language deficits.

TREATMENT PLAN

5. AUTISTIC DISORDER

Definition: The main features of autistic disorder are abnormal or impaired development in social interaction and communication as well as a strict regimen of repetitive behaviors.

Signs and Symptoms to Note in the Record:

- Lack of interest in other people.
- Failure to develop appropriate interpersonal relationships.
- Delays in communication skills and language development.
- Repetition of rituals or self-stimulating behaviors, such as rocking.
- Self-injurious behaviors, such as head banging or biting.
- Overreaction to changes in routine or environment.
- Impairment in both intellectual and cognitive functioning.

Goals:

1. Develop basic language and communication skills.
2. Parents should accept their child's capabilities and limitations.
3. Decrease and eventually eliminate all self-injurious behaviors.

Objectives	Interventions
Client will utilize speech and language therapists.	Refer the client to a speech and language therapist to increase the child's development of speech and language skills.
Client will increase interactions with others which will help to improve communication skills.	Parents should utilize positive reinforcement or modeling techniques to encourage interaction with others and better communication skills.
Client will decrease self-injurious behaviors.	Teach the parents behavioral management techniques to decrease their child's self-injurious behaviors.
	Refer the parents and the child to a therapist who is knowledgeable about aversive therapy, which can also be used to decrease self-injurious behaviors.
Parents will develop an understanding of their child's illness.	Educate the parent about autism, inform them of the difficulties they will encounter while taking care of the child as well as realistic expectations of the disorder and the extent of their child's abilities.
	Refer the clients to a support group where they can receive support and guidance from other families with autistic children.
	Encourage parents to use respite care when needed.

TREATMENT PLAN

6. SEPARATION ANXIETY DISORDER

Definition: The main feature of separation anxiety disorder is an excessive anxiety and worry over being separated from parents or caregivers.

Signs and Symptoms to Note in the Record:

- High level of distress when separated from parents or other caretakers.
- Excessive worry about losing child's parents or something happening to them while they are away from the child.
- Fear of being alone without parents nearby.
- Frequent nightmares about separation from parents.
- Lack of participation in social activities due to excessive fear of being separated from parents.

Goals:

1. Decrease the anxiety and fear when a separation is anticipated or occurs.
2. Resolve the underlying issues that may be contributing to the fear.
3. The child should participate in activities with peers and spend time playing independently, away from parents.
4. Parents should establish clear boundaries and set firm limits on their child's acting out behaviors which occur when separation is near.

Objectives	Interventions
Client will describe fears and how those fears are irrational.	Encourage the child to explore the reasons why separation from parents is feared.
	Encourage the child to express how fears are irrational.
Parents will set limits on their child's crying, clinging, pleading, and temper tantrums when separation occurs.	Teach the parent to set consistent limits on their child's temper tantrums, crying, and clinging.
	Educate the parents about the need for space and privacy.
Client will increase the amount of time spent away from parents.	Encourage the child to spend progressively longer periods of time playing independently or with peers.
	Parents should positively reinforce autonomous behaviors.
Both the client and parents will examine why the anxiety occurs and the factors that may be contributing to its occurrence.	Encourage the child to examine and verbally express how fear may be related to past separations, trauma, or abuse.
	Encourage the parents to examine how they may be contributing to or reinforcing their child's anxiety and fears.

TREATMENT PLAN

7. BULIMIA NERVOSA (PURGING TYPE)

Definition: The main features of bulimia nervosa are binge eating and purging behaviors that are used as a means of preventing weight gain.

Signs and Symptoms to Note in the Record:

- Consumption of large quantities of food at one time.
- Self-induced vomiting, abuse of laxatives, or excessive exercise to prevent weight gain.
- Preoccupation with body image and body size.
- Fear of becoming overweight.
- Electrolyte imbalance and dental problems resulting from the eating disorder.

Goals:

1. Stop the pattern of binge eating and purging behavior.
2. Restore a more healthy eating pattern with appropriate nutrition to maintain a healthy weight.
3. Develop understanding of the cognitive and emotional struggles that have resulted in the eating disorder and develop alternative coping strategies.
4. Change the perception of oneself so that it does not focus on body weight or size as the primary means of self-acceptance.

Objectives	Interventions
Client will cooperate with a complete physical and dental exam.	Refer client to physician for a physical exam and to dentist for a dental exam.
Client will keep a food journal of food consumption and any methods used to control gaining weight.	Discuss with the client the dysfunctional eating patterns that may have resulted in physical problems.
	Monitor the client's bingeing and purging behaviors, develop a nutritional eating plan, and positively reinforce healthy eating patterns.
Client will identify the relationship between low self-esteem, a drive for perfectionism, a fear of failure, and the eating disorder.	Assist the client in exploring how a drive for perfectionism and a need for control led to the eating disorder.
	Encourage the client to identify positive qualities and positively reinforce all of the client's accomplishments.
Client will develop alternative coping strategies for dealing with the underlying emotional issues.	Assist the client to develop assertive behaviors which will allow healthful expression of emotions and refer the client to an eating disorder support group.
Client will state a basis for identity that is not based on body weight or size but on personal character, values, or personality traits.	Assist the client to identify a basis for self-worth that is not based on body size by assessing her talents, positive traits, and importance to significant others in her life, such as family and friends.

TREATMENT PLAN

8. SCHIZOPHRENIA (PARANOID TYPE)

Definition: Schizophrenia of the paranoid type is characterized by delusions and auditory hallucinations. The delusions are primarily persecutory and grandiose and the hallucinations are usually related to the theme present in the delusions.

Signs and Symptoms to Note in the Record:

- Delusions and auditory hallucinations which are typically persecutory and/or grandiose.
- The individual typically has a patronizing and superior manner toward others and interactions with others are either extremely formal or intense.
- Suicidal ideation as a result of the persecutory delusions.
- Anger which may result in violence toward others.
- Extreme distrust of others without sufficient basis.
- A pattern of suspiciousness toward others without reason.
- Expectation of being harmed by others.

Goals:

1. Maintain proper medication treatment for delusions and hallucinations.
2. Demonstrate more trust of others by verbalizing positive beliefs and attitudes about them.
3. Interact with others without defensiveness and/or anger.
4. Reduce suspiciousness about others by interacting with others in a more trusting, open, and relaxed manner.

Objectives	Interventions
Client will take medication as prescribed.	Monitor patient's medications for compliance and report effectiveness and side effects to the client's psychiatrist.
Client will identify those individuals the client distrusts and why.	Assist the client in exploring the nature of the paranoia.
Client will examine the belief that others are untrustworthy.	Review the client's social interactions and explore the distorted beliefs directed at others.
	Encourage the client to assess the distorted perceptions by verifying those conclusions with others.
Client will decrease accusations against others based on the belief that they will cause harm.	Provide alternative explanations for others' behaviors besides planning to bring harm to the client.
Client will increase interaction with others without expression of mistrust, fear, or suspicion.	Use role playing to increase the patient's empathy for others.
	Refer the client to a support group for people suffering from schizophrenia.

TREATMENT PLAN

9. MAJOR DEPRESSIVE DISORDER, RECURRENT

Definition: Major depressive disorder is characterized by one or more major depressive episodes. These episodes last for a period of at least two weeks and are characterized by depressed mood and/or a loss of interest or pleasure in most activities.

Signs and Symptoms to Note in the Record:

- Depressed mood most of the day for nearly every day.
- Markedly diminished interest or pleasure in all or most activities.
- Changes in appetite, eating too little or too much.
- Insomnia or hypersomnia.
- Psychomotor agitation.
- Fatigue or loss of energy.
- Feelings of worthlessness or excessive guilt.
- Difficulty with concentrating.
- Suicidal thoughts.

Goals:

1. Lessen depressed mood and return to an effective level of functioning.
2. Develop the ability to recognize and cope with feelings of depression.
3. Develop healthier cognitive patterns and more positive beliefs about self and the future.
4. Reduce suicidal thoughts.

Objectives	Interventions
Client will identify the source of depressed mood.	Ask the client to make a list of what is causing the depression and process this list in psychotherapy.
Client will identify any dysfunctional self-talk that is perpetuating the depression and replace those negative thoughts with more positive and realistic self-talk.	Ask client to keep a daily record of dysfunctional thoughts. Challenge each of the client's negative thoughts through cognitive therapy.
Client will verbalize more positive, hopeful statements about the future.	Ask client to write at least one positive statement daily about self and the future and discuss them in psychotherapy.
Client will engage in a regular exercise and/or meditation.	Assist the client in developing an exercise routine and teach the client meditation and/or relaxation techniques.
Client will reduce suicidal ideation.	Assess and monitor client for suicide ideation and arrange for hospitalization when client is judged to be a threat to self.
Client will take medication as prescribed by psychiatrist	Monitor patient's medications for compliance and report effectiveness and side effects to the client's psychiatrist.

TREATMENT PLAN

10. Bipolar I Disorder, Most Recent Episode Manic

Definition: Bipolar I disorder, most recent episode manic, is characterized by the presence of a manic episode. There has previously been at least one major depressive episode, manic episode or mixed episode but the client is presently in a manic episode. A manic episode consists of a period of elevated, expansive, and irritable mood that lasts at least one week.

Signs and Symptoms to Note in the Record:

- Inflated self-esteem or grandiosity.
- Decreased need for sleep.
- Pressured speech.
- Flight of ideas or racing thoughts.
- Distractibility.
- Psychomotor agitation.
- Excessive involvement in pleasurable activities that may have harmful consequences, such as sexual promiscuity or impulse buying.

Goals:

1. Reduce uncontrollable energy, return to a normal activity level, and increase good judgement.
2. Reduce agitation, impulsive behaviors, and pressured speech and increase sensitivity to consequences of behaviors.
3. Cope with underlying feelings of low self-esteem and fears of rejection or abandonment.
4. Increase controlled behavior, achieve a more stable mood, and develop more deliberate speech and thought processes.

Objectives	Interventions
Client will cooperate with a psychiatric evaluation and take medications as prescribed.	Arrange for a psychiatric evaluation for psychotropic medications and monitor patient's reaction to the medication.
Client will reduce impulsive behaviors.	Psychotherapy to address consequences of behaviors.
Client will decrease grandiosity and express self more realistically.	Confront the client's grandiosity through psychotherapy and reinforce more realistic self-statements.
Client will be able to sit calmly for 30 minutes without agitation or distractibility.	Reinforce client's increased control over hyperactivity and help the client set attainable goals and limits on agitation and distractibility.
Client will speak more slowly and maintain focus on one subject at a time.	Provide structure for the client's thought processes and actions by directing the course of the conversation and developing plans for the client's behaviors.
Client will acknowledge the low self-esteem and fear of rejection that underlies their grandiosity.	Psychotherapy to explore the psychosocial stressors that are precipitating the client's manic behaviors, such as rejection by peers or past traumas.

TREATMENT PLAN

II. GENERALIZED ANXIETY DISORDER

Definition: Generalized anxiety disorder is characterized by excessive anxiety and worry about a number of events or activities that lasts for at least six months.

Signs and Symptoms to Note in the Record:

- Restlessness or feeling keyed up or on the edge.
- Easily fatigued.
- Difficulty concentrating.
- Irritability.
- Muscle tension.
- Sleep disturbance, such as restless sleeping or difficulty falling asleep.
- Difficulty controlling the worry.

Goals:

1. Reduce overall intensity and frequency of the anxiety.
2. Increase ability to function on a daily basis.
3. Resolve the core issue that is causing the anxiety.
4. Develop coping skills to better handle anxieties encountered in the future.

Objectives	Interventions
Client will complete a psychiatric evaluation and take medications as prescribed.	Arrange for a psychiatric evaluation for psychotropic medications and monitor patient for side effects of the medication.
Client will identify causes of anxious feelings.	Assign the client homework assignments to identify cognitive distortions that are causing anxiety.
	Psychotherapy to address client's cognitive distortions.
Client will identify how worries are irrational.	Psychotherapy to assist client in developing an awareness of the irrational nature of fears.
Client will utilize thought-stopping techniques to prevent anxiety.	Teach client thought-stopping techniques to prevent anxiety-producing thoughts.
Client will decrease level of anxiety by increasing positive self-talk.	Cognitive therapy to assist the client in developing more realistic thoughts which will increase self-confidence in coping with anxiety.
Client will identify alternative, more positive views of reality that oppose the anxiety-producing view.	Reframe the client's fears and anxieties by suggesting another way of looking at it and helping the client to broaden the client's perspective.
Client will develop a relaxation and regular exercise program to decrease anxiety level.	Teach client the technique of guided imagery.
	Encourage regular exercise as a means of reducing anxiety.

TREATMENT PLAN

12. ANTISOCIAL PERSONALITY DISORDER

Definition: A persistent pattern of contempt and violation of the rights of others characterized by deceit and manipulation.

Signs and Symptoms to Note in the Record:

- Failure to conform to social norms.
- Pattern of law violations and authoritative noncompliance.
- Impulsivity.
- Repeated acts of aggression against others.
- Difficulty keeping a job.
- Financially irresponsible (i.e., fails to pay bills, child support, etc.).
- Limited understanding of cause and effect.
- Little or no conscience regarding their violent behavior.

Goals:

1. Client will take responsibility for parental, financial, and occupational obligations.
2. Client will demonstrate an understanding of and compliance with social norms.
3. Client will demonstrate respect for the rights of others.
4. Client will accept responsibility for decisions and actions.

Objectives	Intervention
Client will list negative consequences of antisocial behavior.	Identify jobs and relationships lost or negatively impacted by antisocial behavior.
Client will recognize and accept responsibility for illegal and socially deviant behavior.	Identify 10 antisocial behaviors performed in the past and the consequences for self and others of each.
	Client will define social norm by identifying 25 acceptable behaviors which had previously been challenged or broken by the client.
Client will contract to adhere to rules and regulations defined by social norms.	Client will create and sign a behavioral contract indicating intent to comply with the laws and rules of society.
	Client will attend work regularly and cooperate with coworkers.
Client will acknowledge the benefits to compliance with social norms.	Client will verbalize ways in which the client and others are benefited by compliance with the laws and rules of society.
Client will verbalize and offer restitution for incomplete participation in parental, financial, and occupational obligations.	Assist client in learning the value of empathy and the necessity of apology for wrongdoing.
	Client will identify individuals deserving of restitution and role play the apology for each.

TREATMENT PLAN

13. BEREAVEMENT

Definition: Clinical attention focusing on an individual's reaction, emotionally, behaviorally, and cognitively, to the death of a loved one.

Signs and Symptoms to Note in the Record:

- Characteristics of a major depressive episode including problems sleeping, and eating, weight gain or loss.
- Guilt surrounding the death of the loved one.
- Conversational superficiality with respect to the loved one's death.
- Excessive emoting when the loved one's death is discussed.
- Feelings of worthlessness.
- Difficulty concentrating due to domination of thoughts surrounding loved one's death.
- Possible psychomotor retardation.
- Functional Impairment.

Goals:

1. Client will acknowledge and accept the death of loved one.
2. Client will begin the grieving process.
3. Client will resolve feelings over the death of loved one.
4. Client will reconnect with old relationships and activities.

Objectives	Interventions
Client will identify and state steps in the grieving process.	Therapist will educate the client on the grieving process, specifically, the stages of grief.
	Client will seek out others who have experienced the loss of a loved one to evaluate coping mechanisms used in dealing with this loss, and evaluate the use of these in individual therapy.
Client will explore and express emotions and feelings associated with this loss.	Client will create a journal of emotions related to this loss to be discussed in individual therapy.
	Client will participate in "empty chair" exercise where the client will verbally express feelings not verbalized to the deceased loved one in life.
Client will resolve feelings of anger and guilt associated with loss of loved one.	Client will write a letter to the lost loved one expressing feelings and emotions, memories and regrets associated with loss to be discussed in individual therapy.
	Client will attend a bereavement support group.
Client will interact with and discuss the death of loved one with others.	Client will interact with one mutual friend of the client and the deceased and share feelings about this loss, discussing the impact it has had on the living.

TREATMENT PLAN

14. MALE ERECTILE DISORDER, ACQUIRED TYPE, GENERALIZED TYPE, DUE TO PSYCHOLOGICAL FACTORS

Definition: A disorder whose essential feature is a persistent inability to achieve or maintain an adequate erection throughout sexual activity, which follows a period of normal sexual functioning, is not limited to a specific type of stimulation, situation or partner, and is not due to a medical condition.

Signs and Symptoms to Note in the Record:

- Recurrent lack of physiological response to sexual intimacy.
- Inability to maintain an erection in the initial stages of sexual activity.
- Loss of rigidity during the act of sexual intercourse.
- An ability to attain an erection only during masturbation.
- Total inability to attain an erection.

Goals:

1. Client will achieve an erection in response to sexual activity.
2. Client will maintain an erection throughout sexual intercourse.
3. Client will increase desire for intimate relations and pleasure derived from sexual intercourse.

Objectives	Interventions
Client will openly share feelings regarding intimate relationship with significant other.	Conjugate therapeutic session to address open line of communication regarding sex, conflict resolution, and feelings.
Client will identify negative feelings regarding previous sexual experiences.	Client will develop a detailed sexual history (experiences, practices, knowledge of sex, and frequency) to be discussed in individual therapy.
Client will identify positive feelings regarding previous sexual experiences.	Client will develop a list of sexual situations in which the inability to become erect did not manifest itself to be discussed in individual therapy.
Client will journal sexual fantasies that result in penile erection.	Individual therapy to focus on the integration of sexual fantasies, successful in the attainment of an erection, into current intimate relationship.
Client and significant other will experiment with new and varying types of stimuli during sexual relations.	Encourage client to explore varying positions, types of foreplay, and different venues in an effort to increase and sustain the arousal response.
Client will verbalize desire for and enjoyment of sexual activity to partner.	Client will verbally express enjoyment of intimate relations to partner in order to reinforce positive sexual relations.
	Individual therapy to address reactions and feeling associated with this verbal acknowledgment.

TREATMENT PLAN

15. POSTTRAUMATIC STRESS DISORDER (PTSD)

Definition: The development of fear, helplessness, or horror in response to an event including actual or threatened death to self, the witnessing an event involving the death or threat of harm to another, or learning of the death or threat of injury to a family member or friend.

Signs and Symptoms to Note in the Record:

- Persistent re-experiencing of the traumatic event—flashbacks.
- Continuous avoidance of persons, places, and things, emotions and feelings associated with the traumatic event.
- Physiological response when exposed to stimuli associated with traumatic event.
- Difficulty sleeping and possible nightmares.
- Difficulty concentrating.
- Angry outbursts.

Goals:

1. Client will return to level of functioning prior to traumatic event.
2. Client will learn and utilize coping skills to assist in maintaining close relationships.
3. Client will be able to cognitively re-experience the traumatic event without a physiological response.
4. Client will exhibit acceptance of traumatic event.

Objectives	Interventions
Client will identify ways in which PTSD has impaired occupational or social functioning.	Explore in individual therapy the limiting effects PTSD has had on intimate relationships, work, and recreational activities.
Client will describe traumatic event in detail.	Therapist will assist client in safely recalling details of the traumatic event utilizing E.M.D.R.
Client will utilize relaxation and anger management techniques to help cope with PTSD.	Client will learn and implement imagery and deep muscle relaxation, positive self-talk, and/or deep breathing techniques in coping with physiological effects of PTSD.
Client will increase ability to talk about traumatic event while decreasing physiological or emotional response.	Client will engage in the repeated retelling of the story of the traumatic event in order to gradually increase ability to verbalize the traumatic event in individual therapy session.
Client will confront physical stimuli associated with event while remaining calm.	Use of systematic desensitization to reduce emotional and physiological reactions to mentally picturing the traumatic event and physical aspects of the traumatic event.
Client will interact with others experiencing PTSD and for support.	Refer client to a PTSD support group.

TREATMENT PLAN

16. Dementia of the Alzheimer's Type

Definition: A gradual onset of cognitive deficits, and at least one cognitive disturbance or a disturbance in executive functioning, resulting in an impairment of social or occupational functioning which is indicative of a decline from a previously higher functional level.

Signs and Symptoms to Note in the Record:

- Spatial disorientation.
- Poor judgment and poor insight regarding capabilities and risk assessment.
- Memory loss present though often not apparent to the individual.
- Cognitive impairments including disturbances in anxiety, mood, and sleep patterns.
- Possible motor skill disturbances resulting in falls.
- Disinhibited behaviors including neglect of hygiene and disregard for social norms.
- Symptomology does not fluctuate.

Goals:

1. Client and family will seek out educational material regarding Dementia and its associated features including memory loss, poor judgment, and cognitive deficits.
2. Client will maximize his/her capacity for independent living.
3. Client and family will accept and understand the extent of memory loss while incorporating compensatory coping strategies.
4. Client will take medication as prescribed by a physician.
5. Client will have in place an established support system.

Objectives	Interventions
Client and family will read dementia related articles and pamphlets as suggested by therapist.	Individual and family therapy to discuss information and answer questions regarding Dementia of the Alzheimer's Type.
Client will utilize compensatory strategies for irreparable aspects of memory loss.	Create a bulletin board for identifying and consolidating activities of daily living, appointments and outside activities.
Client will routinely complete activities of daily living including bathing, eating, hygiene, and dressing.	Create a daily living checklist and check off activities of daily living as they are completed: place in a central living area.
	Encourage family members and friends to establish a routine pattern of communication with the client.
Client will take medication in appropriate dosages and at specified times.	Utilize a weekly or monthly pillbox to assist client in the proper consumption of medications.
	Include medication in daily living checklist.
Client and Family will develop a consistent and reliable pattern of communication.	Family will establish a routine pattern of calling and visitations in an effort to assist client with reality orientation.

References

Abbott Health Care Worldwide. (1997). In News in Mental Health Nursing. *Journal of Psychosocial Nursing, 35*(2), 6.

Abramowitz, J. S. (1998). Does cognitive-behavioral therapy cure obsessive-compulsive disorder? A meta-analytic evaluation of clinical significance. *Behavioral Therapy, 29,* 339–355.

Addolorato, G., Cibin, M., Caprista, E., Beghe, F., Gessa, G., Stefanini, G. F., et al. (1998). Maintaining abstinence from alcohol with gamma-hydroxybutyric acid [Research letters]. *Lancet, 351*(9095), 38.

Allen, J. P. (1998). Project, MATCH: A clarification (Behavioral interventions for alcoholics). *Behavioral Health Management, 18*(4), 42–44.

Alperin, R. M. (1994). Managed care versus psychoanalytic psychotherapy: Conflicting ideologies. *Clinical Social Work Journal, 22*(2), 137–148.

Altschule, M. D., Bigelow, L. B., Liss, E. L., Cancro, R., Cohen, G., Kety, S., et al. (1976). The genetics of schizophrenia. In S. Wolf (Ed.), *The biology of the schizophrenic process.* New York: Plenum Press.

American Psychiatric Association. (1952). *Diagnostic and statistical manual of mental disorders.* Washington, DC: Author.

American Psychiatric Association. (1968). *Diagnostic and statistical manual of mental disorders* (2nd ed.). Washington, DC: Author.

American Psychiatric Association. (1980). *Diagnostic and statistical manual of mental disorders* (3rd ed.). Washington, DC: Author.

American Psychiatric Association. (1987). *Diagnostic and statistical manual of mental disorders* (3rd ed., rev.). Washington, DC: Author.

American Psychiatric Association. (1994). *Diagnostic and statistical manual of mental disorders* (4th ed.). Washington, DC: Author.

American Psychiatric Association. (1995). *Diagnostic and statistical manual of mental disorders* (4th ed., rev). Washington, DC: Author.

American Psychiatric Association. (2000). *Diagnostic and statistical manual of mental disorders.* (4th ed., text rev.). Washington, DC: American Psychiatric Press.

Anderson, D. F., Berlant, J. L., Mauch, D., & Maloney, W. R. (1997). Managed behavioral health care services. In P. R. Kongstvedt (Ed.), *Essentials of managed care* (pp. 248–273). Gaithersburg, MD: Aspen.

379

Anthenelli, R., & Schuckit, M. (1993). Affective and anxiety disorders and alcohol and drug dependence: Diagnosis and treatment [CD-ROM]. *Journal of Addictive Diseases, 12*(3), 73–87. Abstract retrieved from PsychLIT: AN 81–13797.

Antonousky, A., & Sourani, T. (1988). Family sense of coherence and family adaption. *Journal of Marriage and Family, 50,* 79–92.

APA Online. (2001a). Practice coding. Retrieved from www.apa.org/practice /medcoding.html

APA Online. (2001b). Practice coding. Retrieved from www.apa.org/practice /medbilling.html

Araoz, D. L., & Carrese, M. A. (1996). *Solution-oriented brief therapy for adjustment disorders: A guide for providers under managed care.* New York: Brunner/Mazel.

Armenteros, J. L. (1997). Risperidone in adolescents with schizophrenia: An open pilot study. *Journal of the American Academy of Child and Adolescent Psychiatry, 36,* 694, 697.

Aronson, E. (1988). *The social animal* (5th ed.). New York: Freeman.

Arredondo, P. (1998, July). Integrating multicultural counseling competencies and universal helping conditions in culture-specific contexts (Reconceptualizing multicultural counseling). *Counseling Psychologist, 26*(4), 592–602.

Association of Psychiatrists in Africa. (1974). *Alcoholism and drug addiction* (International Council on Alcohol and Addictions). Johannesberg, South Africa: Association of Psychiatrists.

Austrian, S. G. (1995). *Mental disorders, medications and clinical social work.* New York: Columbia University Press.

Awad, A. G., & Lakshmi, V. (1999). Quality of life and new antipsychotics in schizophrenia: Are patients better off? *International Journal of Social Psychiatry 45*(4), 268–275.

Ayuso-Gutierrez, J. L., & del Rio Vega, J. M. (1997). Factors influencing relapse in the long term course of schizophrenia. *Schizophrenia Research, 28,* 199–206.

Badger, L. W., & Rand, E. H. (1998). Mood disorder. In J. B. W. Williams & K. Ell (Eds.), *Mental health research: Implications for practice* (pp. 49–117). Washington, DC: National Association of Social Workers Press.

Barker, R. L. (1995). *The social work dictionary* (3rd ed.). Washington, DC: National Association of Social Workers Press.

Baron, M., Gruen, R., Rainer, J. D., Kane, J., Asnis, L., & Lord, A. A. (1985). A family study of schizophrenia and normal control probands: Implication for the spectrum concept of schizophrenia. *American Journal of Psychiatry, 142*(4), 447–455.

Bateman, A., & Fonagy, P. (1999). Effectiveness of partial hospitalization in the treatment of borderline personality disorder: A randomized controlled trial. *American Journal of Psychiatry, 156*(10), 1563–1569.

Bateman, A., & Fonagy, P. (2001). Treatment of borderline personality disorder with psychoanalytically oriented partial hospitalization: An 18-month follow-up. *American Journal of Psychiatry, 158*(1), 36–42.

Beck, A. T. (1967). *Depression: Clinical, experimental, and theoretical aspects.* New York: Hoeber Medical Division, Harper & Row.

Beck, A. T., Freeman, A., & Associates. (1990). *Cognitive therapy of personality disorders.* New York: Guilford.

Benedetti, F., Sforzino, L., Colombo, C., Marrei, C., & Smeraldi, E. (1998). Low-dose clozapine in acute and continuation treatment of severe borderline personality disorder. *Journal of Clinical Psychiatry, 59*(3), 103–107.

Benedict, N. J. (1998). Reactive attachment disorder: A neuropsychological study. *Dissertation Abstracts International, 59*(7B), 3680. (UMI Libraries No. 717).

Bentley, K. J., & Walsh, J. (1996). *The social worker and psychotropic medication: Toward effective collaboration with mental health clients, families, and providers.* Pacific Grove, CA: Brooks/Cole.

Bernheim, K. (1992). Supportive family counseling. *Schizophrenia Bulletin, 8.*

Bernstein, B. E., & Hartsell, T. L. (1998). *The portable lawyer for mental health professionals.* New York: Wiley.

Bloom, B. L. (1992). *Planned short-term psychotherapy: A clinical handbook.* Boston: Allyn & Bacon.

Bloom, M., Fischer, J., & Orme, J. (1999). *Evaluating practice: Guidelines for the accountable professional* (3rd ed.). Boston: Allyn & Bacon.

Blow, F. C. (1998). *Substance abuse amongst older adults* (Technical Assistance Publication Series 26, Publication No. SMA 98–3179). Rockville, MD: U.S. Department of Health and Human Services.

Bohus, M., Landwehrmeyer, M., Stiglmayr, C., Limberger, M., Bohme, R., & Schmahl, C. (1999). Naltrexone in the treatment of dissociative symptoms in patients with borderline personality disorder: An open-label trial. *Journal of Clinical Psychiatry, 60,* 598–603.

Bonn, D. (1999). New treatments for alcohol dependency better than old (News). *Lancet, 353*(9148), 213.

Boris, N. W., & Zeanah, C. H. (1999). Disturbances and disorders of attachment in infancy: An overview. *Infant Mental Health Journal, 20*(1), 1–9.

Bowlby, J. (1982). *Attachment.* New York: Basic Books.

Bowlby, J. (1988). *A secure base.* London: Routledge.

Boyd-Franklin, N. (1989). *Black families in therapy.* New York: Guilford Press.

Braithwaite, K., Duff, J., & Westworth, I. (1999). *Conduct disorder in children and adolescents.* Behavioural Neurotherapy Clinic. Available from www.adhd.com.au /conduct.html

Brekke, J. S., & Barrio, C. (1997). Cross-ethnic symptom differences in schizophrenia: The influence of culture and minority status. *Schizophrenia Bulletin, 23*(2), 305–316.

Broberg, A. G. (2000). A review of interventions in the parent-child relationship informed by attachment theory. *Acta Paediatrica Supplement, 434,* 37–42.

Brower, A. M., & Nurius, P. S. (1993). *Social cognitions and individual change: Current theory and counseling guidelines.* Newbury Park, CA: Sage.

Brown, K. W., McGoldrick, T., & Buchanan, R. (1997). Body dysmorphic disorder: Seven cases treated with eye movement desensitization and reprocessing. *Behavioural and Cognitive Psychotherapy, 25,* 203–207.

Brown, S. (1985). *Treating the alcoholic: A developmental model of recovery.* New York: Wiley.

Browning, C. H., & Browning, B. J. (1996). *How to partner with managed care.* Los Calamitous, CA: Duncliff's International.

Bruner, J. (1991). *Acts of meaning.* Cambridge, MA: Harvard University Press.

Brunk, M. (1999). *Effective treatment of conduct disorder.* Juvenile Forensic Evaluation Resource Center. Available from http://ness.sys.virginia.edu/juv/ConDis.html

Brzustowicz, L., Hodgkinson, K., Chow, E., Honer, W., & Bassett, A. (2000, April 28). Location of major susceptibility locus for familial schizophrenia on chromosome 1q21–q22. *Science, 288,* 682–687.

Buchanan, R. W., & Carpenter, W. T. (1997). The neuroanatomies of schizophrenia. *Schizophrenia Bulletin, 23*(3), 367–372.

Buchanan, R. W., Stevens, J. R., & Carpenter, W. T. (1997). The neuroanatomy of schizophrenia: Editors' introduction. *Schizophrenia Bulletin, 23*(3), 365–366.

Budman, S., & Gurman, A. (1988). *Theory and practice of brief therapy.* New York: Guilford Press.

Bullers, A. C. (2001). Living with AIDS—20 years later. *EDA Consumer 35*(6), 29–35.

Burck, C., & Speed, B. (1995). Introduction. In C. Burck & B. Speed (Eds.), *Gender power and relationships* (pp. 1–6). New York: Routledge.

Burke, A. C., & Clapp, J. D. (1997). Ideology and social work practice in substance abuse settings. *Social Work, 42*(6), 552–563.

Burner, S. T., Waldo, D. R., & McKusick, D. R. (1992). National health expenditures projections through 2030. *Health Care Financing Review, 14*(1), 1–29.

Burns, D. (1983). *Ten days to self-esteem.* New York: Morrow.

Burns, L. E., Thorpe, G. L., & Cavallaro, L. A. (1986). Agoraphobia eight years after behavioral treatment: A follow-up study with interview, self-report, and behavioral data. *Behavior therapy, 17,* 580–591.

Byely, L., Archibald, A. B., Graber, J., & Brookes-Dunn, J. (2000). A prospective study of familial and social influences on girls' body image and dieting. *International Journal of Eating Disorders, 28,* 155–164.

Caetano, R., Clark, C. L., & Tam, T. (1998). Alcohol consumption among racial/ethnic minorities. *Alcohol Health and Research World, 22*(4), 233–241.

Carlton, T. O. (1984). *Clinical social work in health care settings: A guide to professional practice with exemplars.* New York: Springer.

Carlton, T. O. (1989). Classification and diagnosis in social work in health care. *Health and Social Work,* 83–85.

Carpenter, W. T., Conley, R. R., & Buchanan, R. W. (1998). Schizophrenia. In S. J. Enna & J. T. Coyle (Eds.), *Pharmacological management of neurological and psychiatric disorders.* New York: McGraw-Hill.

Carroll, K. M. (1997, Fall). New methods of treatment efficacy research: Bridging clinical research and clinical practice (Alcoholism treatment). *Alcohol Health and Research World, 21*(4), 352–360.

Casas, J. M. (1984). Policy, training, and research in counseling psychology: The racial/ethnic minority perspective. In S. D. Brown & R. W. Lent (Eds.), *Handbook of counseling psychology* (pp. 785–831). New York: Wiley.

Case, L. P., & Lingerfelt, N. B. (1974). Name-calling: The labeling process in the social work interview. *Social Service Review, 48,* 75–86.

Cash, T. F. (1996). Treatment of body image disturbances. In J. K. Thompson (Ed.), *Body image, eating disorders and obesity* (pp. 83–107). Washington, DC: American Psychological Association.

Cassano, G. B., Pini, S., Saettoni, M., & Dell'Osso, L. (1999). Multiple anxiety disorder comorbidity with patients with mood spectrum disorders with psychotic features. *American Journal of Psychiatry, 156,* 474–476.

Chambless, D., Cherney, J., & Caputo, G. (1987). Anxiety disorders and alcoholism: A study with inpatient alcoholics [CD-ROM]. *Journal of Anxiety Disorders, 1*(1), 29–40. Abstract retrieved from PsychLIT: AN 75–26791.

Cheisa, M., & Fonagy, P. (1999). Cassel personality disorder study methodology and treatment effects. *British Journal of Psychiatry, 176,* 485–491.

Chen, S. (1997). *Measurement and analysis in psychosocial research.* Brookfield, VT: Ashgate.

Chengappa, K., Elbeling, T., Kang, J., Levine, J., & Parepally, H. (1999). Clozapine reduces severe self-mutilation and aggression in psychotic patients with borderline personality disorder. *Journal of Clinical Psychiatry, 60,* 477–484.

Chopra, D. (1994). *Alternative medicine: The definitive guide.* Fife, WA: Future Medicine.

Ciminero, A. R., Calhoun, K. S., & Adams, H. E. (1986). *Handbook of behavioral assessment* (2nd ed.). New York: Wiley.

Cline, F. W., & Helding, C. (1999). *Can this child be saved? Solutions for adoptive and foster families.* Milwaukee, WI: World Enterprises.

Colby, I., & Dziegielewski, S. F. (2001). *Introduction to social work: The peoples' profession.* Chicago: Lyceum Books.

Concian, F. M. (1991). Feminist science: Methodologies that challenge inequality. *Gender and Society, 6*(4), 623–642.

Cone, J. D. (1998). Psychometric considerations: Concepts, contents and methods. In A. S. Bellack & M. Hersen (Eds.), *Behavioral assessment: A practical handbook* (4th ed., pp. 22–46). Boston: Allyn & Bacon.

Congress, E. (1997). *Multicultural perspectives in working with families.* New York: Springer.

Cooper, M. (1999). Treatment of persons and families with obsessive compulsive disorder: A review article. *Crisis Intervention, 5,* 25–36.

Corcoran, K., & Fischer, J. (1999a). *Measure of clinical practice: A sourcebook. Vol 1: Couples, families, and children* (3rd ed.). New York: Free Press.

Corcoran, K., & Fischer, J. (1999b). *Measures of clinical practice: A sourcebook. Vol. 2: Adults* (3rd ed.). New York: Free Press.

Corey, G. (2001a). *Theory and practice of psychotherapy* (6th ed.). Belmont, CA: Brooks/Cole.

Corey, G. (2001b). *Case approach to counseling and psychotherapy* (5th ed.). Belmont, CA: Brooks/Cole.

Cormier, W. H., & Cormier, L. S. (1991). *Interviewing strategies for helpers* (3rd ed.). Pacific Grove, CA: Brooks/Cole.

Cowles, L. A., & Lefcowitz, M. J. (1992). Interdisciplinary expectations of medical social worker in the hospital setting. *Health and Social Work, 17*(1), 58–65.

Cunningham, J. A. (1999, July). Resolving alcohol-related problems with and without treatment: The effects of different problem criteria (ST). *Journal of Studies on Alcohol, 60*(4), 463.

Curtis, O. (1999). *Chemical dependency: A family affair.* Pacific Grove, CA: Brooks/Cole.

Dassori, A. M., Miller, A. L., Velligan, D., Saldana, D., Diamond, P., & Mahurin, R. (1998). Ethnicity and negative symptoms in patients with schizophrenia. *Cultural Diversity and Mental Health, 4*(1), 65–69.

Davis, K. (1998). Managed health care: Forcing social work to make choices and changes. In G. Shamess & A. Lightburn (Eds.), *Humane managed care?* (pp. 409–429). Washington, DC: National Association of Social Workers Press.

Davis, S. R., & Meier, S. T. (2001). *The elements of managed care: A guide for helping professionals.* Belmont, CA: Brooks/Cole.

Dawson, D. A. (2000, September). The link between family history and early onset alcoholism: Earlier initiation of drinking or more rapid development of dependence? (Statistical data included). *Journal of Studies on Alcohol, 61*(5), 637.

Deitch, D. E. (1998). *Addiction counseling competencies: The knowledge, skills, and attitudes of professional practice* (Technical Assistance Publication Series 21, Pub. No. SMA 98–3178). Rockville, MD: U.S. Department of Health and Human Services.

deShazer, S. (1985). *Keys to solution in brief therapy.* New York: Norton.

Diagnostic and Statistical Manual of Mental Disorders. 2000. (4th ed., text rev.). Washington, DC: American Psychiatric Association.

DiClemente, C. C., Bellino, L. E., & Neavins, T. M. (1999). Motivation for change and alcohol treatment. *Alcohol Research and Health, 23*(2), 86–92.

Dumont, F., & Lecomte, C. (1987). Inferential processes in clinical work: Inquiry into logical errors that affect diagnostic judgments. *Professional Pathology: Research and Practice, 18,* 433–438.

Dumont, M. P. (1987). A diagnostic parable: First edition—Unrevised. *Journal of Reviews and Commentary in Mental Health, 2,* 9–12.

Duncan, T. E., Duncan, S. C., & Hops, H. (1998, July). Latent variable modeling of longitudinal and multilevel alcohol use data. *Journal of Studies on Alcohol, 59*(4), 399–409.

Dupper, D. (1992). Separate schools for Black males. *Social Work in Education, 14*(12), 75–76.

Dziegielewski, S. F. (1996). Managed care principles: The need for social work in the health care environment. *Crisis Intervention and Time-Limited Treatment, 3*(2), 97–110.

Dziegielewski, S. F. (1997a). Time limited brief therapy: The state of practice. *Crisis Intervention and Time Limited Treatment, 3*(3), 217–228.

Dziegielewski, S. F. (1997b). Should clinical social workers seek psychotropic medication prescription privileges? Yes. In B. A. Thyer (Ed.), *Controversial issues in social work practice* (pp. 152–165). Boston: Allyn & Bacon.

Dziegielewski, S. F. (1998). *The changing face of health care social work: Professional practice in the era of managed care.* New York: Springer.

Dziegielewski, S. F. (2002). Social work practice and herbal medicine. In A. R. Roberts & G. J. Greene (Eds.), *Social Workers Desk Reference* (pp. 651–660). New York: Oxford University Press.

Dziegielewski, S. F., & Holliman, D. (2001). Managed care and social work: Practice implications in an era of change. *Journal of Sociology and Social Welfare, 28*(2), 125–138.

Dziegielewski, S. F., Johnson, A., & Webb, E. (in press). *DSM-IV,* knowledge and application with social work professionals: A continuing education evaluation. *Social Work in Health Care.*

Dziegielewski, S. F., & Leon, A. M. (2001a). *Psychopharmacology and social work practice.* New York: Springer.

Dziegielewski, S. F., & Leon, A. M. (2001b). Time-limited case recording: Effective documentation in a changing environment. *Journal of Brief Therapy, 1*(1).

Dziegielewski, S. F., & Powers, G. T. (2000). Designs and procedures for evaluating crisis intervention. In A. R. Roberts (Ed.), *Crisis intervention handbook: Assessment, treatment and research (2nd ed.).* New York: Oxford University Press.

Dziegielewski, S. F., Resnick, C. A., & Krause, N. (1995). Shelter-based crisis intervention with battered women. In A. Roberts (Ed.), *Helping battered women: New perspectives and remedies* (pp. 159–172). New York: Oxford University Press.

Dziegielewski, S. F., & Wolfe, P. (2000). EMDR as a time-limited intervention for body image disturbance and self-esteem: A single subject case study design. *Journal of Psychotherapy in Independent Practice, 1*(3), 1–16.

Easing the emotional cost of schizophrenia. (1997). In News in Mental Health Nursing. *Journal of Psychosocial Nursing, 35*(2), 6.

Ecker, B., & Hulley, L. (1996). *Depth-oriented brief therapy: How to be brief when you were trained to be deep—and vice versa.* San Francisco: Jossey-Bass Publishers.

Eddy, M. F., & Walbroehl, G. S. (1998, April). *Recognition and treatment of obsessive-compulsive disorder.* Retrieved from www.aafp.org/afp/980401ap/eddy.html

Egan, G. (1998). *The skilled helper: A problem management approach to helping* (6th ed.). Pacific Grove, CA: Brooks/Cole.

Ellis, A. (1971). *Growth through reason.* Palo Alto, CA: Science and Behavior Books.

Ellis, A., & Grieger, R. (Eds.). (1977). *Handbook of rational-emotive therapy.* New York: Springer.

Epstein, L. (1994). Brief task-centered practice. In R. Edwards (Ed.), *Encyclopedia of social work* (19th ed., pp. 313–323). Washington, DC: National Association of Social Workers Press.

Ethics meet managed care. (1997, January). *NASW NEWS, 42*(1), 7.

Fanger, M. T. (1994). Brief therapies. In R. Edwards (Ed.), *Encyclopedia of social work* (19th ed., pp. 323–334). Washington, DC: National Association of Social Workers Press.

Federici, R. S. (1998) *Help for the hopeless child: A guide for families.* Alexandria, Virginia: Hennage Creative Printers.

Fiesta, J. (1995). Managed care: Whose liability? *Nursing Management, 26*(2), 31–32.

Fimerson, S. S. (1996). Individual therapy. In V. B. Carson & E. N. Nolan (Eds.), *Mental health nursing: The nurse patient journey* (pp. 367–384). Philadelphia: Saunders.

Findling, R. L. (2000). A double-blind pilot study of risperidone in the treatment of conduct disorder. *Journal of the American Academy of Child and Adolescent Psychiatry, 39*(4), 509–516.

Finfgeld, D. L. (1997). Resolution of drinking problems without formal treatment. *Perspectives in Psychiatric Care, 33*(3), 14–24.

First, M. B., Frances, A., & Pincus, H. A. (1995). *DSM-IV handbook of differential diagnosis.* Washington, DC: American Psychiatric Press.

Fischer, J. (Ed.). (1999). *Measures for clinical practice a sourcebook.* (3rd ed., Vol. 2). New York: Free Press.

Fischer, J., & Corcoran, K. (1994). *Measures of clinical practice: A sourcebook. Vol. 2: Adults* (2nd ed.). New York: Free Press.

Fischer, J. S. (2000). Taking the shock out of electroshock. *U.S. News & World Report, 128*(3), 46.

Flack, H. S. (1981). *The social status examination in health care.* Richmond: Virginia Commonwealth University, School of Social Work, Department of Continuing Education.

Flaum, M. (1995). Schizophrenia. In C. L. Shriqui & H. A. Nasrallah (Eds.), *Contemporary issues in the treatment of schizophrenia* (pp. 83–108). Washington, DC: American Psychiatric Press.

Frager, S. (2000). *Managing managed care.* New York: Wiley.

Frances, A., Pincus, H. A., Davis, W. W., Kline, M., First, M. B., & Widiger, T. A. (1991). The *DSM* field trials: Moving towards an empirically derived classification. *European Psychiatry, 6,* 307–314.

Frances, A., Pincus, H. A., Widiger, T. A., Davis, W. W., & First, M. B. (1990). *DSM-IV:* Work in progress. *American Journal of Psychiatry, 147,* 1439–1448.

Frances, A., & Ross, R. (1996). *DSM-IV case studies: A clinical guide to differential diagnosis.* Washington, DC: American Psychiatric Press.

Friedman, S. (1997). *Time-effective psychotherapy: Maximizing outcomes in an era of minimizing resources.* Needham Heights, MA: Allyn & Bacon.

Fuller, R. K., & Hiller-Sturmhofel, S. (1999). Alcoholism treatment in the United States: An overview. *Alcohol Research and Health, 23*(2), 69–77.

Garner, D. M. (1991). *Eating Disorders Inventory: Manual*. Odessa, FL: Psychological Assessment Resources.

Garner, D. M., & Garfinkel, P. E. (1997). *Handbook of treatment for eating disorders*. New York: Guilford Press.

Garner, D. M., Olmsted, M. P., & Polivy, J. (1983). Development and validation of a multidimensional eating disorder inventory for anorexia and bulimia. *International Journal of Eating Disorders, 2,* 15–34.

Gassman, R. A., Demone, H. W., & Abilal, R. (2001, Winter). Alcohol and other drug content in core courses: Encouraging substance abuse assessment (Statistical data included). *Journal of Social Work Education, 37*(1), 137.

Gaw, A. C. (1993). *Culture ethnicity, and mental health illness*. Washington, DC: American Psychiatric Press

George, A. A., & Tucker, J. A. (1996, July). Help-seeking for alcohol-related problems: Social contexts surrounding entry into alcoholism treatment or Alcoholics Anonymous. *Journal of Studies on Alcohol, 57*(4), 449–458.

George, C. (1996). A representational perspective of child abuse and prevention: Internal working models of attachment and caregiving. *Child Abuse and Neglect, 20*(5), 411–424.

Getz, W., Wiesen, A., Sue, S., & Ayers, A. (1974). *Fundamentals of crisis counseling*. Lexington, MA: Lexington Books.

Ghizzani, A., & Montomoli, M. (2000). Anorexia nervosa and sexuality in women: A review. *Journal of Sex Education and Therapy, 25,* 80–88.

Gilbert, L. A. (1991). Feminist contributions to counseling psychology. *Psychology of Women Quarterly, 15,* 537–547.

Gilbody, S. M., Kirk, S. F., & Hill, A. J. (1999). Vegetarianism in young women: Another means of weight control? *International Journal of Eating Disorders, 26,* 87–90.

Gilliland, B., & Gilliland, J. R. (1993). *Crisis intervention strategies*. Pacific Grove, CA: Brooks/Cole.

Gottesman, I. I. (1991). *Schizophrenia genesis: The origins of madness*. New York: Freeman.

Grant, J., & Cash, T. F. (1995). Cognitive-behavioral body-image therapy: Comparative efficacy of group and modest-contact treatments. *Behavior Therapy, 26,* 69–84.

Grim, P. (2000, July). Cut to the quick. *Discover, 21,* 38.

Griswold, K. S., & Pessar, L. F. (2000). Management of bipolar disorder. *Family Physician, 62,* 1343–1353, 1357–1358.

Gross, R., Rabinowitz, J., Feldman, D., & Boerma, W. (1996). Primary health care physicians' treatment of psychosocial problems: Implications for social work. *Health and Social Work, 21,* 89–94.

Gur, R. E., & Pearlson, G. D. (1993). Neuroimaging for schizophrenia research. *Schizophrenia Bulletin, 19*(2), 337–353.

Hales, D., & Hales, R. E. (1996). *Caring for the mind the comprehensive guide to mental health*. New York: Bantam Books.

Hales, R. (1995). Anxiety disorders. In D. Hales & R. Hales (Eds.), *Caring for the mind* (pp. 119–153). New York: Bantam Books.

Hall, L. L. (1997). Fighting phobias: The things that go bump in the mind. *FDA Consumer, 31*(13), 13–15.

Hanson, R. F., & Spratt, E. G. (2000). Reactive attachment disorder: What we know about the disorder and implications for treatment. *Child Maltreatment, 5*(2), 137–145.

Harrison, D., Thyer, B., & Wodarski, J. (1996). *Cultural diversity and social work practice.* Springfield, IL: Charles C Thomas.

Harrow, M., Goldberg, J. F., Grossman, L. S., & Meltzer, H. Y. (1990). Outcome in manic disorders: A naturalistic follow-up study. *Archives of General Psychiatry* (47), 665–671.

Hartmann, D. E. (1995). *Neuropsycological toxicology* (2nd ed.). New York: Plenum Press.

Harvard Medical School. (1999, January). In brief: Olanzapine preferred. *Harvard Mental Health Letter, 15,* 7.

Harvard Medical School. (2000a). Treatment of alcoholism: Part I (ITEM00130001). *Harvard Mental Health Letter, 16,* 11.

Harvard Medical School. (2000b). Treatment of alcoholism: Part II (ITEM00172001). *Harvard Mental Health Letter, 16,* 12.

Harvard Medical School. (2001). Bipolar disorder: Part I. *Harvard Mental Health Letter, 17*(10), 1–4.

Hayashida, M. (1998, Winter). An overview of outPatient and inPatient detoxification. *Alcohol Health and Research World, 22*(1), 44–47.

Helms, J. E. (Ed.). (1990). *Black and White racial identity: Theory, research, and practice.* Westport, CT: Praeger.

Henderson, R., Landry, M., Phillips, C., & Shuman, D. (1994). *Intensive outpatient treatment for alcohol and other drug abuse: Treatment improvement protocol (TIP)* (Series No. 8, Publication No. SMA 94B2077). Rockville, MD: U.S. Department of Health and Human Services.

Hepworth, D. H., & Larsen, J. A. (1993). *Direct social work practice: Theory and skills* (4th ed.). Pacific Grove, CA: Brooks/Cole.

Hepworth, D. H., Rooney, R. H., & Larsen, J. (1997). *Direct social work practice: Theory and skills* (5th ed.). Pacific Grove, CA: Brooks/Cole.

Herman, J. L. (1992). *Trauma and recovery: The aftermath of violence from domestic abuse to political terror.* New York: Basic Books.

Hill, S. Y., & Yuan, H. (1999, January). Familial density of alcoholism and onset of adolescent drinking. *Journal of Studies on Alcohol, 60*(1), 7.

Hirschfeld, R. M., Williams, J. B., Spitzer, R. L., Calabrese, J. R., Flynn, L., Keck, P. E., et al. (2000). Development and validation of a screening instrument for bipolar spectrum disorder: The mood disorder questionnaire. *American Journal of Psychiatry, 157*(11), 1873–1875.

Hodson, D. S., & Skeen, P. (1994). Sexuality and aging: The hammerlock of myths. *Journal of Applied Gerontology, 13,* 219–234.

Hoffman, R. E. (2000, March 25). Transcranial magnetic stimulation and auditory hallucinations in schizophrenia. *Lancet, 355,* 1073–1076.

Holcomb-McCoy, C. C., & Myers, J. E. (1999). Multicultural competence and counselor training: A national survey. *Journal of Counseling and Development, 77,* 294–302.

Hollandsworth, J., Jr. (1986). *Physiology and behavior therapy: Conceptual guidelines for the clinician.* New York: Plenum Press.

Hong, C. J., Lee, Y. L., Sim, C. B., & Hwu, H. G. (1997). Dopamine D4 receptor variants in Chinese sporadic and familial schizophrenics. *American Journal of Medical Genetics (Neuropsychiatric Genetics), 74,* 412–415.

Hudson, W. W. (1990). *The WALMYR Assessment Scale Scoring manual.* Tempe, AZ: WALMYR Publishing.

Hughes, D. A. (1997). *Facilitating developmental attachment: The road to emotional recovery and behavioral change in foster and adopted children.* Northvale, NJ: Aronson.

Hughes, D. A. (1998). *Building the bonds of attachment: Awakening the love in deeply troubled children.* Northvale, NJ: Aronson.

Hughes, D. A. (1999). Adopting children with attachment problems. *Child Welfare League of America, 77*(5), 541–560.

Hughes, D. A. (2000, August). [Letter to the editor]. *Connections,* 2.

Jacobs, M. H. (1995). What is schizophrenia. In S. Vinogradov & Yalom, I. D. (Eds.), *Treating schizophrenia* (pp. 1–25). San Francisco: Jossey-Bass.

Jaffe, D. J. (1998, January). *Research begins to yield understanding of childhood schizophrenia* (NAMI/NYC Home Page). Retrieved from www.schizophrenia.com/ami /diagnosi/kidSZ.html

Jehu, D., Klassen, C., & Gazan, M. (1986). Cognitive restructuring of distorted beliefs associated with childhood sexual abuse. *Journal of Social Work and Human Sexuality, 4,*(1), 49–69.

Johnson, B. A., & Ait-Daud, N. (1999). Medications to treat alcoholism. *Alcohol Research and Health, 23*(2), 99–106.

Johnson, R. S., & Berger, C. S. (1990). The challenge of change: Enhancing social work services at a time of cutback. *Health and Social Work, 15*(3), 181–190.

Johnstone, L. (1999, February). Adverse psychological effects of ECT. *Journal of Mental Health, 8*(1), 69–86.

Jones, E. (1995). The construction of gender in family therapy. In C. Burck & B. Speed (Eds.), *Gender power and relationships* (pp. 7–23). New York: Routledge.Jongsma, Jr., A. E., & Peterson, L. M. (1995). *The complete psychotherapy treatment planner.* New York: Wiley.

Jones, K. (1969). *Drugs and alcohol.* New York: Harper & Row.

Jongsma, Jr., A. E., & Peterson, L. M. (1995). *The complete psychotherapy treatment planner.* New York: Wiley.

Kane, J. (1993). Future directions in schizophrenia research. *Psychiatric Annals, 23*(4), 222–225.

Kaplan, A., & Dziegielewski, S. F. (1999). Graduate social work students' attitudes toward spirituality and religion: Issues for education and practice. *Social Work and Christianity: An International Journal, 26*(1), 25–39.

Kaplan, H. I., Sadock, B. J., & Grebb, J. A. (1994). *Synopsis of psychiatry: Behavioral sciences clinical psychiatry.* Baltimore: Williams & Wilkins.

Kaplan, M. (1983a). A woman's view of *DSM-III. American Psychologist, 38,* 786–792.

Kaplan, M. (1983b). The issue of sex bias in *DSM-III:* Comments on articles by Spitzer, Williams, and Kass. *American Psychologist, 38,* 802–803.

Karasu, T. B., Docherty, J. P., Gelenberg, A., Kuper, D. J., Merriam, A. E., & Shadoan, R. (1993). Practice guidelines for major depressive disorder in adults. *American Journal of Psychiatry, 150*(Suppl.), 1–26.

Karls, J. M., & Wandrei, K. M. (Eds.). (1996a). *Person-in-environment system: The PIE classification system for social functioning problems.* Washington, DC: National Association of Social Workers Press.

Karls, J. M., & Wandrei, K. M. (1996b). *PIE manual: Person-in-environment system: The PIE classification system for social functioning problems.* Washington, DC: National Association of Social Workers Press.

Kass, F., Spitzer, R. L., & Williams, J. B. W. (1983). An empirical study of the issue of sex bias in the diagnostic criteria of *DSM-III* Axis II personality disorders. *American Psychologist, 38,* 799–801.

Keck, G., & Kupecky, R. (1995). *Adopting the hurt child.* Colorado Springs, CO: Pinton Press.

Kelly, J. J., & Rice, S. (1986). The aged. In H. L. Gochros, J. S. Gochros, & J. Fischer (Eds.), *Helping the sexually oppressed* (pp. 99–108). Englewood Cliffs, NJ: Prentice-Hall.

Keltner, N. L., & Folks, D. G. (Eds.). (2001). *Psychotropic drugs* (3rd ed.). St. Louis, MO: Mosby.

Kendler, K. S., & Diehl, S. R. (1993). The genetics of schizophrenia: A current, genetic epidemiological perspective. *Schizophrenia Bulletin, 19*(2), 261–286.

Kendler, K. S., Gruenberg, A. M., & Tsuang, M. T. (1985). Psychiatric illness in first degree relatives of schizophrenic and surgical control patients: A family study using *DSM-III* criteria. *Archives of General Psychiatry, 42*(8), 770–779.

Kendler, K. S., McGuire, M., Gruengerg, A. M., O'Hare, A., Spellman, M., & Walsh, D. (1993). The Roscommo family study. 1: Methods, diagnosis of probands and risk of schizophrenia in relatives. *Archives of General Psychiatry, 50*(7), 527–540.

Keshavan, M., Marshall, W., Shazly, M., & Paki, M. (1988). Neuroendocrine dysfunction in schizophrenia: A familial perspective. *Psychiatry Research, 23*(5), 345–348.

Keshavan, M. S., Montrose, D. M., Pierri, J. N., Dick, E. L., Rosenberg, D., Talagala, L., et al. (1997). Magnetic resonance imaging and spectroscopy in offspring at risk for schizophrenia: Preliminary studies. *Progressions in Neuro-Psychopharmacological and Biological Psychiatry, 21,* 1285–1295.

Kessler, S. (1979). The genetics of schizophrenia. *Social Biology, 26*(2), 142–153.

Kilpatrick, A. C., & Holland, T. P. (1999). *Working with families: An integrative model by level of need.* Boston: Allyn & Bacon.

King, G., & Lorenson, J. (1989, June). Alcoholism training for social workers. *Social Casework: The Journal of Contemporary Social Work, 375–385.*

Kirschfeld, R. M., Williams, J. B., Spitzer, R. L., Calabrese, J. R., Flynn, L., Keck, P. E., et al. (2000). Development and validation of a screening instrument for bipolar spectrum disorder: The Mood Disorder Questionnaire. *American Journal of Psychiatry, 157*(11), 1873–1875.

Klerman, G. L., Weissman, M. M., Markowitz, J. C., Glick, I., Wilner, P. J., Mason, B., et al. (1994). Medication in psychotherapy. In A. E. Bergin & S. B. Garfield (Eds.), *Handbook of psychotherapy and behavior change* (4th ed., pp. 734–782). New York: Wiley.

Koerner, K., & Linehan, M. (2000). Research on dialectical behavior therapy for patients with borderline personality disorder. *Psychiatric Clinics of North America, 23*(1), 151–167.

Kramer, M. (1978). Population change and schizophrenia. In L. Wynee, R. Cromwell, S. Matthysse, M. Tooher, B. Spring, & L. Sugarman (Eds.), *The nature of schizophrenia: New approaches to research and treatment* (pp. 1970–1985). New York: Wiley.

Kushner, J. N., & Associates. (1995). *Purchasing managed care services for alcohol and other drug treatment: Technical Assistance Protocol (TAP)* (Series No. 16, Publication No. SMA 96–3091). Rockville, MD: U.S. Department of Health and Human Services.

Kutchins, H., & Kirk, S. A. (1986). The reliability of *DSM-III:* A critical review. *Social Work Research and Abstracts, 22,* 3–12.

Kutchins, H., & Kirk, S. A. (1988). The business of diagnosis. *Social Work, 33,* 215–220.

Kutchins, H., & Kirk, S. A. (1993). *DSM-IV* and the hunt for gold: A review of the treasure map. *Research on Social Work Practice, 3*(2), 219–235.

Lambert, L. (1998). New medications aid cognition in schizophrenia. *Journal of the American Medical Association, 280*(11), 953.

Larimer, M. E., Palmer, R. S., & Marlatt, G. A. (1999). Overview of Marlatt's Cognitive Behavioral Model. *Alcohol Research and Health, 23*(2), 151–160.

Latorre, M. A. (2000, April/June). A holistic view of psychotherapy: Connecting mind, body, and spirit. *Perspectives in Psychiatric Care, 36*(2), 67.

Lauver, P., & Harvey, D. R. (1997). *The practical counselor: Elements of effective helping.* Pacific Grove, CA: Brooks/Cole.

Lefley, H. P., & Pederson, P. B. (1986). *Cross-cultural training for mental health professionals.* Springfield, IL: Charles C Thomas.

Lehmann, H. E., & Ban, T. A. (1997, March). The history of the psychopharmacology of schizophrenia. *Canadian Journal of Psychiatry, 42*(2), 152–162.

Leon, A. M., & Dziegielewski, S. F. (1999). The psychological impact of migration: Practice considerations in working with Hispanic women. *Journal of Social Work Practice, 13*(1), 69–82.

Levy, T. M., & Orlans, M. (1998). *Attachment, trauma, and healing: Understanding and treating attachment disorder in children and families.* Washington, DC: Child Welfare League of America.

Lewinsohn, P. M. (2000). The OADP-CDS: A brief screener for adolescent conduct disorder. *Journal of the American Academy of Child and Adolescent Psychiatry, 39*(7), 888–895.

Libassi, C., & Parish, M. S. (1990). Strengthening the "bio" in the biopsychosocial paradigm. *Journal of Social Work Education, 26,* 109–123.

Liberman, R. (1973). Behavioral approaches to family and couple therapy. In J. Fischer (Ed.), *Interpersonal helping: Emerging approaches for social work practice* (pp. 200–229). Springfield, IL: Charles C Thomas.

Lieberman, J. A., Alvir, J. M. J., Woerner, M., Degreef, G., Bilder, R. M., Ashtari, M., et al. (1992). Prospective study of psychobiology in first-episode schizophrenia at hillside hospital. *Schizophrenia Bulletin, 18*(3), 351–371.

Lieberman, J. A., & Koreen, A. R. (1993). Neurochemistry and euroendocrinology of schizophrenia: A selective review. *Schizophrenia Bulletin, 19*(2), 371–430.

Lin, K., & Kleinman, A. M. (1988). Psychopathology and clinical course of schizophrenia: A cross-cultural perspective. *Schizophrenia Bulletin, 19*(2), 371–430.

Lindeman, M., Stark, K., & Latvala, K. (2000). Vegetarianism and eating-disordered thinking. *International Journal of Eating Disorders, 8,* 157–165.

Linehan, M. (1993). *Skills training manual for treating borderline personality disorder.* New York: Guilford Press.

Linehan, M., Schmidt, H., Dimeff, L., Craft, C., Kanter, J., & Comtis, K. (1999). Dialectical behavior therapy for patients with borderline personality disorder and drug-dependence. *American Journal of Addictions, 3*(8), 279–292.

Linehan, M., Tutek, D., Heard, H., & Armstrong, H. (1994). Interpersonal outcome of cognitive behavioral treatment for chronically suicidal borderline patients. *American Journal of Psychiatry, 151*(12), 1771–1775.

Linehan, M. N., Goldstein, J. L., Nielsen, S. L., & Chiles, J. A. (1983). Reasons for staying alive when you are thinking of killing yourself: The Reasons for Living Inventory. *Journal of Counseling and Clinical Psychology, 51,* 276–286.

Long, P. W. (2000). *Schizophrenia: A handbook for families: Schizophrenia youth's greatest disaster.* Retrieved from www.mentalhealth.com/book/p40-sc02.html

Longabaugh, R., & Morgenstern, J. (1999). Cognitive behavioral coping skills therapy for alcohol dependence: Current status and future directions. *Alcohol Research and Health, 23*(2), 78–85.

Lorr, M., & Wunderlich, R. A. (1988). A Semantic Differential Mood Scale. *Journal of Clinical Psychology, 44,* 33–38.

Lott, B. (1991). Social psychology: Humanist roots and feminist future. *Psychology of Women Quarterly, 15,* 505–519.

Lowery, M. (1996). Total quality management. In V. B. Carson & E. N. Arnold (Eds.), *Mental health nursing: The nurse patient journey* (pp. 1173–1192). Philadelphia: Saunders.

Lukoff, D., Wallace, C. J., Liberman, R. P., & Burke, K. (1986). A holistic program for chronic schizophrenic patients. *Schizophrenia Bulletin, 12*(2), 274–282.

MacCluskie, K. C., & Ingersoll, R. E. (2001). *Becoming a 21st century agency counselor.* Belmont, CA: Brooks/Cole, Thompson Learning.

MacKeen, D. (1999). *The outer limits of schizophrenia treatment* (Salon.com Health & Body). Retrieved from www.salon.com/health/feature/1999/12/01 /schizophrenics/?CP=110

MacPhillamy, D. J., & Lewinsohn, P. M. (1982). The Pleasant Events Schedule: Studies on reliability, validity and scale intercorrelation. *Journal of Consulting and Clinical Psychology, 50,* 363–380.

Maier, W., Hallmeyer, J., Minges, J., & Lichtermann, D. (1990). Morbid risks in relatives of affective, schizoaffective, and schizophrenic patients: Results of a family study. In A. Maneros & M. T. Tsuang (Eds.), *Affective and schizoaffective disorders: Similarities and differences.* New York: Springer-Verlag.

Malhotra, A. K., Pinsky, D. A., & Breier, A. (1996). Future antipsychotic agents: Clinical implications. In A. Breier (Ed.), *The new pharmacotherapy of schizophrenia* (pp. 41–56). Washington, DC: American Psychiatric Press.

Mancoske, R., Standifer, D., & Cauley, C. (1994). The effectiveness of brief counseling services for battered women. *Research on Social Work Practice, 4*(1), 53–63.

Manisses Communication Group Incorporated. (1999, March). Mood stabilizers effective in children with mania. In What's new in research. *Brown University Child and Adolescent Behavior Letter, 15*(3), 4.

Manisses Communication Group Incorporated. (2001, March). Venlafaxine may be effective for bipolar depression. *Psychopharmacology Update, 12*(1), 1.

Marin, G. (1993). Defining culturally appropriate community interventions: Hispanics as a case study. *Journal of Community Psychology, 21,* 149–161.

Marks, I. M., & Mathews, A. M. (1979). Brief standard self-rating for phobic patients. *Behaviour Research and Therapy, 17,* 263–267.

Mattick, R. P., & Newman, C. R. (1991). Social phobia and avoidant personality disorder. *International Journal of Psychiatry, 3,* 163–173.

Mattick, R. P., & Peters, L. (1988). Treatment of severe social phobia: Effects of guided exposure with and without cognitive restructuring. *Journal of Consulting and Clinical Psychology, 56,* 251–260.

Maxmen, J. S., & Ward, N. G. (1995). Schizophrenia and related disorders. In J. S. Maxmen & N. G. Ward (Eds.), *Essential psychopathology and its treatment* (pp. 173–194). New York: Norton.

Maxmen, J. S., & Ward, N. G. (1996). *Essential psychopathology and its treatment* (2nd ed., pp. 419–449). New York: Norton.

May, P. R. (1976). When, what, why? Psychopharmacotherapy and other treatments in schizophrenia. *Comprehensive Psychiatry, 17.*

McAllister, R., & Caltabiano, M. L. (1994). Self-esteem, body image and weight in noneating-disordered women. *Psychological Reports, 75,* 1339–1343.

McCaulay, M., Mintz, L., & Glenn, A. (1988). Body image, self-esteem, and depression-proneness: Closing the gender gap. *Sex Roles, 18*(7/8), 381–391.

McElroy, S. L., Strakowski, S. M., West, S. A., & Keck, P. E. (1997). Phenomenology of adolescent and adult mania in hospitalized patients with bipolar disorder. *American Journal of Psychiatry, 154*(1), 44–49.

Meeks, S. (1999). Bipolar disorder in latter half of life: Symptom presentation, global functioning, and age of onset. *Journal of Affective Disorders, 52*(2), 161–167.

Mendelson, B., & White, D. (1985). Development of self-body-esteem in overweight youngsters. *Developmental Psychology, 21*(1), 90–96.

Mendelson, J., & Mello, N. (1992). *Medical diagnosis and treatment of alcoholism.* New York: McGraw-Hill.

Merck. (2000). *The physician guide to diagnosis and treatment.* Whitehouse Station, NJ: Merck.

Milkman, H., & Sederer, L. (1990). *Treatment choices for alcoholism and drug abuse.* New York: Lexington Books.

Miller, N. S., & Gold, M. S. (1998, July). Management of withdrawal syndromes and relapse prevention in drug and alcohol dependence. *American Family Physician, 58*(1), 139–147.

Mitchell, R. W. (1991). *Documentation in counseling records.* Washington, DC: American College Association.

Modesto-Lowe, V., & Kranzler, H. R. (1999). Diagnosis and treatment of alcohol-dependent patients with comorbid psychiatric disorders. *Alcohol Research and Health, 23*(2), 144–150.

Mohandle, K., & Duffy, J. E. (1999). Understanding subjects with paranoid schizophrenia. *FBI Law Enforcement Bulletin, 68*(12), 8–16.

Moise, F. N., & Petrides, G. (1996). Case study: Electroconvulsive therapy in adolescents. *Journal of the American Academy of Child and Adolescent Psychiatry, 35*(3), 312–319.

Moore, D. P., & Jefferson, J. W. (1997). *Handbook of medical psychiatry.* St. Louis, MO: Mosby.

Morales, A. T., & Schaefer, B. W. (1998). *Social work: A profession of many faces* (8th ed.). Boston: Allyn & Bacon.

Moras, K. (1997, May). Potential applications of behavioral decision research to treatments for drug abuse, related risky behaviors, and other problems: A comment on Fischhoff and Downs (Response to article by Baruch Fischhoff and Julie Downs in this issue, p. 154, Special section: Behavior Therapy and Psychological Science). *Psychological Science, 8*(3), 159–162.

Morey, L. C. (1996, Winter). Patient placement criteria: Linking typologies to managed care. *Alcohol Health and Research World, 20*(1), 36–45.

Munby, J., & Johnson, D. W. (1980). Agoraphobia: The long term follow-up of behavioural treatment. *British Journal of Psychiatry, 137,* 418–427.

Myers, D. (1992). *Psychology* (3rd ed.). New York: Worth.

Myrick, H., & Anton, R. F. (1998, Winter). Treatment of alcohol withdrawal. *Alcohol Health and Research World, 22*(1), 38–44.

National Clearinghouse for Alcohol and Drug Information. (1994). *ATOD resource guide: Women.* K. Zuckerman (Ed.), Center For Substance Abuse Prevention. Rockville, MD: Author.

National Clearinghouse for Alcohol and Drug Information. (1995a). *Fact sheet on domestic violence and alcohol and other drugs* (Inventory No. ML001). Rockville, MD: Author.

National Clearinghouse for Alcohol and Drug Information. (1995b, Spring). *Making the link fact sheet: Alcohol, tobacco, and other drugs and women's health* (Inventory No. ML011). Rockville, MD: Author.

National Institute of Mental Health. (1999). *Schizophrenia* (chap. 9). Retrieved from NIMH Web site: www.nimh.gov/publicat/schizoph.htm

National Institute on Mental Health. (2000). *Bipolar disorder research at the National Institute of Mental Health* (NIH Publication N0. 00–4500). Bethesda, MD: Author.

Nugent, W. R., & Thomas, J. W. (1993). Validation of the self-esteem rating scale. *Research on Social Work Practice, 3,* 191–207.

Obsessive-Compulsive Disorder Treatment. (2000). Retrieved from http://www.mentalhelp.net/poc/view_index.php/?idx=37&id=197

O'Connor, K., Todorov, C., Robillard, S., Borgeat, G., & Brault, M. (1999). Cognitive-behavioral therapy and medication in the treatment of obsessive-compulsive disorder: A controlled study. *Canadian Journal of Psychiatry, 44,* 64–70.

O'Donnell, M. P. (1994). Preface. In M. P. O'Donnell & J. S. Harris (Eds.), *Health promotion in the work place* (pp. ix–xvi). Albany, NY: Delmar.

O'Hanlon, W. H., & Weiner-Davis, M. (1989). *In search of solutions: A new direction in psychotherapy.* New York: Norton.

Olson, R., Ganley, R., Devine, V., & Dorsey, G. (1981). Long-term effects of behavioral versus insight-oriented therapy with inPatient alcoholics. *Journal of Consulting and Clinical Psychology, 49*(6), 866–877.

Pande, P. (1987). Personality patterns of alcoholics [CD-ROM]. *Journal of Psychological Research, 31*(1), 1–3. Abstract retrieved from PsychLIT: AN 75–36076.

Parad, H. J., & Parad, L. G. (1990). *Crisis intervention: The practitioner's sourcebook for brief therapy.* Milwaukee, WI: Family Service America.

Pato, M. T., Pato, C. N., & Gunn, S. A. (1998). Biological treatments for obsessive-compulsive disorder: Clinical applications. In R. P. Swinson, M. M. Antony, S. Rachman, & M. A. Richter (Eds.), *Obsessive-compulsive disorder: Theory, research, and treatment* (pp. 327–347). New York: Guilford Press.

Paul, A. M. (1999). *Painting insanity black.* Retrieved from Salon.com Health & Body Web site: www.salon.com/books/it/1999/12/01/schizo/?CP=SAL&DN=110

Peele, S. (1996, September/October). Recovering from an all-or-nothing approach to alcohol. *Psychology Today, 29*(5), 35–42.

Perlman, H. H. (1957). *Social casework: A problem solving process.* Chicago: University of Chicago Press.

Perry, A., Tarrier, N., Morriss, R., McCarthy, E., & Limb, K. (1999). Randomised controlled trial of efficacy of teach patients with bipolar disorder to identify early symptoms of relapse and obtain treatment. *British Medical Journal, 218*(7177), 149–154.

Perry, C., Banon, E., & Ianni, F. (1999). Effectiveness of psychotherapy for personality disorders. *American Journal of Psychiatry, 156,* 1312–1321.

Perry, P. (1997, July/August). Personality disorders: Coping with the borderline. *Saturday Evening Post, 269,* 44–54.

Petrakis, I., & Krystal, J. (1997, Spring). Neuroscience: Implications for treatment. *Alcohol Health and Research World, 21*(2), 157–161.

PDR: Medical dictionary. (1995). Montvale, NJ: Medical Economics.

Physician's Desk Reference. (2000). *Physician's desk reference* (54th ed.). Montvale, NJ: Medical Economics.

Physician's Desk Reference. (2001). *Physician's desk reference* (55th ed.). Montvale, NJ: Medical Economics.

Pickle, P. (2000). Community-focused attachment services. *Handbook of Attachment Interventions,* 261–277.

Pliner, P., Chaiken, S., & Flett, G. (1990, June). Gender differences in concern with body weight and physical appearance over the life span. *Personality and Social Psychology Bulletin, 16*(2), 263–273.

Pollak, J., Levy, S., & Breitholtz, T. (1999, Summer). Screening for medical and neurodevelopmental disorders for the professional counselor. *Journal of Counseling Development, 77,* 350–357.

Pomeroy, C. (1996). Anorexia nervosa, bulimia nervosa, and binge eating disorder: Assessment of physical status. In J. K. Thompson (Ed.), *Body image, eating disorders and obesity* (pp. 83–107). Washington, DC: American Psychological Association.

Powers, G. T., Meenaghan, T., & Toomey, B. (1985). Practice-focused research. Englewood Cliffs, NJ: Prentice-Hall.

Queralt, M. (1996). *The social environment and human behavior: A diversity perspective.* Boston: Allyn & Bacon.

Rabak-Wagener, J., & Eickhoff-Shemek, J. (1998). The effect of medial analysis on attitudes and behaviors regarding body image among college students. *Journal of American College Health, 47*(1), 29–36.

Rankin, E. A. (1996). Patient and family education. In V. B. Carson & E. N. Arnold (Eds.), *Mental health nursing: The nurse patient journey* (pp. 503–516). Philadelphia: Saunders.

Rauch, J. (1993). Introduction. In J. Rauch (Ed.), *Assessment: A sourcebook for social work practice.* Milwaukee, WI: Families International.

Raz, S., & Raz, N. (1990). Structural brain abnormalities in the major psychosis: A quantitative review of the evidence from computerized imaging. *Psychological Bulletin, 108*(1), 93–108.

Reamer, F. G. (1994). Social work values and ethics. In F. Reamer (Ed.), *The foundations of social work knowledge* (pp. 195–230). New York: Columbia University Press.

Reamer, F. G. (1998). The evolution of social work ethics. *Social Work, 43*(6), 488–500.

Reber, K. (1996). Children at risk for reactive attachment disorder: Assessment, diagnosis and treatment. *Progress: Family Systems Research and Therapy, 5,* 83–98.

Reid, W. H. (1997). Anxiety disorders. In W. H. Reid, G. U. Balis, & B. J. Sutton (Eds.), *The treatment of psychiatric disorders* (3rd ed., pp. 239–262). Bristol, PA: Brunner/Mazel.

Reid, W. H., Keller, S., Leatherman, M., & Mason, M. (1998). ECT in Texas. *Journal of Clinical psychiatry, 59,* 5–13.

Reiss, R. K. (1995). *Assessment and treatment of patients with coexisting mental illness and alcohol and other drug abuse* (DHHS Publication No. 95–3061). Rockville, MD: U.S. Department of Health and Human Services.

Resnick, C., & Dziegielewski, S. F. (1996). The relationship between therapeutic termination and job satisfaction among medical social workers. *Social Work in Health Care, 23*(3), 17–35.

Resnick, W. M., & Carson, V. B. (1996). The journey colored by mood disorders. In V. B. Carson & E. N. Arnold (Eds.), *Mental health nursing: The nurse patient journey* (pp. 759–792). Philadelphia: Saunders.

Ridley-Siegert, D. (2000). Anorexia nervosa: Treatment with olanzapine. *British Journal of Psychiatry, 177,* 87.

Roberts, A., & Dziegielewski, S. F. (1995). Foundation skills and applications of crisis intervention and cognitive therapy. In A. Roberts (Ed.), *Crisis intervention and time-limited cognitive treatment* (pp. 3–27). Thousand Oaks, CA: Sage.

Rosen, J. (1995). Assessment and treatment of body image disturbance. In K. Brownell & C. Fairburn (Eds.), *Eating disorders and obesity a comprehensive handbook* (pp. 369–373). New York: Guilford Press.

Rosen, J. C., Srebnik, D., Saltzberg, E., & Wendt, S. (1991). Development of a body image avoidance questionnaire. *Psychological Assessment, 3,* 32–37.

Ross, M. F. (1999, March). *UF researchers cite possible link between autism, schizophrenia and diet.* Retrieved from University of Florida: Health Science Center Web site: www.health.ufl.edu/hscc/storiesmar99/autism.html

Roth, A., & Fonagy, P. (1996). Anxiety disorders I: Phobias, generalized anxiety disorder, and panic disorder with and without agoraphobia. In A. Roth & P. Fonagy (Eds.), *What works for whom? A critical review of psychotherapy research* (pp. 113–144). New York: Guilford Press.

Rounsaville, B. J., O'Malley, S., Foley, S., & Weissman, M. M. (1988). Role of manual-guided training in the conduct and efficacy of interpersonal psychotherapy for depression. *Journal of Consulting and Clinical Psychology, 56*(5), 681–688.

Rudman, W. J. (2000). *Coding and documentation of domestic violence.* Retrieved from endabuse.org/programs/display.php3?DoclD=54

Rudolph, C. S. (2000). Educational challenges facing health care social workers in the twenty-first century. *Professional Development, 3*(1), 31–41.

Saklad, S. R. (2000). APA studies focus on side effects, efficacy of antipsychotics. *Psychopharmacology Update, 11*(1), 1.

Salesby, D. (1994). Culture, theory and narrative: The intersections of meanings in practice. *Social Work, 39*(4), 351–359.

Schlundt, D. G. (1989). Computerized behavioral assessment of eating behavior in bulimia: The self monitoring analysis system. In J. W. Jornson (Ed.), *Advances in eating disorders 2: Bulimia* (pp. 1–23). New York: JAI Press.

Schneider, A. W., Hyer, K., & Luptak, M. (2000, November). Suggestions to social workers for surviving in managed care. *Health and Social Work, 25*(4), 276.

Schram, B., & Mandell, B. R. (1997). *Human services: Policy and practice* (3rd ed.). Boston: Allyn & Bacon.

Schulz, S. C. (2000). New antipsychotic medications: More than old wine and new bottles. *Bulletin of the Menninger Clinic, 64*(1), 60–75.

Schutte, N. S., & Malouff, J. M. (1995). *Sourcebook of adult assessment strategies.* New York: Plenum Press.

Schwartz, G. E., Davidson, R. J., & Goleman, D. J. (1978). Patterning of cognitive and somatic processes in self-regulation of anxiety: Effects of meditation versus exercise. *Psychosomatic Medicine, 40*(1), 321–328.

Seibert, S., & Gruenfeld, L. (1992). Masculinity, femininity, and behavior in groups. *Small Group Research, 23*(1), 95–112.

Shapiro, F. (1995). *Eye movement desensitization and reprocessing: Basic principles, protocols, and procedures.* New York: Guilford Press.

Shapiro, F. (1997). *EMDR in brief.* Retrieved from www.emdr.com/brief.htm

Shapiro, S. (1981). *Contemporary theories of schizophrenia.* Hightstown, NJ: McGraw-Hill.

Sheafor, B. W., Horejsi, C. R., & Horejsi, G. A. (1997). *Techniques and guidelines for social work practice* (4th ed.). Needham Heights, MA: Allyn & Bacon.

Sholomskas, A. J., Chevron, E. S., Prusoff, B. A., & Berry, C. (1983). Short-term interpersonal therapy (IPT) with the depressed elderly: Case reports and discussion. *American Journal of Psychotherapy, 38*(4), 552–566.

Shore, D. (Ed.). (1993). *Special report: Schizophrenia* (DHHS Publication). Washington, DC: U.S. Government Printing Office.

Siegelman, L. (1990). *Selecting effective treatments.* San Francisco: Jossey-Bass.

Sifton, D. (Ed.). (1998). *The PDR pocket guide to prescription drugs* (3rd ed.). New York: Pocket Books.

Simon, E. P., Showers, N., Blumenfield, S., Holden, G., & Wu, X. (1995). Delivery of home care services after discharge: What really happens. *Health and Social Work, 20*(1), 6–14.

Simpson, E., Pistorello, J., Begin, A., Costello, E., Levinson, J., Mulberry, S., et al. (1998). Use of dialectical behavior therapy in a partial hospital program for women with borderline personality disorder. *Psychiatric Services, 49*(5), 669–673.

Siris, S. G. (2000). Management of depression in schizophrenia. *Psychiatric Annals, 30*(1), 13–17.

Skidmore, R. A., Thackeray, M. G., & Farley, O. W. (1997). *Introduction to social work* (7th ed.). Boston: Allyn & Bacon.

Skinner, B. F. (1953). *Science and human behavior.* New York: Macmillan.

Slomski, A. J. (2000, January 5). Group practice economics. *Medical Economics Archive.*

Smyrnios, K. X., & Kirkby, R. J. (1992). Brief family therapies: A comparison of theoretical and technical issues. *Journal of Family Therapy, 13*(3), 119–127.

Sobal, J. (1995). Social influences on body weight. In K. Brownell & C. Fairburn (Eds.), *Eating disorders and obesity a comprehensive handbook* (pp. 73–77). New York: Guilford Press.

Spitzer, R. (1980). Introduction. In *Diagnostic and statistical manual of mental disorders.* Washington, DC: American Psychiatric Press.

Sroufe, L. A., Carlson, E. A., Levy, A. K., & Egeland, B. (1999). Implications of attachment theory for developmental psychopathology. *Development and Psychopathology, 11,* 1–13.

Steinglass, P. (1976). Experimenting with family treatment approaches to alcoholism, 1950–1975: A review [CD-ROM]. *Family process,* 97–123. Abstract retrieved from PsychLIT: AN 3882.

Steps taken to watchdog managed care. (1997, January). *NASW NEWS, 42*(1), 12.

Substance Abuse and Mental Health Services Administration. (1998). *Treatment Episode Data Set (TEDS).* Available from www/dasis.samhsa.gov/teds.htm

Sutton, M. (2000, October). Cultural competence: It's not just political correctness: It's good medicine. *Family practice management* (pp. 1–6). Available on line: http://www.afp.org/fpm/20000000/58cult.html

Swartz-Kulstad, J. L., & Martin, W. E. (1999). Impact of culture and context on psychosocial adaption: The cultural and contextual guide process. *Journal of Counseling and Development, 77,* 281–293.

Taylor, S. (1996). Meta-analysis of cognitive-behavioral treatments for social phobia. *Journal of Behavioral Therapy and Experimental Psychiatry, 27*(1), 1–9.

Terry, L. L. (1992). Gender and family therapy: Adding a bi-level belief systems component to assessment. *Contemporary Family Therapy: An International Journal, 14*(3), 199–210.

Thomas, N. L. (2000). Parenting children with attachment disorders. *Handbook of attachment interventions* (pp. 261–277; DHHS Publication) *Healthy people 2000: National health promotion disease and prevention objectives.* Washington, DC: Department of Health and Human Services.

Thomas, V. (1989). Body-image satisfaction among Black women. *Journal of Social Psychology, 129*(1), 107–112.

Thyer, B. A., & Wodarski, J. S. (1998). *Handbook of empirical social work practice: Mental disorders* (Vol. 1). New York: Wiley.

Timko, C., Moos, R. H., Finney, J. W., Moos, B. S., & Kaplowitz, M. S. (1999, July). Long-term treatment careers and outcomes of previously untreated alcoholics (ST). *Journal of Studies on Alcohol, 60*(4), 437–445.

Tonnigan, J. S., Conners, G. J., & Miller, W. R. (1998). Special populations in Alcoholics Anonymous. *Alcohol Health and Research World, 22*(4), 281–285.

Turner, F. J. (Ed.). (1996). *Social work treatment: Interlocking theoretical approaches* (4th ed.). New York: Free Press.

Van Balkom, A. J. L. M., & Van Dyck, R. (1998). Combination treatments for obsessive-compulsive disorder. In R. P. Swinson, M. M. Antony, S. Rachman, & M. A. Richter (Eds.), *Obsessive-compulsive disorder: Theory, research, and treatment* (pp. 349–366). New York: Guilford Press.

Van Balkom, A. J. L. M., Van Oppen, P., Wermeulen, A. W. A., Van Dyck, R., Nauta, M. C. E., & Vorst, H. C. M. (1994). Meta-analysis on the treatment of obsessive-compulsive disorder: A comparison of antidepressants, behavior, and cognitive therapy. *Clinical Psychology Review, 14,* 359–381.

Van den Bergh, N. (Ed.). (1991). *Feminist perspectives on addictions.* New York: Springer.

Walitzer, K. S., & Connors, G. J. (1999, Fall). Treating problem drinking. *Alcohol Research and Health, 23*(2), 138–145.

Walker, T. (2000). MCOs begin to recognize the reality of schizophrenia. *Managed Healthcare, 10*(6), 43–46.

Wallace, J. (1989). A biopsychosocial model of alcoholism. *Social casework: The journal of contemporary social work,* 325–331.

Walsh, B. T. (1995). Pharmacotherapy of eating disorders. In K. D. Brownell & C. G. Fairburn (Eds.), *Eating disorders and obesity* (pp. 313–317). New York: Guilford Press.

Walsh, J. (2000). *Clinical case management with persons having a mental illness: A relationship-based perspective.* Belmont, CA: Wadsworth/Thompson Learning.

Walter, J. L., & Peller, J. E. (1992). *Becoming solution-focused in brief therapy.* New York: Brunner/Mazel.

Wambach, K. G., Haynes, D. T., & White, B. W. (1999). Practice guidelines: Rapprochement or estrangement between social work practitioners and researchers. *Research on Social Work Practice, 9*(3), 322–330.

Ware, J. E., & Sherbourne, C. D. (1992). The MOS 36 Item Short Form Health Survey (SF-36): Conceptual framework and item selection. *Medical Care, 30*(2), 473–483.

Watson, L. (1991). Paradigms of recovery: Theoretical implications for relapse prevention in alcoholics [CD-ROM]. *Journal of Drug Issues, 21*(4), 839–858. Abstract retrieved from PsychLIT: AN 79–17576.

Weaver, H., & Wodarski, J. S. (1996). Social work practice with Latinos. In D. F. Harrison, B. A. Thyer, & J. S. Wodarski (Eds.), *Cultural diversity and social work practice* (2nd ed.). Springfield, IL: Charles C Thomas.

Weisman, A. G. (1997). Understanding cross-cultural prognostic variability for schizophrenia. *Cultural Diversity and Mental Health, 3*(1), 23–35.

Welch, M. G. (1988). *Holding time.* New York: Fireside.

Welch, M. G. (1999). Four tape video series: Creating and repairing attachment with direct synchronous bonding [Video]. (Available through the Martha G. Welch Centers, 952 Fifth Avenue—Suite 7C, New York, NY, 10021)

Welfel, E. R. (1998). *Ethics in counseling and psychotherapy: Standards, research and emerging issues.* Pacific Grove, CA: Brooks/Cole.

Wells, R. A. (1994). *Planned short-term treatment* (2nd ed.). New York: Free Press.

Wells, R. A., & Phelps, P. A. (1990). The brief psychotherapies: A selective overview. In R. A. Wells & V. J. Giannetti (Eds.), *Handbook of the brief psychotherapies* (pp. 3–26). New York: Plenum Press.

Wesson, D. R. (1995). *Detoxification from alcohol and other drugs* (Publication No. SMA 95–3046). Rockville, MD: Department of Health and Human Services.

West, M., Prado, R., & Krystal, A. D. (1999). Evaluation and comparison of EEG traces: Latent structure in nonstationary time series. *Journal of the American Statistical Association, 94*(446), 375–394.

Westermeyer, J. (1990). Treatment for psychoactive substance use disorder in special populations: Issues in strategic planning [CD-ROM]. *Advances in Alcohol and Substance Abuse, 8*(3/4), 1–8. Abstract retrieved from PsychLIT: AN 24228.

Whitaker, L. P. (1992). *Schizophrenic disorders: Sense and nonsense in conceptualization, assessment and treatment.* New York: Plenum Press.

Whiting, L. (1996). Forward. In J. M. Karls & K. M. Wandrei (Eds.), *Person-in-environment system: The PIE classification system for social functioning problems* (pp. xiii–xv). Washington, DC: National Association of Social Workers Press.

Wild, T. C., & Cunningham, J. (2001, January). Psychosocial determinants of perceived vulnerability to harm among adult drinkers [Abstract]. *Journal of Studies on Alcohol, 62*(1), 105.

Wilfley, D., & Rodin, J. (1995). Cultural influences on eating disorders. In K. Brownell & C. Fairburn (Eds.), *Eating disorders and obesity a comprehensive handbook* (pp. 78–82). New York: Guilford Press.

Wilhelm, F., & Margraf, J. (1997). A cognitive-behavioral treatment package for panic disorder with agoraphobia. In W. T. Roth (Ed.), *Treating anxiety disorders* (pp. 205–244). San Francisco: Jossey-Bass.

Wilkes, J. (1995). The social construction of a caring career. In C. Burck & B. Speed (Eds.), *Gender power and relationships* (pp. 232–247). New York: Routledge.

Williams, J. B. W., & Spitzer, R. L. (1983). The issue of sex bias in *DSM-III*: A critique of "A woman's view of *DSM-III*" by Marcie Kaplan. *American Psychologist, 38,* 793–798.

Willie, C., Kramer, B., & Brown, M. (1973). *Racism and mental health.* Pittsburgh, PA: University of Pittsburgh Press.

Willoughby, C. L., Hradek, E. A., & Richards, N. R. (1997). Use of electroconvulsive therapy with children: An overview and case report. *Journal of Child and Adolescent Psychiatric Nursing, 10*(3), 11–18.

Wilson, N., & Blackhurst, A. E. (1999). Food advertising and eating disorders: Marketing body dissatisfaction, the drive for thinness, and dieting in women's magazines. *Journal of Humanistic Counseling Education and Development, 38*(2), 11–12.

Wodarski, J. S., & Megget, K. E. D. (1996). Social work practice with African Americans. In D. F. Harrison, B. A. Thyer, & J. S. Wodarski (Eds.), *Cultural diversity and social work practice* (2nd ed.). Springfield, IL: Charles C Thomas.

Worden, M. (1999). *Family therapy basics* (2nd ed.). Pacific Grove, CA: Brooks/Cole.

Wynne, L. C. (1987). A preliminary proposal for strengthening the multi-axial approach of the *DSM-III:* Possible family-oriented revisions. In G. L. Tischler (Ed.), *Diagnosis and classification in psychiatry: A critical appraisal of DSM-III* (pp. 477–488). Cambridge, England: Cambridge University Press.

Yalisove, D. (1998, July). The origins and evolution of the disease concept of treatment. *Journal of Studies on Alcohol, 59*(4), 469–477.

Young, A., Macritchie, K., & Calabrese, J. (2000). Treatment of bipolar affective disorder: New drug treatments are emerging, but more clinical evidence is required. *British Medical Journal, 321*(i7272), 1302–1303.

Zeanah, C. H. (2000). Disturbances of attachment in young children adopted from institutions. *Developmental and Behavioral Pediatrics, 21*(3), 230–236.

Zimberg, S. (1996, October). Treating alcoholism: An age-specific intervention that works for older patients. *Geriatrics, 51*(10), 40–45.

Zimmerman, M. (1988). Why are we rushing to publish *DSM-IV? Archives of General Psychiatry, 45,* 1135–1138.

Zuckerman, E. L. (1995). *Clinician's thesaurus* (4th ed.). New York: Guilford Press.

Zung, W. K. (1965). A self-rating depression scale. *Archives of General Psychiatry, 12,* 63–70.

About the Author

Sophia F. Dziegielewski, PhD, LCSW, is a professor in the School of Social Work, University of Central Florida, Orlando, Florida. She also has joint appointments in Health Services Administration and Sociology. Prior to this appointment, Dr. Dziegielewski had faculty appointments in the School of Social Work, The University of Alabama, Tuscaloosa, Alabama, the Departments of Family and Preventive Medicine and Psychiatry at Meharry Medical College, Nashville, Tennessee, The School of Social Work at the University of Tennessee, and in the U.S. Army Military College at Fort Benning, Georgia. Throughout her social work career, she has been active in health and mental health clinical practice.

Dr. Dziegielewski has her MSW and PhD in Social Work from Florida State University, Tallahassee, Florida. Professional honors include the College and University Award for Excellence in Graduate Teaching at the University of Central Florida (2002), the University Faculty Leadership Award (2002), the National Association of Social Workers (NASW) Social Worker of the Year in 1995 for the State of Tennessee, and numerous other professional recognitions.

Her professional social work interests primarily focus on two major areas: health and mental health issues and time-limited empirically based practice strategy. As a licensed clinical social worker, she is firm on the importance of joining practice and research and applying the concepts of measurement to establish treatment effectiveness in time-limited intervention settings. She supports her research and practice activity with over 70 publications and five books in the area of health and mental health (including medications and the use and abuse of substances). Her practice interest centers primarily on the establishment of outcome-based interventions in health and mental health settings. Relying on experience in practice and research, she has served as the methodologist on numerous research and grant writing projects. In addition, she has also conducted over 500 workshops and community presentations on mental health counseling practice and strategy in today's managed care environment.

Author Index

Subject Index

413

mr|27 K
1